3

ENTOMOLOGY
FOR
STUDENTS OF MEDICINE

BY

R. M. GORDON

O.B.E., M.D., Sc.D., F.R.C.P.

Late Emeritus Professor of Entomology and Parasitology, Liverpool School of Tropical Medicine, University of Liverpool; formerly Professor of Tropical Diseases of Africa and Director of the Sir Alfred L. Jones Laboratory, Freetown, Sierra Leone.

AND

M. M. J. LAVOIPIERRE

B.Sc., M.B., Ch.B.

Formerly Lecturer in Medical Entomology, the Liverpool School of Tropical Medicine, University of Liverpool; now in the Department of Medicine, and the George Williams Hooper Foundation for Medical Research, the San Francisco Medical Center, University of California.

Illustrated by
MARGARET. A. JOHNSON

THIRD PRINTING

Blackwell Scientific Publications
Oxford and Edinburgh

© 1962 by Blackwell Scientific Publications
5 Alfred Street, Oxford, England and
9 Forrest Road, Edinburgh, Scotland

ISBN 0 632 06190 1

First published 1962
Reprinted 1969, 1972

Distributed in the U.S.A. by
F. A. Davis Company, 1915 Arch Street,
Philadelphia, Pennsylvania

Printed in Great Britain by
Lowe & Brydone (Printers) Ltd., London
and bound by
The Kemp Hall Bindery, Oxford

PREFACE

THIS book is intended for the use of medical practitioners, particularly for those studying for the Diploma in Tropical Medicine & Hygiene, who have no specialised knowledge of entomology and whose knowledge of general zoology does not extend beyond that acquired in pre-clinical years. We believe that it may also prove useful to the increasing number of laymen seeking knowledge of a subject which under modern conditions of widespread travel is becoming of almost universal interest.

The term "Medical Entomology" is a misnomer since it is generally accepted to include the study of a wide variety of arthropods in addition to the insects. The present work does not claim to give a comprehensive account of these various arthropods a proper understanding of the morphology, alone, of which would entail anatomical studies far beyond the scope of a textbook intended for the use of medical practitioners; but rather it is intended to serve as an introduction to Medical Entomology and to form a companion volume to some similarly simple treatise on Medical Parasitology.

An introduction to Medical Entomology, no matter how brief, must include accounts not only of how to recognise the species, genus or family of the arthropods referred to but also of the part played by a particular species or group of species in causing injury to man, together with a sufficiently ample description of their life-cycle and habits, to give a proper understanding of their relationship to disease, and of how best to effect their control. To deal with all these aspects of each individual species would be impossible in an introductory textbook and we have tried to achieve the necessary brevity without the omission of essential information by emphasising the general morphological and biological characteristics of certain groups of medically important arthropods and only dealing with individual species in a few special instances.

The separation of tropical medicine from general medicine is an entirely artificial division, so that a practitioner attending courses in tropical medicine is addressed in terms the majority of which are familiar to him since his undergraduate days. On the other hand, when his attention is transferred from "tropical medicine" to "tropical parasitology and entomology" he finds himself confronted with a bewildering number of names and terms which he is encountering for the first time. In order to lighten the student's load we have reduced the use of such scientific terms to a minimum and at the same time we have simplified the morphological presentation to an extent which, although allowing the student to understand and apply the use of simple keys for the recognition of certain genera of medically important mites and fleas and of certain species of mosquitoes and tsetse flies, does not necessarily include the numerous anatomical details required for the recognition of each particular species.

We have used line drawings and occasional photographs to illustrate this book, the former almost entirely in diagrammatic form and the latter to illustrate the appearance when seen alive of some of the more important vectors of disease. The use of illustrations in a textbook on medical entomology is of course desirable, indeed it is almost essential, but pictures cannot take the place of the preserved specimens nor can these, in their turn take the place of the much truer impression gained by seeing the living creatures in captivity or better still, in their natural environments, and we would emphasise our belief that it is impossible to teach the subject without the student having access not only to preserved but also to living material.

It is appropriate here to mention a number of other points regarding our treatment in this book of certain aspects of Medical Entomology. The average medical officer proceeding to the tropics for the first time is keen to collect material which he wishes to identify, or have identified at some suitable institution. Such collections are of very great value, not only to the collector but also to the workers in the institute to which they are sent for identification. Unfortunately, however, the worker in the tropics is often discouraged from making such collections because he thinks the work will necessitate the possession of much elaborate equipment and that successful results are only achieved by the expert. In order to correct this erroneous impression we have included chapters describing simple methods of collecting, labelling and preserving various types of arthropods, together with notes on techniques which may be used for breeding them. For the same reason we have included accounts of simple methods of dissecting certain arthropods in order to demonstrate in them the presence of parasites at different stages of development. Our experience is that the student is agreeably surprised at the simplicity of these techniques and rapidly becomes an enthusiast when he finds how quickly he can learn to dissect successfully such insects as mosquitoes and tsetse flies and to recognise the presence in them of the developing forms of the parasites which they transmit.

Considerable experience of teaching medical graduates and undergraduates has convinced us that the average student believes that the application of the rules of zoological nomenclature are only understandable by, and of value to, the expert. In order to dispel this illusion we have included a short account of binominal nomenclature for we have found that such an explanation interests students and gives them an understanding of the essential simplicity and practical value of the system. Finally we have included a short guide to the literature, particularly books of reference and abstracting journals generally available to the student of Medical Entomology.

As regards omissions we have thought it inadvisable in a book not directly concerned with the preventive aspects of arthropod-borne infections, to discuss such methods of control as the use of insecticides, although references to biological methods of control, arising from a knowledge of the life-cycle and habits of a particular species, are sometimes considered. Similarly, in order to avoid duplication with the teaching of parasitology, although we have discussed the part played by various arthropods as vectors of parasites communicable to man, we have omitted any detailed reference to the development of such parasites in the vector.

R.M.G. / M.M.J.L.

ACKNOWLEDGEMENTS

We acknowledge with great gratitude our indebtedness to a host of colleagues both at home and abroad for much information and advice. It would be impossible to name all those who have assisted us, but we offer particular thanks to our friends at the Liverpool and London Schools of Tropical Medicine, and we wish especially to put on record our indebtedness to Miss G. Phillips, Librarian at the Liverpool School.

Mr. Harold Oldroyd has advised us on many points in taxonomy, and has kindly allowed us to reproduce a map from his book, *Collecting, Preserving and Studying Insects,* Hutchinson & Co. (Publishers) Ltd.

Dr. C. A. Hoare, F.R.S., has permitted us to quote extensively from his work on zoological nomenclature.

Dr. J. B. Busvine has read, brought up to date, and improved those sections of our book which refer to insecticides and the development of insecticide resistance.

We are also very grateful to the following journals, commercial firms and individuals for permission to reproduce various photographs: the *Transactions of the Royal Society of Tropical Medicine and Hygiene,* the *Annals of Tropical Medicine and Parasitology,* the *American Journal of Tropical Medicine and Hygiene,* the Shell Photographic Unit No. 1, Kingsway, London, Mr. J. P. Brady, Dr. W. Crewe, Dr. B. R. Laurence, Dr. Marshall Hertig, Mr. Eric Norman, Mr. W. Petana, Mr. S. A. Smith.

Finally, we owe a very real debt of gratitude to our publishers, and in particular to Mr. Per Saugman, for constant help and kindness, and for exemplary patience in enduring an exasperating series of delays (most of which were due to mishaps beyond our control) in submitting our finished manuscript.

To Our Wives
who have helped us so much

CONTENTS

CHAPTER

I   A brief survey of the development of Medical Entomology .   11

II   Some remarks on the influence of injurious and beneficial
arthropods on human welfare   14

III   The ways in which injurious arthropods affect the health of man   15

IV   The use in insect-borne disease of various methods of control
directed against the parasite   22

V   The use in insect-borne diseases of various methods of control
directed against the animal reservoir   25

VI   The use in insect-borne diseases of various methods of control
directed against the arthropod vector.   27

VII   A description of the phylum Arthropoda and its division into
various classes containing creatures of medical importance. .   37

VIII   The general structure and external anatomy of insects . . .   42

IX   The internal anatomy and physiology of insects   52

        The integument and its relation to growth   52

        The nervous system and the senses   54

        The respiratory system and the oxygen requirements   . .   55

        The digestive and excretory systems   57

        The "fat body"   60

        The circulatory system   61

X   The internal anatomy and physiology of insects (cont.) . . .   63

        The reproductive system and fertilisation   63

        The egg and its development   65

        The development of the insect (holometabolous and
hemimetabolous life-cycles)   68

XI   The adaptation of insects to climatic conditions   71

XII   The orders of medical importance in the class Insecta   75

XIII   The order Diptera   77

XIV   The suborder Nematocera and its division into families of
medical importance   81

XV   The family Culicidae. Definition of the subfamily Culicinae.
The external and internal anatomy of an adult mosquito . .   83

XVI   The subfamily Culicinae (cont.) . . . .
A brief outline of the life-cycle and habits of a true mosquito   91

XVII   The subfamily Culicinae (cont.). Its division into three tribes   95

XVIII   The tribe Anophelini and its division into three genera . . .
The genus Anopheles   99

XIX   The tribe Culicini and its division into five groups   115

XX   The family Psychodidae. The genus Phlebotomus   131

XXI   The family Simuliidae. The genus Simulium   140

XXII   The family Ceratopogonidae. The genus Culicoides   148

XXIII   The suborder Brachycera and its division into families of
medical importance   153

9

XXIV   The family Tabanidae. The genus *Chrysops* 155
XXV   The suborder Cyclorrapha and its division into families of medical importance 162
XXVI   The family Muscidae. 164
XXVII   The family Muscidae (cont.). *Musca domestica* and related species 165
XXVIII The family Muscidae (cont.). *Fannia* spp. and *Muscina stabulans* 174
XXIX   The family Muscidae (cont.). *Glossina* spp 177
XXX   The family Muscidae (cont.). *Stomoxys calcitrans* 186
XXXI   The family Calliphoridae 189
XXXII   The family Oestridae 199
XXXIII Myiasis in man 204
XXXIV   The order Siphonaptera. The characters of the order and the life-cycle 208
XXXV   The order Siphonaptera (cont.). The classification of fleas and the association of certain species with disease 216
XXXVI   The order Anoplura. The lice parasitising man: their anatomy, life-cycle and association with disease. 223
XXXVII The order Hemiptera 231
XXXVIII The order Hemiptera (cont.). The family Cimicidae 233
XXXIX   The order Hemiptera (cont.). The family Reduviidae, with special emphasis on the subfamily Triatominae 237
XL   Definition of the class Arachnida 242
XLI   The order Acarina. 244
XLII   The family Argasidae 247
XLIII   The family Ixodidae 254
XLIV   *Sarcoptes scabiei*. Recognition, life-cycle and medical importance 261
XLV   The family Trombiculidae. Recognition, life-cycle and medical importance 267
XLVI   Miscellaneous mites of medical importance together with observations on those members of the class Pentastomida which sometimes parasitise man 273
XLVII   Arthropods directly affecting health, including the so-called venomous arthropods 280
XLVIII Collecting arthropods of medical importance 288
XLIX   Labelling and recording collections of arthropods of medical importance 300
L   The preservation of arthropods of medical importance . . . 302
LI   The rearing and maintenance of arthropods of medical importance 309
LII   The dissection of arthropods of medical importance 313
LIII   The use of keys for the identification of arthropods of medical importance 323
LIV   Zoological nomenclature 332
LV   On consulting the literature. 336

CHAPTER I

A BRIEF SURVEY OF THE DEVELOPMENT OF MEDICAL ENTOMOLOGY

ALTHOUGH many of the important and widespread diseases of the tropics, such as malaria, yellow fever, trypanosomiasis and relapsing fever are transmitted by arthropods it is only within the span of a human life-time that the part played by these creatures in the epidemiology of such diseases has been fully appreciated.

The realisation, during the latter part of the nineteenth century, that arthropods are important and efficient transmitters of disease, brought about during the subsequent years an intensive study of insects, ticks and mites by many investigators, not only as regards the recognition and biology of these creatures, but also with respect to those aspects of their life-cycles which could render control methods efficacious. Today, many of the insect-borne diseases transmissible to man are under partial control and it is at last possible to envisage their almost complete control in the not too distant future. Nor must it be forgotten that these discoveries in human medicine were accompanied by similar discoveries by workers concerned with arthropod-borne diseases of domestic stock, and that today many of the problems, for example trypanosomiasis, presented to medical entomologists are so closely knit with those presented to veterinary entomologists that it would be disastrous for either to pursue their investigations in isolation. On the other hand, however desirable it may be to remember this close link between medical and veterinary entomology it would not be possible to deal with the veterinary aspect in a book intended mainly for the use of medical practitioners and in consequence no further reference will be made to the subject.

It is reasonable to believe that from the very earliest times man has been aware of the beneficial as well as the injurious effects of insect life. As regards the beneficial effects, although primitive man cannot have realised the dependence of plant growth on insect life, nevertheless he must have augmented his meagre food supplies by honey obtained from wild bees and, in times of adversity, devoured locusts and white ants. As regards the injurious effects, from the time of man's earliest attempt at the cultivation of crops he must have been harassed and often brought to a state of starvation by the depredations of insects, while although he cannot have had any conception of the relationship between insects and disease, nevertheless, he must have suffered annoyance and minor injuries by the attacks of parasitic and venomous arthropods. With the passage of time knowledge of the effects of beneficial and injurious insects slowly increased, and by the close of the 18th Century the important part played by insects in the fertilisation of foodcrops became known. Some 50 years later suspicion began to be aroused that insects might be concerned in the spread of certain diseases, a notion which was advanced by writers such as Beauperthuy, who, in 1853, suggested that yellow fever was transmitted by mosquitoes. A few years later, in 1857, David Livingstone, during his exploration of Africa, recorded his belief that the tsetse fly, when sucking the blood of cattle injected some form of poison which resulted in the development of a usually fatal disease—"Nagana"—a few weeks later.

It was not until 1870, however, following Fedschenko's discovery of the transmission of the guinea-worm through the agency of *Cyclops*, that a remarkable and inspiring series of researches was initiated by biologists and physicians into the mode of transmission of arthropod-borne diseases. In 1878, a helminth parasite, *Wuchereria bancrofti*, which has an almost world wide distribution and which is the cause of filarial fever and elephantiasis in man, was shown by Manson to develop to the infective stage in the mosquito, but the first proof of the transmission of a protozoan parasite by an arthropod vector was not made until 1893 when the American workers Smith and Kilbourne proved that *Babesia bigemina*, the cause of red water fever in cattle, an often fatal disease, was transmitted by ticks. These researches paved the way for Ross's epoch making discovery in 1898 of the transmission of malaria by the mosquito and during the next half century led to a series of brilliantly successful studies by research workers of many nationalities concerning the transmission of various tropical and subtropical diseases. Thus in 1900, Walter Reed and his colleagues proved that yellow fever was transmitted by *Aedes aegypti*, while three years later Bruce and Nabarro (1903) showed that human trypanosomiasis was transmitted by the tsetse fly. In 1905 Dutton and Todd demonstrated that the transmission of endemic relapsing fever was effected by ticks belonging to the genus *Ornithodoros*, although the vector of epidemic relapsing fever was not known until two years later when Mackie, working in India, incriminated the louse. In 1909 Nicoll and his co-workers proved that lice transmitted epidemic typhus, while in 1916 Cleland and his collaborators in Australia demonstrated that mosquitoes belonging to the genus *Aedes* transmitted dengue fever.

These are only a few of the more important landmarks in the history of medical entomology which, during the 50 years following Ross's discovery of the transmission of malaria, resulted in an accumulation of knowledge of such outstanding value to humanity that it led not only to a great reduction of disease in Europe, but also to the spread of civilisation in the tropics and to the colonization of vast areas previously believed to be uninhabitable by the white man, a long held belief founded on the fallacy that certain tropical climates were in themselves the main cause of ill health.

At about the same time that these remarkable developments were taking place various systematists, amongst others Theobald, Austen, Newstead and Rothschild, began to collect, study, describe and catalogue the various groups of arthropods, and the species included in these groups, which had been proved by other workers to be important transmitters, or in some instances the direct cause, of certain diseases. This publication by the systematists of exact descriptions of particular arthropods was essential to the progress of medical entomology for it enabled the early medical and veterinary investigators to recognise the type of arthropod concerned in the transmission of a particular disease and to distinguish the important species in any particular group. Today the combined knowledge gained by the work of biologists and systematists when placed at the disposal of the hygienist is enabling him to correlate the epidemiology of many arthropod-borne diseases with the distribution and ecology of their vectors and to plan effective methods for their control.

CHAPTER II

SOME REMARKS ON THE INFLUENCE OF INJURIOUS AND BENEFICIAL ARTHROPODS ON HUMAN WELFARE

BEFORE considering the various ways by which injurious arthropods affect the health of man and the different methods of control—some involving the wholesale destruction of insect life—which may be used against the relatively few species concerned, it is obviously advantageous to weigh together their beneficial and harmful aspects.

On the one side, many species of arthropods are injurious in their role as destroyers of man's crops both growing and stored, so they have been responsible for vast famines and long sustained malnutrition over wide areas; whilst as vectors of disease both to man and to his domestic stock they have caused great suffering and great mortality and today still determine the extent of some of the world's most important epidemic and epizootic diseases. On the other side against these harmful aspects must be weighed not only the benefits bestowed by insects as fertilisers of plants of economic importance, but also the part played in nature by many species of arthropods as scavengers of decaying organic matter and as predators of injurious insects.

From the human viewpoint, this balance between injurious and beneficial arthropods dips, in undisturbed nature, in favour of the beneficial, and Duncan* was probably correct when he wrote: "It has long been apparent to biologists, whenever insects and human relations are viewed in the entirety, that the insect species which are injurious or antagonistic to human welfare actually constitute only a small proportion of the total of insect life, and that the great majority of insects are either directly or indirectly beneficial to man or enjoy a neutral status".

It would seem, therefore, when considering the effect of injurious insects on the health of man and when planning methods for their control, that due account must be taken of the co-existence of a vast assemblage of different types of arthropods which are directly or indirectly beneficial to man or which play an essential role in the general economy of nature, and that, contrary to the view held by the ill-informed, a widespread and indiscriminate destruction of insect life would prove detrimental to human existence.

Until fairly recently man had little power to effect any such widespread and indiscriminate destruction, but with the introduction of new and immensely powerful insecticides the situation has altered. Today man can alter the balance of nature by exterminating a proportion of the arthropod population over a particular area, so that much care must be exercised when using these dangerous weapons, a subject which will be more fully discussed when considering in later chapters various methods of control directed against the vectors of insect-borne diseases.

---

* Duncan, C.D. (1948). Rep. Smithson. Instn., 1947, p. 339

CHAPTER III

THE WAYS IN WHICH INJURIOUS ARTHROPODS AFFECT THE HEALTH OF MAN

IT is customary to consider the arthropods injurious to human welfare under three headings: firstly, those which adversely affect the health of man by damaging or destroying his food supplies, secondly, those arthropods which are directly injurious to health, either because of their parasitic habits or because they sting, bite or provoke allergic manifestations, and thirdly, those arthropods which are injurious in their role as transmitters of disease. The first group of injurious insects, the destroyers of food supplies, has already been referred to and their important connection with malnutrition has been stressed, for, as Sir John Boyd-Orr has written, "If we plan for human welfare, we should begin with food". Nevertheless, the problem of protecting food supplies while growing, and after storage, is essentially the concern of the agricultural entomologist and it will receive no further consideration in this book.

We are left then with two main divisions of injurious arthropods; those which are directly injurious to health and those which are injurious in their role as vectors of disease.

(1) DIRECTLY INJURIOUS ARTHROPODS.

The pathogenic effects produced by arthropods directly injurious to man usually fall into certain well-defined groups and can be classified in one of four categories: (a) lesions due to mechanical trauma; (b) lesions due to secondary infections; (c) lesions due to the injection or absorption of substances which are normally harmless, but to which the host has become sensitized as a result of previous exposure; and (d) lesions due to the injection or absorption of directly injurious substances. Although these pathogenic effects are considered separately, they may, and often do, occur in conjunction—a fact which is sometimes overlooked by the clinicians.

(a) *Lesions due to mechanical trauma*. In the case of the puncture or abrasion made by a blood-sucking arthropod, the extent of the lesion produced will depend on the size and nature of the insect's mouthparts and the manner in which they are used. Some blood-sucking insects, such as the mosquito, with long and delicate mouthparts, may feed with the proboscis lying in the lumen of a capillary; whereas the proboscis of larger flies, such as the tsetse (*Glossina* sp.), is usually too bulky to enter the lumen and is used to suck up the blood which results from numerous lacerations of small subcutaneous vessels. It is, of course, obvious that the large and relatively clumsy skin-piercing organs of some of the horse flies (Tabanidae) will produce a more extensive wound than will the small and delicate mouthparts of the midges (*Culicoides* spp.); but the difference in the final result is not so great as might be expected, since both insects tend to probe the tissues until a pool of blood, more than sufficient for their purpose, has been produced. From the clinician's point of view it would seem that the uncomplicated trauma produced by any type of blood-sucking arthropod is seldom severe enough to cause any serious disturbance in the host.

When, however, the parasitic arthropod extends its activities from sucking blood to tissue invasion the resultant trauma may be more extensive. Thus, in the tropics, myiasis caused by the larvae of certain flies, such as the "berne fly" (*Dermatobia hominis*), can result in the deep invasion of the subcutaneous tissues by a number of larvae, each of which may be as much as an inch in length, while the invasion of the turbinal mucous membrane, or even of the frontal sinuses, by the so-called "screw-worm" larvae of other flies, such as *Callitroga* sp. and *Chrysomyia* sp., may produce even more serious injury. Extensive invasions by such large arthropods are obviously not only painful but are bound to interfere seriously with health.

On the other hand, the invasion of the host's tissues by a parasite so minute as *Sarcoptes scabiei,* and one which never penetrates below the stratum corneum, cannot be regarded as causing any serious mechanical trauma, and the extensive lesions sometimes associated with its presence must be ascribed to some other cause. Between these extremes there are a host of tissue-invading parasites, mostly larvae of two-winged flies which in the tropics, and more rarely in this country, cause varying degrees of mechanical trauma in the tissues of their host.

As already mentioned, a few species of myiasis-causing larvae may produce serious lesions, but with these exceptions, and in the absence of complications, most of the tissue-invading arthropods, so long as they confine themselves to their normal host, seldom produce any marked reaction. Occasionally, of course, an invading parasite finds itself in the tissues of an unusual host, and in such instances both parasite and host may react abnormally. In the majority of such cases the reaction produced in the host is the result of the invasion of certain skin-piercing nematode larvae, which finding themselves in the wrong environment fail to pursue their normal course of development and wander aimlessly in the subcutaneous tissues of the host, the course of their journeyings being demarcated by a characteristic serpiginous line of limited inflammation, a condition which is often regarded as a clinical entity and has received the appellation "larva migrans". In only a very limited number of instances has the causal organism been recovered and, whereas it is probably true that in the tropics the condition is usually caused by invasive nematode larvae, it should be remembered that in all parts of the world similar lesions are known to follow the penetration of the human skin by the larvae of the warble fly (*Hypoderma* sp.), the usual host of which is cattle, or by the larvae of the bot-fly (*Gasterophilus* sp.) which is normally an intestinal parasite of equines.

(b) *Lesions due to secondary infections.* It has been noted that the larvae of a few, mainly tropical, species of Diptera may, when in the tissues of the human host, produce considerable mechanical trauma. Usually, however, the most serious results of myiasis are those which follow the subsequent invasion by bacteria of the wound previously made by the dipterous parasite, and the term "myiasis" generally conjures up a picture of a septic lesion for the cause of which the bacteria are more responsible than are the Diptera.

16

It sometimes happens that these pathogenic bacteria are introduced by the parasite when piercing the skin, but it seems to be more usual for them to gain access after the abrasion has been made, and such abrasions do not appear to be any more prone to infection than similar lesions caused by other means. Indeed, the secondary bacterial invasion is often rendered less severe by the presence of dipterous larvae and in the past blow fly (*Calliphora* sp. and *Lucilia* sp.) larvae have been employed for the treatment of osteomyelitis and for cleaning up septic wounds. Although the active substance, allantoin, produced by fly larvae, is sometimes prescribed, the utilization of living larvae as a therapeutic measure has now been largely abandoned, as the distaste produced by this rather repulsive form of therapy probably outweighs any benefits derived from its use, whilst the difficulty of ensuring that the larvae are free from anaerobic bacteria has been known to result in tetanus.

(c) *Lesions due to the injection of normally harmless substances into a previously sensitized host.*

The picture just presented of a more or less trivial traumatic injury caused by an arthropod, and which may or may not be followed by a more serious bacterial infection, is often thought to be further complicated by the injection by the parasite of a substance inimical to the host: in the case of the skin-piercing arthropods it is generally believed that the responsible substance is derived from the salivary glands of the parasite, although some workers consider that in certain instances it originates from some other part of the insect's digestive tract. Recent observations do not support the view that immediate reactions to insect bites are due to the injection of a poison; they suggest rather that such reactions are most commonly of an allergic nature and that only a very limited number of parasitic arthropods secrete a directly toxic substance, and that when this does occur the reaction produced is usually more delayed and trivial and never results in the immediate well-marked weal so often associated with the bites of blood-sucking arthropods. A varied assortment of such arthropods have been allowed to feed on volunteers, and, so long as these volunteers have never previously been exposed to the bites of the particular kind of arthropod under investigation (for instance, if imported tsetse flies are fed on persons who have never visited the tropics), either no reaction follows the infliction of their bites or else it is so slight as to be clinically negligible. As regards the anatomical source of the irritating substance, it has been shown that, in the case of the tsetse fly at any rate, it must be derived from the salivary glands, for if these are removed from the living insect, and it is then fed on a person known to react violently to the bite of the intact insect, the fly feeds to repletion but the host shows no subsequent reaction.

It has been mentioned that persons not previously exposed to the bites of a particular species of blood-sucking arthropod show little or no reaction when bitten for the first time. The pertinent point now arises as to what happens if such non-reacting persons continue to be exposed at various intervals of time to the attacks of a particular species of arthropod. The answer appears to be that if they receive the bites at more or less regular intervals (as commonly occurs, particularly in the tropics, in the case of persons constantly working in an area where there is no very marked seasonal fluctuation in the density of the biting arthropod in question) the persons so exposed will usually remain free from any marked reaction. On the other hand if such individuals are exposed to the bites of a particular species of arthropod at irregular intervals (as commonly occurs in the case of persons moving from one area to another, or living in an area where there is a marked variation in the seasonal density of the arthropod, as is usual in temperate zones) a proportion of persons so exposed will develop a reaction which may or may not be severe in character.

It should be realised that these allergic reactions are often highly specific, and that persons who react to one species of insect do not necessarily react in a similar manner when bitten by a different species, although both may be so closely related as to belong to the same genus. These findings may explain why it is not unusual to encounter persons who state that while they sometimes react violently to flea-bites at other times they remain unaffected, or that they react to the bites of mosquitoes in one part of the country but not in another. In the first instance the individual may have become sensitized to the bites of the "human flea" *(Pulex irritans)* but not to those of the "dog flea" (*Ctenocephalides* sp.) while in the second instance he may have become sensitized to the bites of anophelines but not to those of culicines.

Although allergy caused by arthropods is usually the result of the injection of their salivary secretions yet in some instances the arthropod responsible is not a biting insect and sensitisation of the individual may develop following the stings of wasps and bees or as the result of the inhalation, ingestion, or mere contact with the secretions or excretions of a particular arthropod. The former type of sensitisation is, of course, common amongst bee-workers and may have serious and sometimes fatal consequences. The latter type of sensitisation is commonly encountered amongst industrial workers handling mite-infested material such as copra, flour or grain and results in a dermatitis to which the appropriate eponym of "copra itch", "miller's rash", or "grain shoveller's itch" becomes attached. When dealing with such a wide variety of causes it would be unwise to dogmatise, but in general it may be stated that the pattern of sensitisation and desensitisation following the absorption of such arthropod antigens is similar to that observed in the case of antigens derived from the saliva of blood-sucking insects.

An individual who has become sensitized to an antigen contained in the secretions or excretions of a particular arthropod does not necessarily remain in this condition, on the contrary, the majority of such sensitized persons gradually become desensitised when persistently exposed. This loss of reaction is a common experience among residents in the tropics, some of whom claim that, in addition, they are no longer subject to attack from a particular species of insect. Such persons may exist but in the majority of instances their apparent freedom from attack can be traced to the fact that they do not react to the bite of the insect and therefore fail to notice its presence.

(d) *Lesions due to the injection or absorption of directly injurious substances.*
The association between man and arthropods so far considered has been that of host and parasite and, since it is always to the disadvantage of the parasite to cause any incapacitating injury to its host, most of the injuries of a serious character arising from this association have been in the nature of accidents caused by the arthropod in its capacity as a vector of disease, or else, as a producer of a violent reaction following the injection of a normally harmless substance into a previously sensitized person. On the other hand, certain arthropods which are non-parasitic and in no way dependent on man for their existence have developed weapons of defence which they use to protect themselves from interference. These defensive weapons produce harmful effects which vary from the comparatively trivial discomfort caused by a wasp sting to the serious symptoms which may follow the sting of a scorpion or the bite of certain species of spiders. It must not be forgotten, however, that the stings or bites of usually only mildly pathogenic arthropods may take on a serious aspect if inflicted in a previously sensitized person.

The use of venom as a means of protection has been developed by arthropods of so widely different character that species of medical importance occur in at least seven different zoological groups:—(1) Orders HYMENOPTERA (bees, wasps and ants); (2) Order LEPIDOPTERA (butterflies and moths); (3) Order COLEOPTERA (beetles); (4) Order ARANEIDA (spiders); (5) Order SCORPIONIDA (scorpions); (6) Class CHILOPODA (centipedes); and (7) Class DIPLOPODA (millipedes). The description of these various arthropods and of the lesions they produce will be referred to in the appropriate section of this book, but it may be stated here that although serious and, on rare occasions, even fatal injuries may follow the bites or stings of certain species of spiders and scorpions, nevertheless the part played by such venomous arthropods, and indeed by directly injurious insects in general, is usually more irritating than serious and that their ill-effect on the health of mankind is trivial when compared with the vast indirect injuries caused by arthropods in their role as vectors of disease.

(2) INDIRECTLY INJURIOUS ARTHROPODS.
Although the term may be taken to include arthropods causing the spread of deficiency diseases by the destruction of growing crops or stored food supplies, it is usually understood to refer to arthropods as vectors of disease, and it will be used in this sense in the following account.

Arthropods may act as indirect vectors of disease either by mechanically transferring the infective organism from one mammalian host to another, without any intervening period of development being necessary—such a form of transmission being known as "mechanical transmission"—or they may do so only after an intervening incubation period during which the parasite undergoes development to the infective stage—the latter form of transmission being known as "cyclical transmission".

(a) *Mechanical transmission of disease.* In the case of mechanically transmitted infections the responsible parasite undergoes no obvious morphological or biological changes and, although there may be multiplication of the parasite, this is not essential so that there is no obvious enforced latent period during which the vector is incapable of successfully transferring the infection to a new host. Many bacterial, protozoal, helminthic and virus infections are thus mechanically transmitted to the human host through the agency of a wide variety of insects but, whatever the species of the organism or of the vector, the mechanism of transmission is very similar. Thus the house fly (with its equal liking for human excretions and human food supplies) may take up pathogenic viruses, bacteria, protozoa or helminth ova and convey these directly either on its feet, or in its faeces and vomit to the human host; and since the house fly has a worldwide distribution and a high density it has come to rank with the louse and the mosquito as a vector of disease.

In the example just given the organisms (viruses, bacteria, protozoa and helminths) mentioned were not solely dependent on an arthropod vector for their establishment in a fresh mammalian host; on the other hand some blood-inhabiting protozoa, notably many species of trypanosomes highly pathogenic to domestic stock, can, in nature, only pass from one host to another through the mechanical agency of biting flies. In connection with the close relationship between cyclical and mechanical transmission of disease it should be remembered that it is not always possible to distinguish sharply between the two types; thus the transmission of tularaemia by arthropods appears to lie between mechanical and cyclical transmission, for although an incubation period is not essential, the persistence of the causal organism and, in certain species of arthropods, its passage through the eggs to the next generation, suggests cyclical development. Certain authorities class the transmission of plague by fleas as mechanical, but in view of the incubation period and other factors it is more usual to class it under cyclical transmission.

Finally, it must be remembered that laboratory investigations have suggested that many virus and protozoal infections which normally require a period of development in a specific arthropod vector may on occasions be transmitted accidentally, so to speak, by the vector being crushed and the contained parasite escaping into an abrasion at a time when its normal incubation period has not been completed. To quote an example; the transmission of yellow fever normally only occurs after the ten days necessary for the virus to have multiplied in the body of the insect and invaded the salivary glands; but throughout this ten day period there is an ever increasing chance of infection following the inoculation of the crushed mosquito into the tissues of a susceptible mammalian host.

(b) *Cyclical transmission of disease*. The indirect injury caused by arthropods in their role as cyclical transmitters of disease is immense, indeed, malaria alone is stated to be responsible for more illness throughout the world than any other single disease, while louse-borne typhus has caused more deaths than have the two world wars during the same period.

These two diseases, malaria and typhus, are representative of a large group of infections caused by organisms which in nature, are, for all practical purposes, only transmitted to man after they have undergone some form of biological development in an arthropod host. The development of such parasites in their arthropod vectors may take the form of multiplication unaccompanied by any obvious morphological change, as occurs in the case of the parasitic viruses, rickettsiae, spirochaetes and bacteria, or the parasite may change its morphology but undergo no increase in its numbers, as occurs in the case of helminth larvae undergoing development in arthropod vectors, or both multiplication and morphological change may occur together, as is usual in the case of the cyclically transmitted protozoa. Whichever of these forms of development takes place the term cyclical transmission always implies an intermediate period during which the parasite is developing, but since it has not yet become infective it cannot be successfully transmitted by the vector. It must be remembered, however, that many blood-inhabiting parasites which normally only pass from one mammalian host to another after cyclical development in an arthropod may, on occasions, be directly transferred by blood-sucking insects, as occurs in the case of human sleeping sickness which may be transmitted cyclically or on rare occasions mechanically.

In an earlier chapter an outline has been given of the sequence of events which resulted in the discovery that many important parasitic diseases were insect borne. Prior to this discovery attention was focussed on the destruction of the causative organism, for example the use of quinine in malaria, but with the discovery that a particular species or group of arthropods were solely responsible for the transmission, attention became centred on measures directed against the vector, in this instance the anopheline mosquito. At a still later date it became known that although no animal reservoir existed for the malaria parasite, in other insect-borne diseases, such as trypanosomiasis, there was an important animal reservoir and in such instances control measures must be devised not only against the parasite and its vector but also against the animal reservoir.

CHAPTER IV

THE USE IN INSECT-BORNE DISEASES OF VARIOUS METHODS OF CONTROL DIRECTED AGAINST THE PARASITE

OUR acquaintance with arthropods as vectors of disease extends over little more than half a century, and although the amount of knowledge acquired during this period is impressive, and although it has enabled the hygienist to reduce the suffering caused by arthropod-borne diseases in a remarkable way, nevertheless, the main result of this extensive study has been to allow medical officers of health to instruct certain educated and well-equipped individuals (who, in the tropics, represent only a minute fraction of the total population) how to protect themselves from acquiring infection, while it has not greatly reduced the total incidence of any arthropod-borne infection, except in localized areas.

There is no doubt that with the spread of education and with a raising of the standard of living, personal protection will gradually extend to a larger section of the community, and the incidence of certain arthropod-borne infections will gradually diminish over wide areas. These improvements will follow the use of various methods of control directed against (1) the parasite, (2) the vertebrate reservoir and (3) the arthropod vector. The present work on medical entomology is concerned essentially with the arthropod vectors of disease but if methods of control directed against the vector are to be employed to their best advantage it is essential to possess knowledge, or at least some general concept, of methods of control directed against the parasite and against the particular animal reservoirs from which many of these parasites are acquired. It is only when this combined knowledge is available that the hygienist can best decide which methods should be employed under various circumstances against the vector and to what extent these methods should be used independently or in combination with methods of control directed against the parasite and against its animal reservoir.

CONTROL MEASURES DIRECTED AGAINST THE PARASITE.

These may be considered under three headings :- (a) chemotherapeutic measures aimed at the destruction by drugs of the parasite when already established in the vertebrate host, (b) chemoprophylactic measures which involve the use of drugs to prevent the further development of the parasite which has entered, but which has not become established in the vertebrate host, and (c) the use of various forms of vaccination the object of which is to develop by means of antigens a resistance and finally an immunity to the parasite, an immunity which normally can only be acquired as a result of prolonged natural infection.

(a) *Chemotherapeutic measures.* In insect-borne infections, as in other diseases, attention was at first directed mainly towards the cure of the patient, and knowledge in this direction has progressed so satisfactorily that at the present time the arthropod-borne infections, with but few exceptions, can be regarded as rapidly curable so long as they receive skilled attention at any early stage of infection. With increased knowledge and experience, however, it has become clear that the cure of the individual, although vitally important from the humanitarian standpoint, is economically unsound if, although temporarily cured, he is unprotected as a result of his treatment and has to return to an environment where he will inevitably again contract the infection; for not only will the patient suffer again, but his return may prove a danger to the general community in a variety of ways. In the first instance, it appears far more difficult completely to rid the human host of many of the arthropod transmitted parasites, both protozoan and metazoan, than was formerly believed. Thus, whereas it is true that all the recognized anti-malarial drugs, when properly used, can reduce all known species and strains of the malaria parasite to a sub-clinical level, and in a proportion of cases, can entirely eradicate the parasite, yet, no known drug can be guaranteed to eradicate the parasite in every instance and so prevent the human host becoming a reservoir of infection from which the mosquito, and subsequently the human population, may acquire the disease. In the second instance, such unsatisfactorily treated carriers may be a means of establishing a drug-resistant strain in the area. The development of drug-resistant strains of metazoa and protozoa is of considerable importance, but in the case of the arthropod-borne infections with which we are concerned, this is of little practical importance so long as the drug resistance is not transmitted through the arthropod vector. That resistance can be transmitted through the arthropod has long been known in cases of trypanosomiasis treated with arsenicals, and the success or failure of other recently introduced, highly promising drugs as a preventive of trypanosomiasis in man and his domestic stock, is largely dependent upon whether drug-fastness transmissible through the tsetse will become established with their use,

(b) *Chemoprophylactic measures.* Although chemoprophylaxis has been employed mainly in malaria, it has also been used to protect against African trypanosomiasis. For many years search has been made for true causal prophylactics which will destroy the parasites before they have undergone development, and which will be sufficiently innocuous and cheap to allow of use by all classes of the population. So far, however, no drug fulfilling these conditions has been made available for use against any of the arthropod-borne infections. It is true that the prophylactic use of certain drugs for the control of malaria has proved of very great service, but the drugs so far employed have not proved equally effective against all species and all stages of the parasite, so that although they control they do not always prevent infection, while their cost, although relatively small, often precludes their use by the poorest and, as a result, most exposed section of the indigenous population.

(c) *Vaccination.* Yellow fever is the only instance, amongst the known arthropod-borne infections affecting man, in which completely successful prophylaxis has followed the use of vaccines; while in the one bacterial disease which is an essentially arthropod-borne infection, bubonic plague, the value of a vaccine to afford protection, as distinct from modifying the course of the infection, is still in doubt. In many of the rickettsial and protozoal infections, the use of vaccines has been shown to modify the course and severity of infection, but in no instance has complete protection always followed their use. In metazoan infections, although the injection of extracts prepared from the parasite has been followed by some degree of resistance, and in a few instances by complete immunity to subsequent infection, nevertheless, none of the vaccines so far prepared have given promise of being able to reduce the incidence of any of the diseases due to metazoa and transmitted by arthropods.

It would appear from these observations that whereas advances in knowledge of parasites and of chemotherapeutic and chemoprophylactic measures for their control have proved very successful in curing and, in certain instances, protecting the individual, they have in no measurable way, with the possible exception of yellow fever, reduced the total incidence of arthropod-borne diseases nor are they likely to eradicate an arthropod-borne disease from a particular area.

Various methods of control directed against the animal reservoir and against the arthropod vector are considered in the following two chapters.

CHAPTER V

THE USE IN INSECT-BORNE DISEASES OF VARIOUS METHODS OF CONTROL DIRECTED AGAINST THE ANIMAL RESERVOIR

FOLLOWING the use of the yellow fever virus vaccine previously referred to, hopes at first were entertained that the disease might disappear from the endemic foci, on the supposition that if a sufficient number of persons were thus immunized, the vector would lack a source from which to obtain its infection. Several millions of people have now been successfully vaccinated against yellow fever but although this disease is no longer reported from many of the areas in which they live, yet it is the considered opinion of recognized authorities that this widespread immunization has failed to eradicate the disease from such areas. The reasons for the persistence of yellow fever are twofold; firstly, because in Africa and South America a proportion of the indigenous human population, although susceptible to yellow fever, is so tolerant of this disease that its occurrence passes unnoticed until revealed by the protection test, and, secondly, because there is another and still greater reservoir of the disease in the animal population, mainly in the primates.

The existence of an animal reservoir for yellow fever has been known for many years, although at first its vast extent was not recognized. Prior to this it had been established that bubonic plague and scrub typhus were really diseases of rodents and man's infection only an accident in the train of transmission. In addition it has long been known that animal reservoirs exist for most forms of trypanosomiasis which afflict the human population. On the other hand, many other arthropod transmitted infections were believed to be specific to the human host, and hence the hope was expressed that in such diseases effective chemotherapeutic and chemoprophylactic measures might result in sterilizing the human reservoir and eliminating the disease. With increased knowledge however, it has become clear that, with one or two important exceptions, man is only a sharer in the arthropod-borne infections, and that, short of exterminating the animal reservoir, the disease must, as in the case of yellow fever, remain present in the area even if unobservable in the human population. It is now known that certain forms of trypanosomiasis, leishmaniasis, spirochaetosis, viral and bacterial infections, and many forms of rickettsial infections, although they infect man and often cause serious epidemics are, nevertheless, essentially diseases of the animal, mainly rodent, population. This animal reservoir is sometimes limited in its extent and may involve only one type of animal host; more often, however, the reservoir is widely distributed and includes such dissimilar groups as primates, carnivores, marsupials and rodents. When man enters such an area, he may be infected by an arthropod vector that has itself become infected from a wild animal, and once in the human host the disease may pass to man by the same or by another species of vector.

In spite of this increasing awareness that the majority of human arthropod-borne infections were widespread in the animal population, there remained, until very recently, a limited number of insect-borne diseases which were considered by most authorities to be confined to the human race. These diseases included such important infections as louse-borne typhus, louse-borne relapsing fever, certain forms of filariasis, and the four types of malaria recorded in man. As regards the last named, it would appear certain that malaria is one of the few arthropod-borne infections causing disease in man which has no extensive animal reservoir. In the case of filariasis, no reservoir for *Wuchereria bancrofti* and *Onchocerca volvulus* has been discovered, but there is reason to believe that *Brugia malayi, Dipetelonema perstans* and *Loa loa* may have animal reservoirs. As regards the louse-borne diseases, it was formerly believed that there was no animal reservoir for *Treponema recurrentis,* whereas there was a large animal, mainly rodent, reservoir for *Treponema duttoni* transmitted to man by the tick. It has now been shown that an *S. duttoni* infection originally derived from the tick may be transmitted from man to man by the louse, and that, similarly, *S. recurrentis* infections originally derived from the louse may be transmitted by ticks. Under these circumstances, it appears possible that these two organisms may come to be regarded as strains of the same species which can be maintained in either human or animal reservoirs. In the case of typhus, no animal reservoir has been found for *Rickettsia prowazeki,* nor, in view of the habits of the louse and its early death following infection, is it likely that there is any immediate reservoir other than man where the infection might be maintained. But it is possible that there may be a "stem" strain virus in animals from which certain rickettsial and viral infections borne by arthropods can originate and to which they may revert.

There remain certain virus infections, such as sandfly fever and dengue, which cause disease in man, but for which no animal reservoir has, as yet, been demonstrated. In view of the fact, however, that certain of the insect vectors of these diseases feed on a wide variety of animal hosts and that relatively few experiments have been undertaken to establish whether such hosts are susceptible to the human strain of the disease, it would be unwise to believe that these diseases differ from the majority of the arthropod-borne infections in lacking an animal reservoir.

Since the parasite ensconced in the animal reservoir is not usually open to attack by chemotherapeutic measures, the only means available for controlling its spread is to break the contact between it and the human host, or else to destroy the animal reservoir. When the extent of the reservoir is limited and where the animals composing it are relatively accessible, as occurs in the case of big game harbouring *Trypanosoma rhodesiense,* the driving away or destruction of such animals is possible, and sometimes practicable. In other instances, and these comprise the majority of the arthropod-borne diseases, the animal reservoir is extensive and is composed of such inaccessible animals as rodents. Under these circumstances, attempts to control the parasite by measures directed against the reservoir are unlikely to prove successful.

CHAPTER VI

THE USE IN INSECT-BORNE DISEASES OF VARIOUS METHODS OF CONTROL DIRECTED AGAINST THE ARTHROPOD VECTOR

THE discovery of vast and often inaccessible animal reservoirs for most of the arthropod-borne infections and the realisation that chemotherapeutic and chemoprophylactic measures (which involve the use of vaccines, as well as drugs) seldom rid the general community of such infections, has resulted in increased attention being paid to the control of these diseases by measures directed against the vector. This change of attitude must not be taken as implying any weakening of faith in the necessity for continued research in chemotherapeutic and vaccinal techniques, but merely as showing that advances in methods for arthropod control have progressed more rapidly and that at the present time they are more likely to prove swiftly successful. Until such time, however, as complete control of the vector has been achieved the use of the former methods must not be abandoned.

Measures for controlling the arthropod vectors of disease may be considered in two categories, the first comprising measures which may be employed to prevent the vector coming in contact with the human host and the second comprising chemical or biological measures of control which are aimed at the destruction of the vector during some stage of its development.

(I) METHODS WHICH MAY BE EMPLOYED TO PREVENT THE VECTOR COMING IN CONTACT WITH THE HUMAN HOST.

This subject is far too complex for detailed discussion here but its scope can be outlined by giving examples of certain (1) biological, (2) mechanical and (3) chemical barriers which are commonly employed to separate the vector from its human host.

(1) BIOLOGICAL BARRIERS.

A wide variety of biological barriers may be employed but the most usual is the interposition of an area of land, usually a cleared area, between the human host and the breeding and resting places of the vector, the extent of the area and the nature of the clearing being dependent on the species of arthropod and its general ecological background. The use of biological barriers is often dependent on various complex factors, but as simple examples might be mentioned the siting of habitations well away from mosquito breeding places, and the interposition of a cleared area of land between the human population and the resting places of the tsetse fly.

(2) MECHANICAL BARRIERS.

Under the heading of mechanical barriers are included the use of protective clothing and the employment of screening; in the former category may be placed such simple but very important measures as the wearing of long-sleeved shirts and long trousers and the donning of mosquito boots in the evening; while in the latter category may be included the rendering of habitations proof against the invasion of biting flies, particularly mosquitoes, by the use of screening.

(3) CHEMICAL BARRIERS.

Under the heading of chemical barriers may be considered the use of a wide variety of naturally occurring repellent substances such as oil of citronella. These naturally occurring repellents have been largely replaced by synthetic preparations which are effective in preventing, although only for a limited period, the bites of a wide variety of potentially infected arthropods. There exists a wide range of such synthetic repellents, amongst which dimethyl phthalate and *n, n*-diethyl toluamide are outstanding examples. Under certain circumstances these mechanical barriers and chemical repellents may be advantageously combined. Thus, protective clothing is rendered much more efficient by previously proofing with dimethyl phthalate; while the physical discomfort involved in using fine mesh netting in the tropics to protect against sandflies and midges may sometimes be avoided by the employment of wide mesh netting previously impregnated with a repellent.

The use of mechanical and chemical barriers has greatly reduced the individual risk of contracting certain insect-borne infections, but their employment involves a certain standard of education and affluence and, even when widely adopted by persons possessing these advantages, does little to reduce the incidence of disease amongst the general population.

On the other hand biological barriers, when used in the control of arthropod vectors of disease, may be maintained at a relatively low cost (although the initial expense is often great) and thus have a more constant and lasting effect and a wider application as regards the protection of the general population.

(II) METHODS WHICH MAY BE EMPLOYED TO DESTROY THE VECTOR.

In the preceding section the use of biological, mechanical and chemical barriers to separate the vector from the human host were described. It would be possible to discuss methods aimed at the destruction of the arthropod vector under similar headings, but in practice mechanical methods such as fly traps, a wide variety of which have been used against not only the house fly but also against mosquitoes and tsetse flies, have little lasting effect on the density of the general vector population. Although these devices have no appreciable effect on the general insect population, nevertheless they have considerable value when used to destroy localised populations which are not receiving reinforcements from outside sources. Thus, fly traps designed against the house fly may destroy all these insects when they are living within a closed room or dwelling, while similar traps, when used out of doors and directed against the tsetse fly, have proved of considerable value when they were employed in isolated areas from which the flies could not escape.

28

Methods of control directed against the vector

If it is agreed to omit mechanical methods of control from further general consideration, then the remaining methods which may be employed to destroy the vector can be considered under the two headings (1) chemical methods of destruction and (2) biological methods of destruction. It must be remembered, however, that this division is artificial and that the two methods are often employed in combination. This is particularly true in the case of holometabolous insects in which the adult and larval forms differ markedly in their biological requirements so that one type of control may prove most effective for the imago and the other type of control for the larval stages.

(1) CHEMICAL METHODS OF DESTROYING THE VECTOR.

Here, as in the case of chemotherapeutic measures designed to destroy the parasite, great advances in knowledge have taken place during the past fifteen years concerning various methods which may be employed for the destruction of arthropod vectors of disease, particularly concerning their control by recently introduced insecticides, but whereas increase in knowledge concerning the parasite and its control has resulted mainly in benefits being conferred on the individual, increase in knowledge concerning the vector and its control has proved of far greater value to the general community. As in the case of the first estimation of the chemotherapeutic drugs, so in the case of the first estimation of the new insecticides too optimistic a view was taken of their applicability to the control of all insect-borne infections. Nevertheless, so spectacular have been some of the successes achieved that for the first time in history it would appear possible to predict that we have seen the last of the great louse-borne typhus epidemics and, quite possibly, the last of the great flea-borne bubonic plague epidemics. Such claims do not, of course, imply the disappearance of endemic typhus or plague, but merely that the disease, although present, can be prevented from reaching epidemic proportions in the human population.

The successful control of a disease in an area by the use of insecticides alone at once raises the question—is it possible not only to control but to eliminate a disease from an area by the destruction of the vector in that area without seriously interfering with the beneficial aspects of insect life?

We began our discussion by quoting the generally accepted view that arthropods as a whole are more benefical than harmful; if we agree that this is true we must dismiss as unjustifiable any scheme which is directed to the indiscriminate destruction of insect life in general over a wide area. It follows, therefore, that the insecticides employed must either have a selective action against the vectors of disease or else they must be capable of being employed in a selective manner. Unfortunately, none of the efficient insecticides possess such a selective action to an extent which renders possible their use for this purpose, and efforts at confining the destructive action of any insecticide to a particular arthropod or group of arthropods are limited to employing the insecticide in such a way that it will not materially affect the general community of beneficial or harmless arthropods. In certain instances, this limitation of insecticidal action to the destruction of obnoxious arthropods is relatively simple. The head and body louse which infest man, since they are permanent ectoparasites, can be destroyed without in any way affecting other insects, and since the methods used for destroying the louse are simple, inexpensive and unobtrusive, and since the louse appears to have no other host than man, it seems highly probable, providing resistance to insecticides does not occur, that it will disappear from many parts of the world, and, quite possibly, may become extinct. With its passing will disappear louse-borne diseases of man although, as already suggested, they may persist under a different guise in some animal reservoir.

If the lethal area is widened from the host to the host's domicile the insecticide can still be employed without materially affecting other forms of insect life. This form of control has proved highly efficient and is now practised on a wide scale for the destruction of various house-haunting arthropod vectors, particularly mosquitoes. That it is of great value in reducing the adult anopheline population in houses there is no doubt, but the first optimism which believed that persistent residual spraying would eventually destroy the total anopheline population in an area is now giving place to a more well-balanced view. This view, while recognizing the great value of residual spraying, considers that its efficacy varies greatly with the habits of the species against which it is used, and believes that if any really substantial reduction in the total anopheline population is to be affected, then for the most part (although not in all instances) measures directed against adult mosquitoes in houses must be combined with anti-larval measures in the field. The use of insecticides in the field for the destruction of arthropod vectors of disease has, of course, not been confined to the control of mosquitoes but has been successfully extended to measures directed against the larval stages of *Simulium* and against the adult forms of the tsetse fly. In spite of the extensive nature of these campaigns, there is little evidence of any great injurious effect having been produced on the beneficial insect or animal population. It must be remembered, however, that although the insecticides employed in these medical campaigns have not often been recorded as proving directly poisonous to beneficial insects and other animals, they may yet prove indirectly injurious by destroying some food factor necessary for the continued well-being of the beneficial species, and sufficient time may not have elapsed for this deleterious effect to have been observed. Although the extensive use of insecticides in the field when directed against medically important insects has not so far proved deleterious to the community, nevertheless it should be realised that their employment on a still larger scale is by no means free from objection. Insecticides directed against agriculturally injurious insects are now being used on a vast scale, and a large number of instances have been reported in which a particular contact insecticide has destroyed not only the species against which it was directed but also the predator or predators which, previous to its use, had exerted a beneficial controlling effect on potentially harmful arthropods, one or more of which were insusceptible to the insecticide. Once freed from the control of the predators, these injurious species, since they were resistant to the insecticide, multiplied so prolifically that they eventually caused more damage than the original susceptible pest which had been succesfully destroyed.

Finally, reference must be made to one other factor which appears to be steadily increasing in importance and which mitigates the successful use of certain insecticides. Just as the parasite can develop resistance to the drug, so the vector may develop and transmit to succeeding generations resistance to the insecticides employed for its destruction. Instances of resistance to the new insecticides were observed (in two species) for the first time in 1947. Since then the number and variety of species acquiring resistance has steadily increased and at the present time reports from widespread sources have involved nearly fifty species of public health importance, including most genera except *Phlebotomus, Glossina* and *Simulium*. There is as yet no evidence of diminution in this spread; and at the present time about twenty species of anophelines are known to be resistant, while the resistance of body lice in Korea and Egypt is sufficient to interfere seriously with successful control both by DDT and *gamma*-BHC.

(2) BIOLOGICAL METHODS OF DESTROYING THE VECTOR.
Although biological methods of control are primarily aimed at limiting the multiplication of the vector, rather than at its immediate destruction—which is the aim of chemical methods of control—nevertheless this distinction is theoretical rather than practical and it is usual to employ both methods simultaneously.

Biological methods of control as used today in agriculture and hygiene depend for their success on the application of the knowledge derived from the work of generations of entomologists who have studied the essential environmental conditions necessary for the successful existence of particular species of arthropods. In so far as hygiene is concerned, although it is true that prior to the introduction of the new insecticides certain chemicals (such as the pyrethrins for the destruction of adult mosquitoes, copper aceto-arsenite (Paris Green) for killing anopheline larvae and the thiocyanates for getting rid of lice) provided powerful weapons with which to enhance the effects of biological control nevertheless, until the coming of the new insecticides, biological control was regarded as the more generally effective method and one which had an almost universal application. However, with the coming of immensely more powerful insecticides such as DDT and *gamma*-BHC, many hygienists began to neglect the sound and well established biological methods of insect control and in their place to employ a wide range of insecticides, all of which were capable of causing a rapid and spectacular reduction in certain insect populations. At first the results obtained were so impressive that certain authorities, not perceiving that each new insecticide, although meeting the immediate need, almost invariably introduced a new problem, were rash enough to suggest that continued success from chemical control could be relied upon and that biological methods of control were now obsolete. Later, however, it was

31

discovered that many species of insects of medical importance were capable of developing resistance to some of the most effective insecticides, while at the same time similar observations were made in agriculture and, in addition, it was noted that many predators of plant pests were themselves more susceptible to insecticides than the pests they fed upon.

These discoveries have caused the balance of opinion to shift, or at any rate to show signs of shifting, in favour of a return to the use of biological methods of controlling arthropod vectors of disease and agricultural pests. This increasing emphasis on biological control is not so much due to any immediate failure on the part of contact insecticides as to the realisation that at any time in the future the development of drug resistance, or of any one of the many factors known to mitigate the use of such insecticides, may force a return to the admittedly slow but remarkably effective biological methods which aim at limiting the multiplication of the vector rather than at its immediate destruction.

Since no one method of effective biological control can have a universal applicability a vast literature has grown up concerning the various methods, and the local modifications of such methods, which have been successfully employed to control particular species of medically important arthropods in different parts of the world. In a work of this present type it would not be possible to consider in any detail individual methods of control directed against a particular species of arthropod, or even those directed against particular groups of arthropods. Nevertheless, it is possible to outline the principles on which these various methods of biological control are founded and if this is done it will at once become evident that the governing principles of biological control are designed to reproduce and accentuate the adverse conditions sometimes encountered by the arthropod in nature. These natural adverse conditions and man's adaptation of them for purposes of control, although overlapping, can be classified into three broad groups, (i) alterations in the fauna which affect the vector, (ii) alterations in the flora which affect the vector, (iii) alterations in the physical constitution of the environment which affect the vector.

(i) *Alterations in the fauna which affect the vector.*

The propagation of arthropod vectors of disease will be affected by the local fauna in a variety of ways. Thus, most arthropods concerned in the transmission of diseases are, in their adult form, partially dependent on vertebrates for their blood meal while the larvae of these and of many other species are dependent for their food, and in many instances for their shelter, on the local fauna. In addition the presence or absence of predators and parasites in the local fauna will play some part in determining the density of the vector population.

Various methods of control founded on studies of the food requirements of the vector, in its adult and larval stages, and of the effects of predators and parasites on the density of the vector population, have been employed with varying degrees of success.

(a) *Alterations in the fauna affecting the food supply and shelter of the vector.* In every insect-borne disease, with the exception of those which are transmitted by vectors which feed exclusively on man, alterations in the local fauna are

32

bound to affect the vector population and man has made use of this fact in various ways of which the following are typical examples. As the first example might be quoted the reduction in the density of the tsetse fly, *Glossina morsitans,* the vector of *Trypanosoma rhodesiense,* which follows the driving away or destruction of "big game" (mainly ungulates) which form the vector's main food supply. As a second example one might quote the reduction in the density of plague fleas which follows the destruction of the rodent population; in this latter instance the vector is dependent on its host not only for shelter and blood meals in the adult stage, but in its larval stages for shelter in the host's burrow and, for food, on its host's excreta.

(b) *Alterations in the predator and parasite fauna which may affect the vector.* Although remarkably successful results have followed the employment of various species of predators and parasites for the control of agricultural pests, similarly successful results have not up to the present been recorded following their use as a means of controlling the vectors of medically important diseases.

As regards predators: in nature vertebrate and invertebrate predators play a part of some importance in limiting population growth amongst arthropods of medical importance and various schemes have been devised to encourage such creatures as a means of biological control. Amongst vertebrates, various species of fish, birds and some mammals are important predators of certain insect vectors of disease. In almost every tropical country an attempt has been made to foster the breeding of fish, such as *Gambusia* spp., which feed on mosquito larvae, while the encouragement of bat breeding has often been advocated as a means of reducing mosquitoes. It is probable that such birds as bee eaters, in destroying tsetse flies, and swallows, in feeding on mosquitoes, may play some part in helping to control these insects, whilst the "tick-bird" is so important in keeping down the numbers of ticks on cattle that, in some countries, it is protected by law.

Amongst the arthropods there exist a vast number of predatory species which help in destroying the various vectors of disease. For example, it is known that dragonflies and certain predaceous culicine larvae do reduce the mosquito population and that some African spiders trap considerable numbers of tsetse flies in their webs, but the part played by predatory arthropods as a whole is a relatively small one and attempts to encourage their propagation and spread as a means of limiting the population of insect vectors of disease has not proved of practical value.

As regards parasites: the parasitic fauna found in arthropod vectors of disease is extensive, including as it does, various species of insects, helminths, protozoa, bacteria, rickettsiae and viruses, and under the title of naturalistic methods of control one might include the encouragement of those parasites most likely to prove pathogenic to the disease vectors. Here, as in the case of the predators, there is no good evidence that the encouragement of any parasite of arthropods of medical importance has produced any significant reduction in the vector population in any but localised areas.

33

(ii) *Alterations in the flora which may affect the vector.*

The adult forms of many species of insects of medical importance are dependent to a large extent on the local flora for the provision of resting places which will provide a suitable microclimate, while their larvae and those of other species are, in many instances, dependent on the existing aquatic or semi-aquatic vegetation both for shelter and oxygen. In addition some species of plants act as predators, while certain fungi act as parasites of many species of medically important insects. Man's utilisation of the knowledge which has been acquired of the dependence of such insects on the local vegetations is extensively employed by him when planning the control of various species of medically important arthropods.

(a) *Alterations in the flora which may affect the food supply and shelter of the vector.* Altering the flora so as to render the habitat unsuitable for the vector is now a recognised part of the control of such widely differing vectors as tsetse flies, ticks, mites and mosquitoes. A variety of techniques are used in this form of control but, here again, two examples will be sufficient to illustrate the principles employed. The control of African trypanosomiasis is, of course, dependent on the control of the vector, the tsetse fly, and of all the methods used for the control of the tsetse, alterations in the local vegetation have proved the most effective. At one time these alterations took the form of extensive clearing of the bush, but it is now known that in the case of certain important species, e.g. *Glossina tachinoides*, atmospheric conditions at certain times of the year are so adverse that this species can only survive by taking refuge in foliage close to the ground; the removal of this zone of climatic refuge is by itself sufficient to secure effective control. The second example concerns the control of certain species of mosquitoes (*Mansonia*) which are responsible for the transmission of a particular form of filariasis. In some parts of the tropics the larval stages of these insects depend for shelter and oxygen on the presence of certain water plants—such as *Pistia*—and in many areas the removal of these plants has resulted in the partial or even complete control of the mosquitoes transmitting the disease.

(b) *Alterations in the predator and parasitic flora which may affect the vector.* As regards predators, although such plants as *Utricularia exoleta* capture many mosquito larvae, nevertheless, the part played by predaceous plants must be small compared with the part played by predators in the animal kingdom. As regards the part played by parasitic plants, one might mention the introduction of parasitic fungi of the genus *Ceolomyces* into the breeding place of mosquitoes; these parasitic fungi having entered the bodies of the larvae and having persisted to the adult form, invade and destroy the ovaries of the adult female. Nevertheless, as in the case of the part played by animal parasites, there is no good evidence of any significant effect on the total vector population being produced by such measures.

(iii) *Alterations in the physical conditions of the environment affecting the vector.*

In nature the physical conditions of the arthropod's environment are constantly altering and these alterations tend either to stimulate or else to depress the propagation of various species concerned in the transmission of disease. Some of these physical changes—such as the drying up of a lake, alterations in the speed and course of a river, or the urbanisation of a previously rural area— are irregular in their time of occurrence and are usually very slow in development, so that the corresponding changes in the vector population may only be noticeable after many years.

Other physical changes are seasonal in character and cause regular fluctuations in the arthropod density; thus, in the tropics, there is usually a well marked fall in the density of the vector population during the dry season and a corresponding rise in the density of the vector, coupled with an increase in the incidence of disease, during the wet season. This fall in the density of the vector during the dry season is in part due to the disappearance of many of the pools, swamps and small streams which form the breeding places of those species of vectors whose larvae are aquatic. In addition, however, the advent of a prolonged spell of dry weather results in the disappearance of certain microclimates essential for the survival of the adults of many species of arthropods concerned in the transmission of disease, and for the growth and development of those species whose larvae lead a terrestial existence.

In the instances just quoted of seasonal alteration affecting vector density, the change over of the seasons is usually gradual in character and the rise or fall in the vector population not abrupt. In other instances, however, changes in the physical conditions of the vector's environment may be very rapid and result in an abrupt fall in the vector density; thus, in semi-tropical conditions, such as exist in Southern Europe, a sudden drop in temperature temporarily inactivates the larval and pupal stages of the arthropod vectors and causes the adult forms to pass into a state of hibernation or semi-hibernation; while a still more rapid alteration in the vector population may be observed to follow a heavy downpour of rain which has swept away large numbers of anopheline larvae, or a high wind which has carried with it vast numbers of the adult forms.

Man's adaptation of some of these natural variations as a means of controlling vectors of disease may range from vast engineering schemes to the periodic sluicing of anopheline breeding places, or to the simple filling in of cracks and crevices in infested dwellings and the removal of domestic garbage. As examples of great engineering works designed for the control of mosquito-borne diseases one might quote the various drainage schemes which, when combined with other methods of control, made possible the building of the Panama Canal in Central America, and rendered habitable the Pontine Marshes in Italy. As regards small scale measures of control based on altering the arthropod's environment to its disadvantage, it would be possible to quote an almost endless number of examples, but the following will serve as typical of the more important methods which are in almost universal use. In tropical Africa a high proportion of the indigenous population lives in mud huts, the walls and floors of which crack as the mud dries, and in these cracks the African soft tick (*Ornithodoros moubata*), the vector of relapsing fever, establishes itself.

c

The replacement of these mud huts by stone and concrete buildings leads to the almost complete elimination of the tick and the disappearance of relapsing fever. A similar improvement in dwelling accommodation, following the replacement of wooden buildings by brick or stone and concrete houses, has resulted in an enormous reduction in the bed bug population, both in temperate and tropical climates, while in South America similar measures have resulted not only in a reduction in the density of the bed bug but also in the density of the reduviid or "rapacious" bugs, which are responsible for the transmission of Chagas' disease. The various species of sandflies which are responsible for the transmission of such important diseases as kala azar, tropical sore and phlebotomus fever, are dependent in most instances on a warm moist microclimate and the presence of one or more species of vertebrate, for the wellbeing of the larval and adult stages. Sometimes all these requirements are found within a dwelling house or stable but many important species breed in the microclimates existing in the rubbish and rubble surrounding buildings and which harbour a rodent and reptile population. The removal of the rubbish and rubble results in the immediate disappearance of the essential microclimate and a fall in the density of the vector population.

Modern methods of vector control involving the use of highly effective insecticides and highly specialised biological methods of control are now so well recognised and so widely employed that there is a danger of omitting proper emphasis on the value of general and personal hygiene. The well lit, well ventilated and scrupulously clean building will tend to harbour fewer vectors of disease than the neglected habitation. In a similar manner good personal hygiene as exemplified in a person of clean habits is conducive to keeping him free of permanent ectoparasites although unfortunately insuring no immunity against the attacks of occasional blood-suckers.

It is clearly impossible to evaluate each of these various types of biological control in the case of individual species of medically important insects. On the other hand a knowledge of the life-cycle and habits of a particular species generally supplies a guide to the type of control required and, later, when considering the life-cycle and habits of particular species of insects, attention will be drawn to those points, a knowledge of which will aid in devising methods for its control.

CHAPTER VII

A DESCRIPTION OF THE PHYLUM ARTHROPODA AND ITS DIVISION INTO CLASSES CONTAINING CREATURES OF MEDICAL IMPORTANCE

ENTOMOLOGY means the study of insects and is derived from the Greek words "entomon", signifying an insect, and "logos", meaning a science. Strictly speaking, therefore, the term "medical entomology" should be confined to the study of a limited number of insects (Hexapoda i.e. creatures possessing three pairs of legs) which directly or indirectly affect the health of man; for the sake of convenience however, not only insects but other closely related creatures of medical importance, such as certain ticks, mites, spiders, scorpions and crustacea are included in the study of medical entomology.

Although these various medically important creatures differ greatly in their morphology, life cycle and habits, nevertheless they all possess certain anatomical features in common which enable zoologists to classify them in the phylum Arthropoda.* The members of this phylum are characterised, externally, by the possession of a segmented, hard (chitinised) exoskeleton, a proportion of the segments of which bear segmented paired appendages which, like the body, are chitinised. Internally the arthropods are characterised by the possession of a single body cavity, the haemocoele, which is filled with haemolymph in which float the various internal organs; this haemocoele and the contained haemolymph extends into all the appendages.

The ancestral prototype of the arthropod was probably a worm-like creature

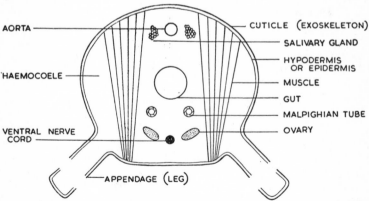

Fig. 1. Transverse section through the thorax of an arthropod. (Diagrammatic).

---

* From the Greek—"arthron" = joint, "pous" = foot, i.e. animals with jointed feet.

living in an aquatic or a semi-aquatic environment and composed of a number of membraneous segments, each bearing a pair of appendages, which were chiefly used for locomotion. During the course of evolution, the integument of the arthropod became hardened by the deposition of chitin and other substances to form an exoskeleton which served to protect and give rigidity to the body. To allow for movement, the hardening process took place separately on the segments, each segment being provided with a chitinous dorsal plate, known as the tergum or notum, and a chitinous ventral plate known as the sternum, these plates being joined by a membrane carrying a lateral plate or pleuron. In order to give stability to the appendages the chitinisation of the pleural plates took place around the base of the appendages.

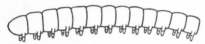

Fig. 2. Diagrammatic representation of a primitive arthropod.

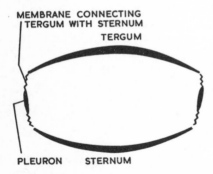

MEMBRANE CONNECTING
TERGUM WITH STERNUM

TERGUM

PLEURON   STERNUM

Fig. 3. Transverse section through the thorax of an arthropod showing the chitinous plates. (Diagrammatic).

The acquirement of a segmented exoskeleton was an essential preliminary to the conquest of the land by the arthropods, for it conferred on these creatures certain characteristics which facilitate their existence in a relatively dry terrestrial environment. Not only does the hard exoskeleton give rigidity to the body and protect the soft internal organs from injury but, since it is almost impermeable to water vapour, it greatly reduces water loss and thereby protects the arthropod from too great dessication in a dry atmosphere. Probably the next most important factor in permitting colonisation of the land by the arthropods was the development of an efficient respiratory system adapted to a terrestrial existence. The most successful forms amongst the higher arthropods have dispensed with the gills and lung books (respiratory pouches or pockets) which characterise some of the lower arthropods, and have developed a breathing system which communicates to the exterior by relatively small openings known as spiracles leading into an extensive system of ramifying tubes and bladder-like structures; in order to guard against water loss the spiracles of many species of arthropods are provided with valves.

The primitive condition of a worm-like body with segments very similar to one another did not, however, persist in the arthropods and during the course of evolution a grouping of the segments into definite regions began to take place. It appears probable that the differentiation of a head region (mainly concerned with direction finding, location of food and feeding) resulted from the separation of the first six segments from the rest of the body, each segment

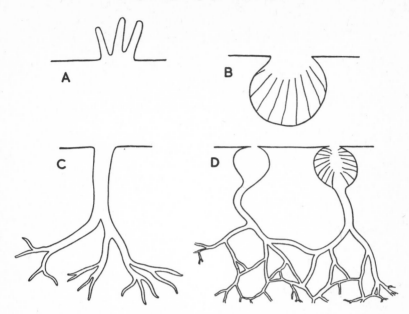

Fig. 4. Diagrammatic representation of different types of breathing systems occurring in arthropods. *A.* gills; *B.* lung books; *C.* unguarded and *D.* guarded types of spiracular openings connecting with a tracheal system.

carrying with it its paired appendages. These appendages which previously were primarily concerned with locomotion became greatly modified and transformed into sensory structures (such as antennae and palps) and into feeding organs (such as the mandibles and maxillae) which served the purpose of seizing and chewing or sucking up the arthropod's food supplies. Although

these evolutionary changes can be traced in embryological material and in fossil remains, in most of the existing terrestial and aquatic arthropods the segments of the head have become coalesced to form a definite head capsule and very little of the previous primitive arrangement can be recognised.

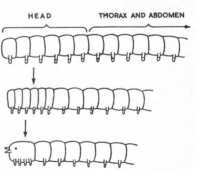

Fig. 5. Diagrammatic representation of the evolution of the head region in a primitive arthropod.

In most arthropods the rest of the body segments have become grouped into a distinct thoracic region and a distinct abdominal region; however, in certain groups of arthropods, such as the centipedes and the millipedes, this division is not clear and it is difficult, and sometimes well-nigh impossible, to distinguish the thorax and the abdomen. In those arthropods in which there is little or no differentiation between the thorax and the abdomen most of the segments bear appendages, a point well illustrated by the centipedes and millipedes; on the other hand, in those arthropods, such as insects, in which the thorax and abdomen are clearly differentiated, the number of segments which bear appendages is reduced.

The number of segments which comprises the thorax varies in different classes of the phylum Arthropoda; thus in the Crustacea the thorax may be comprised of as many as eleven segments bearing appendages, some of which are used for locomotion and others for feeding or respiration or all three functions. In the class Insecta, the thorax is always made up of three segments which are exclusively concerned with locomotion.

In all classes of arthropods in which the thorax and abdomen are distinct the remaining segments of the body have become grouped to form the abdomen. As in the case of the thorax the number of segments making up the abdomen and the functions performed by the attached appendages vary according to the class to which the particular arthropod belongs.

In the case of arthropods occurring in the class Crustacea the number of the abdominal segments and the functions of the attached appendages vary greatly; there may be as few as two or three segments or as many as twenty-one, while the functions of the attached appendages may be concerned with locomotion, reproduction or respiration. In the case of arthropods occurring in the class Insecta there is much less variation in the number of segments and in the functions of the attached appendages, the number of segments usually varying between ten and eleven of which only the terminal segments bear appendages and these with few exceptions are concerned solely with reproduction.

THE DIVISION OF THE PHYLUM ARTHROPODA INTO CLASSES CONTAINING INSECTS OF MEDICAL IMPORTANCE

The great diversity of structure observed amongst the arthropods necessitates the subdivision of the phylum Arthropoda into a number of smaller divisions known as classes. Zoologists differ in opinion as to the number of classes into which the phylum (which comprises 800,000 or so known species of arthropods) may be divided, but although it is not possible in this book to discuss the various classifications which have been proposed, the characters of six of the classes containing creatures of medical importance may be defined as follows:-
Class I.— *Hexapoda or Insecta*. This class contains all the true insects including such medically important groups as the flies, fleas, lice and bugs.

Members of the class Insecta possess a body divided into three regions—a head, a thorax and an abdomen. The head bears, in addition to the mouthparts, a single pair of feelers or antennae, while the three segments of the thorax each bear a pair of legs; one or two pairs of wings may or may not be present. (The Insecta is the only class of the phylum Arthropoda in which wings are found).

Class II.—*Arachnida*. This class includes such medically important arthropods as ticks, mites, spiders and scorpions.

The body of arachnids is divided into two main regions—a cephalothorax (in which the head and thorax are fused together) and an abdomen. The cephalothorax bears six pair of appendages, the first two pairs functioning as mouthparts and the last four pairs as walking legs. There are no feelers or antennae.

Class III.—*Crustacea*. This class includes such arthropods as lobsters, crabs and water fleas, some species of which are intermediate hosts of certain helminths of medical importance.

The Crustacea, which show a great variety of form, have a body which is divided into a head, thorax and abdomen. They may be distinguished from all other arthropods by the presence of two pairs of antennae. In species of medical importance a proportion, at least, of the appendages are branched (biramous).

Class IV.—*Chilopoda*. This class contains the true centipedes.

Centipedes possess a well defined head and a long dorso-ventrally flattened body composed of numerous similar segments; there is no distinction between the thorax and the abdomen. The head, in addition to the mouthparts, bears a pair of antennae and each segment of the body, except the last two, bears a pair of walking legs; the first pair of legs is modified to form poison claws.

Class V.—*Diplopoda*. The class Diplopoda contains all the millipedes or "thousand legs".

Millipedes have a long cylindrical body composed of numerous similar segments; there is no division into a thoracic and an abdominal region. The head in addition to the mouthparts bears a pair of antennae and most of the segments of the body carry pairs of legs. The genital opening of the millipedes is placed at the anterior end of the body, unlike their close relatives the centipedes in which the genital opening is at the posterior end of the body.

Class VI.—*Pentastomida*. The creatures included in this class are highly specialised endoparasitic animals which from time to time are found living in the body of man.

The position of this class in the phylum Arthropoda is uncertain. The adult and nymphs are remarkably worm-like in appearance (indeed at one time, they were classified as nematodes) and bear no recognisable appendages; the larvae of some species however bear appendages and it is largely because of this that they are regarded as being arthropods.

CHAPTER VIII

THE GENERAL STRUCTURE AND EXTERNAL ANATOMY OF INSECTS

THE GENERAL STRUCTURE OF INSECTS.

MEMBERS of the class Insecta (synonym Hexapoda) have the general structure common to all members of the phylum Arthropoda to which they belong, inasmuch as they possess a segmented chitinised exoskeleton bearing appendages, and a single body cavity containing the haemolymph in which the internal organs float. The exact definition of a member of the class Insecta has been provided in the previous chapter, and from this it may be seen that for an arthropod to be defined as an insect—in the strict sense of the term—the adult form must possess, in addition to the general characters just mentioned, three pairs of legs and a body which shows division into three well marked regions. It is clear that this definition at once separates the true insects from the ticks, spiders etc., with which they are often confused.

THE EXTERNAL ANATOMY OF INSECTS.

The three main divisions into which the body of the adult insect is divided are the head, the thorax and the abdomen, and these will now be studied in greater detail.

THE HEAD. It is probable that in insects the head originally consisted of six segments which have become fused together to form a head capsule from which arise appendages; some but not all of these appendages can be associated with certain of the anterior segments of the primitive arthropod.

The head in all adult insects bears a pair of eyes. These eyes, which do not represent appendages, are usually compound and composed of many facets, although simple eyes, ocelli, may also be present; when the compound eyes are close together they are referred to as holoptic and when far apart as dichoptic. The area between the eyes is known as the vertex, while the area below the vertex is known as the frons; from this latter area arise two sensory structures—the antennae. The antennae, which represent the appendages of the primitive second segment, are jointed structures, the number of segments varying according to the type of insect. The area of the head below the frons is known as the clypeus, and the terminal forward prolongation of the head capsule is known as the labrum or upper lip.

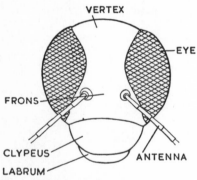

Fig. 6. The head of an adult insect seen from the front.

Before studying the structure of the mouthparts of insects of medical importance, which generally possess highly specialised blood-sucking appendages, it is advisable to consider those of a generalised feeder—such as the cockroach—in which they are relatively simple.

In the case of the cockroach the mouthparts may be regarded as consisting of an upper lip, a pair of upper jaws, a pair of lower jaws, a lower lip and a tongue-shaped structure which conducts the saliva. The upper lip is an unpaired structure known as the labrum; it is not an appendage (hence it is unpaired) and is essentiallly a prolongation forwards of the head capsule. The upper jaws, which are paired and which are probably representative of the appendages borne by the fourth segment of the primitive arthropod, are known as the mandibles; in the cockroach these are massive strongly chitinised structures used for crushing and tearing food. The lower jaws or the maxillae (the 1st maxillae) are paired and each consists essentially of two parts, an outer tactile part, the maxillary palp (which in the Diptera is generally referred to as "the

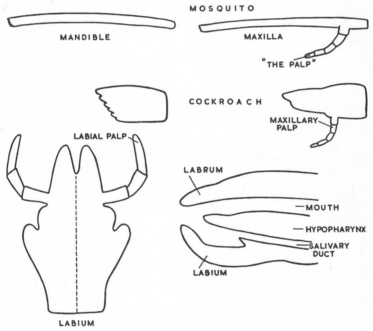

Fig. 7. Diagrammatic representation of the mouthparts of an insect.

palp") and an inner feeding part. The maxillae are probably derived from the appendages on the 5th segment of the primitive arthropod. The lower lip or labium (the 2nd maxillae) is also paired but the two parts have become fused to form a single organ each half of which consists of an outer tactile part, the labial palp, and an inner feeding portion. The fused blades of the labium probably represent the appendages borne on the 6th segment of the primitive arthropod. Lying between the labrum and the labium is the tongue-shaped structure—the hypopharynx—which is always associated with the opening of the salivary duct.

In those insects which have to pierce the skin of their hosts in order to obtain a blood meal, mouthparts of the type possessed by the cockroach are clearly unsuitable, and in all blood-sucking insects—and therefore in most insects of medical importance—these structures have become elongated and stylet-like, and are admirably adapted for probing the skin and tissues and for sucking up the blood from the lumen of a capillary or from the haemorrhage resulting from its severance. This change from the chewing type of mouthparts, as exemplified in the cockroach, to the blood-sucking type exemplified in such insects of medical importance as the mosquito and the horse fly, may be understood more readily if the mouthparts of the cockroach are imagined as consisting of some rubbery and therefore extensible substance which if drawn away from the head by means of a pair of pliers become transformed into the long stylet-like structures which characterize most blood-sucking insects.

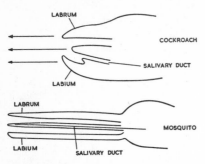

Fig. 8. Diagrammatic representation of the evolution of the mouthparts of a blood-sucking insect, such as the mosquito.

In the case of such insects as the mosquito and the horse fly, to which reference has just been made, it is possible to demonstrate all the essential structures which compose the mouthparts of the cockroach, but in many other blood-sucking insects, for example the tsetse fly, some of these structures —in this instance the mandibles and maxillae—have disappeared during the process of evolution. In addition, it must be realised that amongst different species of blood-sucking insects of medical importance the functions performed by the various structures composing the mouthparts are not always similar. Thus, in the case of both the tsetse fly and the mosquito the labium forms a sheath or scabbard in which are carried the other mouthparts, but, whereas in the case of the tsetse fly this organ forms an efficient skin-piercing weapon which enters deeply into the tissues of the host, in the mosquito the labium serves no such function and remains resting on the skin surface during the meal. Finally, attention must be drawn to the danger of over simplification when trying to trace the evolution of the mouthparts of biting insects of medical importance. Whilst an evolutionary process from the biting or chewing type of mouthparts to the skin-piercing type is clearly discernible in such widely differing insects as the cockroach and the blood-sucking flies, in certain other instances highly specialised mouthparts such as those of the louse present features which defy attempts similarly to homologise their structure with those of other types. This caution regarding the danger of over simplification of evolutionary processes applies not only to the mouthparts but also to other anatomical structures such as the thorax.

THE THORAX. If the head is considered as composed of the first six segments of the body then the thorax may be regarded as being composed of the seventh to the ninth segments.

The thorax of insects is a well defined unit consisting of three segments, the prothorax, the mesothorax and the metathorax, each of which bears a pair of appendages, the legs, which are used for the purpose of walking. In insects which fly, the second and third segments (the mesothorax and the metathorax respectively) bear the wings. In the Diptera (or true flies) the second pair of wings are reduced to vestigial peg-like structures known as halteres.

In wingless insects the three segments of the thorax are approximately equal in size, whilst in those which bear two pairs of wings the wing-bearing segments, i.e. the mesothorax and the metathorax, are much larger than the prothorax, which is wingless. In the Diptera, which only possess one pair of wings arising from the mesothorax, the second pair of wings being represented by peg-like structures, the halteres, this segment of the thorax is greatly developed in order to accommodate the large flight muscles required to operate the single pair of wings, while the prothorax and the metathorax are greatly reduced in size and are relatively insignificant.

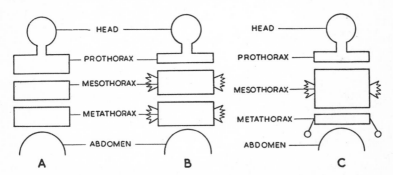

Fig. 9. Diagrammatic representation of the relative sizes of the thoracic segments in *A*. a wingless insect; *B*. a four-winged insect and *C*. a two-winged insect (Diptera).

As has already been explained in the last chapter, each segment of an arthropod is provided with a dorsal plate, the tergum or notum, a ventral plate or sternum and two side plates, the pleura. In the Hexapoda these plates, however, have not remained simple structures and during the course of evolution of insects from primitive types of arthropods to such highly organised insects as the Diptera, the plates covering various portions of the thorax have undergone many modifications and changes.

In the case of the Diptera these modifications and changes have resulted in the thorax presenting a somewhat complicated external anatomy, the various anatomical landmarks of which are used by systematists to separate many closely allied species of Diptera, some of which are of great medical importance. In practice these identifications are usually carried out when using illustrated "keys" prepared by specialists.

The finding of the various anatomical landmarks and the comparison of the structures iden:ified with those illustrated in the keys can usually, although not always, be made without great difficulty, nor is a previous knowledge of the origin of these structures essential. On the other hand the mere geographical identification of anatomical landmarks, without reference to their significance or phylogenetic origin, is not only lacking in interest but, later, may preclude a proper understanding of many interesting problems such as those associated with the transmission of various forms of parasites to the human host. It is for this reason that the following account of the anatomy of the insect contains brief references to the probable phylogenetic and anatomical significance of the various structures referred to.

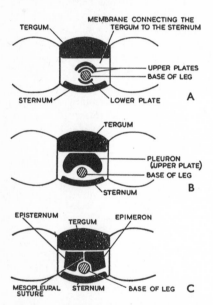

Fig. 10. Diagrammatic representation of the evolution of the pleuron in higher insects. *A.* first; *B.* second and *C.* third stage of development.

The Pleuron. The pleuron or lateral plate of a segment of the insect thorax may be a relatively insignificant and poorly defined structure such as occurs in primitive insects, or it may be a large complex plate, broken up by sutures (or infoldings of the integument) into many subdivisions, as occurs in the case of the higher insects—such as the Diptera.

The evolution of the complex pleuron of the higher insects from the primitive insect type probably took place in the following manner. In primitive insects there were formed around the base of each leg two small upper plates and a lower plate. The two upper plates in higher insects have become fused together to form a single plate which has extended its territory so as to cover most of the lateral wall of the thoracic segment, resulting in the formation of a large plate known as the pleuron, whilst the lower plate has become imperceptibly fused with the sternum and has lost its identity as an independent structure. In winged insects, the pleuron has undergone a further evolution and is divided by a vertical division, the mesopleural suture, into an anterior portion, the episternum and a posterior portion, the epimeron. In certain higher insects, such as the mosquito and the house fly, the pleural region has undergone additional modifications which consist essentially of a subdivision of the episternum and the epimeron into smaller plates or pleurites* which differ in each family of flies.

Although a detailed study of the pleurites is quite beyond the scope of an elementary text book, the student should keep in mind that these plates and the hairs which they bear are used extensively by the systematist in classifying medically important flies such as mosquitoes, house flies and blow flies. Due to the great development of the mesothorax in flies, the mesopleuron is large and its characters are much used in classification, more so than those of the prothorax and metathorax which are greatly reduced. In the various groups of flies

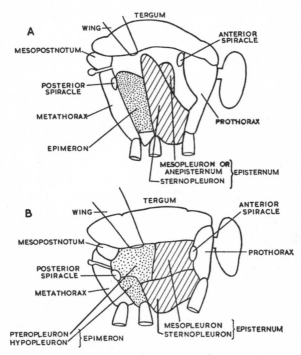

Fig. 11. Diagrammatic representation of the thorax as seen from the lateral aspect of *A*. a mosquito and *B*. a house fly.

---

* The termination—ite—indicates smaller divisions, e.g. the tergum may be divided into smaller plates each of which is known as a tergite. Similarly, the pleuron may comprise several pleurites and the sternum, several sternites.

the breaking up of the pleuron into smaller plates or pleurites shows certain differences; for instance, whereas in the case of the mosquito (see Fig. 11A) the episternum is divided by a diagonal suture into an upper plate and a lower plate and the epimeron does not appear to be divided, in the case of the house fly and the blow fly (see Fig. 11B) the episternum and the epimeron are each divided by a transverse suture into an upper and a lower plate.

The Tergum. In wingless primitive insects each thoracic segment, as in the case of the abdominal segments, bears a dorsal plate known as the tergum or notum, a small anterior portion of which is demarcated off from the main tergal plate by a suture or inward inflection of the integument. In insects which bear wings these sutures assume great importance and are well defined, for they serve as points of attachment for certain of the large flight muscles.

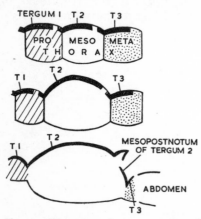

The small anterior portion of the tergum or notum which the suture demarcates off from the rest of the tergal plate is closely associated with the tergum of the preceding segment (particularly in the case of wing-bearing segments) and is known as the postnotum of the segment with which it is associated. For instance, in the Diptera, where only the mesothorax is well developed, its postnotum, which is known as the mesopostnotum, is so closely associated with the mesothorax that it is difficult to trace its connection with the metathorax; it is, however, quite distinct form the main body of the mesothorax and its characters are much used in systematics.

Fig. 12 Diagrammatic representation of the development of the mesopostnotum of a two-winged fly (lateral aspect).

In addition to the changes discussed above, the tergum or notum may be further broken up into smaller divisions due to the formation of sutures to which muscles are attached. In the Diptera it is usual to find a suture, the

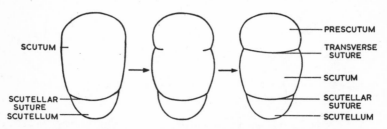

Fig. 13. Diagrammatic representation of the development of the transverse suture in the tergum of the mesothorax of a two-winged fly (dorsal aspect).

scutellar suture, separating off a small postei ɔr portion of the tergum, known as the scutellum, from the larger anterior portion known as the scutum. In certain flies a small anterior portion of the scutum, known as the prescutum, is separated off from it by a suture known as the transverse suture. The number and form of these various sutures are used for purposes of identification.

The Wing. The wing has developed as a lateral prolongation of the tergum carrying with it, outwards, a reflexion from the body wall. The wing is thus seen to be a hollow structure in communication with the haemocoele of the thorax and contains haemolymph, tracheae and nerve fibres. Immediately after the insect has become an adult it forces blood into the wing haemocoele so that the wing becomes expanded, but the two surfaces of the wing soon

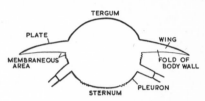

Fig. 14. Diagrammatic representation of a cross section through the thorax of a two-winged fly, showing how the wing has developed as a lateral prolongation of the tergum of the mesothorax.

become apposed, leaving channels enclosing blood spaces, tracheae and nerves, which appear as thickened ridges or lines on the wing membrane and which

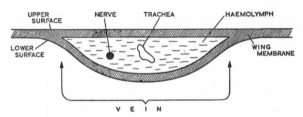

Fig. 15. Diagrammatic representation of a cross section through the wing vein of a fly.

are known as the veins of the wings. Haemolymph flows in the veins of the wings throughout the life of the insect.

Two methods exist for the naming of the veins in the insect wing. One method involves an elaborate system of nomenclature known as the Comstock-Needham method which is applicable to all insects, and the other involves a simpler system which consists in numbering the veins in the wing and which is used mainly by entomologists who specialise in the study of the Diptera. The system of the numbering of the veins is the simpler and it will be adopted in this book, since, for all practical purposes, the medical officer does not require to familiarise himself with the more elaborate Comstock-Needham nomenclature.

In Fig. 16 it is seen that there is a thickening of the anterior edge of the wing out to the apex—the costa. Posterior to the costa and joining it at a point along

the anterior margin is the subcosta. Following the subcosta and running along
the transparent wing membrane to the wing edge is a series of six veins—the
longitudinal veins; these are numbered in sequence from the subcosta back-

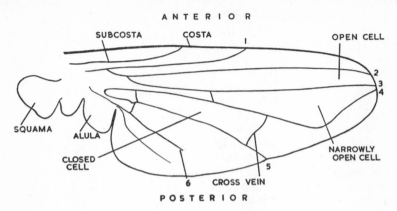

Fig. 16. The wing of a fly showing the venation and the method of
numbering the veins.

wards and are called the 1st longitudinal vein, the 2nd longitudinal vein and so
on up to the 6th longitudinal vein. In addition to veins running along the length
of the wing there are a number of veins running across from one longitudinal
vein to another; these veins are known as cross veins. The areas of transparent
wing membrane enclosed by the veins are called cells; if a cell is completely
surrounded by veins it is called a closed cell, but if it is not completely bounded
by veins and is open on one side, as for instance at the margin of the wing, it is
called an open cell.

In many flies there is a lobe on the hind margin of the wing which is usually
grey in colour and more opaque than the rest of the wing; this is the calypter or
squama. The presence or the absence of the calypter is used by entomologists
in placing flies in certain systematic groups; thus the term "calypterate fly"
means a fly with a calypter, whereas the term "acalypterate fly" means a fly
without a calypter. The student must note the presence of another wing lobe,
the alula, homogeneous in appearance with the wing and which must not be
confused with the calypter (squama).

Fig. 17. The haltere of a
house fly.

In the Diptera, the 2nd pair of wings are replaced by club-shaped structures known as halteres. These are highly modified sensory structures
which are freely moveable and capable of vibration. These halteres are apparently associated
with the co-ordination of the movements of flight.
They are club-shaped in form and have a complicated sensory apparatus at
the base.

Although the pattern of the wing veins is of great use in the classification of insects, this character alone is never self-sufficient for the identification of species, as is often erroneously believed by the beginner, so that in addition to the wing venation the systematist in classifying an insect has to take other characters into consideration.

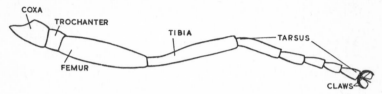

Fig. 18.   The leg of an insect.

The Leg. Each segment of the thorax bears a pair of legs. Each leg consists of a coxa, a trochanter, a femur, a tibia and a tarsus. The tarsus is usually segmented and commonly terminates in a pair of claws although in some insects, such as the louse, there may be only a single claw.

THE ABDOMEN. The abdomen of insects consists of ten or eleven distinct segments. In certain insects, such as the house fly, only the first four segments are normally visible, the remaining segments being telescoped into the body; in the female fly these remaining segments may be protruded to form a long ovipositor. Each abdominal segment consists of a tergum and a sternum; in most insects these segments, with the exception of the 8th and 9th segments which bear the genital organs, possess no pleura. There is usually a pair of spiracular openings on each abdominal segment.

The genital organs may be regarded as modified abdominal appendages which are supported on pleura. The external genitalia of the female are small and inconspicuous and arise from the 8th and 9th segments of the abdomen, whereas the external genitalia of the male, which arise from the 9th segment, are highly complex and are usually large conspicuous structures, which are used for the purpose of grasping the abdominal extremity of the female during the mating act. A fuller account of the external genitalia of the male and the female insect is given in a later chapter when considering the reproductive system of insects. From the 10th segment there arises a pair of sensory structures, having the character of appendages, which are known as cerci. The anus is on the last segment of the body, usually the 10th.

CHAPTER IX

THE INTERNAL ANATOMY AND PHYSIOLOGY OF INSECTS

INTRODUCTION

A S has been explained already, the body of insects consists of a relatively hard integument, the exoskeleton, enclosing a space filled with haemolymph and extending not only into the head, thorax and abdomen, but also into the legs and even into the wings. Floating within this fluid-filled space are the internal organs, including the nervous system, the respiratory system, the digestive and excretory systems, the fat body, the circulatory system, and the reproductive system. In addition insects possess a complex musculature responsible not only for the movements of locomotion but also, by means of the visceral muscles, of those of the gut, and of the reproductive and respiratory systems. It is not proposed to deal with the muscular system in detail although passing reference will be made to it at the appropriate places.

THE INTEGUMENT AND ITS RELATION TO GROWTH

a) *Anatomy and histology of the integument.*

The integument of insects consists of an outer non-living, non-cellular layer, the cuticle, secreted by an inner single layer of epidermal cells, the epidermis (sometimes called the hypodermis), resting on a basement membrane. The cuticle is composed of a thin outer zone, the epicuticle, which is non-chitinous consisting of complex chemical substances such as waxes and lipoproteins and a thicker inner zone, the procuticle, of which chitin, a complex polysaccharide is an important constituent. The epicuticle confers on the integument the property of almost complete impermeability for the escape of fluid from with-

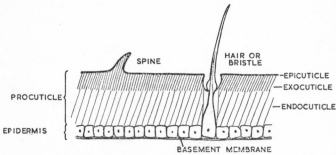

Fig. 19.   Diagrammatic representation of a section cut through the cuticle of an insect.

in the body and the absorption of moisture from without, although it must be remembered that in insects with a thin integument or in organs which are lightly chitinised, such as the anal gills of dipterous larvae, there may be an increased permeability to liquids; if the epicuticle is abraded in any way, water loss seems to become increased and it is for this reason that the admixture of abrasives with certain insecticides often enhances their action. The procuticle confers on the integument amongst other properties those of hardness and strength and is the real skeletal support of the body of the insect.

Arising from the integument are the spines and hairs. Spines may be distinguished from hairs in that they are projections from the cuticle whereas the hairs are products of the epidermal cells and reach the skin surface by canals which penetrate the cuticle. If these hairs are rubbed off, their sites can still be located by means of the canal openings, calyces or sockets. The hairs arising from the epidermis may take various forms, and are named according to the form assumed and the functions performed. When coarse they are usually referred to as bristles, when fine, as setae; when obviously flattened they are referred to as scales and when their function appears to be markedly sensory they are known as sensillae.

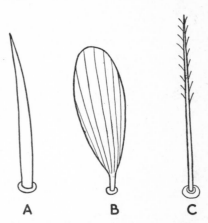

Fig. 20.   *A.* bristle; *B.* scale; *C.* sensilla.

b) *Integument in relation to growth.*

The integument tends to be rigid so that the growth of the young insect can only be achieved by a series of skin casts, the process being known as a "moult" or an "ecdysis". Since ecdysis occurs only at intervals, it follows that the growth of the insect takes place spasmodically, and if we illustrate it by a graph it takes on the form of a series of steps, each rise in which is represented by an ecdysis. The form assumed by an insect between ecdyses is known as an

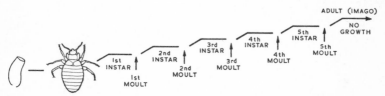

Fig. 21.   Diagram showing how an insect grows by a series of skin–casts or moults.

instar. The number of moults and therefore of instars varies in different types of insects. After its final moult the insect becomes an adult or imago and once this has occurred it undergoes no further variation in size.

The moulting process is achieved by the insect dissolving and digesting the inner layers of the old cuticle and laying down a fresh cuticle, the old and the

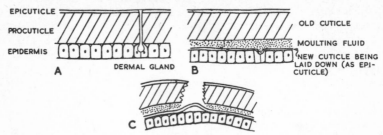

Fig. 22.   *A.* and *B.* diagrams show how an insect lays down fresh cuticle, and
C. the splitting of the old cuticle at the time of moulting.

new cuticle being separated by a thin layer of fluid produced as an exudate of the epidermal cells.

When the time for moulting is reached, the insect absorbs water or air, contracts its muscles and splits the old cuticle, usually along the back. The insect now clambers out of the old skin and it is sometime before the new skin, which is at first thrown into folds, has time to expand and harden.

The period of time occupied by the larva in growing to adult form, that is to say, in passing through the various instars, varies greatly according to the food supply available and the temperature of the environment. Hence it is seldom possible to give exact figures for the length of the life-cycle, except in the case of such insects as the louse which lives in a stable environment and has access to a constant food supply.

THE NERVOUS SYSTEM AND THE SENSES OF INSECTS

The central nervous system consists essentially of a brain and a ventral nerve cord on which ganglia occur at intervals. From these ganglia nerves are given off to the various organs of the body. All the senses possessed by man such as sight, hearing, tactile senses and appreciation of heat and cold, smell and taste, are known to occur amongst insects.

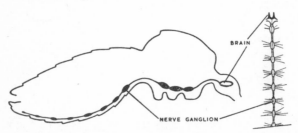

Fig. 23.   Diagrammatic representation of the brain
and ventral nerve cord of an insect.

Insects possess many types of sensory organs, the most conspicuous of which are the eyes. In addition to the organs concerned with the reception of visual stimuli, namely the compound and the simple eyes, almost all hairs of the insect's body serve as sensory end organs (detecting various mechanical and chemical stimuli), whilst a variety of other structures, such as the tympanic organs concerned with hearing, have been described.

In some species, just as amongst vertebrates, one or more senses, such as sight, may be missing, while other senses may be much more highly developed than in man. As examples of highly developed sense organs may be mentioned the temperature receptors of insects, such as occur in bugs and fleas, which enable them to detect small changes in temperature and to orientate themselves to their hosts, while humidity receptors, such as those possessed by lice, assist insects in selecting the optimum microclimate.

Certain smells and colours are repugnant to insects and others act as attractants. Both types are sometimes made use of in control; thus certain lights and odours are used to attract insects into traps in which they are subsequently destroyed. Although this form of trapping has proved of considerable value in reducing agricultural pests, it has not been of much practical value in the destruction of insects of medical importance, nor has the use of repellent colours been very satisfactory although it is worth remembering that certain colours in clothing are slightly repellent to particular species of insects while the painting of walls blue is sometimes used to reduce the fly population in jam factories. Auditory traps for mosquitoes, in which a sound-producing mechanism imitates the note of the female and attracts the males, although theoretically effective, have not proved practical.

On the other hand, the employment of chemical repellents, whether "contact repellents" such as the phthalates or more volatile odoriferous repellents such as oil of citronella, have proved of great value in reducing the risk of acquiring certain insect-borne diseases.

Prior to the introduction of the newer and much more potent insecticides, the previously used insecticidal substances exerted their toxic effects for the most part either after ingestion into the gut or else after they had entered the body through the spiracles and travelled along the tracheae and tracheoles. The newer insecticides such as DDT and BHC owe their lethal action to their effect on the nervous system which they reach via the nerve endings in the integument, or by the legs when the drug is used as a residual insecticide.

THE RESPIRATORY SYSTEM AND OXYGEN REQUIREMENTS

In contradistinction to vertebrates in which the carriage of oxygen to the tissues is dependent on transport by the red cells of the blood, insects rely for their oxygen requirements on simple diffusion. In many aquatic insects and in endoparasites, and also in the case of all eggs, gaseous exchange takes place through the integument, but in the great majority of terrestrial insects and in a proportion of aquatic forms, such as the mosquito larva, respiration is effected by the inward diffusion of oxygen and the outward diffusion of carbon dioxide.

This exchange occurs within the body of the creature by means of the so-called tracheal system, the exchange usually being assisted by muscular contractions of the abdomen.

The tracheal system consists essentially of a series of tubes formed from invaginations of the integument and leading from openings called spiracles or stigmata situated at various points on the surface of the body. These tubes (the tracheae) branch, anastomose and ramify to a remarkable extent while gradually narrowing in diameter as they reach the deeper tissues; in addition to anastomosing with each other they may also communicate with large air sacs. The finest tubes, known as tracheoles, penetrate to the vicinity of every cell in the body of the insect and it it here that the diffusion of oxygen in one

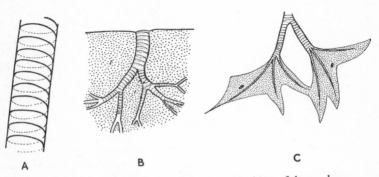

A   B   C

Fig. 24.   A. spiral thread which prevents kinking of the tracheae.
B. tracheal tubes and their bifurcation to form tracheoles.
C. ending of the tracheoles in the cells.

direction, and carbon dioxide in the other, takes place. In order to prevent kinking of the tracheae during active movements by the insect they are for the greater part of their length lined by a spiral thread which gives strength, similar to that resulting from the spiral wire in a hose-pipe.

Insects can accommodate themselves to an existence during which they require very little oxygen and can thus resist asphyxiation for days or weeks with a modicum of air. For this reason attempts to destroy noxious insects by cutting off their air supply, either by replacing the existing atmosphere with an inert gas such as nitrogen or by immersing the insects in a neutral fluid such as water, are generally unsuccessful. On the other hand, the introduction of poisonous substances into the tracheal system via the spiracles is a recognised method of control, indeed, until the adoption of the newer insecticides it was the method most commonly employed; thus spraying with emulsion containing small globules of oil (the globules of oil being themselves insecticidal) charged with an insecticide such as pyrethrum allows the penetration of the oil to the deeper tissues and in the case of the pyrethrum, enables the poison to come in contact with the internal nervous system.* The use of insecticides acting through the tracheal system is not confined to the liquid emulsions; fine dusts containing pyrethrum or rotenone are highly successful when employed against various insects such as fleas and lice.

The lethal action of insecticides operating through the tracheal system is to a marked extent dependent on the size of the oil globules or dust particles carrying the poison; since if these are too large they will fail to pass the spiracles, or if just small enough to pass the spiracular opening they may fail to penetrate deeply into the rapidly narrowing tracheal system. Finally it must be remembered that many insects have the power to close the spiracles by muscular action and this power may, for a time at any rate, render the insect immune to substances which are rapidly lethal once they gain access to the tracheae.

So far we have only considered the tracheal system and the ability of the insect to open and close its spiracles in relation to respiration, but it must be remembered also that the tracheal system plays a highly important part in regulating water loss, a subject which will be referred to again when considering the adaptation of insects to climatic conditions.

THE DIGESTIVE AND EXCRETORY SYSTEMS

(a) *The alimentary canal and digestion.*

Insects feed upon almost every type of organic substance found in nature; some species are parasitic on plants, others on animals, some feed on dead vegetable matter, others on the dead bodies or excretions of animals. Since the diets of different species of insects may be so dissimilar it follows that the digestive and excretory systems of such different species are bound to differ greatly, and it is simpler to discuss these variations when we come to consider individual species of insects of medical importance, and at this stage to give an outline of the basic insect plan.

The alimentary canal consists of a tube of epithelium, formed by a single layer of cells and surrounded by a muscular coat. The alimentary canal may be divided into three primary regions according to their embryonic origin, the fore-gut, the mid-gut and the hind-gut. The fore-gut and hind-gut are really ectodermal invaginations and are lined with chitin. In the mid-gut, however, the cells lining the lumen of the gut are exposed and it is in this region that the main part of the digestive and absorptive processes take place.

The fore-gut is divided into the mouth, buccal cavity, pharynx and oesophagus, the hind part of which often forms a "crop" which may bear diverticula, and the proventriculus which acts as a valve and may have teeth as in the cockroach to grind up food, or break up blood corpuscles as in the flea. If this

---

* The relative failure of heavy inert oils to destroy insect life can be demonstrated by layering medicinal paraffin over water containing culicine larvae. In this instance the larvae remain apparently unaffected for as much as 24 hours although their spiracles are blocked, whereas if they are confined below a layer of light oil which penetrates deeply beyond the spiracles, they rapidly succumb.

valve-like mechanism becomes deranged, as for instance by plague bacilli in the case of the flea, the insect is unable to prevent regurgitation of the stomach contents back into the oesophagus.

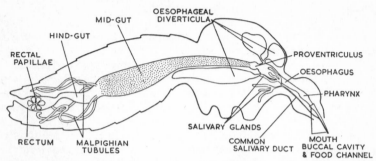

Fig. 25. Diagrammatic representation of the alimentary tract of a mosquito.

The fore-gut is provided with muscles attaching it to the body wall, hence enabling the ingestion of food by suction. Associated with the anterior part of the fore-gut there are the salivary ducts, conveying the secretion from the salivary glands. The salivary glands vary in different insects and may either be simple or lobed. For instance in the tsetse fly they are simple and extend into the abdomen, whereas in the mosquito they lie in the thorax at the level of the first pair of legs, one on each side of the thorax, and are trilobed structures, each lobe provided with a collecting channel down which the salivary excretion passes to the salivary duct which is joined by the duct from the other side to form the common salivary duct.

The nature of the salivary secretion varies in different species of insects; frequently it contains an anti-coagulant and/or a red cell agglutinin which may be specific for certain animal groups. Thus the salivary glands of the tsetse fly secrete a powerful anti-coagulant and if the glands are removed from the fly it eventually perishes as a result of being unable to digest its food.

The injection of the salivary secretion by blood-sucking arthropods during the act of feeding is sometimes followed by a cutaneous reaction in the host which may vary from trivial to very severe. The majority of such reactions appear to be due to previous sensitisation, and they do not tend to occur in persons not previously exposed to the bites of a particular insect while they tend to disappear amongst persons constantly exposed to attack.

The size and shape of the mid-gut varies in different insects, and in some the surface available for digestion is increased by the presence of enteric caeca. The mid-gut secretes various enzymes, which vary in number and type according to the food requirements of the insect; thus omnivorous eaters, like the cockroach, have a full complement of enzymes, while exclusively blood-sucking species have little but proteolytic enzymes, whereas such insects as the butterflies, feeding only on nectar, possess nothing but invertase.

The commencement of the hind-gut is marked by the insertion of the malpighian tubules, which are the excretory organs of the insects. The hind-gut is commonly regarded as consisting of a narrower anterior portion, the ileum, which leads into a wider posterior portion known as the rectum. The rectum is usually more or less globular in shape and is generally provided with rectal papillae or glands which have an important function in that they allow the reabsorption of water from the faeces.

There is one other structure in the alimentary canal of some insects which is of medical importance. This is the peritrophic membrane. It is apparently absent or poorly developed in many insects such as the bug but well developed in other insects such as the tsetse fly. It is a delicate membrane which in the case of the Diptera originates as a viscous secretion in a zone.of cells at the anterior end of the mid-gut and from this point it hangs down as a gossamer mantle which lines all the mid-gut and part of the hind-gut. The medical importance of the peritrophic membrane in the tsetse fly lies in the fact that although it is of extreme thinness and permeable to enzymes and digestive juices, yet it is sufficiently strong to resist penetration by trypanosomes which, in order to develop completely, must pass round the fringe of the peritrophic membrane where it hangs free in the gut.

(b) *The malpighian tubules and excretion.*

Excretion in insects is mainly carried out by the malpighian tubules which act as kidneys and filter off the urine from the body fluids, the separated salts, mainly carbonates, chlorides and phosphates, rendering the tubules opaque and giving them a chalky appearance. The number and length of the malpighian tubules varies according to the species of insect but they always present a large surface area, so that when few in number they are long and when numerous, short. Each tubule consists of a tube closed at its free end, which floats in the haemocoele and at its origin opens into the lumen of the gut, usually at the junction between the mid-gut and the hind-gut. The urine, separated by the cells which line each tubule, is excreted first into the lumen of the tubules and from them into that of the intestine, where it mixes with the faeces and is excreted through the anus. Before excretion takes

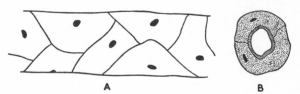

A   B

Fig. 26.   Drawing showing the large cells lining the Malpighian tubules.
A. as viewed from the side and *B.* as seen in cross section.

place, however, much of the contained water is re-absorbed by the rectal glands and retained in the body of the insect thereby reducing water loss. In addition, nitrogen is excreted chiefly as uric acid, an insoluble substance which

59

does not require water for its elimination, unlike urea which in the mammals demands large amounts of water. This power to conserve water, which varies with the species of insect and its stage of development, plays an important part in determining its power to resist desiccation. Not only is this the case but the comparative dryness or moistness of the faecal pellets passed by certain insect vectors of tropical diseases may increase or diminish the chances of the contained parasite being established in a new host. Thus the faeces of the reduviid bugs are usually moist and tend to adhere to the skin so that when they contain infective forms of *Trypanosoma cruzi*, the parasites are easily introduced into lesions caused by scratching or rubbing the site of irritation, in contrast to plague infected faeces from the flea which are usually dry and since they do not tend to adhere to the skin, seldom if ever cause infection by this route.

THE FAT BODY

The fat body consists of groups of cells, loosely connected together by a delicate stroma, and widely distributed throughout the body. These cells, which differ both in morphology and function, occur commonly in masses, sometimes in strands, and occasionally as individual cells, and are freely bathed by the haemolymph. The functions performed by the cells of the fat body are various but an important duty appears to be the storage of reserve food supplies; for this purpose the cells become filled with such substances as protein, fat and glycogen, a wider range of food material than is suggested by the name "fat body". These food reserves are called upon and used up under conditions calling for increased metabolism, as when the insect is moulting or undertaking long sustained efforts, such as prolonged flights. In addition, insects which enter into a state of hibernation or diapause make use of the reserve materials in the fat body, sometimes during the entire period of hibernation and in other instances supplementing the fat body reserves by partaking of food at widely separated intervals. In these conditions the part played by the fat body in maintaining and spreading such parasitic infections as malaria is of considerable significance. Thus it was observed in Salonika during the first World War that cases of primary malaria occurred amongst troops in early spring (at a time when no anopheline breeding had yet started) as a result of the soldiers being bitten by anophelines infected the previous year and hibernating during the winter months. As an example of the spread of malaria by anophelines undergoing interrupted hibernation, one might quote the so-called "winter malaria" which occurs in Holland and results from intermittent feeding

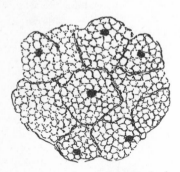

Fig. 27. Portion of the fat body showing the cells loosely connected together with delicate stroma.

of anophelines hibernating in dwelling houses and occasionally "awakening" to partake of a blood meal from the inhabitants.

THE CIRCULATORY SYSTEM

In insects the blood, or more correctly the haemolymph, is a clear fluid which may be either colourless or slightly coloured. As already explained, respiration in insects is carried out independently, or almost independently, of the circulation so that erythrocytes (which in vertebrates are essential for the carriage of respiratory pigments) are absent; on the other hand, the haemolymph does contain cells, generally referred to as haemocytes, which correspond in function with the leucocytes occurring in mammalian blood. Some of these latter cells have an important function as phagocytes and are especially active during the processes of moulting and metamorphosis, when they ingest the discarded cellular tissues; they also play a part in ingesting foreign bodies and may be seen to congregate around such invasive parasites as the larvae of

Fig. 28. Diagrammatic representation of "the heart" and the branched "aorta" of an insect.

filarial worms. The haemocytes also play a part in the repair of damaged insect tissues and by congregating at the site of injury act as plugs to prevent the continued escape of haemolymph.

The haemolymph is kept in a state of more or less constant agitation by the movement of the visceral muscles and by the muscles of locomotion, whilst it is maintained in a constant state of circulation by the action of a muscular pulsating tube, the posterior end of which is situated in the abdomen and is called the heart. The heart is almost always closed at the posterior end and provided with a series of valved openings, ostia, through which the haemolymph enters and is driven forwards in the so-called aorta which terminates in open vessels in the neighbourhood of the brain. The haemolymph pumped out of these openings percolates slowly backwards through the body-cavity and re-enters the heart, once more to be propelled forwards.

The main function of the blood in insects is to carry nutrient materials to the tissues and waste products to the excretory organs, but it also plays a very important part as a source of water reserves for the tissues, and in redistributing pressures, so facilitating respiration, ecdysis and hatching. In winged insects it is essential for the proper expansion of the wings after the insect's emergence from the pupa, and if the wing of a recently emerged insect is cut before it has become fully expanded the haemolymph seeps away so that the insect is crippled and unable to fly. To the medical entomologist the knowledge that the haemolymph bathes all the tissues and is in a state of constant circulation is important, for it explains how the various organs of an insect may become infected with parasites which, having escaped from the insect's gut, must reach some other organ before they can be introduced into a new host. Thus it is by means of the haemolymph that the sporozoites, escaping from the ruptured oocyst lying in the stomach wall of the mosquito, travel to the salivary glands. Similarly, the filarial worms, having bored through the gut of the insect host, travel via the haemolymph first to the thoracic muscles and subsequently to the cavity of the labium.

CHAPTER X

THE INTERNAL ANATOMY AND PHYSIOLOGY
OF INSECTS (cont.)

THE REPRODUCTIVE SYSTEM AND FERTILISATION

REPRODUCTION in insects forms one of the most remarkable chapters in their natural history. The structural adaptation for copulation, the control of the sperms in the body of the female following their introduction by the male, and the means by which they gain access to and fertilise the contents of the egg, vary greatly in different species, and a knowledge of these differences is often of value in studying the taxonomy and biology of insects.

In insects of medical importance the sexes are separate, reproduction being dependent on the previous fertilisation of the female by the male. As in the "higher vertebrates" the act of copulation consists in the introduction of the penis (called aedeagus in insects) into the genital tract of the female, insemination being facilitated by the fact that the tip of the abdomen of the female is grasped by the complex external genital apparatus of the male which acts as a clasping organ. The act of copulation may be brief, or may last for several hours in which case the sexes may often be captured in pairs, a point worth remembering when it is necessary to collect both sexes of a particular species.

Mating may, of course, take place at anytime and in almost any type of environment, but in the case of many insects of medical importance, notably amongst certain species of mosquitoes and horse flies, mating tends to occur only at dawn or dusk and often only when the two sexes meet together in swarms; while the habitat and the height above ground level selected by the swarms also vary according to the species of insect. A knowledge of these mating habits may prove of value in the planning of control measures.

The spermatozoa introduced into the genital tract of the female find their way to the spermatheca (spermathecae in some insects), a chitinised sperm-storing organ associated with the lower female genital tract, from which they are subsequently liberated to fertilise the eggs which have descended into the vagina from the ovaries. In many small insects the spermatheca may be rendered visible when the whole insect is immersed in some clearing agent, such as a mixture of lactic acid and phenol, and since in certain species of insects, notably fleas and sandflies, the morphology of the spermatheca is generally characteristic for each individual species, this clearing technique is made use of in the classification of these and other insects. The stored sperms have a long life, generally as long as that of the insect, so that the female is usually capable of repeated egg production without necessarily undergoing further impregnation. Although prolonged storage in the manner described is common, nevertheless, repeated copulations are the rule rather than the exception.

Male reproductive organs.

The external reproductive organs in the male generally consist of the claspers, below and between which the aedeagus (penis) may be seen protruding.

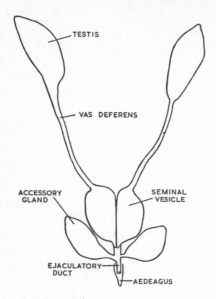

The internal male organs consist of (1) *paired testes*, wherein the sperms are formed, lying in the abdominal haemocoele, one on each side of the alimentary canal, (2) the *vas deferens* conducting the sperms to (3) the *seminal vesicles* which are swellings of the vas deferens for storage of the sperms, (4) the *ejaculatory duct* and the *aedeagus* which together are instrumental in conducting the sperms into the female, (5) the *accessory glands* which secrete a fluid the exact function of which is not clearly known.

Fig. 29. Diagrammatic representation of the male genital organs of an insect (a mosquito).

Female reproductive organs.

In most insects of medical importance, external reproductive organs in the female are either not recognisable or are so insignificant as to be of very

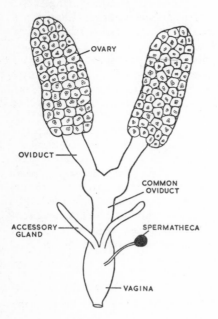

little taxonomic value. The internal reproductive organs of the female consist of (1) a pair of *ovaries* lying in the abdominal haemocoele one on each side of the alimentary canal; (2) the *oviducts* which lead from the ovaries and meet to form (3) the *common oviduct* the lower part of which is called (4) the *vagina*; (5) the *spermatheca*, a darkly coloured structure communicating by a duct with the vagina and (6) one or two pairs of *accessory glands* (known also as cement glands) which open into the posterior limit of the vagina. These glands secrete a mucous substance which may serve to attach the eggs to the hair of the host, as in the

Fig. 30. Diagrammatic representation of the female genital organs of an insect (a mosquito).

case of the louse, to each other as in the case of the eggs of culicine mosquitoes or to some part of the habitat as in the case of the bed bug.

THE EGG AND ITS DEVELOPMENT

Reproduction in insects, as in all metazoan creatures, begins with the fertilized egg but the degree of maturation which may occur within the body of the parent insect varies enormously according to the type of insect, so that the progeny may be produced at any stage of development from that of the unsegmented egg to that of a fully grown larva ready to pupate. For example, many insects such as the house fly and the mosquito lay eggs which are at a very early stage of development, so that the contents have to undergo maturation before giving rise to a larva which, having left the egg, must in its turn undergo further development involving a series of ecdyses before pupating. Other insects such as the carrion flies produce eggs which, when passed out of the body of the fly, contain fully developed larvae which hatch almost immediately. Insects which lay eggs at any stage of development are referred to as oviparous to distinguish them from larviparous insects which produce fully formed larvae, the eggs having hatched within the body of the parent.

Just as the stage of development of the egg when passed out of the body varies in different species of oviparous insects, so also does the stage of development of the larva vary according to the species of the larviparous insect depositing it. Thus, the sheep nostril fly, *Oestrus ovis,* produces an early 1st instar larva, which after its birth must undergo the usual series of ecdyses before pupation. On the other hand, the tsetse fly, *Glossina* sp., produces a single fully developed 3rd instar larva which, after its deposition by the parent fly, pupates almost immediately. With certain notable exceptions, such as the tsetse fly just described, the majority of medically important insects occur in the egg-producing or oviparous group.

As already stated, certain insects produce eggs containing fully developed larvae which hatch almost immediately and independently of the external environment and other things being equal, the more advanced the stage of development, the shorter the incubation period of the egg. In the case of the permanent ectoparasites which lay their eggs on the body of the host, the incubation period remains very constant, but in the case of insects which lay their eggs elsewhere than on the host, the length of the incubation period will vary greatly according to the external environment, the most important influence being temperature. To quote one example amongst many, the eggs of the bed bug kept at an equable temperature of 17.8°C, such as might occur in a house with central heating, will hatch in about 20 days following deposition, but under conditions of lower temperature, such as 13°C, hatching may be delayed for as long as 50 days, or under conditions of higher temperature, such as 35°C, hatching may occur in just under 5 days.

The eggs laid by different species of insects vary greatly not only as regards their stage of development, but also as regards (a) their morphology and their structural adaptations for the emergence of the larva, (b) the numbers laid at a single oviposition, the numbers laid during the lifetime of the female and the manner of their deposition and (c) the site and the stratum on which they are laid.

(a) *The morphology of the egg and the structural adaptation for the emergence of the larva.*

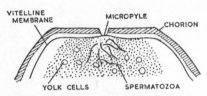

Fig. 31. Diagrammatic representation of the anterior end of a fertilised insect egg.

The eggs laid by insects of medical importance are usually oval or ovoid in outline as those of fleas and bugs respectively, or elongated as those of the mosquito or the house fly. Each egg consists essentially of three parts, the outer shell or chorion which is lined by a delicate vitelline membrane, which in its turn encloses the developing embryo and the yolk cells.

The chorion, which varies in thickness, is chitinous and generally speaking impervious to the penetration of non-volatile insecticides. When thin-walled the contained embryo usually obtains its oxygen by direct diffusion but where the chorion is thick, minute pores are present. If for any reason free access of air to the embryo becomes obstructed, hatching is delayed and it is for this reason that oily substances, although not truly ovicidal, nevertheless prolong the incubation period when applied to louse eggs. The chorion is often sculptured and in the case of some insects such as anopheline mosquitoes which oviposit on water, the chorion is provided with large air cells referred to as floats, while in some culicine mosquitoes, floating of the eggs is achieved by air being retained in minute pits on the surface of the chorion. In addition to the pores which are present in certain insects for the supply of oxygen to the larva, there is an aperture in the micropyle through which the spermatozoa can penetrate to the ovum, along one or more minute canals.

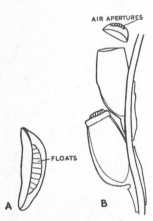

Fig. 32. Operculate and non-operculate eggs.
A. non-operculate egg of the anopheline mosquito.
B. operculate egg of the louse, before and after hatching.

Although the eggs of most insects possess an even chorion which the emerging larva splits, the eggs of a number of species of insects are provided with a well defined lid or operculum which the larva pushes off immediately prior to emergence. In such instances the outline of the previously oval egg becomes truncated and can at once be distinguished from its unhatched fellows, as in the case of the louse.

(b) *Number of eggs laid, and the manner of their deposition.*

Most insects have more than one oviposition during their lifetime. Whereas some insects lay their eggs singly at fairly regular intervals, others deposit them in batches, the periods separating each oviposition varying greatly in different species. In the case of blood-sucking insects, the length of time elapsing between each oviposition is usually dependent on the frequency of the blood meals; thus in the louse, which feeds frequently during the 24 hours, the eggs are produced almost continuously over this time, whilst in horse flies, which only feed to repletion at comparatively long intervals, there are probably only two or three ovipositions separated by periods lasting anything from ten days to several weeks. The number of eggs laid at one oviposition as well as the number produced during the entire life-cycle varies enormously with the different species and does not necessarily coincide with the length of adult life. Thus the louse living under equable conditions throughout its lifetime of about a month lays some 250–300 eggs, whereas the house fly, living under much less equable conditions and with a very variable life span, produces a vastly greater number estimated to be anywhere between 500 and 2,500.

The eggs laid by an insect may be entirely free as occurs in the case of the flea and the sandfly, or they may be free from the substrate but connected together as occurs in the case of the egg rafts laid by certain culicine mosquitoes. Other insects fix their eggs by cement, either singly to the substrate as occurs in the case of the bed bug and the louse, or in masses as occurs in the case of the horse flies.

(c) *The site and stratum on which the eggs are laid.*

The environment and substrate on which insects lay their eggs are extremely varied, the only constant feature being that the female chooses some place where the hatched larva can undergo successful development following emergence from the egg and where its nutritional requirements will be met.

Some completely parasitic insects such as the louse spend all their existence on the host, laying their eggs attached to the hair, or in the case of man, to the hair and clothing. Other insects such as the flea spend most of their adult existence on the host leaving him only in order to lay eggs, which are deposited in the debris of the host's dwelling; in the case of man deposition is in or near a human habitation and in the case of the rodent, in its burrow or nest. Some parasitic insects such as bugs, in which both adults and larvae feed on the host although at no time living on the body of the host, nevertheless live in very close association with him and lay their eggs as do the fleas in or near his habitation. The remaining groups of parasitic insects, such as the blood-sucking flies, although the adult forms are wholly dependent on their host for the blood-meals necessary to mature the eggs, cannot be regarded as more than occasional visitors and lay their eggs in various environments and on widely different substrates.

Up to this only those parasitic insects in which the adults and in some cases the larvae are dependent on the host for their blood-meals have been considered.

There are, however, many insects of medical importance only the larvae of which are parasitic, the adults living a non-parasitic existence and in such cases the eggs are laid in a manner which will ensure the ready access of the emergent larva to its host. Sometimes access to the host is ensured by direct means; thus the so-called "screw worm" flies (such as certain species of *Chrysomyia* and *Callitroga*) only visit the mammalian host to lay their eggs on its body, usually in some abrasion or damaged tissue. But approach to the host is not always direct, thus the female of the tumbu fly of Africa, *Cordylobia anthropophaga,* tends to lay her eggs on ground contaminated with urine in the vicinity of human or rodent dwelling places, while the adult of the "ver macaque" of South America, *Dermatobia hominis,* ensures its progeny reaching a warm-blooded animal by attaching its eggs to the body of a blood-sucking insect, which visits its host to obtain its blood-meal.

THE DEVELOPMENT OF THE INSECT AFTER ITS EMERGENCE FROM THE EGG

Growth amongst the insects as has already been discussed, always takes the form of a series of moults or ecdyses, the periods between which are referred to as instars.

Amongst many insects the form of the newly hatched larva closely resembles the parent and the resemblance continues throughout the various instars, so that the differences between adult and immature stages are mainly those of size and sexual maturity. Such a type of life-cycle, representing as it does an incomplete change or metamorphosis, is referred to as a hemimetabolous life cycle.

Amongst other insects, however, the newly hatched insect bears little or no resemblance to its parent and only after a series of ecdyses and a resting, or pupal stage, is there a sudden and profound alteration in morphology resulting in the emergence of the adult. Such a type of life-cycle, since it involves a complete metamorphosis, is referred to as a holometabolous life-cycle.

As has already been pointed out the rate of growth of insects is determined by such external factors as climate and the availability of food supplies, but co-ordination of the factors leading to an increase of growth, moulting and metamorphosis, are determined by a complex endocrine system.

Examples of hemimetabolous life-cycles.

Typical examples of hemimetabolous life-cycles occurring amongst insects of medical importance are to be found in the case of the louse and the bed bug. In both these examples the immature growing stage of the insect, which in the case of hemimetabolous life-cycles is usually referred to as the nymph, lives in the same environment and partakes of the same food as its parents. In the case of the bed bug, the young growing forms and the sexually mature adults both live in the cracks and crevices of the host's habitation and at frequent intervals leave these refuges and partake of a blood-meal from any warm-blooded host in their vicinity; while in the case of the louse the nymphs and adults live together in colonies on, or in intimate contact with, their host's body, partaking of their blood-meals from the same host and only leaving him when compelled to do so by force of adverse circumstances.

Fig. 33.   Diagrammatic representation of the life-cycle of a hemimetabolous insect (the bed bug).

Examples of holometabolous life-cycles.

Typical examples of insects having holometabolous life-cycles are provided by the house fly and the mosquito. In the case of the house fly the growing stage or larva, a legless maggot, lives and feeds in decaying vegetable or animal organic matter, an entirely different environment from that of the six-legged winged adult. This difference in the food requirements and the environments of larva and adult is of course associated with a correspondingly great difference in their external and internal morphology so that when the time comes for the final ecdysis and the change from maggot to winged adult, this change can

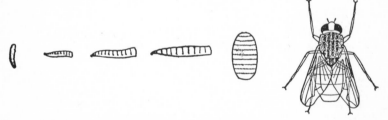

Fig. 34.   Diagrammatic representation of the life-cycle of a holometabolous insect (the house fly), showing the egg, the three larval stages, the puparium, containing the pupa, and the imago.

only be achieved by an extensive histolysis of the larval tissue followed by a histogenesis leading to the formation of adult tissues and organs. Such great changes necessitate a resting or pupal stage during which the creature is unable to feed and movement, in the case of the house fly, is reduced to a minimum. Similar revolutionary changes occur in the life-cycle of the mosquito whose aquatic larva feeds on algae and bacteria, and which neither in morphology nor in habits bears any resemblance to its blood-sucking parent. Here also a resting or pupal stage is required before the full development of the imago but the pupa of the mosquito although, like that of the house fly unable to feed, differs from the latter and all other diptera in that it is endowed with the power of very active movement.

It should be clear from these accounts of hemimetabolous and holometabolous life-cycles that the nature of the relationship established between an insect of medical importance and its human host, and the means of control to be devised against such an insect, will, to a very large extent, be determined by which type of life-cycle is being followed by the particular insect under consideration. In very general terms it may be said that insects following a hemimetabolous life-cycle affect man directly throughout this cycle and methods devised to control the adult forms are likely to prove equally efficacious when employed against the larval stages. On the other hand insects which have adopted a holometabolous life-cycle tend to affect man adversely only during part of their life-cycle, so that it is usually necessary to adopt different methods for successful control of the larval and adult stages.

CHAPTER XI

THE ADAPTATION OF INSECTS TO CLIMATIC CONDITIONS

THE climatic factors in the terrestial insect's environment which effect its behaviour, multiplication and survival are numerous, and include such influences as temperature, humidity, light intensity, chemical composition of the atmosphere, wind force and variations in barometric pressure. Any or all of these factors may, and often do, play a significant part in determining insect behaviour, but temperature and humidity exert so predominant an influence that they merit special consideration.

All warm-blooded animals, including man, possess great powers of adapting themselves to varying climatic conditions; this they achieve by altering their body temperature and their water balance, so that within certain wide (although well defined) limits, they are relatively independent of external variations in temperature and humidity. Insects also possess certain powers of adapting themselves to changes occurring in the surrounding climate but these powers of adaptation are confined within narrower limits and, in consequence, insects are much more dependent on their external environments than are warm-blooded animals.

So marked are these limitations of adaptability that a wide variety of arthropods—including many species of medical importance—can only maintain their normal life-cycle by establishing themselves in circumscribed environments where the prevailing climatic conditions, unlike those in the surrounding atmosphere, are favourable for their existence and propagation. These circumscribed environments, or niches, may be referred to as "climatic pockets" and the atmospheric conditions existing within such pockets are generally spoken of as microclimates.

It follows from these observations that whereas insects can, to some extent, survive adverse climatic conditions by exercising their individual physiological mechanisms of adaptation, nevertheless, they are dependent to a much greater extent on seeking out and temporarily inhabiting, for varying periods, niches or pockets containing the type of microclimate most suitable for their needs. The nature of the pocket selected for habitation or oviposition by the particular species of insect varies not only in relation to the climatic requirements of that particular species, but also in accordance with its own food requirements and with those of its progeny. Within recent years it has become increasingly clear that our understanding of the epidemiology of insect-borne diseases and of the different methods which may be used for their control are to a considerable degree dependent on previous knowledge of the climatic requirements of the vectors of these diseases, and on the extent to which these requirements are met by the vector's physiological mechanisms or, where these are insufficient, the type of microclimate it selects for habitation. These two aspects (the physiological mechanisms concerned with adaptation to climatic changes and the seeking out of certain microclimates), although interdependent, are best considered separately.

THE PHYSIOLOGICAL MECHANISMS CONCERNED WITH ADAPTATION TO CHANGES IN TEMPERATURE AND HUMIDITY

Any climatic change stimulates or tends to stimulate various physiological responses in the affected insect. For the most part these stimuli are concerned with the regulation of the insect's body temperature and with the prevention of excessive water loss and subsequent dehydration. If the conditions of temperature and humidity are long lasting — as occurs in the tropics — other physiological mechanisms, notably those concerned with growth and reproduction, may be stimulated and result in a speeding up or else in a retardation of the normal life-cycle.

(a) *Adaptation to temperature changes.* In general it may be said that insects gain or lose heat in direct relation to the temperature of the surrounding climate. It is true that any form of increased metabolism calling for the burning up of food supplies, such as active movement or the processes of digestion, will tend to raise the body temperature, but the lowering of the body temperature of insects is almost entirely dependent on evaporation of water from the body surface. This loss of fluid takes place mainly through the spiracles which, in the case of most insects of medical importance, are capable of adjustment.

(b) *Adaptation to humidity changes.* As regards insects' power of adaptation to changes in humidity; since insects are relatively minute creatures, whose exposed surface area is out of proportion to their body volume, any increase in the evaporative power of the surrounding atmosphere (measured as the saturation deficiency) will tend to result in dessication. This tendency to dessication will be increased in those species of insects possessing a cuticle which readily allows the escape of water vapour and which lack such efficient compensatory physiological mechanisms as the power to close the spiracles.

Amongst most insects the liability to excessive water loss, and resultant dessication, is counterbalanced by considerable water intake and also by various physiological processes which occur within the insect's body and which are directed towards the conservation of the existing and potential supplies of moisture; these two aspects — the water intake and the water conservation — cannot be sharply differentiated.

It is of course essential for insects — as for all living creatures — to obtain water since this is essential for the maintenance of life. For the most part insects achieve this objective by extracting the water from their ingested food supplies or else by deriving it from the products of metabolism; in addition, many species of insects possess — but only to a limited extent — the power of absorbing, through the cuticle, moisture from a nearly saturated atmosphere.

These methods of compensating for water loss are to some extent common to all insects of medical importance, but the degree to which they are employed varies not only with the species but also, in some instances, with the sex of the arthropod under consideration. To quote a few examples amongst the many available, the females of all blood-sucking insects directly extract water from their relatively large blood-meals, whereas in those species in which the males are not blood-suckers, the latter obtain their water by directly imbibing it from plants, in the case of mosquitoes, and from open pools of water in the case of horse flies (tabanids). This direct gain of water is augmented, or in times of stress temporarily replaced, by the re-absorption of moisture from the hind-gut, a process which in some insects such as the flea is brought to a high state of efficiency by the extraction of water from the faeces by the rectal glands, a process which results in the passage of almost dry pellets of excreta. These physiological mechanisms for regulating the insect's temperature and water loss must not be regarded as working independently of each other, for a tempera-ture which suits a particular insect's requirements at one humidity may cease to be suitable if the humidity is altered. It must be remembered that temperature and humidity are closely inter-related and that due account must be taken of this fact when considering the effects of the evaporative power of the air on the life-cycle and habits of a particular insect.

When used in combination physiological methods of temperature control and regulation of water loss are of considerable value to the insects concerned, nevertheless, by themselves, they are often insufficient to protect the insect from markedly adverse conditions. In these circumstances most insects of medical importance augment the efficiency of their physiological mechanisms for temperature and humidity control by seeking out and inhabiting microclimates in which they can maintain their existence.

THE SEEKING OUT AND INHABITING OF SUITABLE MICROCLIMATES

In the case of all species of permanent ectoparasites the whole of the life-cycle is spent in a reasonably constant temperature and humidity, and it is only when an accident, such as the death of the host, forces migration that the insect suffers climatic stress.

In permanent ectoparasitic insects, such as the human body louse (which spends the whole of its life-cycle on man and which has adapted itself to the range of temperature and humidity pertaining between the clothes and the skin of its host) the mechanism of adaptation to climatic extremes is, as might be expected, poorly developed. In the case of those ectoparasites whose adult stages are spent on the host and whose larval stages are free living—for exam-ple, the flea—we find the mechanism of adaptation limited to the adult forms which require to use such mechanisms only when they leave the micro-climate of the host's body to lay their eggs. In the case just quoted of the flea, since the larval stages are so liable to fall victims to adverse climatic conditions, it is essential that the parent deposits her eggs in an environment where the larvae can carry on their existence in a constantly suitable climate; to achieve this the female drops her eggs in rodent burrows or in the moist debris in cracks and crevices in human or animal habitations.

Many insects, such as all the blood-sucking flies, are parasitic only during the short period when they are obtaining their blood-meal and, in consequence, they are in no wise dependent on the microclimate supplied by the host. Since these blood-sucking flies are all holometabolous creatures they must during their complete life-cycle seek out and inhabit two microclimates, one suitable for the adult forms and one suitable for the larvae, and these microclimates may or may not be similar. Thus the various species of sandflies, all of which are quite unable to exist for any length of time in a hot dry climate, inhabit a wide range of shelters such as cellars and living rooms in human habitations, rodent burrows or caves inhabited by wild animals, the deep cracks and crevices where the soil has been fissured by the tropical sun, and in these or similar situations they lay their eggs, so that the sandfly's entire life-cycle including the partaking of blood-meals can be completed in a climate suitable for her needs and very different from that existing in the outside world.

The tsetse fly, which spends much of its life in the shaded microclimate immediately surrounding the leaf or twig on which it rests, only leaves this climate in order to seek the essential blood-meal, and if when doing so the surrounding climate is particularly unsuitable, the fly is always careful not to put too great a distance between itself and the nearest suitable microclimate.

The house fly, which subsists on a much more rapidly digestible diet than the blood-meal partaken of by the sandfly and the tsetse, cannot afford to spend long resting pauses in suitable climates and has to search continually for her nourishment in a wide variety of exposed localities. In consequence, she loses water very rapidly, and to make up for the water loss incurred, the house fly partakes of frequent, indeed almost constant, meals with a high water content.

CHAPTER XII

THE ORDERS OF MEDICAL IMPORTANCE IN THE CLASS INSECTA

IT is estimated that the phylum Arthropoda contains close on three quarters of a million known species of creatures, while the class Insecta, alone, embraces some half a million described species of insects. It is obvious that the task of identifying all species of insects is beyond the powers of even the most highly trained individual entomologist and that it can only be undertaken by a team of specialists. This being the case the question at once arises how can the average medical officer, who lacks basic training in the systematics of entomology, acquire the knowledge essential for the recognition of those particular species or groups of insects which are of medical importance?

It might at first be thought that the identification of a particular insect of medical importance might be accomplished by means of a generalised description of the species concerned without having resort to details of anatomy and the use of keys. With a few exceptions, however, this method is adequate only for the recognition of certain groups of medically important insects such as the mosquitoes (sub-family Culicinae) and the tsetse flies (genus *Glossina*). With the lapse of time and with better knowledge of arthropod-borne infections it has become increasingly clear that the planning of control measures directed against arthropod vectors of disease must, if they are to be fully effective, take into account not only the particular family or even genus of insect concerned but also the particular species. Thus, if we consider the examples of the mosquitoes and the tsetse flies just referred to, whereas it is true that moderately successful methods of control may be devised against these insects in general, nevertheless the most effective control will depend on the adoption of methods which take into account the bionomics of the particular species of mosquito or tsetse fly concerned in the transmission of disease in that area.

Fortunately nothing more than access to the relevant literature and a generalised knowledge of insect anatomy is required by the medical officer who wishes to identify most insects of medical importance. It is true that the identification of certain medically important flies does present greater difficulties, but these can usually be overcome by acquiring a slightly more detailed knowledge of the anatomy of the group of flies being studied together with an understanding of the terms used for the identification of various surface markings on the bodies of the adults and the larvae.

The identification of medically significant insects is rendered easier by the fact that they occur only in a limited number of the orders comprising the class Insecta. The class Insecta is generally accepted as being divided into about 25 orders; each of these orders includes a number of species which are indirectly beneficial or else indirectly injurious to the health of man, inasmuch as they assist or impede his agricultural or industrial economy. For reasons which have already been discussed, a consideration of insects which cause such agricultural and industrial effects must be omitted from a work on medical entomology, and if this is done, then only four out of the twenty-five orders referred to will be found to contain species which are of medical importance, mainly in their role as vectors of disease but also as the cause of traumatic injury.

The four orders of the class Insecta which contain species of considerable medical importance are the Diptera or two-winged flies, the Hemiptera or bugs, the Anoplura or lice and the Siphonaptera or fleas. In addition, certain stinging or vesicant insects occur in the orders Coleoptera (beetles), Hymenoptera (bees, wasps and ants) and the order Lepidoptera (butterflies and moths); but these insects, to which reference will be made later, seldom produce severe lesions and cannot be regarded as of real medical importance.

Amongst these orders of medically important insects, the order Diptera unquestionably contains the largest number of species (widely distributed in systematic position throughout the order) which are universally recognised as seriously affecting the health of man. The numerical preponderance of medically significant species amongst the Diptera in no way implies a lack of important species amongst the other orders, each of which contains several species which are the cause of widespread disease and suffering.

The order Hemiptera contains a number of species of "kissing" or "assassin" bugs which act as transmitters of disease in South America; while two species of bed bugs (which between them have a worldwide distribution) although they are not known to transmit disease, nevertheless are recognised as being injurious to health, chiefly as the result of the irritation caused by their bites.

The order Anoplura contains two species of lice which are obligatory parasites of the human host; one of these species is pre-eminently important as a vector of disease to man, while both species are responsible for much suffering as a result of the irritation caused by their bites.

The order Siphonaptera contains many species of fleas which although normally parasitic on rodents may, in certain circumstances, leave these hosts and feed on man, thereby causing outbreaks of diseases which are normally confined to the rodent population. In addition to these species of fleas—for which man is an abnormal host—two species of fleas (belonging to different genera) persistently feed on man. One of these species, which has an almost worldwide distribution, is merely a cause of trivial irritation, but the other, which is confined to the tropics, burrows into its host's tissues and is often a cause of serious traumatic injury.

It will be observed that the preceding brief outline of the part played in the causation of human disease by various orders in the class Insecta contains no reference to particular species of insects or to the particular diseases they transmit. In the chapters which follow a systematic account is given, not only of the individual species and their association with disease but also of their life-cycles, together with brief references to such methods of control as may be suggested by a knowledge of their bionomics.

CHAPTER XIII

THE ORDER DIPTERA

THE order Diptera may be defined as comprising insects which in their adult form possess one pair of wings and a pair of structures, known as halteres, which may be regarded as vestigial wings although they no longer bear any resemblance to organs of flight. All members of the order Diptera undergo a holometabolous life-cycle.

Certain true flies, i.e. Diptera, are commonly known by names which give no indication of the insect's systematic position; as a result it comes as a surprise to many students to learn that the mosquito and the midge are as truly flies as the house fly and the blow fly and, indeed, that they are comparatively closely related. On the other hand, members of certain orders of insects which possess two pairs of wings, and which therefore are not Diptera, also bear the eponym "fly" as part of their vernacular name; examples of such insects are the "caddis fly", the "may-fly", the "stone-fly" and the "dragonfly", none of which show any close relationship to the Diptera.

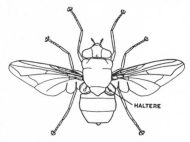

Fig. 35. A fly (the common "blue bottle") belonging to the order Diptera.

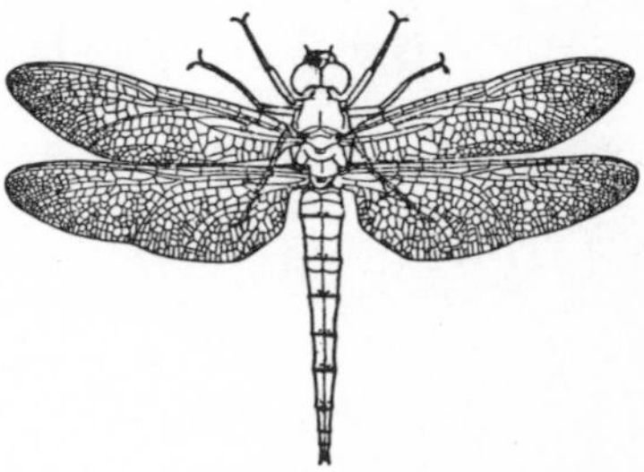

Fig. 36. A four-winged insect (a dragonfly).

The order Diptera, which is one of the largest orders—it contains more than 50,000 species—of the class Insecta, has a worldwide distribution, one or more species being found, sometimes in vast numbers, in every area on the globe. Although the great majority of species contained within the order Diptera are free-living during the whole of the life-cycle, a significant number are parasitic on a wide variety of animals including man either during their adult or their larval stages. Not only do the adults of many species of parasitic flies, particularly the mosquitoes, the biting midges and the buffalo-flies cause great annoyance and suffering, due to the irritation caused by their bites, but certain species are responsible for the mechanical and cyclical transmission of a number of viral, bacterial, protozoal and helminth diseases (but apparently not rickettsial diseases) from infected vertebrate hosts to non-infected persons, and thereby cause millions of human beings to suffer yearly from such widespread diseases as, for example, sleeping sickness and malaria. Finally, a restricted number of species, although free-living in the adult stage, spend their larval existence in natural passages or in wounds of the human body, whilst a few normally penetrate intact human skin and undergo their larval development in the host's tissues. In addition the adults of a few free-living species of Diptera, notably the house flies, although non-parasitic are often responsible for epidemics of bacterial and, to a lesser extent, of protozoal helminth and viral infections; the mechanical transmission of these infections results from the fly's habit of feeding indiscriminately on human excretions and human food supplies.

It must be remembered that not all Diptera are injurious to the health of man; the adults of certain species play a beneficial role in their capacity as fertilisers of various plants and as predators of harmful insects, while the larval forms of many species act as efficient scavengers of decaying organic matter.

The various species of medically important Diptera present a vast variety as regards their size, from and colouration, so that no generalised description is applicable. In size they range from the tiny blood-sucking midges (*Culicoides*) no larger than a pin's head, to the relatively enormous horse flies (Tabanidae), with a wing span of as much as two inches. In form they may be elongate, gnat-like flies, such as the mosquitoes (Culicinae), or heavily built compact flies like the bluebottle flies (*Calliphora*). In colouration they vary from brightly coloured metallic flies (e.g. *Lucilia*, the sheep blowfly) to the dull brown or yellow which is characteristic of most of the house fly group (Muscidae).

OCELLI

Fig. 37. Head of a horse fly showing compound eyes and ocelli (simple eyes).

The head is generally globose but it may, as in the case of the Tabanidae, be semilunar in outline. A large proportion of the surface area of the head in the Diptera is occupied by the eyes which are always compound. In addition, many flies also possess simple eyes or ocelli, the presence or absence of which is used by the systematist in distinguishing one group of flies from another.

The antennae, the characters of which are of paramount importance in the classification of flies, differ greatly in morphology. Amongst flies of medical importance the antenna varies from a simple, many segmented structure with, similar segments, to one which consists of only three recognisable dissimilar segments, the last segment bearing a bristle known as an arista.

All true flies have suctorial mouthparts adapted to the partaking of liquid food. In species which are parasitic the mouthparts are so adapted as to provide an organ suited to the purpose of piercing the integument of their host. Mandibles and maxillae, absent in most species of flies, are present in the female sex of many flies of medical importance, and where these two structures are absent, as in the case of the tsetse fly and the stable fly, the labium becomes transformed into a horny skin-piercing organ. Whilst maxillary palps are present in all flies, including those species lacking maxillae, labial palps are always absent.

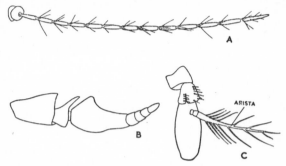

Fig. 38.   Various types of insect antennae. *A.* a mosquito;
B. a horse fly; *C.* a house fly.

The thorax in the Diptera is characterised by the great development of the mesothorax (which has to accomodate the great flight muscles) at the expense of the prothorax and the metathorax. The arrangement of the various plates and sutures has been considered already, and will be refered to again.

The pattern of the wing venation varies considerably throughout the order Diptera, and whilst in some groups of flies it is of great systematic significance, in other groups it is of little importance. For example, in the suborder Nematocera it is of considerable value as a supplementary means of distinguishing flies belonging to different families, whereas in the suborder Cyclorrapha the wing venation is not characteristic of the members of any one family although within the range of the family it may be used as a means of distinguishing certain genera and species.

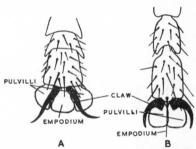

Fig. 39.   *A.* the foot of a horse fly (*Tabanus*) possessing a pad-like empodium. *B.* the foot of a house fly (*Musca*) possessing a bristle-like empodium.

The morphology and colouration of the legs are used in systematics for the identification of certain species or groups of flies, notably the tsetse flies, the mosquitoes and the horse flies. In the Diptera the legs consist of five segments, the coxa, the trochanter, the femur, the tibia and the tarsus (see Fig. 18), the tarsus being further segmented and bearing a pair of claws and two pads (pulvilli), together with a median structure (the empodium) which may be either bristle-like or pad-like.

Amongst the true flies the abdomen is composed of ten segments, the number distinctly visible varying from four to eight, according to the species. The external genitalia are terminal, and when especially prominent as in the males of certain flies, such as the sandflies, this character is extensively used in classification.

Insects belonging to the order Diptera undergo a holometabolous life-cycle in which there is a larval, pupal and adult stage. All flies deposit their eggs or larvae (the latter with certain notable exceptions in an early stage of growth) at the site most favourable to larval development. The number of larval stages varies; for example, all mosquitoes have four larval stages whereas their close relations, the buffalo-flies, have six. The fly larva, which is "worm-like" or "grub-like" in appearance, may or may not possess a recognisable head, according to the suborder to which it belongs. None of the dipterous larvae possess legs but false legs or pseudopods may be present.

The larvae of all flies of medical importance are either aquatic or else they live in an atmosphere of very high humidity. In either case they usually feed on decaying animal or plant matter, although it must be remembered that certain medically important species of flies spend their larval stages as parasites in the living tissues of man and animals.

Most larval Diptera—including the aquatic species—breathe atmospheric air. Although the great majority of the aquatic forms obtain their oxygen from above the water surface, a few species, occurring mainly in the families Simuliidae and Ceratopogonidae, obtain their oxygen from the surrounding water through the thin integument of the larva.

Although the larvae of the Diptera can only develop in water or else in a moist environment, nevertheless just prior to pupation the larvae of certain terrestial species leave the moist habitat to seek drier conditions. Similarly the larvae of certain aquatic species migrate from the water prior to pupating in the surrounding damp earth.

At pupation dipterous larvae may either discard the last larval skin in which case they are known as "naked" pupae, or else they may retain the last larval skin which forms the puparium. In the first group the adult emerges from the naked pupa by means of a longitudinal slit, in which case it is known as an orthorraphous fly; while in the second group the adult emerges from a circular slit in the puparium, in which case it is known as a cyclorraphous fly.

The order Diptera is divided into four suborders—the suborder Nematocera, the suborder Brachycera, the suborder Cyclorrapha and the suborder Pupipara. The suborder Pupipara contains many flies which have become adapted to a highly specialised form of parasitic existence. They very rarely bite man and are of no direct medical importance; on the other hand many species are parasitic on domestic stock and are transmitters of various forms of trypanosomiasis. In direct contrast to the absence of medically important flies in the suborder Pupipara, each of the three remaining suborders contians a number of species of flies which are of very great medical importance and which will be briefly dealt with in subsequent chapters.

CHAPTER XIV

THE SUBORDER NEMATOCERA AND ITS DIVISION INTO FAMILIES OF MEDICAL IMPORTANCE

THE suborder Nematocera may be defined as including two-winged flies, the antennae of which are usually longer than the head and thorax, and composed of many segments, the majority of which are similar. An arista is never present. The palps are usually pendulous and composed of 4-5 segments. No one wing shape or wing venation can be regarded as generally characteristic of flies occurring in the suborder Nematocera; on the other hand both wing shape and wing venation are of great value in separating members of certain families occurring within the suborder. The larvae possess a well developed non-retractile head, which carries horizontally directed mandibles.

The suborder is a large one, and it is usually divided into 15 families containing some 450 genera. Although only a limited number of these genera contain flies of medical importance, nevertheless the suborder is a predominantly significant one since it includes such notable vectors of disease as mosquitoes, sandflies, buffalo-flies and biting midges which are responsible for the transmission of such important diseases as filariasis, malaria, leishmaniasis, yellow fever, dengue and certain of the encephalitides. Whilst sandflies are limited to the warmer regions of the world especially where the climate is dry, mosquitoes, biting midges and buffalo-flies have a worldwide distribution, being found not only in the tropics but also in temperate zones, even where the climatic conditions may be almost arctic.

The characters already given are sufficient to allow the recognition of flies belonging to the suborder Nematocera, but since this suborder contains a vast number of species of no medical significance it would be useful to provide a guide to the recognition of the medically important species. Obviously, it is impossible to provide an exact guide founded on a scientific basis, but the following points concerning the mouthparts, when considered in conjunction with the fact that any nematocerous fly captured when biting man may be regarded as of potential medical importance, will, on most occasions, allow a decision to be made. With the exception of a few species of non-biting midges, such as *Tanytarsus* sp., which are occasionally responsible for localised outbreaks of allergy in the human population, all adult Nematocera of medical importance are blood-suckers and possess mouthparts adapted for piercing mammalian skin. This character is of considerable value in distinguishing the medically important blood-sucking Nematocera from other non-medically important nematocerous flies. It must be realised, however, that many nematocerous flies of medical importance, particularly the midges, possess mouthparts which although well adapted for skin piercing are nevertheless inconspicuous. In addition it must be remembered that certain nematocerous flies, which are not blood-suckers and which are of no medical importance, possess mouthparts adapted for piercing the cuticle of other insects or of plants and that these mouthparts sometimes bear close resemblance to those of the blood-sucking species.

Morphologically the larvae of the Nematocera may be distinguished from those belonging to other suborders of Diptera by the well defined head which cannot be retracted within the thorax. Whereas the great majority of the larvae of species of medical importance are aquatic, those of some species— notably the larvae of sandflies and of certain midges—are exceptional in that they live not in water but in moist soil or decaying vegetation. On pupating, the last larval skin is shed (although not completely in the case of sandflies) and the naked pupa is generally capable of movement.

Only four of the 15 families of the suborder Nematocera contain species of medical importance. The four families of medical importance are the Culicidae which include the mosquitoes, the Psychodidae which include the sandflies, the Simuliidae which are known as buffalo-flies, buffalo-gnats or black flies, and the family Ceratopogonidae which contains the biting midges. In the following chapters each of these families will be discussed in turn.

CHAPTER XV

THE FAMILY CULICIDAE. DEFINITION OF THE SUB-FAMILY CULICINAE. THE EXTERNAL AND INTERNAL ANATOMY OF AN ADULT MOSQUITO

THE FAMILY CULICIDAE

FLIES occurring in the family Culicidae can be distinguished from those occurring in other families in the suborder Nematocera by their characteristic wing venation, in which the third vein is straight and lies between two forked veins.

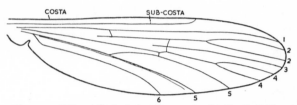

Fig. 40. Wing of a fly belonging to the family Culicidae showing the characteristic venation.

The family Culicidae is divided into three subfamilies—the Culicinae, the Chaoborinae and the Dixinae—only one of which, the subfamily Culicinae (comprising all the true mosquitoes), is of medical importance. The vast majority of true mosquitoes are blood-suckers, but none of the flies occurring in the subfamilies Chaoborinae and Dixinae possess a proboscis capable of penetrating mammalian skin.

THE SUBFAMILY CULICINAE

Members of the subfamily Culicinae, i.e. true mosquitoes, may be distinguished from all other nematocerous flies including those belonging to the related subfamilies Chaoborinae and Dixinae by the fact that only in the subfamily Culicinae are the following two characters always present. (1) The insect possesses a prominent, forwardly projecting proboscis with palps which are held straight and rigid, and which are not pendulous. (2) Scales are present on the body, the legs and the wings.

The colouration of the mosquito is dependent on the colour of the scales. Whereas many species of mosquitoes have inconspicuous colouring, others have black and white bands or patches of coloured scales on the body and legs and sometimes, especially in the genera *Anopheles* and *Mansonia*, on the wings. A few species of mosquitoes are handsome insects with brightly coloured metallic scales on the head and thorax.

Mosquitoes have a worldwide distribution being found in the tropics, in

F

the temperate zones and in the arctic circles. They have been found breeding not only in underground tunnels but also in deep mines, and have been recorded as occurring at altitudes as high as 13,000 feet above sea level. Generally they are more common in the tropics than in the temperate zones but, in certain northern territories such as Lapland and Quebec, they may occur in such vast numbers as to render life almost unbearable.

It was only towards the end of the 19th century that mosquitoes were definitely proved to be vectors of malaria and that their vast importance in the tropics and the urgent need for their control was recognised, a development which served as an impetus to the study of an insect, which until then had been regarded as unimportant. As a result of this realisation a great deal of information has accumulated during the past 50 years concerning the biology of the mosquito, its role as a vector of many diseases and the methods which may be employed for its control. At the present time, although it is true to say that the mosquito is still the most important vector of disease in the tropics, it is equally true to say that the methods available for its control are highly efficient and that, in general, they have proved more successful than those applied to the control of other arthropod vectors of tropical infections.

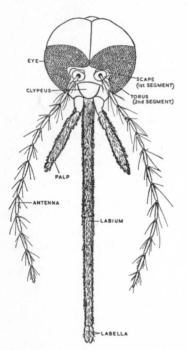

Fig. 41. The head of a mosquito seen from the front, showing the elongated proboscis. The biting fascicle is contained within the labium.

This emphasis on the importance of mosquitoes as vectors of disease and the need for their control should not cause forgetfulness of their significance as irritating creatures which, when they occur in sufficient numbers, add immeasurably to the discomfort of life, particularly in the tropics. Nor should it be forgotten that even a small number of mosquito bites may have serious consequences when received by a highly sensitized person.

THE EXTERNAL ANATOMY OF THE ADULT MOSQUITO

All mosquitoes are small (usually not more than a centimetre in length), slender-bodied flies. The division of the body into head, thorax and abdomen is sharply defined.

The Head.

The head of the mosquito is relatively small in comparison with the thorax and is almost spherical in form. Conspicuous on the surface are the large eyes, the long antennae and the elongated mouthparts.

The two compound eyes (simple eyes, ocelli, are lacking in mosquitoes) are kidney-shaped and occupy a large part of the sides of the head.

The antennae which originate between, and just in front of, the eyes are many-jointed, thread-like appendages with 14-15 segments, of which the first two—the scape and the torus—are dissimilar in form, not only from each other but also from the remaining segments which are similar to each other. In both

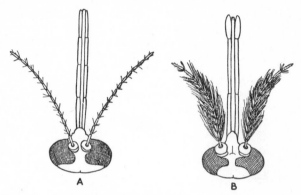

Fig. 42. Head of a mosquito showing *A*. the pilose antennae of the female and *B*. the plumose antennae of the male.

sexes the antennae are adorned with hairs; in the male they are so densely clothed with long hairs as to have the appearance of a test-tube brush and are said to be plumose, while in the female the antennae are provided with far fewer and shorter hairs and are said to be pilose.

The mouthparts, all of which are prolonged forwards to form the much

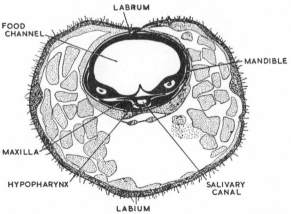

Fig. 43. Cross section of the mouthparts of a mosquito.

elongated proboscis, consist of a flexible, gutter-shaped labium, terminating in two peg-shaped structures, the labella, a pair of maxillary palps and a biting fascicle, the latter being a much more rigid structure than the labium. The fascicle is composed of the labrum, the hypopharynx, a pair of maxillae and a pair of mandibles. Normally these structures lie enclosed within the groove of the labium so that, except when the mosquito is feeding, the only visible portion of the proboscis is the labium. The various structures which make up the fascicle normally remain in close apposition, forming a compact bundle, but, if the fascicle is disengaged from the labial groove with a fine needle the various organs comprising it may be separated and will present the appearance shown in Fig. 44. When the organs thus separated are examined with the

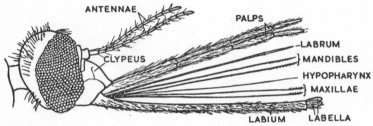

Fig. 44.   Side view of the head of a mosquito showing the mouthparts, disengaged from the labium.

compound microscope it will be seen that the labrum, up which the blood passes, has the form of a split tube which terminates in a nib-like extremity, while the hypopharynx, through which the saliva passes on its way to the host's tissues, also is tube-like in structure, but with a far finer lumen than that of the labrum. The mandibles and the maxillae, which are both cutting instruments, possess scalpel-like blades which are serrated, the serrations on the maxillae being much coarser than those on the mandibles.

Although the mouthparts of the two sexes resemble each other superficially, it is only the female which possesses mandibles and maxillae which are sufficiently developed to enable her to cut the host's skin and obtain a blood-meal; in consequence, only female mosquitoes are concerned in the transmission of disease.

The behaviour of the female mosquito when obtaining her blood-meal from the mammalian host is usually as follows. The mosquito after alighting on the skin generally moves about for a few seconds, applying its labella at various points on the surface; having selected a suitable site, the mandibles and maxillae are used to cut a tunnel through the stratum corneum and the underlying tissues. Into the aperture thus made pass the labrum and the hypopharynx, but the labium remains on the surface and becomes gradually more kinked as the head of the mosquito is thrust closer to the skin. The relatively flexible fascicle of the mosquito now probes, in all directions, the host's subcutaneous tissues in search of a blood-meal. The first action of a mosquito when biting is not

86

suction but the injection of the salivary secretion through the hypopharynx (the injection being accomplished by means of the salivary pump) from which droplets of saliva are ejected intermittently throughout the probing and feeding processes. Once a capillary has been penetrated by the cutting mandibles and

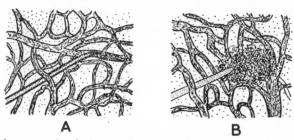

Fig. 45. *A.* a mosquito feeding with the fascicle lying in the lumen of a capillary. *B.* a mosquito feeding from a pool of blood forming from a lacerated capillary.

maxillae the mosquito may feed either with the fascicle lying in the lumen of a capillary, or else—less commonly— with the tip of the labrum resting in a pool of blood which has escaped from a previously lacerated blood vessel. *The thorax.*

The thorax of the mosquito is stoutly built and slightly humped, being oval in cross-section. The pleurites of the pro-, meso- and metathorax bear setae, the nature and arrangement of which are of value in classifying the various species. The thorax is covered with scales, the shape, colouration and arrangement of which are also made use of in the identification of the species. In life, the wings are carried folded over the abdomen.

The wing, the venation of which has been described previously, is of the narrow type (being much longer than broad) and is provided with scales along the veins and along the posterior edge. When coloured scales are present, they are often arranged in a definite pattern, which—as in the case of the thorax—may be used to assist in the identification of the species.

The legs are long and slender, terminating in claws which may or may not be toothed, and may be ornamented with patches of light and dark scales, often in the form of rings. *The abdomen.*

In the unfed mosquito the abdomen is long and slender, but when the female is fully fed, or when the ovaries are well developed, the abdomen becomes distended and ovate. The

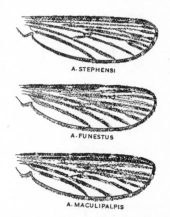

Fig. 46. The scale patterns on the wings of three species of anopheline mosquitoes.

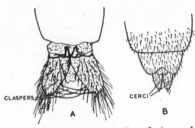

Fig. 47. External genitalia of *A*. a male mosquito and *B*. a female mosquito.

abdomen, like the thorax, is provided with scales, but the form, colouration and arrangement of these are relatively unimportant as a means of recognising the species. The external genitalia, which are borne at the tip of the abdomen in both male and female mosquitoes, are illustrated in Fig. 47. The morphology of the conspicuous male organs is often used in classifying the various species,

but the genitalia of the female are inconspicuous and are unimportant in classification.

THE INTERNAL ANATOMY OF THE ADULT MOSQUITO

The internal anatomy of the adult mosquito conforms to the general plan of insect anatomy as described in Chapters IX and X.

The digestive and excretory systems.

The alimentary canal is divided into three primary regions—the fore-gut, the mid-gut (or stomach) and the hind-gut.

The fore-gut consists of the buccal cavity, the pharynx (the suction pump) and the oesophagus. The hypopharynx, which helps to form the floor of the buccal cavity, is in direct communication with the common salivary duct, which divides in the thorax to form the two salivary ducts communicating with the salivary glands. The salivary glands of the mosquito lie at the level of the first pair of legs, one on each side of the thorax. They are trilobed structures and each is provided with a collecting channel down which the saliva

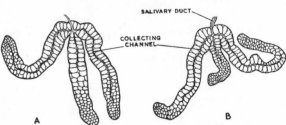

Fig. 48. Salivary glands dissected from *A*. a culicine mosquito and *B*. an anopheline mosquito.

passes to the duct which joins with the duct from the other side of the thorax to form the common salivary duct. It is probable that the chemical composition of the saliva varies in different species of mosquitoes; it is known that the saliva of certain species of mosquitoes contains a haemagglutinin and, or, an anticoagulin, whereas in other species those substances appear to be absent. The reactions which are observed sometimes to follow the injection of saliva into the human host are discussed in a later chapter. Coming off the hind portion of the oesophagus are two small and one large oesophageal diverticula; the two small diverticula are confined to the thorax, but the large diverticulum extends well into the abdomen. The junction of the fore-gut and mid-gut, which in the mosquito is situated about the middle of the thorax, is guarded by the proventriculus which prevents regurgitation of food from the distended stomach into the oesophagus.

The mid-gut has the form of a straight tube which expands somewhat after its entrance into the abdomen.

The hind-gut is usually considered as consisting of the ileum, the colon and the rectum, and its junction with the mid-gut is marked by the insertion of the malpighian tubules, which in the mosquito are of moderate length and five in number. The hind-gut like the mid-gut commences as a straight tube, but its termination is expanded to form the large and almost spherical rectum which contains six prominent rectal glands (see Fig. 25).

The females of all species of mosquitoes of medical importance are blood-suckers and, although they will feed on fruit juice and take up various liquids from plants, their digestive system is adapted to a protein diet. When the mosquito is feeding on the vertebrate host, the insect's powerful pharyngeal muscles cause the host's blood to rush up the narrow bore of the labrum and into the fly's oesophagus with surprising speed. When the mosquito partakes of a blood-meal the ingested fluid passes from the oesophagus directly to the stomach, so that the whole abdomen is soon distended with blood; it is only when fluid other than blood—for example, fruit juice—is ingested that the meal passes into the oesophageal diverticulum prior to entering the stomach.
The fat body.

Fat body, in varying amounts, is always present in the body cavity of the adult mosquito. When dissecting mosquitoes under a simple lens, the fat body can usually be seen as a loose whitish material lining the inner walls of the abdomen and surrounding the gut and the reproductive organs. The amount of fat body present in the mosquito, as in the case of most other insects, is markedly increased as a prelude to hibernation.
The reproductive system.

The male reproductive organs consist of a pair of testes, the ducts of which, together with the ducts of the accessory glands, open into a common ejaculatory duct. The ejaculatory duct leads to the aedeagus (or penis) which opens on the 9th segment of the mosquitoe's abdomen (see Fig. 29).

The female reproductive organs consist of paired ovaries, the ducts of which unite to form a common oviduct, the lower portion of which is known as the vagina. The vagina—into which open the ducts from the spermatheca and from the accessory gland—not only receives the aedeagus of the male during copulation, but also acts as a channel by which sperms previously stored in the spermatheca may reach and fertilize the eggs. During oviposition the vagina acts as the portal of exit of the eggs, and it is in the vagina that they are coated with a substance, produced by the accessory gland, which in the case of many species serves to glue the eggs together in the form of a raft.

The ovary in the non-gravid mosquito is spindle-shaped and consists of numerous elongated tube-like structures in which the eggs are formed and develop. When the mosquito is gravid the ovaries become greatly increased in volume, due to the presence of maturing eggs in the ovarioles, and at this stage the ovaries take up much space in the abdomen and give it a distended appearance. The spermathecae are spherical, chitinised, sperm-storing organs which vary in number from one to three in various species of mosquitoes.

The degree of development of the ovaries and the appearance of the oviducts are made considerable use of in estimating the age of mosquitoes captured during mosquito surveys.

CHAPTER XVI

THE SUBFAMILY CULICINAE (cont.)

A BRIEF OUTLINE OF THE LIFE-CYCLE AND HABITS OF A TRUE MOSQUITO

ALL mosquitoes have a holometabolous life-cycle, the immature stages being aquatic and not resembling in any way the adult forms which are terrestial.

The females of all mosquitoes of medical importance (with the exception of the megarhine mosquitoes) are blood-suckers and, once they are fertilised, they are wholly, or in part, dependent on obtaining a blood-meal before they can lay the eggs necessary for the propagation of the species, the source of the blood meal varying according to the species and even, sometimes, according to the subspecies of the mosquito.

Since most of the mosquito-borne diseases transmissible to the human host are carried by the insect vector from man to man, it is usual to find that the more important vectors are those which show a close association with man and which prefer him to animals as a source of food. On the other hand many species of mosquitoes which bite man and animals indiscriminately not only play a part in transmitting from man to man certain diseases which exist also in an animal reservoir, but in addition play a part in transmitting these diseases from the animal reservoir to the human host. Finally, it must be remembered that certain species of mosquitoes which seldom, if ever, bite man and which therefore are unimportant as direct vectors of disease to the human population, nevertheless play a vital part in the epidemiology of such medically important diseases as yellow fever (where monkeys constitute the main reservoir), and certain encephalitides (where the reservoirs are birds and domestic animals such as horses and sheep).

Selectivity amongst different species of mosquitoes is not limited to the source of the blood-meal, but is noticeable also with regard to the time at which the meal is taken, and the nature of the environment in which it is sought. As regards the time of feeding, many species are nocturnal in their feeding habits, some are crepuscular, some are diurnal, while others feed indiscriminately by day or night. As regards the environment in which the meal is sought, it is obvious that this will be associated with the host's habits and with any preference shown by the vector to feed at a particular time. Thus, most anophelines are night-feeders and the diseases they transmit are most commonly acquired during the night and therefore, in the case of man, are more often contracted indoors than out of doors. On the other hand most species of *Aedes* are ready to feed either by day or by night and the diseases, such as yellow fever, which they transmit to man may be acquired by him at any time of the day or night and "out of doors" as well as "indoors". These preferences regarding sites and times of feeding have given rise to the use of such terms as "outdoor biters", "indoor biters", "forest mosquitoes", "night biters", "day biters", etc.

Whatever the site and time of the blood-meal, the mosquito which is fully fed will remain quiescent for a variable period, usually 2-4 days, during which time the ovaries mature, the first batch of eggs taking a little longer to ripen than the subsequent batches. The resting place selected by the gorged female during this period varies greatly, not only according to the species of mosquito concerned but also according to the environment in which the meal was obtained. In spite of this variability it can be stated that, in general, the house-haunting species tend to spend at least part of the gestation period in the room or house in which the blood-meal was obtained, while the outdoor biters rest in a wide variety of sheltered situations, such as outhouses, caves, and, often, on the under surface of foliage.

The eggs having fully matured the female leaves her resting place to seek a collection of water (a few species of medical importance oviposit on damp surfaces) on which to lay her eggs. Each individual species of mosquito shows some degree of preference with regard to the type of water which she selects for oviposition. These preferences are always subservient to the overriding urge to lay the eggs as soon as possible after they are fully formed, so that when the preferred oviposition site is not available she will lay her eggs on almost any collection of water which is not too saline and which is not subject-ed to high winds or rough wave motion.

The manner of deposition of the eggs differs somewhat amongst various species of mosquitoes. Most species rest on the surface of the water whilst ovipositing and lay their eggs either scattered about the surface or attach them together in the form of floating rafts, whilst a smaller proportion of species drop their eggs on to the surface of water, one at a time, whilst performing a "hovering dance" or else when resting above the water. Certain species of medically important mosquitoes, some of which occur in the Aedes group and others in the Mansonia group, have a rather specialised oviposition behaviour which will be discussed later.

The number of eggs laid at each oviposition varies greatly according to the species of the mosquito concerned; thus the females of some species may lay as many as 300 eggs on a single occasion, whereas the females of certain other species seldom deposit more than twenty. Not only does the number of eggs deposited vary according to the species of the mosquito but the number produced by individual females of the same species also shows marked dif-ferences which are apparently dependent on various factors, notably the nature and amount of the previous blood meals. In spite of these species and individual differences it can be stated in general terms that most mosquitoes lay 50-150 eggs at each oviposition.

The total number of eggs laid by a mosquito during its lifetime is, of course, directly related to the fly's longevity, but it is dependent also on many other factors such as the food supply available to the adult and the temperature of the environment, but it may be stated that under optimal conditions the females will oviposit once a fortnight and it is unusual for more than four batches of eggs to be laid by any one mosquito.

The eggs laid by the female on the surface of the water usually hatch in 2 or 3 days but in cold weather this time may be prolonged. In addition, the eggs of certain species, in particular those which deposit their eggs on moist surfaces, can remain dormant and viable for much longer periods.

The larva emerges from the egg, by tearing a circular rent in the egg shell with its "egg breaker", only in the presence of free water. There are always four larval stages (instars) in the life-cycle of the mosquito, the larva casting its skin (which is also known as the "pelt") four times before transforming into a pupa. The larval life lasts, under optimum conditions, 1-3 weeks, depending on the species, the temperature of the water and the availability of the food supply.

The type of habitat in which mosquito larvae may be found varies widely and depends, of course, mainly on the site of oviposition. It may be said that, by far and large, mosquito larvae are usually found inhabiting natural collections of water, although many species thrive readily in man-made habitats, and some have become so domesticated as to breed in water-filled utensils in, or in close proximity to, human dwellings. Although each species of mosquito tends to have a predilection for a certain type of habitat, most species are fairly ubiquitous and may be found in a wide range of breeding sites. Habitats vary from large expanses of water such as swamps, ponds and lakes to much more restricted collections of water in tree-holes, leaf bases, depressions in the ground, rock pools, hoof marks, crab holes, discarded tins, water barrels, etc. Springs, streams and rivers—particularly when they are fast flowing—are less commonly the site of mosquito breeding.

In many of these sites mosquito larvae are found living in association with plants. In some instances the association satisfies the larva's need for shade and for protection from water currents, while in other instances the association is much closer, the larva being dependent on the presence of the plant for such essentials as food or oxygen.

Most species of mosquito larvae feed indiscriminately on micro-organisms by sweeping these into the mouth by means of water currents set up by the mouth brushes, and from these micro-organisms the larvae appear to derive all the food substance necessary for growth. A certain number of species, however, browse on submerged objects (the surface of which they abrade) whilst others are predatory on the larvae of other species of mosquitoes and have the mouthparts modified in accordance with this habit.

The larvae of all species of mosquitoes breathe atmospheric air through spiracles which are located on the upper surface of the eighth segment, but a few species which spend much of their life in the mud at the bottom of their habitat, augment this supply by absorbing, through the cuticle, oxygen dissolved in the water. Mosquito larvae are stimulated by changes in light intensity, vibrations, or any disturbances of their environment. They move very actively, usually by means of a wriggling backward motion, although they may also "creep" at the surface of the water or along the surface of a submerged object.

At the end of the fourth instar the now fully grown larva casts its skin and becomes a pupa. The mosquito pupa is always found in free water, in the same sites as the larva. Although the pupa often remains motionless at the water surface it is capable of very active movement and reacts to the same stimuli as does the larva. The pupa is a stage in the mosquito life-cycle during which the larva undergoes transformation to the adult. The length of the pupal life, during which time the insect does not feed, is always very short, usually a few days, but in adverse conditions it may be prolonged.

When the adult is ready to emerge, the pupa flattens out on the surface of the water, a T-shaped slit is torn in its back and the adult mosquito wriggles out of the pupal skin. Having emerged, the mosquito balances itself on the water, the floating pupal case or some nearby floating object until its wings are dry and then flies off.

The total length of the mosquito life-cycle, from the laying of the eggs to the emergence of the adults, is variable and depends not only on the species but also on environmental conditions such as temperature and the availability of food supplies to the growing stages. In general, it may be said that, under optimum conditions, mosquito life-cycles vary between about ten days and one month.

The lengths of life of adult male and female mosquitoes (other things being equal, the females always outlive the males) depend on a wide variety of factors, but, in general, it may be stated that the longevity of a particular species is very closely associated with the temperature and humidity in which it lives. In temperate zones mosquitoes may live up to six months, whereas in the tropics they seldom survive for more than a month.

The length of life of the adult female mosquito under natural conditions has an important bearing on its ability to act as a vector of cyclically transmitted diseases. To be a vector of such diseases, the mosquito must not only survive after its infecting meal for a period sufficient to allow the ingested organism to reach its infective stage, but it must also survive for a further period during which time it obtains another blood-meal from a host susceptible to the infection.

In the following Chapter, the division of the subfamily Culicinae into its three tribes and the distinction between mosquitoes belonging to each of the three tribes is dealt with briefly.

CHAPTER XVII

THE SUBFAMILY CULICINAE (cont.).
ITS DIVISION INTO THREE TRIBES

THE subfamily Culicinae is conveniently divided into three tribes—the Anophelini (the anophelines), the Culicini (the culicines) and the Megharinini (the megharines). Members of the tribe Megharinini (often called "elephant mosquitoes") are easily distinguished from all other mosquitoes by their large size and by their distinctly curved proboscis which is incapable of piercing mammalian skin. The megharine mosquitoes play no part in the transmission of disease and their only claim to being of medical importance lies in the fact that their larvae are predaceous and destroy the larvae of other and more dangerous species. In contradistinction to the harmless—indeed beneficial—members of the tribe Megharinini, members of the tribes Anophelini and Culicini include species which are amongst the most important vectors of disease in the world. Amongst these diseases malaria ranks very high and, since it is normally transmitted to man only through the agency of the anopheline mosquito, it is of fundamental impor-

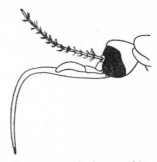

Fig. 49. Head of a megarhine mosquito showing the curved proboscis.

tance that the medical officer should be able to recognise members of this tribe and distinguish them from the culicines, which, although of vast importance in the transmission of various virus and helminth infections, are not concerned in the spread of human malaria.

In the present chapter, it is proposed only to discuss the methods to be used for distinguishing adult mosquitoes occurring in the tribe Anophelini from those occurring in the tribe Culicini, the differences between their respective eggs, larvae and pupae being considered in later chapters.

The method employed to distinguish members of the two tribes is based on an examination of the palps, but before this is done, it is necessary to differentiate between the sexes by examining the antennae; if the antennae are damaged the sex can be established by an examination of the external genitalia (see fig. 47).

Having determined the sex of the mosquito, the differentiation between the two tribes is made by examining the palps, preferably with a low power hand lens (x 10), and noting the points illustrated in the diagram shown below.

In the case of the female culicine, the palps are short, peg-like structures, much shorter than the proboscis and are carried closely applied to the base of the intervening proboscis, giving the appearance of a basal thickening. In the case of the female anopheline, the palps are as long, or nearly as long, as the proboscis. In dead specimens, the palps are usually separated from the proboscis and are clearly visible; but in the live anopheline the palps are often closely applied to the proboscis and therefore more difficult to see. However, if the insect is watched for a few moments, the palps can usually be seen to separate.

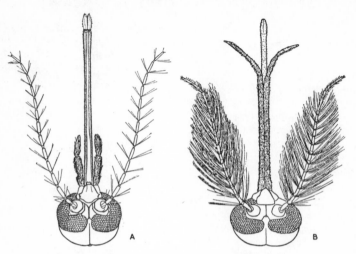

Fig. 50.   Head and mouthparts of *A*. a female culicine mosquito and *B*. a male culicine mosquito.

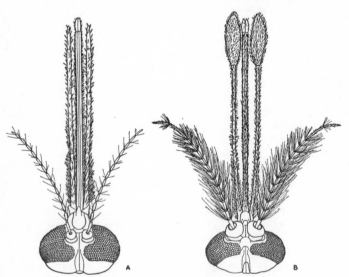

Fig. 51.   Head and mouthparts of *A*. a female anopheline mosquito and *B*. a male anopheline mosquito.

In the case of the male culicine, the palps are usually as long as, or longer than, the proboscis, but in some species in certain genera, such as *Haemogogus*, they are short. The male culicine palp is characterised by the absence of any marked thickening ("clubbing") at its tip. In the case of the male anopheline, the palps are as long as, or longer than, the proboscis and show thickening ("clubbing") at the tip. It should be noted that the terminal segments of the palps of certain male culicines have a broom-like appearance due to the presence of long hairs and this must not be confused with the palpal thickening characteristic of the male anopheline.

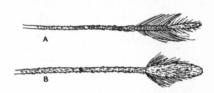

Fig. 52. Showing the differences in the palps of male anopheline and culicine mosquitoes, *A.* the "broom-like" palp of the male culicine and *B.* the "club shaped" palp of the male anopheline.

There are other, but much less reliable, characteristics which help in differentiating the tribes. (1) Most species of mosquitoes belonging to the tribe Anophelini show the presence of patches of coloured scales on the wings (hence the popular name "dapple-winged mosquito") whereas, most, although by no means all, species of mosquitoes occurring in the tribe Culicini lack this characteristic. (2) In life the resting attitude adopted by the adult anopheline generally differs from that adopted by the adult culicine. Anophelines usually rest with the head, thorax and abdomen in a nearly straight line, and with the long axis of the body at an angle of about 45° to the surface on which they have alighted, and so present a tilted appearance. Culicines in contrast assume a position nearly parallel to the resting surface and with the abdomen slightly drooping. (3) The shape of the scutellum can usually be relied upon as a means of distinction; in the culicines it is always trilobed, whereas in the anophelines it is usually simple. (4) The thorax of the culicine mosquito is generally more humped than that of the anopheline.

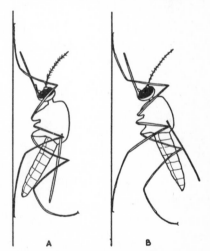

Fig. 53. Diagram showing the resting attitude of a mosquito belonging to *A.* the tribe Culicini and *B.* the tribe Anophelini.

As regards the internal anatomy, with the following two exceptions, no obvious morphological differences are observable:—(1) The middle lobe of the trilobed salivary gland of the anopheline is always shorter than the lateral lobes, whereas in the culicine mosquito the three lobes are approximately equal in length (see Fig. 48). (2) In the female anopheline only one spermatheca is present, whereas the female culicine possesses, according to the species, either two or else three spermathecae.

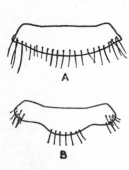

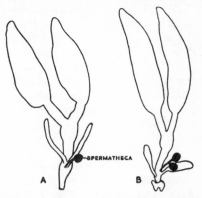

Fig. 54. Scutellum of *A*. an anopheline mosquito and *B*. a culicine mosquito.

Fig. 55. Diagrammatic representation of the female genital organs in a mosquito belonging to *A*. the tribe Anophelini and *B*. the tribe Culicini.

CHAPTER XVIII

THE TRIBE ANOPHELINI AND ITS DIVISION INTO THREE GENERA. THE GENUS ANOPHELES

THE tribe Anophelini is composed of three genera, *Chagasia*, *Bironella* and *Anopheles*, of which only one—the genus *Anopheles*—contains species of medical importance.

The genus *Chagasia*

Members of the genus *Chagasia* are limited in their distribution to South America. Only three species are recognised; two of these are known to bite man, but there is no evidence to suggest that they act as vectors of disease. Members of the genus *Chagasia* can be distinguished from other anophelines by the outline of the scutellum, which is trilobed.

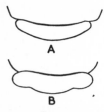

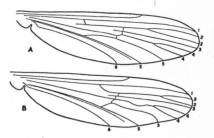

Fig. 56. Scutellum of a mosquito belonging to *A*. the genus *Anopheles* and *B*. the genus *Chagasia*.

Fig. 57. Wing of a mosquito belonging to *A*. the genus *Anopheles* and *B*. the genus *Bironella*.

The genus *Bironella*

The genus *Bironella* occurs in New Guinea and its neighbouring islands, and in Northern Australia. It is composed of seven species, only one of which is known to bite man, and then only very rarely; there is no evidence to suggest that it is a vector of disease. The genus *Bironella* may be separated from the genus *Anopheles* by the details of the wing venation, the 4th vein being straight in *Anopheles*, but wavy in *Bironella*.

The genus *Anopheles*

Members of the genus *Anopheles* have a worldwide distribution. More than 200 species and varieties have been described.

The genus *Anopheles* was so named in 1818, but it was not until some 80 years later that the particular association of anophelines with the transmission of mammalian malaria (in contrast to the part played by culicine mosquitoes in the transmission of avian malaria) was demonstrated. The discovery that culicine mosquitoes allowed the development of *Wuchereria bancrofti* (an im-

G

portant cause of filariasis) to the infective stage was made prior to the discovery of the transmission of human malaria by anophelines, but the discovery that anopheline as well as culicine mosquitoes were responsible for the transmission of this form of filariasis came much later. Although anopheline mosquitoes are predominantly important as vectors of malaria to man, in some parts of the tropics they are also important vectors of filariasis. They are not known to transmit infections other than these, and it is a remarkable fact that, whereas more than 30 species of culicine mosquitoes have been shown to be vectors of at least nine of the viruses affecting man, no species of anopheline has so far been similarly incriminated.

The external and the internal anatomy of the adult mosquito has been described in previous chapters and attention has been drawn to those points which are characteristic of the tribe Anophelini. The morphological characters of the three genera comprising the tribe have been given, but their habits, life-cycles and medical importance have not yet been discussed. Members of the genera *Chagasia* and *Bironella* are of little if any medical importance, so that it is necessary only to consider the life-cycles and habits of those mosquitoes which belong to the genus *Anopheles*.

The life-cycle of the anopheline mosquito

Following fertilization and the partaking of a blood-meal, the female anopheline lays her eggs. These are always deposited singly, and in the majority of instances they are laid on the surface of free water, although a few species oviposit on the surface of damp soil. The anopheline egg, which is about 1 mm. in length and therefore visible to the naked eye, is white when laid but changes to a dull brown or black colour within a few hours of oviposition. The eggs, which often arrange themselves in a distinct pattern on the surface of the water, are always canoe-shaped and are provided with a pair of distinct lateral floats. These floats, which represent an air-filled space between the exochorion and the endochorion of the eggshell, enable the egg to float and resist submersion, even during heavy rain. Culicine eggs never possess floats.

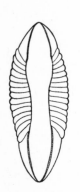

Fig. 58. Egg of an anophe-line mosquito as seen from above.

Oviposition is generally undertaken at night, when 50-150 eggs are laid on the water surface; sometimes all the eggs are deposited at a single sitting, but on other occasions oviposi-tion is prolonged over two or more successive nights.

The time elapsing between the deposition of the egg and the hatching of the first instar larva varies very little with the species, but greatly with variations in temperature. In the warm conditions commonly encountered in the tropics the eggs usually hatch within 2-3 days, but under conditions of cold, such as are often encountered in Europe, the hatching of the eggs of certain important vectors of malaria (for example *A. maculipennis*) may be delayed for several weeks.

The first instar larva emerges from the egg by cutting a circular slit in the shell by means of its egg-breaker. Having pushed off the resultant cap and having become free in the water, the larva grows with a speed which is directly proportional to the suitability of the environment to its requirements. These requirements vary considerably according to the species of anopheline concerned, but always include a suitable food supply and certain suitable physical conditions, particularly those relating to water movement, temperature and light intensity.

The food requirements of all surface-feeding anopheline larvae include bacteria and various minute plants (algae etc.) together with animacules, such as protozoa and rotifers.

Almost every species of anopheline has its own requirements as regards the physical conditions of the larval habitat. Sometimes these requirements are similar not only for different species of anophelines but also for different species of culicines in which case many species of anophelines and culicines may be found breeding in the same collection of water. Other species, however, have such highly specialised requirements that

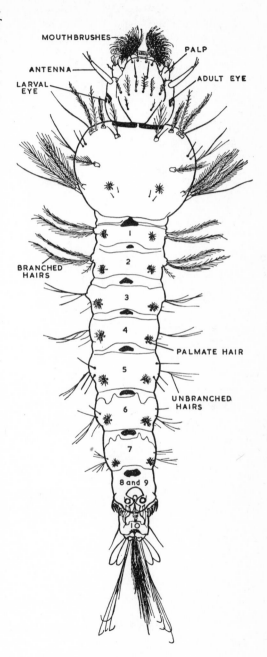

Fig. 59. Dorsal view of a fourth stage anopheline larva.

it is unusual to find them in association with other species and it is useless to search for them in the more commonly favoured habitats. Amongst the some 200 species of anophelines almost every type of water is favoured by at least one species and it can truly be said that no type of water is potentially free from breeding except, (1) water in domestic utensils, (2) evanescent puddles of water, (3) collections of water subject to marked wave action, (4) fast running currents in streams, (5) highly polluted water and (6) water, the salt content of which is considerably higher than that of the sea. In view of the great diversity of these breeding-places it is not possible to do more than consider, as has been done at the end of this chapter, the favourite breeding-sites of some of the more important anopheline vectors of malaria and filariasis.

The fourth instar larva (which has undergone three ecdyses since its emergence from the egg, some three weeks previously) when full-grown and ready to pupate measures about a centimetre and presents the appearance shown in the drawing.

Anatomy of the larva.

As shown in the drawing the anopheline larva, like all mosquito larvae, possesses a well-defined head, thorax and abdomen.

The head. The head, which is more chitinised than the thorax or the abdomen, is broadly ovate in dorsal view and is compressed dorso-ventrally. It carries a pair of peg-like antennae, two pairs of eyes (for in the fourth stage larva, the eyes of the future adult can be seen through the larval skin), and a pair of mouth-brushes with which it sweeps food towards the mandibulate (chewing) mouthparts. The resting anopheline larva lies with its body parallel to, and just below, the surface film. When about to feed, it turns its head through an angle of 180°, thereby

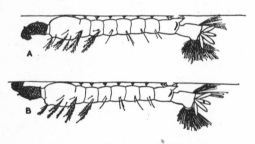

Fig. 60.   Drawing of an anopheline larva in *A.* the resting position and *B.* the feeding position.

bringing the mouth-brushes into contact with the surface of the water. This mode of feeding has an important bearing on certain methods commonly employed for anopheline—as distinct from culicine—control. The horizontally suspended anopheline larvae are essentially surface feeders (as distinct from the culicine larvae which hang head downwards from the surface film and which, therefore, feed mainly below the surface), so that control measures employing the use of floating particles of copper acetoarsenite (Paris Green) are highly effective when used against anopheline larvae, but almost useless when used against culicine larvae.

The thorax. The prothorax, the mesothorax and the metathorax are fused together to form a compact mass. Although the three thoracic segments cannot be recognised individually, a group of conspicuous branched hairs, corresponding to each of the three segments, is present laterally.

The abdomen. The abdomen consists of nine distinct segments, the first seven of which are very similar to one another. Arising laterally, on each side of the

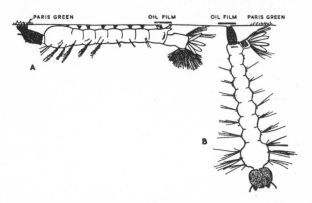

Fig. 61. Feeding attitudes of *A* anopheline and *B.* culicine larvae showing why a film of oil is efficient in controlling members of both tribes, whereas floating particles of Paris green are more often ingested by anopheline larvae.

first seven abdominal segments, there is a group of long hairs, the hairs of the first few segments being conspicuously branched whilst those of the remaining segments are unbranched. In addition the anopheline larva bears, on the dorsal surface of the first six (sometimes the first seven) abdominal segments, a pair of fan-shaped hairs—"the palmate hairs"—which are peculiar to members of the tribe Anophelini. When the palmate hairs are protruded through the surface film they suspend the anopheline larva in its characteristic horizontal position and thereby play an important part in determining the method of feeding and the method of breathing adopted by the larva. The eighth segment bears on its dorsal aspect a large chitinised plate known as the "stigmal plate" on which may be recognised an anterior plate (sometimes called "the fan-shaped plate"), a posterior plate (part of which is known as "the scoop"), two lateral plates (often called "the lateral flaps") and, lying between the lateral flaps, two openings, the spiracles, which lead into the tracheal system of the larva. On each side of the eighth segment and just below the stigmal plate, there is a row of "teeth" arising from a single chitinised base, the whole structure being known as "the pecten".

Throughout its life the anopheline larva must have oxygen and this it obtains by periodically resting horizontally (by means of its palmate hairs) just below the surface film, so that the eighth segment is brought into contact with the air-water interface and a meniscus is formed around the edges of the spiracular plate; in consequence the spiracles are in direct contact with atmospheric air. This dependence of the anopheline larva on repeated breaking of the surface film is made use of in control measures designed to kill the larvae either by introducing a toxic substance into the tracheae or, much less efficiently, by the use of a "heavy oil" which mechanically interferes with the breaking of the surface film. (See Fig. 61).

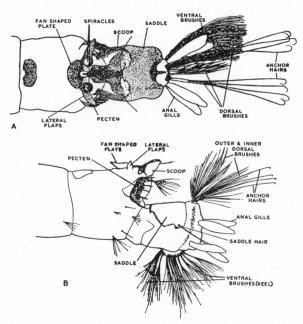

Fig. 62. Terminal segments of the larva of an anopheline mosquito as seen *A.* from above and *B.* from the lateral aspect.

The ninth segment leaves the eighth segment at a downward angle; it carries a dorsal plate, "the saddle", which bears at each posterior angle a hair ("the saddle hair") which, although relatively inconspicuous, is much used in classification. Terminally, the ninth segment is provided with four anal gills, two pairs of "dorsal brushes" consisting of numerous branched hairs, and a pair of "ventral brushes" comprised of similarly branched hairs. The "ventral brushes" are sometimes collectively known as "the ventral fin" or "the keel". In the case of most species of anopheline larvae, many of the hairs composing the outer dorsal brushes are hooked and are used by the larvae to anchor themselves to vegetation, thereby enabling them to resist currents of water capable of sweeping away other larvae, such as those of the culicines, which are not so protected.

When the fourth instar larva casts its skin it becomes a pupa, which is a comma-shaped creature, the fused head and thorax (cephalothorax) forming the upper thickened portion, while the segmented abdomen forms the tail-like extremity. The cephalothorax bears on its dorsal surface a pair of trumpet-shaped breathing tubes and a pair of palmate hairs. At the lateral margins of most of the abdominal segments there are a pair of spines the presence of which is confined to anopheline pupae, only hairs being present on culicine pupae. The abdomen terminates in a pair of flap-like structures known as the paddles. Immediately after its emergence from the larval skin the pupa is ivory in colour, but the pupal skin enclosing the almost completely formed imago darkens rapidly, although remaining sufficiently transparent to allow the pigmented eyes and the general form of the future mosquito to be seen through it.

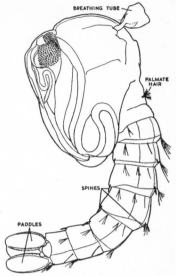

Fig. 63. Pupa of an anopheline mosquito.

The pupa spends most of its short existence at the surface of the water supported by the palmate hairs. The pupa is incapable of feeding and therefore unaffected by insecticides, such as Paris Green, which depend on being ingested for their toxic effect; but since the pupa rests with its breathing trumpets above the surface film and in contact with the atmospheric air it is vulnerable to oils which block its spiracular openings and to larvicides capable of entering its tracheal system. Although the anopheline pupa spends most of its time at the water surface it is capable, like all mosquito pupae, of active movements and if disturbed descends through the water with a characteristic jerky movement, by alternately extending and flexing the abdominal portion and by moving the paddles.

Two to three days after the formation of the pupa and shortly before the imago is ready to emerge, air collects between the imago and the enclosing pupal skin, conferring on the pupa an added buoyancy which lifts it high in the water. Immediately prior to the emergence of the adult from the pupal skin, the pupa straightens out just below the surface film, to which it is attached by the palmate hairs, and the imago escapes through a T-shaped slit torn through the dorsum of the pupal skin. Emergence having been completed, the mosquito usually rests either on the surface of the water, or else on the empty pupal case which it uses as a raft. The insect now expands its wings and when these have hardened, about an hour after its emergence, it takes flight. Until the wings have expanded and hardened the mosquito is incapable of flight and if, during this resting period, winds or waves disturb the water surface, the newly-emerged mosquitoes are liable to be drowned; in such circumstances the surface of the breeding place may be seen to be covered with drowned mosquitoes.

Copulation between the sexes usually takes place shortly after emergence and, therefore, generally near to the breeding site. The preliminaries to mating vary considerably according to the species of anopheline concerned. The more usual method of mating is for the males and females to meet in a "swarm" (the "dance of the gnats") during which the male seizes the female with the aid of its claspers. Insemination takes place and the joined couple fall from the swarm, to separate a few minutes later. The site and time of swarming varies with the species; the majority of anophelines swarm in open places commonly at dusk or dawn and the swarm can usually be seen as a small cloud of mosquitoes, hovering in the open, sometimes over an object such as a bush, some feet above ground level. Although this method of mating is generally adopted by anophelines certain species have recourse to very different mating habits, swarming not in open spaces, but in sheltered spots such as in the mouths of caves or high up in forest vegetation.

Once fertilisation has been effected the sexes part to seek food, the males looking for plant juices and similar substances, and the females for the blood meal, which is an essential preliminary to the maturation of the ovaries. During this search most species of anophelines, although they may be dispersed widely by wind, seldom fly far from their breeding places, and more often than not they limit their hunt for a host to distances varying from a few hundred feet to half a mile. It would be very unwise, however, to regard control measures carried out over a radius of such a short distance as half a mile as always sufficient to prevent anophelines travelling from their breeding places to human habitations, and malariologists in Europe know that anti-larval measures, to be successful, must extend about 2 to 3 miles from any centre requiring protection.

Most species of anophelines require only one blood-meal to mature each batch of eggs, although some species are known to take two or more such meals prior to oviposition.

Although the vast majority of anopheline mosquitoes prefer to feed in darkness, and normally do so at night, their attacks are not necessarily confined to the hours of darkness and most species will bite readily during the half-light of dusk or dawn. Certain species of anophelines, some of which are important vectors of malaria, do not conform to this pattern of behaviour; thus, to quote two examples, *A. bellator*, a South American species, bites virtually at all hours of the day and night, while *A. leucosphyrus*, an important vector of malaria in Borneo, does not enter houses to feed on man until after midnight and leaves the habitation well before dawn.

The fascicle of the anopheline mosquito is capable of penetrating such materials as a moderately thick shirt or linen trousers, particularly when these are put on the stretch; hence the danger of contracting mosquito-borne diseases when sitting on the perforated cane chairs commonly used in the tropics. Similarly anophelines can bite through all but very thick socks and, since the ankles are the favourite site of attack, canvas or leather mosquito boots afford the best protection. As in the case of all other blood-sucking insects the time taken to gorge varies considerably, but the anopheline generally completes its meal within 3-5 minutes. Most anophelines, when given the opportunity, will feed every two or three days.

These attacks on the human host may be made by anophelines which have a tendency to feed out of doors ("outdoor biters") or by those which show a preference for feeding indoors ("indoor biters") and these tendencies are so closely connected with preferences for feeding on particular species of vertebrates, that the two aspects are best considered together. Certain species of anophelines (such as *A. gambiae*, in Africa, and *A. darlingi* in America) which readily enter human dwellings, and which markedly prefer the blood of man to that of animals, are often responsible, sometimes to an exclusive degree, for the transmission of malaria over very considerable areas. Other species, such as *A. stephensi* in India, which have an equal liking for animal and human blood and which readily enter both human and animal habitations, may be presented with so many more opportunities of feeding on animals that the frequency with which they bite man is so reduced as to render them unimportant when compared with less common but more anthropophilic species. Finally, some "wild" species, such as *A. algeriensis*, although very ready to feed on man, have such restricted opportunities to do so that they are of no importance as vectors of disease.

The dependence of certain species of anopheline mosquitoes on human blood as a source of food is an important factor in the epidemiology of malaria and filariasis, for it is well recognised that some of the so-called "wild" anophelines, although not vectors in nature are capable, in laboratory conditions, of allowing the development of malarial and filarial parasites to the infective stage. Such "wild anophelines" would be a potential danger to human health were it not for the fact that they are not dependent on man for their blood-meals.

Having taken her blood-meal the replete female seeks a resting place in which to digest the meal and allow the ovaries to ripen. The sites of choice for the anopheline resting places are sheltered, dark and not too dry situations, usually not far from the source of the blood-meal. Most "outdoor" biters after the meal rest, usually near ground level, on the under surface of leaves, on the bark of trees or in rot holes, but some species although biting out of doors subsequently rest in human or animal habitations. In the case of those species which are indoor feeders, some species leave the dwelling immediately after the blood-meal, others delay their departure until dawn, while some species tend to remain in the dwelling where they obtained the blood-meal for twenty-four hours or longer. Once the ovaries have ripened, following the obtaining of one or more blood-meals, the ovigerous female leaves the resting place to search for a suitable collection of water on which to lay her eggs. The length of life of anophelines does not appear to differ essentially from that of other mosquitoes, being up to six months in the temperate zones, but very much less in the tropics.

The medical importance of anopheline mosquitoes

Whilst a limited number of species of anophelines are important vectors of filariasis, it is as the sole transmitter of malaria that the anopheline has established itself as probably the most important vector of human disease in the world. In the case of both diseases, transmission is only possible after cyclical development of the parasite, and occurs directly as a result of the bite.

At the present time, only four species of *Plasmodium*—*P. falciparum*, *P. vivax*, *P. ovale* and *P. malariae*—are recognised as causing malaria in man. In the case of the first three species there is no evidence that any animal reservoir exists, but in the case of the last named species (*P. malariae*) it seems probable that the chimpanzee shares the infection with man. In addition, certain species, such as *P. knowlesi*, which normally parasitise monkeys, can be transmitted to man under laboratory conditions, but there is no evidence that this occurs in nature.

In the case of filariasis, only *Wuchereria bancrofti* and *Brugia* (=*Wuchereria*) *malayi** are known to be transmitted by anophelines. At the present time no animal reservoir for *W. bancrofti* is known, but recent investigations have shown that there is an animal reservoir for *B. malayi*.

The anopheline mosquito, in addition to acting as a vector of disease, often causes much discomfort and loss of sleep. The fascicle of the insect is so fine that the amount of trauma produced by the bite is negligible. On the other hand the injection of saliva in a previously sensitised person may be followed by an immediate and/or delayed reaction. The immediate reaction is usually much more severe than the delayed and the pruritus with which it is associated often results in scratching and may be followed by secondary infection.

---

* *Brugia malayi* (Buckley. 1960).

TABLES

THE DISTRIBUTION, LARVAL HABITAT AND ADULT
BEHAVIOUR OF SOME IMPORTANT ANOPHELINE VECTORS
OF MALARIA AND FILARIASIS

THE DISTRIBUTION, LARVAL HABITAT AND ADULT BEHAVIOUR OF SOME IMPORTANT ANOPHELINE VECTORS OF MALARIA

N.B. A column has been added to show whether the anopheline in question is known also to be a vector of filariasis and if so, whether of *Wuchereria bancrofti* or *Brugia malayi*. It must be remembered that knowledge on this point is often lacking. The sign + indicates a vector not at present regarded as important. ++ indicates an important vector.

SPECIES	GEOGRAPHICAL DISTRIBUTION	LARVAL HABITAT	ADULT BEHAVIOUR	WHETHER KNOWN TO BE A VECTOR OF: W. bancrofti	B. malayi
A. albimanus	Southern United States to northern parts of S. America.	Fresh water with floating plants or matted vegetation. Also found in brackish or stagnant water. Sunlight or partial shade	Feeds on man and domestic animals. Mainly nocturnal feeder but also bites during day. Usually returns outdoors after feeding.	+	–
A. aquasalis	Central America, Trinidad and the neighbouring islands and coast of S. America.	Brackish water in tidal swamps, in lagoons, and irrigation water exposed to tidal action. Rarely in fresh water. Sunlight or shade.	Feeds on man and domestic animals inside and outside houses and shelters. Feeds at night, particularly early evening. Resting places, chiefly outdoors.	+	–
A. bellator	Trinidad to Brazil.	In collections of water retained by the axils of leaves of certain species of bromeliads. Some shade.	Man (preferred host) and domestic animals. Feeds chiefly in shaded woods (day time). Invades dwellings in smaller numbers at night. Returns outdoors after meal.	–	–
A. claviger	Europe, Asia Minor and Turkestan	Marshes, rock pools, wells and cisterns. Sunlight or shade.	Feeds on man and domestic animals. A crepuscular invader of houses, and bites whenever its haunts are invaded. Usually remains indoors after feeding. (Important only in Middle East).	–	–

A. culicifacies	South East Arabia. Pakistan to Indo-china. Extends also south to Ceylon.	Great variety of sites in clean or polluted water – rarely brack-ish water. Often in man-made collections of water such as ir-rigated fields (rice fields). Found in unshaded sites with little or no floating mats of algae and only sparse vegetat-ion. Sunlight or partial shade.	Feeds on man and bovines at night. Remains indoors after feeding.	–	–
A. darlingi	Central America and South America to the Argentine.	Large collections of fresh water (rice fields, flooded cane fields, pastures, seepage swamps). Ponds, lakes and streams along forested course of large rivers. Shade.	Highly anthropophilic species. Nocturnal biter. Enters human habitations to feed and re-mains indoors after feeding.	++	–
A. farauti (= A. punctu-latus molucc-ensis)	New Guinea, New Britain, Solomons, New Hebrides and Northern Australia.	Large collections of water such as pools and swamps. Slow flowing streams and river mar-gins, also vehicle and animal tracks. Water may be either fresh or brackish, or polluted. Sunlight or shade.	Feeds on man readily and on a wide range of mammals and birds. Bites nocturnally and rests outdoors and indoors after meal.	++	–
A. fluviatilis	Iraq to Hongkong. Extending south to S. India.	Chiefly in clear running water, particularly at edges of irriga-tion canals, streams and springs overgrown with grass. Prefers sunlight.	Man and cattle usual hosts. Night feeder, and remains in-doors after meal.	–	–
A. freeborni (= A. maculi-pennis free-borni)	Western U.S.A.	Semi-permanent or permanent water such as seepage in rice-fields, irrigation schemes and flooded pastures. Clear water exposed to sunlight but with some protection (flotage, emer-gent vegetation or algae).	Feeds on man readily and on domestic animals. Rests indoors after meal.	–	–

TABLE (cont.)

SPECIES	GEOGRAPHICAL DISTRIBUTION	LARVAL HABITAT	ADULT BEHAVIOUR	WHETHER KNOWN TO BE A VECTOR OF: W. bancofti	B. malayi
A. funestus	Southern Sudan to South Africa.	In weedy parts of large collections of more or less permanent clear water such as swamps, edges of streams, rivers, ditches, ponds. Shade (but not deep forest shade).	A markedly anthropophilic species. Nocturnal feeder. Enters habitations to feed and rests indoors after feeding.	++	—
A. gambiae	Widely distributed in Africa from Abyssinia and Fr. West Africa in the north to Natal in the South.	Small collections of water completely or partially exposed to direct sunlight. Particularly temporary collections of water and man-made habitats.	Highly anthropophilic species. Nocturnal feeder. Enters human habitation to feed and usually remains indoors after feeding.	++	—
A. melas (= A. gambiae melas)	Same distribution as A. gambiae but not extending so far South.	Brackish water, particularly lagoons and tidal swamps.	Feeding on man. Enters human habitations and remains after feeding.	—	—
A. labranchiae labranchiae (= A. maculipennis labranchiae)	Countries on western and central Mediterranean littoral. Dalmatia and central Mediterranean islands.	Many sites. Brackish coastal marshes. Fresh water of rice-fields and upland streams. Sunlight.	Prefers human blood to that of domestic animals. Nocturnal biter. Rests indoors after meal.	—	—
A. labranchiae atroparvus (= A. maculipennis atroparvus)	From England, east to Japan and south to Spain and Northern Italy.	Fresh or brackish marshes and swamps. Sunlight.	Feeds on man and domestic animals. Nocturnal biter. Rests indoors after feeding.	—	—

Species	Distribution	Breeding habitat	Feeding and resting habits		
A. maculatus	India to Southern China, Indonesia and the Phillipines.	Among algae in small pools, in sunny exposed parts of streams and river beds with clear flowing water. Seepage, rice fields, ditches. Chiefly sunlight.	Feeds on man and domestic animals; in some localities feeds with preference. Rests outdoors after meal.	++	−
A. minimus (several subspecific variants)	India to China. Phillipines and Indonesia.	Margins of clear, cool, slow flowing irrigation ditches with grassy margins. Sunlit water.	Feeds with preference on man and also feeds on bovines. Feeds at night and rests indoors after feeding.	−	−
A. pseudo-punctipennis	From Southern U.S. to Chili and Argentine.	Clear, slow flowing streams, and clear pools rich in algae. Sunlight.	Man and domestic animals. Numbers feeding on man high in certain localities. Most return outdoors after feeding.	−	−
A. punctulatus	New Guinea, Solomons and neighbouring islands, Eastern Indonesia and Northern Australia.	Stream margins, small rain pools. Animal and vehicle tracks. Water exposed to sunlight.	Man and domestic animals. Where domestic animals absent man is preferred host. Nocturnal feeder. Most return out of doors after feeding.	++	+
A. quadrimaculatus	Canada and the Eastern U.S.A.	Chiefly small expanses of water and puddles, with vegetation; when in large expanses of water, marginal and associated with emergent vegetation. Partial shade.	Man and domestic animals. Nocturnal feeder. Some remain indoors and some return outdoors after feeding.	−	−
A. sacharovi (= *A. elutus*)	Italy, Balkans, Near East, through Central Russia to China.	Fresh or brackish marshes, coastal or inland marshes. Sunlight.	Feeds on man readily also on domestic animals. Nocturnal. Rests in shelters after feeding.	−	−
A. sinensis (= *A. hyrcanus sinensis*)	Burma, China, Indochina and other parts of S.E. Asia.	Ground pools such as ponds, pools, swamps. Also rice-fields and canals. Clean water with emergent vegetation. Chiefly sunlight.	Feeds on man and domestic animals. Nocturnal biter. Returns outdoors after feeding.	+	++

TABLE (cont.)

SPECIES	GEOGRAPHICAL DISTRIBUTION	LARVAL HABITAT	ADULT BEHAVIOUR	WHETHER KNOWN TO BE A VECTOR OF: W. bancrofti	B. malayi
A. stephensi (with several subspecific variants).	From Eastern Arabia to Burma.	Temporary and permanent water in cavities and containers of many types such as cisterns, wells and gutters. Also less commonly in fresh or saline ground water. A domestic species, requires some shade.	Feeds readily on man and bovines. Nocturnal feeder. Rests in human dwellings and cow-sheds, after feeding.	+	—
A. sundaicus	India, Burma, Thailand and Indonesia.	Salt or brackish water in natural or artificial basins where tidal and fresh water intermingle, particularly where purefying masses of algae and other weeds occur: chiefly a coastal species. Sunlight but tolerates some shade.	Feeds on man and cattle. Night feeder. Remains indoors after feeding.	+	—
A. superpictus	South East Asia and S. Europe.	Clear water exposed to sunlight such as shallow hill streams with sandy bottoms. Not in actual running water but in pools and crevices. Chiefly in hilly country.	Man and domestic animals. Nocturnal feeder. Remains indoors after feeding.	—	—
A. umbrosus	Eastern India, Indochina, Malaya, Indonesia.	Stagnant jungle pools and morasses. Shade.	Feeds on man and mammals, outdoors.	—	—

CHAPTER XIX

THE TRIBE CULICINI AND ITS DIVISION INTO FIVE GROUPS OF RELATED GENERA

THE tribe Culicini which contains about 2,000 species and varieties of mosquitoes is divided into about 25 genera.

Although culicine mosquitoes were recognised by the early naturalists, less than 150 of the 2,000 species known at the present day had been studied and described up to the end of the 19th century. Until Manson's discovery in 1877 of the development of the larval stages of *Wuchereria bancrofti* in a female culicine, these insects had been regarded only as a nuisance because of their blood-sucking habits and were of scant interest to the medical officer and the applied zoologist. The work of Manson and, later, that of Ross in malariology, led to intensive collecting of mosquitoes which culminated in the publication in 1901 of the first volume of Theobald's "A monograph of the Culicidae of the World". By 1910, ten years after the demonstration of the transmission of yellow fever by *Aedes aegypti*, Theobald published the 5th and last volume of his monumental work which continues to serve as the mainspring of systematic studies on the mosquito.

Since the turn of the 20th century the association of many species of culicine mosquitoes with the transmission of various diseases to man has been firmly established. Certain species of culicines, together with a few species of anophelines to which attention has already been drawn in a previous chapter, play an essential role in the epidemiology of filariasis caused by *Wuchereria bancrofti* and *Brugia malayi*, whilst a number of species are the only known vectors of certain viral diseases of man, the most important of which are yellow fever and dengue together with certain of the mosquito-borne encephalitides. Although many species of culicines are established vectors of avian malaria and other protozoal infections to birds, no species has so far been proved capable of the cyclical transmission of any protozoal disease to mammals. In addition to their importance as vectors of disease, culicines, both in cold and warm regions of the world, may constitute a serious public health problem as a result of their persistent attacks and of the severity of the lesions following the bites inflicted on previously sensitised persons.

The characteristics of an adult culicine mosquito and the distinction between adult members of the tribe Culicini and the tribe Anophelini have been discussed in a previous chapter. In the present chapter attention is confined to the characteristics distinguishing the immature forms of the culicines from those of the anophelines and to a detailed consideration of the medically important genera of culicines and of such characters which they possess as will enable the medical officer (with only an elementary knowledge of mosquito morphology) to distinguish one genus from another. The relationships of culicine mosquitoes to the transmission of disease is discussed and short notes are given on the life history and habits of the more important species.

Characteristics of the immature stages of the Culicine mosquito

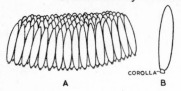

COROLLA

A   B

Fig. 64.   *A.* Egg raft and *B.* single egg of a culicine mosquito (*Culex pipiens*).

The eggs of Culicine mosquitoes, although often laid on the surface of water and provided with some mechanism to prevent submersion, never possess the lateral floats which are such a characteristic feature of the eggs of anopheline mosquitoes.

Culicine larvae resemble anopheline larvae in possessing a distinct head, thorax and abdomen and in their general form; they can, however, be easily and immediately distinguished from anopheline larvae by the presence of a siphon tube situated at the posterior extremity, as well as by other although not so obvious characters.

As in anophelines, the opening into the respiratory system of the culicines is situated on the dorsum of the 8th abdominal segment, but whereas in the anophelines the spiracles open to the exterior on a depressed chitinised plate, in the culicines the opening of the tracheal trunks is at the tip of a conspicuous elongated chitinous process known as the "siphon tube". The two rows of spines, known as the "pecten teeth", which in the anopheline lie one on each side of the spiracular plate are also present in the culicine larva where they have come to lie one on each side of the siphon. One or more ventral tufts of hairs

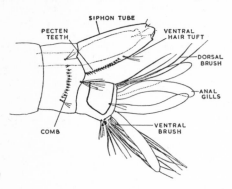

SIPHON TUBE

PECTEN TEETH

VENTRAL HAIR TUFT

DORSAL BRUSH

ANAL GILLS

COMB

VENTRAL BRUSH

Fig. 65.   Terminal segments of a culicine larva. The species depicted is *Aedes aegypti.*

are also present on the siphon tube. In addition, the 8th segment bears laterally on each side a group of spines known collectively as the comb, a structure which is absent in the anophelines. The morphology of the 9th abdominal segment of the culicine larva resembles that of the corresponding segment in the anopheline. In the anopheline larva the hairs on the thorax and abdomen are always distinctly branched, but in the culicine these hairs are not usually branched, although in some species inconspicuous branching may be present. The palmate hairs, always present on anopheline larvae, are absent from culicine larvae (see Fig. 66B).

In consequence of a siphon tube and the absence of palmate hairs, the larvae of culicines always hang downwards when taking air at the water surface so that the mouthparts are never brought into contact with the surface film; it is for this reason that stomach poisons dusted on the surface of water are usually ineffective as a means of culicine control (see Fig. 61).

116

THE DIVISION OF THE TRIBE CULICINI INTO GROUPS OF RELATED GENERA

As already stated the tribe Culicini is comprised of some 25 genera which can only be separated by a consideration of detailed anatomy outside the scope of this book. It is convenient, however, to consider the general characteristics of five groups into which these genera may be segregated and to discuss the recognition and biology of certain important genera in each group.

The five groups into which the tribe Culicini is divided are namely, (1) the Aedes group (2) the Culex group (3) the Mansonia group (4) the Sabethine group and (5) the Urotaenia group.

THE AEDES GROUP

The Aedes group comprises some seven genera of which the most important are the genus *Aedes* and the genus *Haemogogus*. Of the remaining genera only the genus *Eretmapodites* and the genus *Psorophora* include species, few in number, which are of medical significance.

Mosquitoes belonging to the Aedes group show much superficial variation, so that it is difficult to characterise the group as a whole. It may be said however, that in general members of this group are medium sized mosquitoes, with patterns of various designs on the body due to the presence of patches of dark and light (often white, silver or yellow) scales and with banded legs; certain members of the Aedes group are exceptional in that they are brilliantly coloured, thus resembling the sabethine mosquitoes. The wing veins do not bear heavy scaling, and the wings appear unspotted.

The genus *Aedes*

Some members of the genus *Aedes* have an almost worldwide distribution, whilst other species are strictly local.

In 1900 Reid and his colleagues proved that the urban vector of epidemic yellow fever was *Aedes aegypti*. Since that date not only have other species of *Aedes* been shown to be capable of transmitting yellow fever under rural and sylvan conditions, but certain species have been shown to be vectors of other viral diseases and of *W. bancrofti* in many parts of the world.

Members of the genus *Aedes* are black or dense brown, medium sized mosquitoes with silver or white scales forming patterns on the thorax and bands on the legs. The abdomen usually has a banded appearance due to the presence of silver or white scales forming rings round each abdominal segment. The wings are unspotted.

The eggs—which are usually cigar-shaped, although in a few species they are spindle-shaped—are never deposited in the form of a raft, but are laid singly on damp surfaces or else on stagnant water. The habit of ovipositing on damp surfaces which will later become submerged is widespread amongst members of the Aedes group, but it so happens that all—or nearly all—the medically important members of this group oviposit on free water, although they may occasionally lay above the water level on surfaces which will become submerged after heavy rain. This habit of ovipositing on surfaces other than free water has resulted in members of the group producing eggs which are able to resist drying for long periods extending to many months.

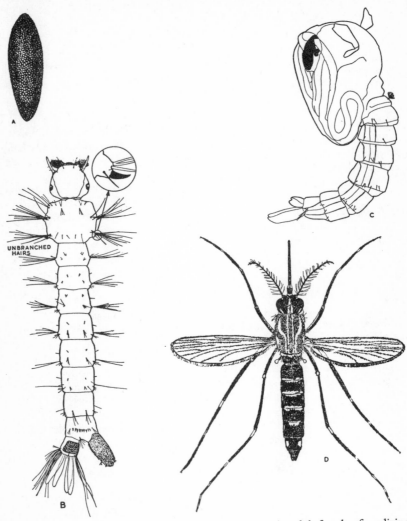

Fig. 66. *A.* the egg, *B.* the larva, *C.* the pupa, and *D.* the adult female of a culicine mosquito. The species depicted is *Aedes aegypti*, a typical member of the Aedes group.

The larvae of *Aedes* are found typically in transient collections of water such as water in tree holes or in the axils of plants, or in rock pools and artificial containers. The larvae feed chiefly on micro-organisms in the water of the habitat and are not predaceous.

The fourth and final instar larvae have a characteristic dark short siphon, contrasting with the much paler body. The siphon always bears a row of pecten teeth and has only one pair of ventral hair tufts which arise at the middle or on the distal half of the siphon. The ventral brush arises posteriorly to the saddle or chitinous ring on the 8th segment (see Fig. 65). In some species a saddle is absent. There may be either one or several rows of teeth to the comb.

The pupa is generally similar to that of other culicine larvae and has a relatively short pair of breathing trumpets.

The females of nearly all species of *Aedes* require a blood-meal for the maturation of their ova. Whilst some species are highly domesticated, living in close association with and feeding readily on man, other members of the genus are found in areas only rarely frequented by human beings and obtain their blood meals by biting wild animals; certain other species feed both on man and animals indiscriminately. The medically important species of the genus *Aedes* feed indiscriminately at night or during the day, but in the latter instance prefer biting under shaded conditions.

Although the pre-eminently important vector of yellow fever — *Aedes aegypti* — is essentially a house-haunting species and although most species of *Aedes* will enter human habitations to feed, nevertheless members of the genus *Aedes* may in general be regarded as outdoor feeders. Whatever the site of feeding the engorged females are usually found resting in its neighbourhood.

The genus *Aedes* is divided into a number of sub-genera, of which the sub-genus *Stegomyia* contains many of the medically important species. Since one of these species, *A. aegypti*, is of outstanding medical significance and since its recognition in both the adult and larval stages is relatively simple it appears appropriate at this point to describe its morphology and habits. Brief references will be made later in this chapter to the other species in the genus which are vectors of disease, but their recognition, unlike that of *A. aegypti*, is often difficult.*

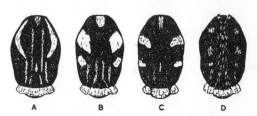

A   B   C   D

Fig. 67. Characteristic scale patterns on the thoraces of four species occuring in the genus *Aedes* (*Stegomyia*). A. *A. aegypti*, B. *A. simpsoni*, C. *A. africanus*, D. *A. vittatus*.

Aedes (Stegomyia) aegypti has a very wide distribution in the tropics and

---

* Many species of mosquitoes in the genus *Aedes* have characteristic scale patterns on the dorsum of the thorax, some of which are represented in Fig. 67. By comparing the actual specimen with the illustrations it is often possible to identify a particular species of *Aedes* with reasonable certainty, but in the case of other species, and for the exact identification of all species the application of specialised knowledge is required.

subtropics, being found in America, Africa, Asia and in Australia and the Pacific. Whereas it is the commonest species of *Aedes* in America, Africa and to a lesser extent in Asia, it is largely replaced in importance by other species of the same genus in south east Asia and the Pacific. The adult of *A. aegypti* may be recognised by the presence on its thorax of characteristic silver markings in the form of a lyre. The cigar-shaped eggs are scattered singly on the surface, usually at the edge, of small transient collections of water such as occur in tin cans, cisterns, water tanks, ditches, hoof-prints, etc. It is a highly domestic species and breeds in the neighbourhood of human dwellings throughout its range of distribution, except in central Africa where it is a tree-hole breeder and apparently does not normally feed on man. The larva is a typical *Aedes* larva in appearance. It possesses one row of comb spines and may be recognised and differentiated from other species of *Aedes* larvae by the well developed spine which arises in association with the third group of thoracic hairs and by the morphology of the spines of the comb (see Fig. 66B).

The adult females seek their hosts, particularly during the late afternoon and early evening, and are persistent and voracious biters of man both indoors and out of doors. In houses they may be found resting behind curtains, hanging clothes and in dark corners of rooms.

The genus *Haemogogus*

The genus *Haemogogus* is found only in South and Central America, where within the last twenty years several species have been shown to act as important vectors of yellow fever to man under sylvan conditions.

Although mosquitoes belonging to the genus *Haemogogus* are closely related to mosquitoes belonging to the genus *Aedes*, members of both genera differ markedly in general appearance. Whereas species of *Aedes* are black or brown with silver or white scales, species of *Haemogogus* are brilliantly coloured and have a metallic appearance. In the genus *Haemogogus*, the prothoracic lobes are prominent and although many species resemble sabethines in possessing setae on the mesopostnotum, such setae are absent in the species which have been shown to transmit yellow fever to man. The males of most species of *Haemogogus* have short palps, an almost unique character amongst male culicines.

The eggs which are oval in shape are laid singly on the margins of rot-holes and in bamboo stems.

The larvae which hatch from the eggs show much variation amongst different species. Most of the important species possess a medium sized siphon tube while the body is covered with fine hairs, giving the larva a downy appearance. Except for one species *(H. mesodentatus)*, the comb spines of the medically important species are borne on a chitinous plate.

The adult mosquitoes are found chiefly in forested areas and show a marked preference for the upper part of the forest canopy. Species of *Haemogogus* feed mainly at midday, chiefly on the monkeys and marsupials which live in the trees. If given the opportunity, as during tree-felling operations, they will readily feed on man.

The genus *Eretmapodites*

Mosquitoes belonging to the genus *Eretmapodites* occur only in Africa. Until recently no member of the genus was considered to be of importance in the transmission of disease (although capable of transmitting yellow fever under laboratory conditions) but the demonstration in 1949 that a species of *Eretmapodites (E. chrysogaster)* was capable of acting as a vector of Rift Valley fever under natural conditions, has increased the interest of the epidemiologist in this group of mosquitoes.

The adult forms of *Eretmapodites* may generally be recognised by the yellow and black scales on the thorax and by the general appearance of the abdomen which is adorned with silver and black scales, forming bands on the dorsal surface, and with golden yellow scales on the ventral surface. Most species, including the only species known at present to be a vector of disease *(E. chrysogaster)*, bear a tuft of hairs on the mesopostnotum, a character which aids in distinguishing members of the genus *Eretmapodites* from all other African mosquitoes.

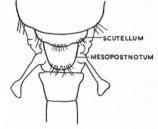

Fig. 68. Posterior portion of the thorax of *E. chrysogaster* seen from above, showing the characteristic tuft of hairs on the mesopostnotum.

The eggs are laid in small collections of water in large fallen leaves, in axils of plants, in old tins, bottles, etc. The larvae resemble those of *Aedes* but may be distinguished from them by the possession of not more than four teeth on the pecten, whereas in *Aedes* the number of teeth is usually more than four. The adult females are usually encountered in swamps and rain-forest areas, and bite chiefly in the late afternoon.

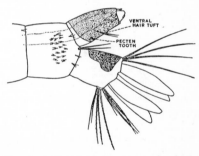

Fig. 69. Terminal segments of a larva belonging to the genus *Eretmapodites*. In the species depicted there is only one tooth on the pecten.

The genus *Psorophora*

Members of the genus *Psorophora* are found only in the American continent. Certain species have been shown to be capable of transmitting yellow fever under laboratory conditions, and under natural conditions they have been found harbouring certain other virus infections known to be transmissible to man. Several species are transport-hosts for the eggs of *Dermatobia hominis*, a fly responsible for myiasis in man. It is possible that they play some part in the transmission of filariasis since it has been shown that the microfilariae of *W. bancrofti* can reach the infective stage after ingestion by certain species of *Psorophora*.

Species of *Psorophora* are medium sized to large mosquitoes. There is much variation in superficial appearance between the various species, some being covered with bright metallic, generally blue or green, scales, whilst others are adorned with patches of dull scales usually yellow in colour. The distinction of the genus *Psorophora* from certain other members of the *Aedes* group is dependent on minutiae and is a matter for the specialist in mosquitoes.

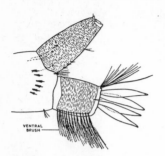

The eggs, which are elongated and which in many species are provided with numerous spines, are laid either in transient collections of water or on moist ground. They are able to resist adverse conditions, including drying, for long periods.

Fig. 70. Terminal segments of a larva belonging to the genus *Psorophora* showing the insertion of the ventral brush in the saddle.

The larvae, many species of which are predaceous, resemble those of *Aedes* but may be distinguished from the latter by the fact that the ventral brush in *Psorophora* is wholly or partly inserted in the saddle whereas in *Aedes* it is separated from the saddle.

The adults readily attack human beings and are vicious daylight biters.

THE CULEX GROUP

The Culex group is composed of two genera. The genus *Deinocerites* is restricted to the Caribbean area and contains no species which bite man; it will not be considered further. The genus *Culex* has a worldwide distribution and contains many species of mosquitoes which bite man and act as vectors of human disease.

The genus *Culex*

Members of the genus *Culex* are found both in temperate and tropical zones throughout the world. Several species occur over very large geographical areas and the group which forms the *Culex pipiens* complex is cosmopolitan.

The genus *Culex* was early shown to be of medical importance, when Manson in 1877 discovered the developing stages of *Wuchereria bancrofti* in a *Culex* mosquito. These mosquitoes are now recognised to be not only important transmitters of filariasis but also vectors of several of the mosquito-borne encephalitides.

Adult mosquitoes belonging to the genus *Culex* are generally dull and inconspicuous insects with unspotted wings. Most species are a light brown colour and lack any striking ornamentation of the body. They do not have prominent bands or patterns on the palps or the legs sufficiently marked to be seen by the naked eye, although when examined with the aid of a simple hand lens the presence of such markings can often be detected. A characteristic which distinguishes the genus *Culex* from all other genera belonging to the

PLATE I

FIG. 1. A male anopheline mosquito (*Anopheles stephensi*) in the resting position.
[*Courtesy Shell Photographic Unit, No. 1 Kingsway, London, W.C.2*]

FIG. 2. A male culicine mosquito (*Culex molestus*) in the resting position.
[*Courtesy Shell Photographic Unit, No. 1 Kingsway, London, W.C.2*]

PLATE II

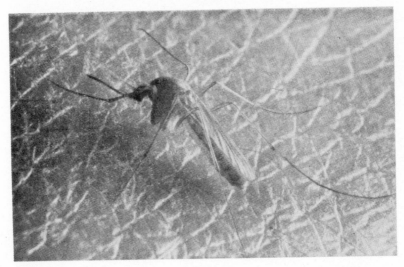

FIG. 1. A female culicine mosquito (*Culex pipiens*) resting on the skin preparatory to feeding.

[*Courtesy Mr. J. P. Brady*]

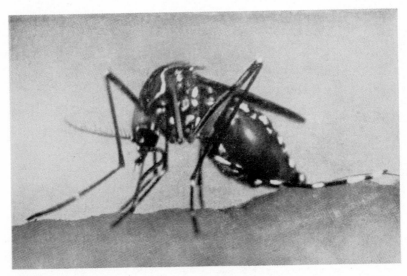

FIG. 2. A female culicine mosquito (*Aedes aegypti*) at the completion of its blood-meal.

[*Courtesy Mr. S. A. Smith*]

PLATE III

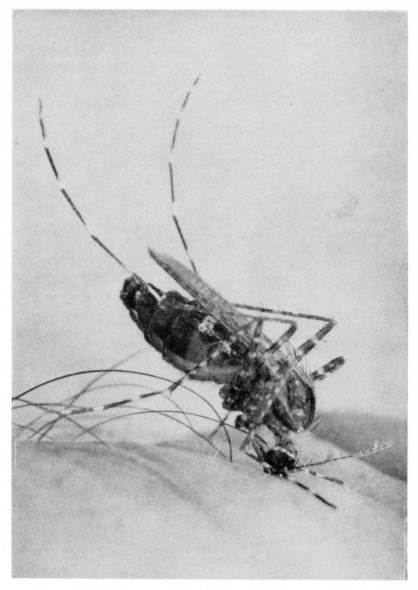

A female culicine mosquito (*Mansonia* sp.) in the act of feeding.

[*Courtesy Transactions of the Royal Society of Tropical Medicine and Hygiene, and Mr. S. A. Smith*]

PLATE IV

FIG. 1. A female sandfly (*Phlebotomus verrucarum*) in the resting position.
[*Courtesy the American Journal of Tropical Medicine and Hygiene, and Dr. Marshall Hertig*]

FIG. 2. A male sandfly (*Phlebotomus verrucarum*) in the resting position.
[*Courtesy the American Journal of Tropical Medicine and Hygiene, and Dr. Marshall Hertig*]

tribe Culicini is the presence of a pair of broad pads (or pulvilli) below the claws.

The eggs are cigar-shaped, and provided with a corolla (a cap-shaped structure surrounding the micropyle) at one end, and are usually brown in colour (see Fig. 64). The eggs are always cemented together to form a raft which floats on the surface of the water. They are unable to withstand adverse conditions, and will not resist dessication. All species of *Culex* deposit their eggs only on free water, never on damp surfaces. The nature of the water selected for oviposition varies from clear water of great purity such as wells and springs to collections of muddy, brackish or polluted water.

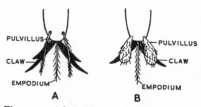

Fig. 71. *A.* hair-like pulvilli which, when present, are commonly seen in culicine mosquitoes other than *Culex* sp. *B.* Pad-like pulvilli only seen in the genus *Culex*

The larvae which hatch from the eggs may usually be readily recognised by the presence of a long, narrow siphon and several pairs of ventral hair tufts; they are never predaceous.

The pupae cannot be distinguished, for all practical purposes, from those of other Culicines.

The females of most species of *Culex* require a blood meal for the maturation of the ova, and attack a wide range of animals in order to obtain blood. Whilst several species feed readily on man and various mammals, it is true to say that the majority of species prefer avian hosts to mammalian hosts as a source of blood. *Culex* mosquitoes feed chiefly during the hours of darkness but will bite in shaded localities during the day.

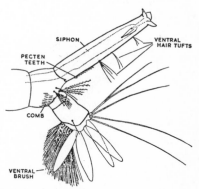

Fig. 72. Terminal segments of a larva belonging to the genus *Culex*.

The most important species is *Culex pipiens*, which occurs all over the world and of which there are several varieties, including *C. p. fatigans*, *C. p. pipiens* and *C. p. molestus*. *C. pipiens* is an important vector of *Wuchereria bancrofti*. In addition, the genus *Culex* contains other species of medical importance, several of which have been shown to transmit certain of the more recently recognised virus diseases. The distinction of one species of *Culex* from another is difficult and can only be undertaken by a specialist.

THE MANSONIA GROUP

The Mansonia group of mosquitoes is considered to include five genera, only two of which, *Mansonia* (= *Taeniorhynchus*) and *Theobaldia* (= *Culiseta*) are of medical importance. Although these five genera are closely related, there is much superficial variation. Since it is not possible to give easily recognisable features to distinguish, as a group, members of the Mansonia group from other mosquitoes, the recognition and characteristics of the two medically important genera will be discussed in turn.

The genus *Mansonia*

The genus Mansonia has a worldwide distribution. Members of this genus have been recognised since 1930 as important vectors of *Brugia malayi* and in certain areas, of *Wuchereria bancrofti*. It is generally accepted that certain species play a minor role in the dissemination of yellow fever and certain of the viral encephalitides.

All species of *Mansonia* are brown or black, medium sized mosquitoes which usually have a banded abdomen and banded legs, due to the presence of dark and light scales (see Plate III). The wings are covered with flat, broad scales (some of which are heart or pear shaped) and which give the wings a speckled appearance, as if they had been dusted with mixed peppers.

The eggs are spindle shaped or barrel shaped in appearance. They are always laid in clusters, either in the form of rafts which float on the surface of the

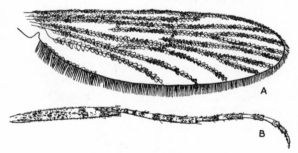

Fig. 73. *A.* wing, and *B.* leg, of a mosquito belonging to the genus *Mansonia*.

water, or they are fixed to the under surface of the leaves of certain species of water plants.

Mansonia larvae have a short pointed siphon tube (sometimes provided with a pair of prehensile hairs) which is modified so as to be capable of piercing plant tissues. The newly emerged larva having driven its siphon tube into the stem of a water plant—the species of plant selected varying with the locality—obtains its oxygen directly from the plant cells, and has no need to relax its hold and come to the surface to obtain oxygen, although it must do so at each ecdysis.

The pupa, like the larva, is found attached to plant stems, but in this instance it is the breathing trumpets which are modified for the purpose of piercing submerged plant stems and obtaining oxygen. When the adult mosquito is ready to emerge the pupa detaches itself from the plant stem, rises to the surface and the imago emerges through the usual dorsal slit.

On account of the peculiar breeding habits of *Mansonia* special methods, such as the clearing away or the destruction of aquatic vegetation, are required to control this mosquito as the usual insecticides are largely ineffective.

The adults are savage and persistent biters of man. They are particularly active during the hours of darkness and, although essentially outdoor biters, readily enter human dwellings in order to obtain a blood-meal.

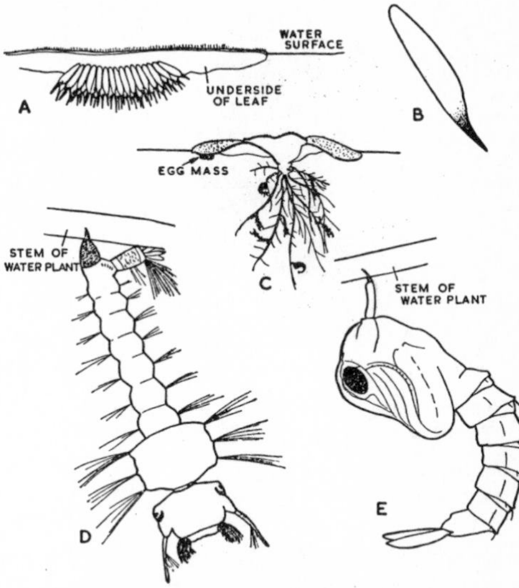

The genus *Theobaldia*

Members of the genus *Theobaldia* are found in all parts of the world, with the exception of South America. Although they bite man readily, no species of *Theobaldia* is at present regarded as being responsible for the transmission of disease to man.

Fig. 74. Eggs, larvae and pupae of mosquitoes belonging to the genus *Mansonia*
A. Egg mass; B. single egg; C. larvae and pupae attached to water plant; D. larva; E. pupa.

The adults are generally large robust mosquitoes of a light brown colour. The wings may be either unspotted or provided with a few patches of dark scales giving them a lightly speckled appearance. Unspotted species in this genus may be distinguished from members of the genus *Culex* by the absence of a pad or pulvillus between the claws of the legs, while those species possessing speckled wings can be separated from members of the genus *Mansonia* by the absence of heart or pear shaped scales on the wings. Although the speckled wing type of *Theobaldia*

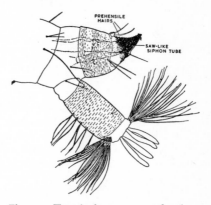

Fig 75. Terminal segments of a larva belonging to the genus *Mansonia*.

commonly bites man in the temperate zones, in the tropics most culicines with speckled wings which are caught coming to bite man belong to the genus *Mansonia*.

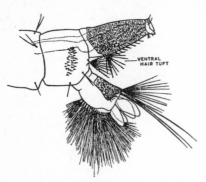

VENTRAL HAIR TUFT

Fig. 76. Terminal segments of a larva belonging to the genus *Theobaldia*.

The eggs are laid either singly or in the form of rafts and may be distinguished from those of *Culex* by the absence of a corolla at one end. The larvae are in general similar to those of other culicines but have a single pair of ventral hair tufts, arising near the base of the siphon. The larvae of certain other species of culicines also possess a single pair of ventral hair tufts, but in such instances these always arise from a site well separated from the base of the siphon.

The adult females feed chiefly on animals but will bite man if the opportunity offers.

THE SABETHINE GROUP

Mosquitoes belonging to the sabethine group are found only in the New World, chiefly in Central and South America. They are so distinctive that some modern authorities do not regard them as a group of the tribe Culicini but as a tribe within their own right (the tribe Sabethini). It has been recently demonstrated that at least one species of sabethine is of importance in the epidemiology of sylvan yellow fever in Central America.

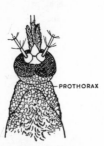

PROTHORAX

Fig. 77. Head and thorax of a sabethine mosquito showing the enlarged prothorax.

Sabethine mosquitoes vary in appearance from moderately large metallic-coloured species to small dull-coloured mosquitoes. Many of the brightly coloured species have a striking appearance due to the presence of paddle-like scales on the legs. All sabethine mosquitoes bear a tuft of hairs on the mesopostnotum. The prothoracic lobes are always well developed and in certain species this feature is marked so as to give the appearance of a collar.

The eggs are oval in shape and laid in collections of water trapped in tree holes, rot holes or in the axils of plants. The larvae are typical culicines in general appearance but lack a ventral brush.

The adults frequent forested regions and are active in the day time when they seek their hosts in order to obtain their blood-meal. Several species bite man readily in the open, but are not known to enter dwellings.

THE GROUP UROTAENIA

This group is comprised of very small mosquitoes which may be distinguished from all other mosquitoes by the absence of the minute hairs (microtrichiae) which are present on the wing membrane of all other culicine mosquitoes. Most species show the presence of peculiar notched scales on the wings. The eggs are laid in rafts. The larvae resemble other Culicine larvae, except that the comb spines are always borne on a definite chitinous plate, absent in most culicines.

No species of mosquito belonging to the group Urotaenia has been shown to bite man and the group is not regarded as of any medical importance.

The medical importance of culicine mosquitoes.

The medical importance of one species of culicine, *Aedes aegypti,* has already been discussed; reference has also been made to the fact that certain culicines act as transport hosts of *Dermatobia hominis.* The following is a brief résumé of the part played by culicine mosquitoes as vectors of helminth and viral infections to man.

Filariasis

The only species of filariae parasitising man which have been shown to be transmitted by mosquitoes are *Wuchereria bancrofti* and *Brugia malayi.* In a previous chapter attention has already been drawn to the important anopheline intermediate hosts of these nematodes and in the present chapter only the important culicine transmitters of filariasis will be considered. As in the case of anophelines, although many species of culicine mosquitoes have been shown capable of allowing development of *W. bancrofti* and *B. malayi* to the infective stages, only a small number are regarded as important natural vectors.

Members of the cosmopolitan *Culex pipiens* complex, and in particular the subspecies *Culex pipiens fatigans* which is a night-biting mosquito, are the most important vectors of the nocturnally periodic form of *W. bancrofti.* In addition to these mosquitoes certain other species of *Culex* and some species of *Aedes* are considered to be of regional importance; of these, one species, *A. pembaensis,* has excited interest because of its peculiar association with certain water-crabs on the carapace of which it lays eggs.

The chief vector of the non-periodic form of *W. bancrofti* is *A. polynesiensis* which has a wide distribution in the Pacific region.

The culicine transmitters of *Brugia malayi* belong almost entirely to the genus *Mansonia* of which the most widespread appear to be *M. uniformis, M. indiana* and *M. annulifera,* while *M. dives* (=*M. longipalpis*) and *M. annulata,* although somteimes of local importance, have a more limited distribution.

Yellow Fever.

Yellow fever is a viral disease which is acquired by susceptible human beings and animals following the bite of a mosquito which has previously fed on an infected person or animal. The infection is widespread in Central and South America and in tropical Africa; it does not occur in any part of Asia although potential mosquito vectors are present. There is an extensive animal reservoir in primates, mainly monkeys and lemurs.

The disease exists in two epidemiological forms. The first form, which is transmitted from man to man almost entirely through the agency of *Aedes aegypti,* is found to occur in urban areas, and in rural areas where human beings are congregated together in villages and towns. The discovery in 1900 by the American Yellow Fever Commission that this urban type of yellow fever, which occurred in great epidemics, was transmitted by *A. aegypti* led to control measures being carried out with a view to eliminating the breeding places of the vector; the control campaign was so successful that within a few years public health authorities in previously affected areas were able to report the almost virtual disappearance of the disease from many towns and villages. Despite the great success that followed these control campaigns against *A. aegypti* small foci of yellow fever still lingered on and vigilance against possible serious outbreaks of the disease was not relaxed.

As the result of studies carried out in West Africa in 1927 and 1928 the important discovery was made that monkeys were susceptible to yellow fever and that mosquitoes other than *A. aegypti* were capable of transmitting the virus. These investigations began to assume great significance when workers in South America in 1932 established the occurrence of yellow fever in man in the absence of *A. aegypti.* These discoveries subsequently led to the recognition, both in South America and in Africa, of a second form of yellow fever, which has become designated as sylvan yellow fever, transmitted by mosquitoes other than *A. aegypti,* and which occurs primarily in certain forest monkeys, man only becoming secondarily infected.

Urban and rural yellow fever in Central and South America and in western Africa is transmitted from man to man by the domesticated *Aedes (Stegomyia) aegypti.* In the Sudan, however, where a serious outbreak of the disease was reported in 1941, it was shown that other species of *Aedes,* in particular *A. (Stegomyia) vittatus,* were the important vectors, so that the classical picture of urban or rural yellow fever always being associated with *A. aegypti* has had to be somewhat modified.

The situation as regards sylvan yellow fever is much more complex than in the case of urban and rural yellow fever. In Africa, the virus is passed from monkey to monkey by *A. (Stegomyia) africanus.* This species is a forest mosquito which breeds in tree holes often at a high level. The females become active soon after sunset and feed throughout the night on monkeys living in the higher foliage of the forest. These forest monkeys frequently leave the canopy and come to ground level to raid plantations, such as banana plantations situated on the forest fringe or in clearings in the forest. In these circumstances they are exposed to the day-biting mosquito *A. (Stegomyia) simpsoni* which breeds chiefly in the leaf axils of banana plants. *A. (Stegomyia) simpsoni* readily bites man, so that persons working in the plantations or frequenting the forest fringe, readily acquire the virus, if bitten by mosquitoes which have previously fed on infected monkeys. Although other African mosquitoes have been experimentally infected with yellow fever virus and are able to transmit the virus by their bite, it is noteworthy that the only species which have been incriminated as important vectors in nature are members of the genus *Aedes* (subgenus *Stegomyia*).

In South America two species of *Haemagogus*, *H. spegazzini* (and its variety *H. spegazzini* var. *falco*, and *H. capricornis* together with *Aedes (Finlaya) leucocelaenus* play an important role in the epidemiology of sylvan yellow fever. These mosquitoes live in the forest canopy and transmit the virus amongst monkeys and possibly marsupials. A proportion of the mosquitoes thus infected with yellow fever descend to ground level—particularly during tree-felling and bush-clearing operations—and bite persons, such as wood-cutters, cocoa planters and others, whose occupations cause them to enter the forest.

In Central America, other species of *Haemagogus*, in particular *H. mesoden-tatus* and a sabethine mosquito *(Sabethes chloropterus)* have recently been proved to be important vectors of sylvan yellow fever. In addition to these species other species of mosquitoes are suspected of playing a minor role, both in South and Central America, in the epidemiology of the disease.

Thus the picture of the epidemiology of yellow fever is that of a disease which exists normally in an animal reservoir in which it is maintained by several species of forest mosquitoes, man acquiring these infections by frequenting forests or their neighbourhood where he is exposed to the bites of infected wild mosquitoes. Human beings thus infected return to villages and towns, where the virus is propagated amongst non-infected persons by domesticated mosquitoes.

Dengue.

Dengue is a virus disease of man which occurs throughout the warm parts of the world and is acquired only following the bite of certain species of *Aedes* all of which belong to the subgenus *Stegomyia*. In view of the ease with which certain monkeys can be infected in the laboratory by the bite of *Aedes* mosquitoes it is considered that these animals may constitute a reservoir of the virus in nature.

A. aegypti throughout its range of distribution serves as a vector of dengue. In the Central Pacific and in certain parts of the Far East, three other species of *Aedes*, *A. albopictus*, *A. polynesiensis* and *A. scutellaris*—all of which also belong to the subgenus *Stegomyia*—are locally more important than *A. aegypti*, although not replacing it entirely.

Mosquito-borne encephalitides.

In many parts of the world, both in the tropics and in temperate zones, there occur a number of viral encephalitides of man which have been shown to be transmitted by mosquitoes. The viruses of most of these diseases have been isolated from wild and domestic animals as well as from man, and it is thought probable that such animals act as a reservoir from which man usually acquires his infection. The most important vectors of these diseases appear to be mosquitoes belonging to the genera *Culex* and *Aedes,* although species of mosquitoes belonging to other genera of mosquitoes are involved to a lesser extent. As has been pointed out in a previous chapter no mosquito belonging to the tribe Anophelini has been shown to be a vector in nature of any of the viral encephalitides.

Japanese B encephalitis, which has a wide distribution in the Far East and which has caused large scale epidemics, is transmitted chiefly by *Culex tritaeniorhynchus,* although other species of culicines are involved. As regards western equine encephalomyelitis and St. Louis encephalitis, which from time to time appear as sporadic outbreaks in the New World, the important vector appears to be *Culex tarsalis.* There is still some doubt as to which mosquito is the chief vector of eastern equine encephalomyelitis, but it seems certain that in the Eastern United States the important species is *Aedes sollicitans.* In Africa, West Nile virus is chiefly transmitted by *Culex univittatus,* whilst *Aedes caballus* in South Africa and *Eretmapodites chrysogaster* in East Africa, have been shown to be the vectors of Rift Valley fever. In Australia it seems likely, from the rather meagre evidence that is available, that Murray River virus is transmitted by *Culex annulirostris;* more proof is needed, however, before the association of the virus and the mosquito is finally accepted.

It may be truly said that our knowledge of the role of mosquitoes as vectors of certain of the viral encephalitides is still in its early stages. Work on these organisms is being actively pursued; and, even as this book is being written, new types of viruses are being isolated and their possible transmission by various species of mosquitoes are being intensively studied by new techniques and methods. The results of these studies are certain to alter our present concept of the mosquito-borne viral encephalitides.

CHAPTER XX

THE FAMILY PSYCHODIDAE

FLIES belonging to the family Psychodidae are small very hairy flies rarely exceeding 5 mm. in length with wings which are so heavily clothed with hairs or scales that the wing venation is usually obscured.

The family Psychodidae is usually regarded as consisting of four subfamilies, only one of which, namely the subfamily Phlebotominae, contains species of medical importance. Members of the subfamily Phlebotominae, are commonly known as sandflies and may be distinguished from flies belonging to the other three subfamilies, which are known as moth flies or owl midges, by the wing venation of the same general type as shown in Fig. 78, and by the presence of biting mouthparts. The subfamily Phlebotominae comprises three genera, namely *Phlebotomus*, *Warileya* and *Hertigia*. The genera *Warileya* and *Hertigia* which consist of only a few species, are limited in distribution to South and

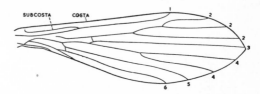

Fig. 78. The wing of a fly belonging to the subfamily Phlebotominae: the hairs which obscure the venation have been rubbed off.

Central America, and since no species have been incriminated as vectors of disease to man no further reference will be made to them. On the other hand, the genus *Phlebotomus*, which has a worldwide distribution and numbers many vectors of disease to man, is of such great medical importance that the recognition of its various stages, its life cycle and habits and its relationship to disease are fully discussed below.

The genus *Phlebotomus*

Members of the genus *Phlebotomus* have a cosmopolitan distribution in the tropics, subtropics and warmer parts of the temperate zones. Over 350 species are known and their habitats range from localities in arid and semi-arid zones to localities in regions of heavy rainfall such as tropical rain forests.

Although as long ago as 1691 sandflies were described as being a biting nuisance it was not until the beginning of the twentieth century that members of the genus *Phlebotomus* were suggested as the possible vectors of a disease to man, namely cutaneous leishmaniasis. The possibility that sandflies might indeed play a part in the transmission of disease induced entomologists to initiate a study of these hitherto little known insects, and in 1911 Newstead published the first systematic study of the genus *Phlebotomus*. Whilst considerable advances in the knowledge of sandflies followed Newstead's work, the identifications of these flies (and in particular those of the female sex), owing to the failure to find good taxonomic characters, continued to present great difficulties until the work of Adler and Theodor in 1926. In that year, these two investigators published a classical paper in which they showed that the morphology of the buccal armature and of the spermatheca was of much taxonomic importance. This discovery was of great significance in that it revolutionised the classification of sandflies and enabled entomologists to carry out accurate identifications, an essential preliminary step in associating a particular species of *Phlebotomus* with a disease which it was suspected of transmitting.

Although the incrimination of sandflies as vectors of disease to man has been a long and difficult task, which has occupied the attention of many workers in different parts of the world, it has fullfilled its purpose, for it has now proved that these insects are the vectors not only of several forms of leishmaniasis but also of a viral infection, papatasii or sandfly fever, and of a bacterial disease, Oroya fever, caused by *Bartonella bacilliformis*. It should not be forgotten that in addition to the role they play as vectors of disease, sandflies may constitute a serious biting nuisance since, in previously sensitised persons, the bites may give rise to a severe skin reaction, which is known in the Near East as "Harara".

External anatomy of the adult Phlebotomus

The adult *Phlebotomus* has a characteristic appearance. It is a small, fuzzy, delicately proportioned fly about 2-3 mm. in length and of a light yellow

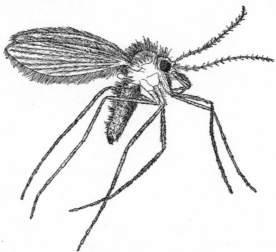

Fig. 79. *Phlebotomus* sp., female. Note the erect hairs on the dorsal surface of the abdomen.

or grey colour with large conspicuous dark eyes. The head, thorax and abdomen are densely covered with long hairs and the legs which are long and slender give it the appearance, after alighting on a surface, of walking on stilts. When at rest all species of sandflies hold their wings erect and do not keep them folded over the body as in the case of other psychodids.

The head. The head which hangs downwards from the thorax is rather elongated and covered with long hairs. The antennae, which are similar in both sexes, consist of sixteen segments which are long and thread-like, with deep constrictions between the segments giving them a rather bead-like appearance; since the antennae are similar in both sexes these structures are of no assistance in distinguishing between the males and females. The eyes are unusually large and because of their dark appearance contrast markedly with the pale colour of the head. The mouthparts which are short and about the same length as the head are adapted for biting and consist of a labrum, a pair of mandibles, a pair of maxillae and a hypopharynx, all of which are stylet-like, and a fleshy labium. As in the case of the mosquito the labium does not penetrate the skin of the host when the fly sucks blood. The presence or the absence of teeth in the buccal cavity and the pharynx (and the

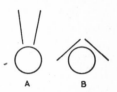

Fig. 80. Diagram showing how in the case of sandflies (subfamily Phlebotominae) the wings are carried erect when the fly is at rest, whereas in the case of other psychodids they are folded tent-wise, as shown in B.

morphology of the teeth when present) are used by the systematic entomologist when indentifying species of sandflies. Although the buccal cavity and the pharynx are internal structures it is not always necessary to dissect these organs from the head of the insect since they can often be easily seen in cleared preparations. The mouthparts are flanked by a pair of five-segmented pendulous palps.

The thorax. The thorax is humped and covered with long hairs. The wings which are somewhat pear-shaped and pointed at the apex are heavily clothed with hairs along the margins and veins, masking a wing venation which is characteristic. If the wing is mounted on a slide and examined with the aid of a microscope, the veins are seen to be subparallel and the second longitudinal vein is seen to fork twice. The legs are long and slender and bear hairs.

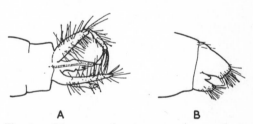

Fig. 81. Diagrammatic representations of the external genitalia of flies belonging to the genus *Phlebotomus*. *A.* male genitalia, *B.* female genitalia.

The abdomen. The abdomen is moderately long. Whereas in the female fly it has a rounded extremity, in the male fly the presence of prominent terminal claspers give it the appearance of being turned up at the tip, a character which can be seen easily and is therefore useful in distinguishing the sexes.

Like the head and thorax the abdomen is covered with long hairs; on the dorsal aspect of the abdomen the hairs may either lie flat (a condition described as recumbent) or they may be raised (in which case they are described as erect), whilst in a few species both recumbent and erect hairs occur together. In the case of the Old World sandflies, the disposition of the abdominal hairs, that is to say whether they are erect or recumbent, may serve as a useful guide to the medical officer in recognising whether a particular fly which is being examined is likely to belong to a group which includes vectors of disease, for, in general, it is true to say that all the sandfly vectors of disease in the Old World have erect hairs on the dorsal surface of the abdomen.

The life-cycle of sandflies

Following fertilisation and the partaking of a blood-meal the female lays her eggs. These are always deposited singly on moist soil, in cracks and holes in the ground, in masonry and rubble heaps, and other protected sites wherever conditions are suitable for the subsequent development of the larvae. The sandfly egg, the shell of which is patterned, and provided with a very thin coating of mucus attaching it to the substrate, is ellipsoidal in outline with rounded ends and measures between 0.3 and 0.4 mm. in length. Immediately following oviposition the egg is white or yellow in colour but soon deepens in hue so that it becomes brown or black when mature. Through the shell of the mature egg, particularly in the case of those species of *Phlebotomus* which lay light brown-coloured eggs, two dark parallel lines may be seen extending in the interior of the egg, from pole to pole; these two lines are the caudal bristles (described below) of the developing larva.

Fig. 82.
Egg of a
sandfly.

The number of eggs laid at each oviposition usually varies from 15 to 40, several such batches being deposited by the female during her lifetime. Oviposition usually takes place during the hours of darkness, but the process is so prolonged that it may be extended well into the following day. In order to deposit her eggs the female fly alights on the ground and lowers her abdomen so that its ventral surface is in contact with the ground. She then turns up the last few segments of the abdomen, to an angle of about 45°, and an egg is extruded from the tip of the abdomen, the whole movement occupying no more than a few seconds. The egg is usually forcibly expelled for a short distance, about equal to the length of the fly, or it may be dropped. After having laid a few eggs the female fly usually pauses, as if exhausted, and after an interval of time, which varies from several minutes to a few hours, the oviposition is continued.

The eggs hatch in 1 to 2 weeks under optimal conditions, an important requirement being the presence of a thin film of capillary water covering the egg shell. Whilst the eggs are not laid in free water, the flooding of the breeding places does not appear to have an adverse effect on their viability, although the time taken by the eggs to hatch may be prolonged. A short time before they are due to hatch, movements of the larvae may be seen through the egg shells. Emergence of the larva from the egg is effected by means of the egg-breaker, a minute chitinous spine-like structure, on the head of the insect, which produces a dorso-lateral split in the egg shell, extending from one end of the egg down to a distance of about a third to a half of its length. Emergence is slow and lasts about 5 to 10 minutes.

The newly emerged larva is capable of only very slow movements at first but within a few hours it begins to crawl about on the surface of the soil and to search for food. Progression is affected by means of a caterpillar-like motion, the advancing head seizing some particle of the substrate with its mouthparts, followed by a contraction of the rest of the body, a movement which is assisted by the presence of false legs, or pseudopods, on the abdomen. The food of the larva consists of decaying organic matter, particularly dead leaves and vegetable debris, although they will also feed on animal faeces and the decaying bodies of dead arthropods.

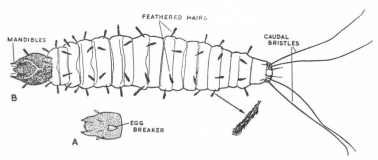

Fig. 83. *A.* head of a first instar sandfly larva showing the egg breaker and *B.* a full grown fourth instar larva.

The larvae of *Phlebotomus*, even in arid regions, are found living in moist soil in situations where the microclimatic conditions approach saturation. They are found thriving typically in dark damp recesses where the humidity is high, as in cellars in human habitations, outhouses for domestic stock, in animal burrows, under masses of rubble, in crevices in stone walls and in the ground, and in the tunnels of termite nests. Although *Phlebotomus* larvae are not adapted to an aquatic existence nevertheless some species appear capable of withstanding immersion in water for many days, a fact which explains their survival in their breeding places following heavy rains. The larvae are always hard to find particularly as they readily sham death when disturbed, and very often the only indication that a likely site is a breeding place is the finding of adults in a gauze cage, or on sticky paper, which has been placed over a crack or crevice overnight.

There are four larval instars, the time taken to complete the larval life usually varying from 3 to 5 weeks in good conditions; this period may be lengthened in unfavourable circumstances such as a lowering of temperature or scarcity of food.

The fourth stage larva is a small caterpillar-like creature measuring 4 to 6 mm. in length. It possesses a dark well defined head which is provided with mandibles and a pair of minute antennae. The head is followed by 12 light coloured, rugose body segments separated from one another by well marked constrictions; the first three body segments comprise the thorax and the remaining 9 segments, seven of which bear small false legs or pseudopods, form the abdomen. The body segments are provided with characteristic bristles ("matchstick hairs") with feathered stems which terminate in thickened tips. In addition to possessing "matchstick hairs" the last segment also bears, on its dorsal surface, a small chitinous plate from which arise four long and conspicuous bristles known as caudal bristles (the first and second stage larvae possess only two caudal bristles).

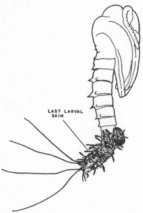

LAST LARVAL SKIN

Fig. 84. Pupa of a sandfly.

When fully grown the fourth stage larva becomes motionless with its head and most of the body raised in an erect attitude and the pupa then wriggles out of the larval skin which however is not completely discarded, as in the case of the mosquito, but remains attached to the hind end of the pupa. The pupa which has a very characteristic appearance remains in an upright attitude, with the shrivelled crumpled larval skin and its conspicuous caudal bristles attached to the tip of the pupal abdomen. Through the thin integument of the pupa, the developing adult with its prominent dark eyes is clearly visible.

Development of the adult within the pupa is completed in one to two weeks, the fly emerging by means of a slow wriggling motion from a dorsal longitudinal slit in the pupal skin. Having emerged from the old pupal skin, the insect rests on some nearby object while hardening and darkening of its integument takes place during the few hours following emergence.

Once mating has been effected, the flies go in search of food, the females looking for an animal host in order to obtain blood which is necessary for the maturation of the ovaries whilst the males, which do not suck blood, seek plant juices and other similar substances in order to feed. This search for food is restricted to a radius of no more than 150-200 yards from their breeding sites, since sandflies are weak fliers progressing by means of short "hopping" flights of a few inches at a time; so weak indeed is their power of sustained flight that they do not remain on the wing in the presence of a slight wind, nor are they usually able to fly to any height, being found on the ground floor of premises rather than in the upper stories. Due to their restricted range of flight it is not uncommon to encounter them in considerable numbers in a localised area, while neighbouring localities may be entirely free of their presence. The knowledge that sandflies progress by means of short "hopping flights" is of considerable importance, since it explains the remarkable efficacy of contact insecticides and the complete disappearance of *Phlebotomus* from areas in which systematic spraying of such substances as DDT and *gamma*-BHC has been carried out.

Although most species of sandflies are nocturnal feeders, attacking their hosts either outdoors or indoors, they will bite readily in darkened habitations or shelters during the hours of daylight. Whilst a considerable number of species of *Phlebotomus* feed on man, it is true to say that in no case is any species known to be exclusively anthropophilic, the host range of species which feed on man including other mammals such as dogs and rodents and sometimes birds and reptiles. Since several important diseases caused by various species of *Leishmania* and transmitted by sandflies have a natural reservoir in mammals, such as dogs and rodents, the feeding habits of certain species of *Phlebotomus,* such as *P. perniciosus* which bites both man and dog and *P. papatasii* which feeds both on man and rodents, has proved to be of great epidemiological significance. Notwithstanding their wide range of hosts, sandflies nevertheless do show a certain degree of host preference and many species are known which have never been caught biting man; some of these species however are of interest to the medical epidemiologist since they may help in maintaining, in the natural reservoir, diseases transmissible to man.

Soon after having partaken of a blood-meal, the replete female seeks a sheltered spot where the humidity is high, since the female with ripening ovaries readily succumbs if exposed to low humidities. In consequence the female *Phlebotomus* should be searched for in dark damp corners in water-closets, cellars, caves, piles of broken masonry and in animal sheds. In areas where the atmosphere is particularly dry, as in arid or semi-arid zones, the flies retire to the protection of cracks and fissures in the soil or to animal burrows.

In the tropics, where breeding goes on all the year round, the entire life cycle of *Phlebotomus* lasts anything from one and a half to two and a half months in the summer, but is probably extended somewhat during the winter months due to a lowering of temperature. In the temperate zones, all the adults die with the onset of the winter and the 4th stage larvae cease to be active and enter a period of rest, known as diapause, until the arrival of spring when they pupate. It is difficult to obtain exact information as regards the length of life of adult sandflies in nature but it appears likely that some species at least may live as long as one and a half months when the prevailing climatic conditions are optimum.

Sandflies and disease

Attention has been drawn earlier in this chapter to the severe reactions which follow the attacks of sandflies in persons previously exposed and sensitised to their bites, a condition known as "Harara". In addition to being a severe biting nuisance, sandflies are responsible for the transmission to man of several forms of leishmaniasis, a sandfly fever and Oroya fever or Carrion's disease.

Kala-azar or visceral leishmaniasis.

This disease is widely distributed in the tropics and occurs in Asiatic Russia, India, China, South America and East Africa. In most areas throughout the range of distribution of the disease the domestic dog, and to a lesser extent other carnivores, are important sources of infection, but in India no animal reservoir has been demonstrated. Man acquires the infection following the bite of an infected sandfly, the flagellates being introduced into the puncture wound through the proboscis of the feeding insect.

In the Mediterranean region where the dog is the reservoir of the disease the chief vectors are *P. perniciosus* and *P. major*. In India the vector is *P. argentipes* which acquires the infection by feeding on cases of kala-azar (usually those with post kala-azar dermal lesions) and which on re-feeding transmits the now infective parasite to a new human host. In South America the disease is widely distributed and both the domestic dog and a wild dog *(Lycolopex vetulus)* are reservoirs of the disease; in Brazil the vector has been shown to be *P. longipalpis*. Although the vector is not clearly established in China, where the dog acts as a reservoir, it is almost certainly *P. chinensis*, whilst *P. mongolensis* has also been incriminated. In Kenya, where the disease has recently been discovered, there is presumptive evidence that the vector is a sandfly.

Oriental sore or cutaneous leishmaniasis.

This form of leishmaniasis has a wide distribution in the countries bordering on the Mediterranean and also occurs in Asiatic Russia and India.

In the Middle East, where *P. papatasii* is the vector, and in India where *P. sergenti* is the vector, dogs are probably the most important reservoir of the disease. In Asiatic Russia it has been shown that gerbils and ground squirrels harbour the infection which is perpetuated amongst them by several species of sandflies one of which, *P. papatasii*, acts as a transmitter of the disease from the reservoir to man.

Muco-cutaneous leishmaniasis.

Muco-cutaneous leishmaniasis is strictly limited to South America. Whilst the available evidence would appear to show that one or more species of sandflies are vectors of this disease, no particular species of *Phlebotomus* has as yet been demonstrated to be a vector. The disease is acquired by man particularly in the neighbourhood of forests, so that although the domestic dog is a proved reservoir it is probable that wild animals are also concerned.

Sandfly fever.

Sandfly fever or papatasii fever is a viral disease of man which occurs only in the Mediterranean region and is transmitted by *P. papatasii*. No animal reservoir of the virus is known. Since the infection is only acquired during the warmer months of the year, it is held by some workers that the virus is transmitted transovarially from one generation of sandflies to the next; although the experimental evidence is unsatisfactory, there is some epidemiological evidence that this may occur.

Oroya fever or Carrion's disease.

This disease is found in the Andes and is caused by a minute bacillus known as *Bartonella bacilliformis*. It is transmitted in Peru by *P. verrucarum*; there is a possibility that other species of sandflies closely related to *P. verrucarum* may also act as vectors of the disease.

CHAPTER XXI

THE FAMILY SIMULIIDAE

MEMBERS of the family Simuliidae are widely known as "buffalo-flies" and "black flies", but in some parts of the world, as in Australia, they are unfortunately designated by other names such as "sandflies" or "midges".* They are small, stout flies measuring between 1 and 5 mm. in length and may be recognised by the strongly humped appearance of the thorax, the short horn-like antennae and the broad clear wings which possess a characteristic wing venation of the type shown in Fig. 88.

Whilst buffalo-flies have long been known to constitute a serious biting nuisance, their particular medical interest dates from 1926 when Blacklock, working in West Africa, first showed that a certain species, *Simulium damnosum*, was a vector of a filarial worm, *Onchocerca volvulus*, the causal parasite of onchocerciasis. Since the studies of Blacklock, further work both in Africa and in America has shown that in addition to *S. damnosum* other species of *Simulium* act as vectors of onchocerciasis. The recognition of the occurrence of the disease, not only over large tracts of Africa but also in considerable areas of Central America and Venezuela, and the recent emphasis on the serious pathogenic lesions (particularly the ocular damage) which may result from the presence of the worms in the human body, has focussed attention on the urgency of devising control measures directed against the insect vector, a task which unfortunately is peculiarly difficult due to the unusual breeding habits of these flies.

The family Simuliidae has a worldwide distribution, species of buffalo-flies being found in the tropical, temperate and arctic zones. They occur from sea level to altitudes over 10,000 feet and a large proportion of species frequent hilly or mountainous country with fast flowing streams and rivers. The family, comprising about 700 species, is composed of seven genera, which are separable mainly on minor characters of the wing venation. Although several of the genera contain species which cause great annoyance and discomfort to man as a result of their bites, only the genus *Simulium* includes vectors of disease to man.

The genus *Simulium*

The account which follows refers to members of the genus *Simulium*, with special reference to those which bite man in the tropics.

External anatomy of the adult fly

The adult buffalo-fly is small, most species attacking man varying between about 2 and 4 mm. in length. Although many species are of a sombre hue,

---

* It should be noted that the term "buffalo fly" as used in Australia refers to *Lyperosia irritans*, a cyclorrhaphous biting fly, and not to a member of the family Simuliidae.

a proportion are brightly coloured being yellow or orange, whilst a few have contrasting bands of black and white and other colours. The markedly humped appearance of the thorax, together with the presence of horn-like

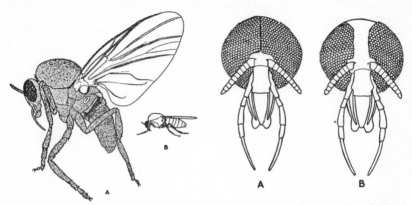

Fig. 85. An adult buffalo-fly. *Simulium* sp., A. drawn from a mounted specimen and B. natural resting attitude.

Fig. 86. Frontal aspect of A. the head of a male *Simulium* sp., and B. the head of a female *Simulium* sp.

antennae and short legs, give the fly ,when seen from the side, the appearance of a miniature buffalo, so that the name buffalo-fly is a very descriptive and appropriate term.

The head. The head, due to the marked arching of the thorax, has the appearance of being borne on the antero-ventral aspect of the prothorax. The eyes are distinctly separated in the midline in the female, but in the case of the male, where they are unusually large, they meet on the vertex; thus the two sexes may very easily be distinguished (see plates VI and VII). The antennae, which are very short, are bare in both sexes and are composed of 11 (rarely 9 or 10) approximately equal, very short and stumpy segments, giving to each antenna a horn-like appearance.

The mouthparts of the female, although adapted for biting, are very short and consist of a labrum, a pair of mandibles, a pair of maxillae and a hypo-

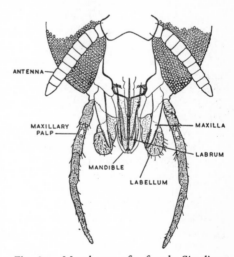

Fig. 87. Mouthparts of a female *Simulium*.

141

pharynx (which together constitute the biting fascicle) and a relatively large labium which terminates in two fleshy labella. Since the individual elements of the biting fascicle are broad and blade-like, and not stylet-like as in the mosquito, they do not penetrate deeply when the fly is feeding but simply fret the surface of the skin until a bloody oozing surface is produced on which the insect feeds. This method of feeding is well adapted to the taking up of the skin-inhabiting microfilariae of *O. volvulus*. After the fly has left its host, the wound continues to ooze blood for a short time afterwards, so that it is often possible to recognise the presence of buffalo-flies in a district by the appearance of little droplets of dried blood on the bare exposed skin of people who have been bitten.

The thorax. The thorax which is arched forwards and humped, bears three pairs of short legs which are somewhat thickened in some species. The wings

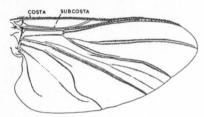

COSTA SUBCOSTA

which are broad and transparent are usually colourless (with the exception of a small proportion of species in which they are uniformly tinged a light yellow or brown) and do not bear scales or readily visible hairs. The wing venation is characteristic, the veins close to the anterior border being well marked, whilst the remaining veins are indistinct.

Fig. 88. Wing of *Simulium* sp.

The abdomen. The abdomen is short and oval in shape and closely attached to the thorax so that the waist-like appearance present in the mosquito is absent. The genitalia are not prominent.

The life-cycle of buffalo-flies

Males and females both feed on plant juices but only the females suck blood, the fertilised females laying their eggs a few days later.

Most species of buffalo-flies lay their eggs at the level of, or just below, the surface of streams and rivers, alighting on partially immersed rocks, vegetation or debris (such as logs and sticks) in order to oviposit. Having settled on the object, the gravid female either deposits her eggs at the water line or crawls below the water surface to some chosen site where she oviposits, sometimes in torrents so swift that it would appear almost impossible for any living thing to remain stationary. Whilst oviposition may be completed in as little a time as 3 to 4 minutes, some species may take up to 15 minutes to lay all their eggs. Even those species which oviposit below the water surface may take a long period of time over the oviposition act, interrupting their laying in order to emerge from the water for a few seconds from time to time. Oviposition is usually undertaken in the late afternoon or early morning and the number of eggs laid at each oviposition varies from about 100 to 500, several such batches of eggs being laid during the lifetime of the female. In the case of several species, including *S. damnosum*, numerous females choose the same spot to deposit their eggs, so that masses of eggs may be found extending over a few square inches. Although most species of buffalo-flies alight on partially immersed objects in order to oviposit, several species, such as *S. ochraceum* and *S. metallicum*, are exceptional in that they drop their eggs on to the surface of water or on floating leaves, whilst they are on the wing during an oviposition flight.

A   B

The eggs, which are covered with a viscous substance, are triangular in shape with rounded corners and have a smooth shell. When first laid they are white or cream in colour but soon darken, so that at the end of 24 hours they are dark brown or black.

Fig. 89. *A.* egg mass of *Simulium*. In this instance the eggs have been laid in a chain-like mass on an underwater reed, but the site of oviposition and the character of the mass varies with the different species. *B.* single egg.

The time taken for the eggs to hatch is extremely variable and differs for each particular species. Whilst the eggs of most tropical species take several days to hatch, the larvae of some species, such as those of *S. damnosum*, emerge from the eggs in as short a time as a few hours to just over a day. In the temperate zones hatching may be delayed for many weeks, whilst in the case of certain northern species, the eggs laid in the late summer or autumn do not hatch until the following spring.

The larvae which hatch from the eggs are always found in free water, the almost universal requirement being moving— usually fast moving— water. The larva remains attached to some submerged object by means of a posterior abdominal sucker and hangs with its head downstream, trapping food by means of a pair of brush-like structures on the head. The food consists almost entirely of microscopic animals and plants but the larvae also ingest small particles of grit and other inert matter, and sometimes graze on the plant life growing on the substrate.

Although simuliid larvae are incapable of swimming they are capable of active movements and, by means of the alternate attachment of the anterior and posterior suckers, progress by creeping in a characteristic manner, somewhat reminiscent of the motion of "measuring worms", over the surface of rocks, leaves, and other submerged objects.

If the larva is disturbed it will deposit saliva on the substrate and allow itself to be carried as much as 2 feet

Fig. 90. Diagrammatic representation of the characteristic creeping movement of the *Simulium* larva.

downstream by the current, the saliva forming a silken thread which serves as an anchoring line, and when the exciting cause has disappeared, the larva finds its way back to its original position by swallowing the thread. Many larvae however allow themselves to be carried to sites further downstream, and it is possible that this is a form of migration.

The habitats of the larvae range from raging mountain torrents, where the current is so strong that a person venturing into the water is likely to be carried away, to very slow-flowing rivers and streams where the movement of the water is barely perceptible. Whilst a great number of species appear to have specific requirements as regards the velocity of the water in which they live, other species, as for instance *S. damnosum*, appear to be more elastic in their habits and may be found in water of such differing types as rapids and slowflowing rivers.

Although the vast majority of simuliid larvae cling either to plants or rocks or to other inert objects in the habitat, a small proportion of African species have developed the specialised habit of attaching themselves to other aquatic insects or to the carapace of crustacea. Of several species which attach themselves to crabs, the most important is *S. neavei* (a vector of *O. volvulus*) which in East and Central Africa lives in association with *Potamon niloticum*.

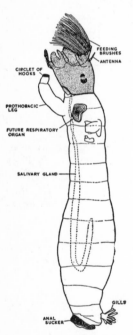

Fig. 91. Full grown larva of *Simulium* sp.

The larva of the buffalo-fly is a curious creature and has such a characteristic appearance that it may readily be distinguished from other aquatic insects, There is a considerable variation in the size of larvae of various species, the range of size varying between 4 and 13 mm. in length. The general appearance of the creature, the cuticle of which is usually smooth, is that of a figure of eight due to the enlarged anterior and posterior extremities and a narrow "waist". It has a well marked head bearing a pair of mandibles, two conspicuous stalked, fan-shaped structures known as the feeding brushes, or cephalic fans, and a pair of slender antennae. The thorax is rounded (forming the anterior bulge of the larva) and bears ventrally, and just behind the head, a distinct pseudopod, known as the prothoracic leg, which is armed with a circlet of hooks. The abdomen is narrow in its anterior half but is bulbous in its posterior half, the terminal portion being provided with a sucking disc (known as the posterior sucker), which is armed with circles of small spines. The posterior end of the abdomen also bears a trilobed, gill-like, structure, known as the blood gill, the three branches of which may show further subdivisions. Although the blood gills have some respiratory function, the term "gill" is to some extent a misnomer, since respiration is largely effected through the thin integument of the larva.

There are six larval instars, the final stage larva being recognisable by the presence of two black marks, the respiratory organs of the future pupa, which are visible through the larval skin. The larval life is generally completed in about 10 days to a little over 2 weeks in the tropics, whilst in the temperate zones the period of development of the larva lasts about 3 to 4 weeeks. Temperature and seasonal influences have a profound effect on the larvae; in exceptionally warm conditions in the tropics, development of the larva may be completed in as little as 5 to 6 days (as sometimes occurs in the case of *S. damnosum*), whilst in the temperate zones the onset of winter causes the larvae of many species to enter a period of rest or diapause which lasts until the following spring.

Pupation takes place in the larval habitat. As a preliminary to pupation the larvae of most species of simuliids spin, with the aid of their mouthparts, a silken cocoon which is firmly attached to rocks, plants, sticks or other objects, while in the case of those larvae which are found on crabs, the cocoons are fixed to the shell. The completed cocoon, which encloses the pupa, measures 2–5 mm. in length and is a pocket-like structure, very variable in form, but generally slipper-shaped in the case of those species, which are of medical importance. The narrow end of the cocoon is closed and directed against the flow of the current whilst the wide, open end faces down stream. A striking feature of the pupa is the presence of a pair of branched respiratory filaments which project conspicuously from the open end of the cocoon and wave about freely in the water; the nature of the filaments and the number of branches they bear are used by the systematist in classifying different species of buffalo-flies. The pupal stage lasts 2 or 3 days to a week but it may be prolonged with a lowering of temperature.

Since the pupa is fixed to objects which are submerged below the surface of water, emergence of the adult takes place under water. During pupal life, air which is expired from the spiracles of the developing adult is trapped within the pupal skin where it surrounds the hairs of the fly, so that when the adult breaks out of the pupal skin the

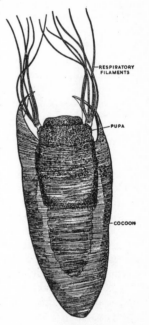

Fig. 92.   Cocoon and pupa of *Simulium*.

entrapped air helps to carry it rapidly to the water surface. The fly then either takes flight from off the water surface or else is swept downstream until it can grasp some object, up which it climbs preparatory to flight.

Copulation has only rarely been observed in nature but it is probable that fertilisation takes place near the breeding sites shortly after the emergence of the adult flies from the pupae.

Once fertilisation has been accomplished both males and females fly off in search of food. Simuliids are exceptionally strong fliers and in contrast to other small biting Nematocera, such as *Culicoides* and *Phlebotomus*, travel very long distances from their breeding-places. Distances of up to 10 miles are not unusual and even longer distances of 25 miles and over, particularly if the fly is aided by wind, have been reported. Occasionally simuliids fly in huge swarms so thick that they appear as great clouds. In their search for food both males and females seek out plant juices and other sources of natural sugars but in addition, the females of most species of buffalo-flies bite mammals or birds in order to obtain blood which is essential for the maturation of the eggs in their ovaries.

Simuliids only attack their hosts during the hours of daylight and are not nocturnal feeders. As a general rule they bite in greatest numbers in the earlier part of the morning or in the later part of the afternoon; although they bite in bright sunlight, making sorties for this purpose from the neighbouring vegetation, they are more active in dull weather. The host range of most species of buffalo-flies is quite extensive but the majority show a predilection for a particular species or group of mammals or birds. Of the 700 or so species of buffalo-flies which have been described only a small proportion are arthropophilic, but the members of this small group are so important, as biting nuisances and as vectors of disease to man, that they have been the subject of intensive study by an ever-increasing number of entomologists and health experts all over the world.

Although simuliids feed on the exposed parts of the body they are so persistent in their efforts to obtain blood that should the hands, legs and face be protected they will make their way down sleeves and other apertures in the clothing in order to bite, whilst they will crawl down the fur of mammals or the feathers of a bird or enter the ears of animals to feed. Several of the anthropophilic species select particular feeding sites on the human body, as for instance *S. damnosum* of Africa which tends to concentrate its attacks on the lower extremities, whilst the Central American species, *S. ochraceum*, bites on the upper part of the body. To what extent these preferences are dependent on environmental conditions is not known.

Following the taking of a blood-meal, simuliids retire to the protection of neighbouring vegetation in order to mature their eggs, a process which occupies 2 or 3 days. Most species fly to low lying vegetation where they rest during digestion of the blood-meal, but in Central America certain important vectors of onchocerciasis have been found resting in large numbers high up in trees.

In the subtropics and tropics, where breeding usually apears to be continuous throughout the year, the life-cycle is completed in about 3 or 4 weeks, although this period is somewhat shortened when the prevailing temperatures are high. In wet regions the population peak of active adults tends to occur in the drier season, whereas in areas of low rainfall where the rivers cease to flow and only leave pools during the dry season, the fly population is greatly reduced until

PLATE V

A house fly (*Musca domestica*) in a resting attitude.
[*Courtesy Shell Photographic Unit, No. 1 Kingsway, London, W.C.2*]

PLATE VI

A male buffalo-fly (*Simulium damnosum*) in the resting attitude.
[*Courtesy Mr. W. Petana*]

PLATE VII

A female buffalo-fly (*Simulium damnosum*) in the resting attitude.

[*Courtesy Mr. W. Petana*]

PLATE VIII

FIG. 1. A female biting midge (*Culicoides nubeculosus*) resting on the
skin preparatory to feeding.
[*Courtesy Mr. J. P. Brady*]

FIG. 2. A female *Chrysops silacea* feeding on a drop of sugar solution.
[*Courtesy Dr. W. Crewe*]

the resumption of the rains. In the temperate zones the life-cycle is generally completed in about 4 to 8 weeks but in northern latitudes where severe winters are common there may be only a single generation a year, the flies over-wintering in the egg stage, or as larvae and pupae. Although it is difficult to determine with any degree of accuracy the average length of life of the adults in nature, it is certain that in the temperate zones they may live for many weeks whilst in the tropics certain species have been found to live up to several months.

The medical importance of buffalo-flies

Simuliids are of importance because of the severe effects of their attacks on human beings in many parts of the world and also because of the role they play as the only known vectors to man of onchocerciasis, a filarial disease due to *Onchocerca volvulus*, affecting many persons in tropical Africa, in Central America and in Venezuela.

The immediate trauma caused by the coarse mouth parts of the feeding *Simulium* is considerably greater than that produced by the relatively fine fascicle of the mosquito and gives rise to great discomfort when the flies are biting in large numbers. It is, however, only in sensitised persons that the bites are of great significance since in such persons persistent attacks by large numbers of flies may lead to very severe reactions. In Canada and Northern Europe simuliids may occur in such vast numbers as to make working in the open virtually impossible, whilst in the Balkans attacks on human beings by the notorious *Simulium columbaschensis* may cause such distress that on parts of the Danube the whole population shifts out of certain districts in the month of May.

It is now known that in addition to *S. damnosum* at least one other species of *Simulium (S. neavei)* also acts as a vector of onchocerciasis in Africa. *S. damnosum* is the more important of the two vectors and is found widely distributed in tropical Africa, whereas *S. neavei* occurs only in Kenya, Uganda and the Belgian Congo. In America onchocerciasis exists in Venezuela and also in Central America where the three chief vectors are *S. ochraceum*, *S. metallicum* and *S. callidum*; of these *S. ochraceum* appears to be the most important transmitter.

CHAPTER XXII

THE FAMILY CERATOPOGONIDAE (= HELEIDAE)

THOSE members of the family Ceratopogonidae which suck blood are known to entomologists as "biting midges", but in some parts of the world they are given local names, such as "punkies" or "no-see-ums" and in Australia "sandflies".

Biting midges are the smallest of the blood-sucking Diptera, measuring between 1 and 4 mm. The wings possess a characteristic appearance of the type shown in Fig. 93. The family Ce-

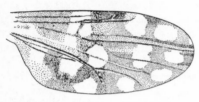

ratopogonidae is sub-divided into four subfamilies and is composed of a large number of genera, three of which, *Culicoides*, *Lasiohelea* and *Leptoconops*, contain species which attack vertebrates. Whilst two of these three genera are only of limited medical importance since they in-

Fig. 93. Wing of *Culicoides* sp.

clude no vectors of disease, the remaining genus (*Culicoides*) includes many species which transmit disease both to man and to domestic animals and which are a source of great discomfort due to their persistent biting habits.

The genus *Culicoides*

Members of the genus *Culicoides* have a cosmopolitan distribution and are found in the tropics and in the temperate zone as far north as Alaska and Northern Europe. Whilst over 400 species have been described, it is certain that many more await discovery since papers describing new forms are being published every year.

Although these flies, because of their severe attacks on man and domestic animals, have long been studied by entomologists, it was not until 1928 that Sharp first showed that two West African species (*C. austeni* and *C. grahami*) act as the intermediate hosts of *Dipetalonema perstans*, a filarial parasite of man. This discovery instigated investigations by other workers into the possible role of biting midges as intermediate hosts of other filarial worms with the result that today several species of *Culicoides* are recognised as allowing development to the infective forms of three relatively benign filarial parasites of man. Although *Culicoides* is a widespread vector of filariasis, nevertheless its medical importance is chiefly derived from its role as a serious biting nuisance. In localities where they occur in immense numbers, as in certain parts of Alaska, Canada and Northern Europe as well as in many areas in the tropics, they will mercilessly and persistently attack human beings in large swarms, biting every exposed part of the body. In heavily infested areas biting rates of over 2,000 an hour are not uncommon and may so deter even accustomed sufferers as to make working in the open impractical at certain times of the year. In the case of persons who are sensitised to the bites of *Culicoides* such severe reactions may follow heavy attacks by the flies as to necessitate admission to hospital.

External anatomy of the adult
Culicoides

Adult *Culicoides* are very small (many tropical species rarely exceed 2 mm. in length), black or dark brown flies with stout bodies and relatively short legs and with mouthparts adapted for biting. They are so minute that their size alone is sufficient to identify members of the genus when caught biting.

The head. The head bears a pair of compound eyes, a pair of conspicuous antennae and biting mouthparts. The antennae in the female are provided with a few short hairs; the antennae of the male are more plum-

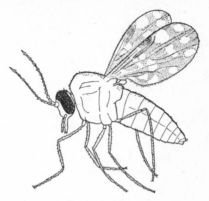

Fig. 94. Adult *Culicoides* female drawn from a mounted specimen. The resting attitude is shown in Plate VIII, fig. 1.

ose. In both sexes the antennae are long and consist of thirteen to fourteen segments, the last few of which are somewhat longer than the others. The mouthparts, which are short, consist of a labrum, a pair of maxillae, a pair of mandibles, a hypopharynx and a fleshy labium. Although the fascicle is short it is capable of penetrating the epidermis of the mammalian host, and drawing blood from the subdermal tissues.

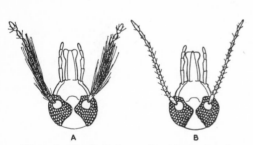

Fig. 95. Head of *A.* a male and *B.* a female *Culicoides* sp.

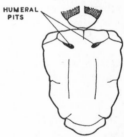

Fig. 96. Thorax of *Culicoides* sp. seen from above, showing the humeral pits.

The thorax. The thorax is stout and slightly humped. On the dorsal surface, at each antero-lateral corner, is a small, sharply defined pit, known as the "humeral pit", a character which serves to distinguish midges of the genus *Culicoides* from most other species of ceratopogonids. The wings, which have a characteristic appearance of the type shown in Fig. 93 are short and moderately broad and in most species of *Culicoides* are distinctly spotted with dark and milky white patches. In the living insect the wings have an irridescent appearance and are kept folded over the back like scissors when the fly is at rest. The legs are short, as compared to those of the mosquito and the sandfly (see Plate VIII fig. 1).

The abdomen. The abdomen is moderately short and bears the external genital organs at its tip. Whereas in the female the external genitalia are inconspicuous, in the male insect they are easily seen at the abdominal extremity. The male external genitalia consist of a conspicuous pair of claspers which are utilised by the fly, during the mating act, to grasp the tip of the abdomen of the female; specialists in the taxonomy of midges use the characters of the male genitalia in classification.

The life-cycle of Culicoides

A few days after the female has been fertilised and has taken a blood-meal she lays her eggs, oviposition usually being undertaken at night. The eggs are deposited either on plants or on objects partially immersed in water, in which case they are arranged in irregular clusters, or rows; or else they are deposited on the surface of mud, moist soil or dung, in which case they are scattered about indiscriminately. The number of eggs laid at each oviposition varies from 30 to 120, according to the species which deposits them. The eggs measure about 0.5 mm. in length and are either banana-shaped or cigar-shaped.

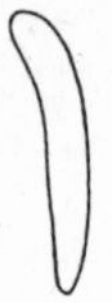

Fig. 97. Egg of Culicoides sp.

The incubation period lasts from 2 days to just over a week, depending on the species of *Culicoides* and on the prevailing temperatures. Seasonal influences exert a profound effect on the ova of some temperate species, the eggs deposited in the late summer or autumn remaining dormant until the following spring.

Emergence of the larva from the egg is effected by means of a circular tear at the anterior pole which is extended as a dorsal slit as the larva wriggles out of the broken shell. The larva is an active creature which progresses by means of a rapid, sinuous, eel-like motion, a characteristic which is useful in distinguishing it from the larvae of other aquatic insects. Most species feed on particulate decaying vegetable matter.

The larval stages of all species of *Culicoides* have a very delicate integument which is not adapted to resist dessication, and they therefore require water—although this may exist only in the form of soil-bound water—in order to breed. Apart from this common requirement of water, each species has its own particular preference regarding the type of breeding place it selects. Sites favoured by *Culicoides* include swamps, salt marshes, ponds, banks of rivers, boggy soil particularly where there is much decaying plant matter, rubbish heaps with much leaf mould, tree holes and a variety of rotting tree stumps such as cut banana-plants, and moist dung or wet soil close to collections of animal faeces. Both *C. austeni* and *C. grahami*, which are the two most important vectors of *D. perstans* and *D. streptocerca*, have their main breeding sites in banana stumps.

The family Ceratopogonidae

There are four larval instars; the time taken to complete the larval stage is short in the tropics and lasts about 3 weeks but in the temperate zones, where most species overwinter in the 3rd and 4th larval instars, it may last as long as 6 to 7 months.

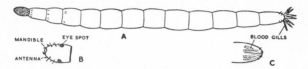

MANDIBLE   EYE SPOT   A   BLOOD GILLS

ANTENNA   B   C

Fig. 98.   A. fourth instar larva of Culioides; B. head of larva; C. terminal segment with blood gills retracted.

The fourth stage larva of Culicoides is a minute elongated cylindrical creature measuring about 5 to 6 mm. in length, with a distinct conical pigmented head, which is yellowish brown to dark brown in colour, and a segmented body which is white or cream. The head bears a pair of eye spots, a pair of mandibles and a pair of antennae, while the body consists of twelve smooth segments each of which bears a few simple hairs. The twelfth segment terminates in retractile, carrot-shaped structures (the so-called blood-gills) each of which is four-lobed. In preserved material the blood-gills are seldom seen since they are usually retracted into the terminal segments.

In the case of semi-aquatic species of Culicoides the larva migrates to drier mud or soil just prior to pupation and once the pupa has formed the creature wriggles into an up-right position by means of active abdominal movements and thereafter remains quiescent. Species of midges living in water do not leave the aquatic environment prior to pupation, the pupa floating to the surface of the water where it remains quiescent until the adult emerges.

The Culicoides pupa measures 2 to 4 mm. and bears a pair of conspicuous breathing trumpets which arise from pedicels, giving the trumpets the appearance of being composed of two segments. The abdomen, which terminates in two small processes, is made up of distinct segments each surrounded by a row of small tubercles bearing hairs.

During its period of development, which varies from three days in the case of tropical species to over a week in the case of temperate species, the pupa remains practically motionless, except for occasional twitching movements of the abdomen. Emergence of the adult fly from the pupa only occupies a few minutes. The newly emerged adults,

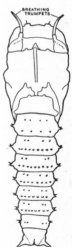

Fig. 99. Pupa of Culicoides.

which are light in colour, rest on the surface of water or on the mud or soil for about an hour, until their integument has darkened and the wings are fully expanded and dried, when they are ready to take to flight.

Following fertilisation, which generally occurs in swarms, the females search for a host in order to obtain a blood-meal which is necessary for the maturation of the ova; the males, on the other hand, do not suck blood and feed only on plant juices. In their search for food, biting midges do not fly far from their breeding places, usually no more than a few hundred yards unless they are carried further by strong breezes. They will fly in light rain and when there is a light breeze but not in heavy rain or high winds, so that wind has comparatively little effect on dispersal.

Most species of *Culicoides* are outdoor biters, and attack their hosts particularly in the early morning or late afternoon, preferably in dull sultry weather when the sky is overcast. A small number of species, however, amongst which are such medically important species as *C. austeni* and *C. grahami* bite mainly at night and readily enter human dwellings in order to feed. Biting midges engorge rapidly, and the replete females retire to the shelter of leaves in the adjacent vegetation and to the protection of rock holes and crevices in the soil, whilst a proportion of the midges which have obtained their blood-meal indoors may rest in corners of a room.

In the tropics *Culicoides* breeds continually throughout the year, although the number of active adults are reduced during the dry season, but in the temperate zones where breeding is interrupted by long winters and where diapause occurs, there may be only one or two generations a year. The longevity of the adults has not been accurately determined but there is evidence to show that they may survive in nature at least for several weeks and even longer.

Medical importance of biting midges

As vectors of disease to man, midges are probably only of limited medical importance, for although three species (out of about 25 known to bite man) act as vectors of filariasis, nevertheless the species of filariae transmitted by these flies are not — up to the present — regarded as being of any great clinical significance. In West Africa, *Dipetalonema perstans* is transmitted by *C. austeni* and *C. grahami*, the latter also acting as a vector of *D. streptocerca*. In the West Indies, where the filarial worm, *Mansonella ozzardi*, parasitises man, *Culicoides furens* has been shown to act as a vector.

In certain areas biting midges occur in such large numbers, and are so persistent in their attacks as to make normal community life, particularly in rural areas, practically impossible.

CHAPTER XXIII

THE SUBORDER BRACHYCERA AND ITS DIVISION INTO FAMILIES OF MEDICAL IMPORTANCE

THE suborder Brachycera contains fairly large, stout, two winged flies, usually with short antennae the morphology of which differs considerably in various genera. The antenna is usually described as three-segmented, the third or terminal segment—which is often enlarged—being either annulated or bearing a terminal bristle known as a style, a structure which is analogous to the arista of cyclorraphous flies. The palps are two-segmented and project forwards. The wings are provided with many veins; although the wing venation is more uniform in the suborder Brachycera than in the suborder Nematocera, there exist some variations amongst the various families composing the Brachycera, but all species which bite man have a venation of the type shown in Fig. 100. In some families the calypter or squama is well developed, in other families it is small or absent.

The suborder Brachycera is composed of 14 families and includes over 10,000 species of flies. Only two families, the Tabanidae and the Rhagionidae, contain species of any medical importance. Whereas the family Tabanidae contains many species which are pests or vectors of disease, the family Rhagionidae—which is briefly referred to later—is of little significance.

Whilst all species of Brachycera which bite man possess mouthparts adapted to piercing the skin, it should be noted that many other brachycerous flies which do not attack vertebrates have well formed biting mouthparts; such flies are predators of other arthropods, particularly insects, from which they suck the body fluids. Thus members of the family Asilidae (the so-called "robber flies") which are bristly insects, have a powerful horny proboscis with which they pierce the cuticle of other arthropods, in order to imbibe the haemolymph, but although they possess piercing mouthparts they never attack vertebrates.

The larvae, which show great diversity of form, are usually elongated with clearly recognisable body segments and a small but distinct head which, excepting in one family, is retractable within the thorax. Whilst most species of brachycerous larvae are characteristically terrestial creatures living in moist soil or leaf mould or decaying wood, the great majority of medically important species are semi-aquatic or aquatic. A very large number of species are predacious, feeding on other arthropods, particularly insects, but a certain proportion are either parasitic or vegetarian.

The family Rhagionidae (Leptidae) which includes about 400 species of flies, known as "snipe flies", has a worldwide distribution. Only about half a dozen species bite man, chiefly in North and South America and in Australia. Members of the genera *Symphoromyia* (in localised areas in the U.S.A.) and *Spaniopsis* (in Tasmania) may be the cause of considerable annoyance as a result of their biting activities, but since they are not known to transmit disease they are only of limited interest to the medical officer. These flies have a wing venation of the tabanid type shown in Fig. 100, but the third segment of the antenna bears a style at its tip. The squama is very poorly developed.

The family Tabanidae (which is discussed in the following chapter) contains species which in contradistinction to those in the family Rhagionidae are of great medical importance since many of them bite man and several tropical species are vectors of disease.

CHAPTER XXIV

THE FAMILY TABANIDAE

MEMBERS of the family Tabanidae are known by such vernacular names as "horse flies", "deer flies", "clegs" or "gad flies". They vary in size from species no larger than a house fly to very large flies measuring up to an inch or more in length. Tabanids are stout flies which lack bristles, being covered only by fine hairs. They may be recognised by the relatively large head (usually semi-lunar in outline), the large eyes, biting mouthparts, easily visible antennae and a wing venation of the type shown in Fig. 100.

Fig. 100. Wing of a tabanid fly showing the many marginal cells characteristic of biting flies of this family.

Tabanid flies have a worldwide distribution and are common pests at all altitudes from sea level to localities as high as 10,000 feet. They frequent a great variety of biotopes and species are known not only from open savannah country but also from such humid habitats as gallery forests. Whilst most species appear to be chiefly active at ground level, a number of forest-living species are known to frequent the forest canopy. Whereas in some sites they may be hard to find, in other localities they may be so numerous and so persistent in their attacks on their hosts as to render normal living activities unbearable for man or animals.

Whilst horse flies have long been known to be a biting nuisance, it is only since Leiper in 1913 showed that certain African species of the genus *Chrysops* act as vectors of loiasis that tabanids have become of serious interest to the medical officer. Some seven years later Francis and Mayne demonstrated that a bacterial disease, tularaemia, was transmitted from its rodent reservoir to man by an American species of *Chrysops*. Although up to the present time these are the only diseases known to be acquired by man following the bite of infected tabanids, there are a number of species which are vectors of diseases to domestic animals, such as surra (caused by *Trypanosoma evansi*), mal-de-caderas (caused by *T. equiperdum*), anthrax and anaplasmosis. In spite of the importance of the family Tabanidae, the life history and habits of only a few of the more common species have been studied. This gap in our knowledge seems mainly due to the very long cycle of development of the flies which makes a complete study of their biology, both in the field and in the laboratory, a particularly difficult task.

The family Tabanidae comprises about 3,000 species and is subdivided into four subfamilies, only three of which, the Chrysopinae, Tabaninae and Pangoninae, contain species which suck blood, whilst the fourth subfamily (Scepsidinae) comprises a small number of rare species which lack biting mouthparts. The subfamily Pangoninae, the members of which usually have a remarkably long forwardly directed proboscis, does not comprise any species of medical importance and need not be considered any further.

The subfamilies Chrysopinae and Tabaninae, on the other hand, contain many such species, and a brief guide to the recognition of the genera containing these species is given at the end of this chapter.

External anatomy of the Tabanids

Horse flies are medium sized to large flies which generally have a stout compact appearance heightened by the close apposition of the semi-lunar head to the anterior border of the thorax. Although they vary considerably in colour, they are usually black, brown, reddish-brown or yellow flies with superimposed darker bands or maculations. In life the eyes of flies belonging to several genera are irridescent and may be coloured bright green to purple, sometimes in the form of banding. When at rest or feeding on the host the wings are either held horizontally at an angle of about 30° to the body (*Tabanus, Chrysops* and other species — see Plate VIII Fig. 2) or are kept folded tent-like over the abdomen *(Haematopota)*.

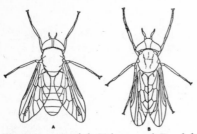

Fig. 101.   A. adult *Tabanus* and B. adult *Haematopota* showing the characteristic carriage of the wings in each genus.

Fig. 102.   Head of *A.* a male and *B.* a female tabanid fly (*Tabanus* sp.).

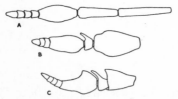

Fig. 103.   Types of antennae belonging to flies in *A.* the genus *Chrysops, B.* the genus *Haematopota* and *C.* the genus *Tabanus.*

The head. The big semi-lunar head carries eyes which are unusually large and generally occupy a considerable area, generally leaving only a narrow frons between them in the case of the female, and meeting in the midline in the case of the male. In the female *Chrysops* the space between the eyes may be quite extensive. The antennae, which are readily visible, are usually shorter than the head, although in the genus *Chrysops* they are distinctly longer. They are often described as being three-segmented with the terminal segment annulated but since the annulations often resemble segments it is advisable to consider the antennae as consisting of 5-10 unequal segments, the first and third being nearly always distinctly stouter and longer than the terminal segments.

The mouthparts of most tabanid flies are adapted for biting and consist of a labrum, a pair of mandibles, a pair of maxillae, a hypopharynx (with its salivary duct) and a labium. The labrum, mandibles, maxillae and hypopharynx (known collectively as the biting fascicle) are drawn out to form stylet-like organs capable of piercing the integument of animals, and are broader, coarser and more blade-like than those of other biting flies, the maxillae being provided with a strong rasp-like set of recurved teeth. The labium, which is grooved anteriorly so as to provide a sheath for the biting fascicle, terminates in two large labella, provided with small tubes known as pseudotracheae; the structure of the labella of tabanids is generally similar to that of the house fly (see chapter XXVII).

The thorax. The thorax, which is stout, bears a pair of moderately broad wings, with a venation of the type shown in Fig. 100, a pair of large squamae and legs of a moderate length. Whilst many horse flies possess clear wings, a considerable proportion have wings with brown or grey markings, imparting to these structures a banded or mottled appearance. Although the wing venation is not a characteristic feature of the family Tabanidae, since certain other brachycerous flies possess a similar pattern, nevertheless, if taken in conjunction with the other characters outlined in the introductory paragraphs of this chapter, the venation is of great value in the recognition of the family.

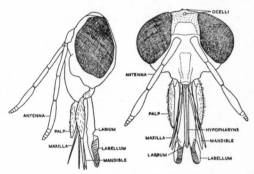

Fig. 104.   Head of a tabanid (*Chrysops*) seen *A*. in profile and *B*. from in front.

The abdomen. The abdomen, which possesses 7 apparent segments, is usually broad and stout and although it is generally flattened dorso-ventrally, it may be, in some species, cylindrical in form. The colour and markings with which it is adorned are often of use in the identification of the species. The external genitalia are inconspicuous.

The life-cycle of the Tabanids

A few days after fertilisation and, in the case of the blood-sucking species, the taking of a blood-meal, the female fly lays her eggs.

The eggs are laid over mud or water on overhanging vegetation such as plant stems or leaves, or on objects such as stones or sticks, on which the fly alights in order to oviposit. As the insect deposits her eggs, by thrusting the tip of her abdomen under her body, she glues them to the substrate, coating each egg with a protective substance which is very impervious to water. The eggs are laid upright, in masses often lozenge-shaped in outline and comprising

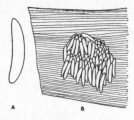

Fig. 105. *A.* a single egg of a tabanid and *B.* an egg mass laid on foliage.

anything from 50 to about 700 ova, the number of eggs in a batch depending on the species of tabanid which has laid them, *Chrysops silacea* for example usually laying between 80-150 eggs at a time.

The eggs, which measure 1 mm.—2 mm. in length are elongated and either torpedo-shaped or cigar-shaped and are usually cream-coloured, although some species lay coloured eggs which may be grey, brown, black or orange.

The time taken for the eggs to hatch varies from a few days to a week, the larva emerging from the egg by tearing a slit in the shell, through which it wriggles to freedom, dropping directly on to the surface of the underlying mud or water.

Tabanid larvae generally move about slowly in the mud or water of their habitat, most species feeding on other aquatic arthropods, such as various species of dragonfly nymphs, mosquito larvae, small crustacea and even other species of horse-fly larvae, which they capture by means of their strong mandibles. A proportion of species, in particular members of the genus *Chrysops*, are not predacious and appear to derive their nourishment from microorganisms or particulate vegetable matter by sifting the mud of their habitat through their alimentary canal.

Tabanid larvae are usually found in shallow water or in wet mud, although a few species have been found living in moist soil some distance from water. They are never found living in deep water, in which they drown if immersed. The larvae of species, which as adults frequent open country or savannah, may be found in mud at the edges of swamps, along the shores of lakes, in the banks of slow-flowing streams and ditches or adhering to floating logs or leaves in open water, whilst forest species are found particularly in mud covered by only a few inches of water and containing large amounts of decaying plant matter, in sites heavily shaded by overhanging vegetation. The immature stages of a small number of tabanids are found inhabiting tree holes, sometimes as high as 20 feet or more above the level of the ground.

The period of time spent in the larval stage is very variable but it is generally noticeably long, the majority of species, both in the temperate zones and in the tropics, taking 1 to 2 years to complete their larval life; in the case of some temperate species, larval development may last as long as 3 years. The number of larval instars appears to vary from seven to nine.

The larval tabanid is a very characteristically shaped creature, but varies greatly in size according to the species; when full grown the length of the creature may vary from a quarter of an inch, in the case of the smaller species, to as much as two inches in the case of largest. The mature larva, which is cylindrical in shape and tapers at both ends, has a very small but distinct head and a body consisting of 11 segments differentiated into a thoracic and an abdominal region; it may be either white, cream or brown in colour, whilst some species have a greenish tinge. The head, which is very small and more darkly pigmented than the body segments, is capable of retraction into the thorax, as occurs when specimens are immersed in alcohol. The first three segments of the body following the head are the thoracic segments, the

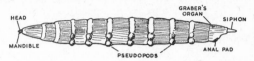

Fig. 106.   Full grown larva of a tabanid. (*Chrysops* sp.).

remaining eight segments forming the abdomen. The first seven abdominal segments usually bear a pair of lateral and two pairs of ventral wart-like protuberances (pseudopods), and in some species of tabanids there may be additional dorso-lateral pairs. The eighth segment bears a single protrusible breathing tube or siphon, by means of which the creature takes in air, and a pair of small papilliform structures between which the anal opening lies. A feature unique to tabanid larvae and which can be seen at the extreme posterior end of the body through the integument of the living larva, is a pyriform organ, known as Graber's organ, containing a varying number of black globular bodies (fifteen or less).

When the larva is mature it migrates to the edge of the breeding place to sites where the mud is drier and there it pupates, the pupa lying upright and partially buried in the mud. The tabanid pupa, which is brown in colour, varies in length from about a third of an inch to one and a half inches and has a distinct cephalothorax and abdomen. The cephalothorax, which comprises the head and thorax, bears large ear-shaped spiracles. There are eight abdominal segments, the second to the seventh bearing near their termination backwardly directed rings of spines. The short eighth segment is provided with six spur-bearing lobes collectively known as the "caudal aster".

In contrast to the long larval development, the pupal life is short and only lasts from a few days to two weeks. The imago emerges from the pupa by wriggling out of the pupal skin through a dorsal Y shaped slit and subsequently rests for about an hour on the surface of the mud until its wings are dried, a point of some practical importance when considering insecticidal methods of control.

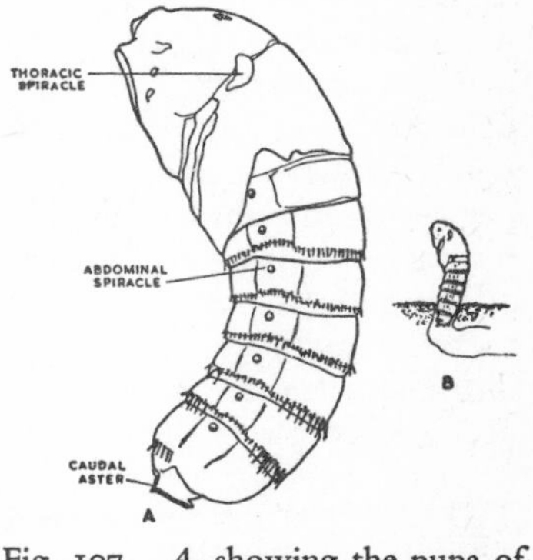

Fig. 107.   *A.* showing the pupa of a tabanid (*Chrysops* sp.) and *B.* showing how, in nature, the pupa is usually found projecting from the mud.

Whilst little is known about the mating habits of horse flies, it seems likely that it generally takes place in the vicinity of the breeding site, usually in the morning. In many instances the sexes appear to mate without a preliminary

swarming with the males, but there is a suggestion that in the case of certain forest-living species swarming may precede mating.

Tabanids are strong fliers and may range several miles from their breeding
sites in their search for food, and they readily follow moving objects, not only
animals but also cars and trains. Both males and females feed on sweet substances, which they obtain from flowers and other natural sources, and they
also take up water from damp mud or soil. While the males never suck blood
and only feed on vegetable sugars, the females of many species in addition to
imbibing plant juices, attack mammals and reptiles (but not birds) from which
they suck blood which is essential to the development of their ovaries.

Horse flies are not markedly host-specific and numerous species which
normally feed on wild and domestic mammals, will readily bite man if given
the opportunity. Whilst the great majority of tabanids only attack their hosts
during the hours of daylight, being active particularly in the earlier part of the
morning or the later part of the afternoon, a small number of species are known
to be nocturnal feeders. Most species (*Chrysops silacea* is an exception) are
strictly outdoor feeders and will not enter human habitations or animal shelters in their search for a host.

Tabanids, owing to their coarse mouthparts, and therefore painful bites,
tend to be intermittent blood-suckers, and this characteristic enhances their
importance as mechanical vectors of disease. Having succeeded in obtaining
a full blood-meal, following the biting of one or more hosts, the fly retires to
the shelter of the undersurface of leaves in the neighbouring vegetation, or
else rests on stones or on walls of nearby buildings or on the bark of trees.

Horse flies both in the tropical and temperate zones appear to be largely
seasonal in activity. In the tropics a general emergence from the pupae corresponds with the onset of the wetter months, the fly population being low
during the drier part of the year. Although the effect of temperature and humidity on the bionomics of the fly is not known it appears that larvae which fail to
pupate before the end of the rainy season will prolong their larval development so as to pupate at the onset of the following wet season. In semi-arid
regions, where the habitat dries out with the cessation of the rains, the larvae
of a number of species make little mud tubes in which they pass the adverse
season. In the temperate zones, adult flies begin to appear on the wing in the
spring, egg laying reaching its maximum in the summer, but with the onset
of the cold weather the flies cease to be active and disappear.

The medical importance of horse flies

In many parts of the world tabanid flies are a pest due to their biting habits
and may seriously interfere with the work of labour teams and other groups
engaged in outdoor activities. The species of tabanids biting man are mainly
confined to one of three genera, namely, *Tabanus*, *Haematopota* and *Chrysops*.
Flies belonging to the genus *Tabanus* are medium sized to very large, thick set
tabanids, with wings which are usually clear (although they may sometimes be
banded) and with short antennae of the type shown in Fig. 103 C. Members of

the genus *Haematopota* are medium sized, dark grey flies about 8 to 10 mm. in length with characteristic mottled wings and with short antennae of the type shown in Fig. 103B. The genus *Chrysops* is composed of medium sized flies, about 9–11 mm. in length with banded wings and with long antennae of the type shown in Fig. 103A. In many species the abdomen is yellow or orange, with black patches or black longitudinal bands.

Only the genus *Chrysops* contains species which transmit disease to man. In West Africa, *C. silacea* and *C. dimidiata* are vectors to man of loiasis, a disease caused by a filarial worm, *Loa loa,* which undergoes cyclical development in the body of the fly; in Central Africa *C. distinctipennis* is a vector of the same disease. In the United States, another species of *Chrysops, C. discalis,* acts as one of the vectors to man of tularaemia, a bacterial disease caused by *Pasteurella tularensis.*

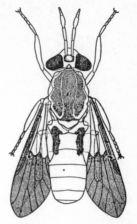

Fig. 108. Female *Chrysops silacea,* vector of *Loa loa.*

CHAPTER XXV

THE SUBORDER CYCLORRAPHA AND ITS DIVISION INTO FAMILIES OF MEDICAL IMPORTANCE

THE suborder Cyclorrapha is composed of a vast assemblage of two-winged flies ranging from minute creatures no longer than a few millimetres to insects as large as the blue bottle and the hover fly, whilst the different species vary in colour from sombre to bright metallic shades. The antenna consists of three segments, the first two of which are difficult to see whilst the third is large and carries on its dorsal surface a conspicuous bristle known as the arista, which may be either bare or hairy. The palps of cyclorraphous flies, unlike those of the suborders Nematocera and Brachycera, are always one-segmented. Whilst the wing venation is very variable throughout the suborder Cyclorrapha and although it is only of limited diagnostic value in the recognition of the families, nevertheless, in certain instances, such as in the case of the tsetse fly, it may prove of generic value.

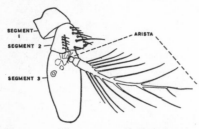

Fig. 109. The antenna of a fly belonging to the suborder Cyclorrhapha. The species depicted is *Musca domestica.*

The suborder Cyclorrapha is very extensive and is divided into a number of divisions, each of which consists of several families. Since this classification of the suborder as accepted by entomologists is somewhat complex, and since it is only amongst the calypterate Cyclorrapha that important vectors of disease occur, it is proposed to use a simpler classification and to consider the Cyclorrapha as being composed of two divisions, the medically unimportant acalypterate Cyclorrapha, in which the calypter (squama) is so poorly developed that it may be regarded as being lacking, and the calypterate Cyclorrapha in which the calypter can easily be recognised.

Although the acalypterates are not considered to be of any great medical significance, it is important to bear in mind that members of the genus *Hippelates* have been linked with the transmission of yaws in the West Indies. In addition, certain species of the genus *Hippelates* and *Siphunculina* have been held responsible for epidemics of conjunctivitis, and the larvae of certain acalypterate flies frequenting fruit have been associated with intestinal disturbances.

The cyclorraphous larva (Fig. 137A) is usually conical in shape, the anterior end forming the apex of the cone, and it is distinctly segmented with 12 apparent segments. The cuticle is commonly provided with rows or bands of minute spines usually along the posterior and anterior margins of each segment; in the case of certain species of blow flies these may be quite conspicuous

162

but normally they are difficult to see. The head is vestigial and the mouthparts, which are situated in the first few segments, consist essentially of a pair of mouth-hooks attached to a complex internal chitinous framework. The latter, which is commonly known as the "cephalopharyngeal skeleton", is distinctly visible through the integument of the larva, and its morphology is sometimes used in the identification of the species. There are two pairs of spiracles—an anterior and a posterior pair. The anterior spiracles are usually small and inconspicuous with finger-like processes but the posterior spiracles, the morphology of which is often of considerable use in classification, are large and situated on the posterior surface of the last segment of the body (Figs. 139 and 140).

When the cyclorraphous larva, unlike the nematocerous larva, metamorphoses to the pupa the last larval skin is retained as a protective covering which, in consequence, is known as the puparium (pl. puparia). In the case of the Cyclorrapha the adult fly emerges by rupturing the puparium along a circular seam at the anterior end, whereas in the Nematocera it emerges through a T-shaped slit in the pupal skin.

Although the suborder Cyclorrapha comprises 32 families of flies, only a small proportion of these contain species of medical importance. The two most important families are the Muscidae and the Calliphoridae which between them include most of the cyclorraphous flies responsible for ill health in man. In addition to these two families, a third family, the Oestridae, which by many authorities is considered to be a complex of families (Cuterebridae, Gasterophilidae, Oestridae (*sensu stricto*) and Hypodermatidae) contains a few species of medical importance.

CHAPTER XXVI

THE FAMILY MUSCIDAE

THE family Muscidae is an extensive family consisting, in the case of all the medically important species, of non-bristly, medium sized flies measuring from a quarter to half an inch in length; the antennae are always provided with an arista which is usually hairy. They are generally of a dull black, grey, or brown colour which is often relieved by darker brown or black markings on the thorax, and by ochreous bands or patches on the abdomen. The squamae are well developed and the mesoposnotum is so reduced as to appear absent. The wing venation, although not uniform enough to characterise the family, serves as a useful means of distinguishing, by differences in the morphology of the 4th longitudinal vein, between the various genera of medical importance within the family. The mouthparts, which lack mandibles and maxillae, consist either of a soft retractile proboscis adapted for the taking up of exposed semi-fluid or fluid food as in the case of the house fly, or are adapted for piercing the skin and sucking the blood of vertebrates, as in the case of the tsetse fly. Although mandibles and maxillae are absent in the blood-sucking species, these flies are able to pierce the skin of the host since the labium has become modified into a rigid, horny structure.

In all flies in the family Muscidae hypopleural bristles are absent, an all-important character in distinguishing them from flies in the family Calliphoridae in which they are present, but since these bristles are very difficult to see, it is usual in the case of the medically important species to depend on the more readily appreciated features of size, colouration, wing venation and morphology of the mouthparts.

The females of the medically important species are usually oviparous but the tsetse flies are exceptional in that they give birth to larvae which are fully developed and ready to pupate. The larvae (with the exception of those of the tsetse) are typical cyclorraphous larvae. The posterior spiracles are always easily seen and are of great assistance in the recognition of various genera of medical interest.

Although the "non-blood-sucking muscids" are non-parasitic, several species, and in particular the domesticated species, of *Musca* are of great importance in public health because of the frequency with which they occur in human habitations, such as houses and restaurants, and their habit of visiting fresh food and faeces indiscriminately. The group of flies known as "the blood-sucking muscids" includes the very important genus *Glossina* (which comprises many species which are vectors of African trypanosomiasis to man and animals) and also flies in the much less significant genus *Stomoxys*, one species of which is a biting pest of man.

The recognition, life-cycle and habits of the more important members of the family Muscidae are discussed in the following and subsequent chapters.

CHAPTER XXVII

THE FAMILY MUSCIDAE (cont.)

THE HOUSE FLY (*Musca domestica*) AND RELATED
SPECIES WHICH FREQUENT HUMAN HABITATIONS

THE genus *Musca*, which consists of about 70 species of flies, has a world wide distribution and is particularly well represented in tropical Asia and Africa. Although the genus consists of a large number of species, only a few have become so closely associated with human dwelling places as to merit the name of "house fly". The most important of these domesticated species is undoubtedly *Musca domestica*, which is found throughout the temperate zones of the world and is the common house fly of Europe, North America, New Zealand, Australia, South Africa and South America. Whilst *M. domestica* is almost completely replaced in tropical and subtropical countries by other domestic species of *Musca*, such as *M. vicina*, *M. nebulo* and *M. sorbens*, it is worthy of note that it has become established in some African and Oriental tropical ports to which it has been carried by ships.

The close association of the house fly with man attracted the attention of the early naturalists and many references to the life-cycle and habits of this ubiquitous insect may be found in early works on Natural History. The earliest detailed account of the life-cycle of a house fly appears to have been that of Gleicher who in 1766 published an excellently illustrated study of *Musca domestica*. Although from time to time many persons speculated on the possible connection of house flies with outbreaks of disease, particularly with regard to enteric infections such as typhoid, bacillary dysentery and summer diarrhoea, it was not until the work of Howard, who began to publish papers on the subject in 1896, that the attention of Public Health officials was focussed on the danger of allowing the breeding of the house fly to go unchecked. The publication of two important books, the first by Howard in 1911, and the second by Hewitt in 1914, in which the relationship of this insect to disease was emphasised, has done a great deal to draw attention to the dangers that the house fly presents to the community, particularly in localities where sewerage is primitive or neglected.

Since house flies possess only a soft retractile proboscis which is incapable of piercing the skin, they do not act as vectors of blood-borne infections, except when these are caused by organisms which also occur in man's excretions. Nevertheless, house flies are of great medical importance as mechanical vectors of many helminth, protozoal, bacterial and viral infections, in the temperate as well as in the tropical zones. The important part now known to be played by members of the genus *Musca* in transmitting these infections is in the main due to their habit of showing a great and indiscriminate liking for alighting on and feeding on human food supplies, and on human excretions, such as faeces, sputum, nasal secretions, pus and urine. Moreover, their habit, whilst they are feeding, of frequently vomiting and defaecating on fresh food and the ease with which they convey micro-organisms on their hairs and sticky tarsal pads makes them peculiarly suitable as conveyers of pathogenic organisms from faeces and other excretions to food.

The external morphology of the adult fly

Musca domestica and the other common species of *Musca* found frequenting human habitations are medium sized flies measuring about 6 to 9 mm. in length and varying in colour from mouse-grey to dark grey with 2 or 4 distinct longitudinal black stripes on the thorax. They can usually be recognised by their general appearance and wing venation.

The head. The head, as viewed from above, is oval, and bears a pair of purple-brown compound eyes, a pair of antennae of the typical cyclorraphous type and retractile suctorial mouthparts. The eyes, which are somewhat larger in the male than in the female, are bare and devoid of hairs. The antennae (see Fig. 109) each of which consists of three segments, are inconspicuous, lying in a depression on the face, and are not readily seen unless carefully looked for. The first two antennal segments are small whilst the third or terminal segment, which is narrowly oval in shape, is relatively much

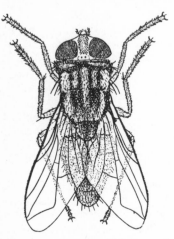

Fig. 110. The housefly *Musca domestica.*

larger and bears on the dorsal surface, near its base, an arista which is provided with dorsal and ventral hairs and is characterised by being swollen above its narrowed base and being attenuated at its tip.

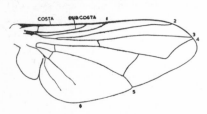

Fig. 111. Wing of the housefly, *Musca domestica.*

The mouthparts, collectively known as the proboscis, are capable of considerable extension and retraction. The proboscis is composed of a bulky labium and labella and a slender labrum and hypopharynx; although the proboscis of the house fly lacks mandibles and maxillae, the maxillary palps are well developed. The labium, which forms a gutter, in which lie the slender labrum and hypopharynx, consists of a chitinous basal portion known as the rostrum and a distensible distal portion known as the haustellum to which is attached a pair of large soft fleshy labella. The labrum is deeply channelled on its inner (posterior) surface, and the resultant gutter, when closed by the apposition of the blade-like hypopharynx, forms a tube up which food is conveyed to the pharynx. Saliva is conveyed to the mouth opening by the hypopharynx which is traversed by a minute tube which opens at the point where the labella are joined to the labium. Surrounding the mouth-opening is a sclerotised ring-like structure which bears ten teeth (the prestomal teeth) which are sometimes used by the fly during feeding, a function which will be described later. Each labellum, which is somewhat oval in shape and partially eversible, is attached independently of its fellow to the haustellum, its long axis lying at right angles to that of the labium. The labellum is covered on its inner surface with a very delicate membrane which is raised into about 30 parallel transverse ridges, marking the presence of small underlying tubes, which, because they are kept patent by means of

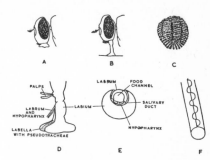

Fig. 112.   Diagrammatic representation of the proboscis of the house fly. *A.* resting position; *B.* feeding position; *C.* imprint of labella on feeding surface; *D.* seen in side view (in nature the labrum lies within the labial gutter); *E.* cross-section of the proboscis showing the labrum and the hypopharynx lying in the labial gutter; *F.* pseudotrachea showing minute openings through which fluid is sucked.

chitinous rings, and thus resemble tracheae, are known as pseudotracheae. Along the length of each pseudotrachea there is a series of small openings, each measuring from 3 to 4 microns in diameter, through which fluid and minute particles are sucked up into the lumen of the pseudotracheae which lead into a common channel opening at the mouth.

The thorax. The thorax is stout and either a mouse-grey or dark grey in colour with 2 or 4 broad, black, longitudinal dorsal stripes; whereas *M. domestica*, *M. vicina* and *M. nebulo* have four such stripes, *M. sorbens* has only two. The wing venation, which is shown in Fig. 111, is characterised by vein 4 which bends sharply to join the costa close to vein 3, leaving a narrowly opened cell between the third and fourth veins. Although this character is not confined to the genus *Musca*, it is, usually, a reliable guide to its identification if taken in conjunction with the general appearance of the insect. The three pairs of legs are similar in appearance, each leg terminating in a five-segmented tarsus, the last segment of which bears a pair of claws and a pair of pad-like structures (the pulvilli) each of which is provided with a large number of glandular hairs. These glandular hairs exude a substance which keep the pads constantly wet and sticky, with the result that particles readily adhere to them so that a fly visiting faeces and subsequently settling on fresh food may act as a direct conveyer of faecal material from human excrement to substances intended for human consumption.

The abdomen. The abdomen, which is usually coloured grey with bands or patches of light orange of varying size, is moderately short and broadly oval in

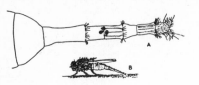

shape and is composed of 4 apparent segments. The remaining abdominal segments are kept withdrawn in the abdomen and are not normally visible. In the female fly the retracted segments are modified to form a segmented tube-like structure which, when extended and protruded from the abdomen, forms an ovipositor which is used in depositing the eggs.

Fig. 113. *A*. The ovipositor of the house fly; *B*. an ovigerous female with the ovipositor extended.

Special aspects of the internal anatomy which are important to an understanding of the role of the house fly as a carrier of disease

The aspects of the internal anatomy of the house fly which are of special interest to the medical officer are concerned almost entirely with the alimentary canal and its associated organs, the malpighian tubules and salivary ducts. The relationships of these various parts are shown in schematic form in Fig. 114.

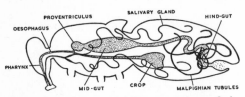

Fig. 114. Diagrammatic representation of the alimentary tract of the house fly.

It will be noted that the pharynx leads into the oesophagus which terminates at the proventriculus. Just before the oesophagus joins the proventriculus it gives off a long slender duct which expands, in the abdomen, to form a distensible thin-walled sac known as the crop, an organ which acts as a reservoir for the liquid food ingested by the fly. The contents of the crop are subsequently regurgitated through the proventriculus into the mid-gut to be digested and absorbed. Waste products find their way into the hind intestine (which is demarcated off from the mid-gut by the insertions of the malpighian tubules) and are then voided to the exterior through the anus. The salivary glands, which lie mainly in the abdomen, are long and coiled, and the salivary ducts, which unite in the thorax to form a common salivary duct, join the hypopharynx in the head.

The life-cycle and habits of the house fly

The life-cycles of all species of true house flies resemble each other so closely that it is unnecessary to describe each separately, and *Musca domestica* may be taken as the type.

About 2 to 3 days following mating the adult female is ready to lay her eggs. As a preliminary to oviposition, which always takes place in daylight, the fly alights on some material to which she is attracted. *Musca domestica, M. vicina,* and *Musca nebulo* are attracted to horse manure, particularly when it is not more than 24 hours old, but human faeces, especially in the form of fresh faeces or night soil is almost equally attractive. They will also deposit their eggs in the dung of other animals, particularly pig faeces, and readily oviposit in garbage dumps, heaps of household refuse and other similar decaying material. In general the material selected for egg-laying must be reasonably fresh, any material which has undergone considerable fermentation or which is "spent" being unsuitable for larval development. Whilst *Musca sorbens* has very similar oviposition habits to the other three species, it appears to favour cow dung if this is available.

After the female has alighted, she walks about on the surface of the material until she finds a crack or crevice. She then depresses her abdomen and having fully extended her ovipositor inserts it into the substrate and extrudes her eggs; sometimes, however, the fly does not wait to find an opening in the substrate but scatters her eggs over the surface.

STRIP OF CHORION

A   B

Fig. 115. Egg of the house fly. A. prior to hatching; and B. the empty egg shell.

The eggs, which are creamy-white in colour and measure 0.8 to 1.0 mm. in length are banana-shaped and are provided on the dorsal surface with two inconspicuous dorsal ridges.

About 100-150 eggs are matured at a time in the fly's ovaries. The gravid female either deposits the whole batch of ova at a single oviposition or she lays several clumps of eggs, sometimes over a period of time lasting as long as 24 hours. During her lifetime an adult fly will deposit anything from 5 to 20 such batches of eggs, depending on the environmental conditions and on the length of time she lives.

The eggs usually hatch in 6-12 hours under optimum conditions. Although an increase in temperature does not significantly shorten the hatching time, a lowering of temperature may prolong it very considerably. The egg is the most vulnerable stage in the life-cycle of *Musca*; it cannot resist drying and very few appear to survive at temperatures above 40°C or below 15°C. When the incubation period is over the larva emerges by forcing upwards the strip of chorion lying between the dorsal ridges of the egg.

The type of material to which house flies are attracted for oviposition is suitable for the future development of the larva, but the speed of development of the larva varies with the nature of the food supply and, under identical climatic conditions, the time occupied by the larval stage will vary from as little as a week in pig dung and horse manure to two weeks in human faeces and nearly three weeks in household refuse. The larva will complete development in a wide range of temperatures between 10° and 45°C., with an optimum at about 36°C. The temperature of the breeding medium is of importance, since it exerts a controlling influence on the speed of growth of the larva. Thus in summer the internal temperature of piles of decaying matter rises steeply and causes the larvae to migrate to the superficial layers where conditions are cooler, a habit which is made use of when employing such control measures as oiling the surface of manure heaps which are known to contain larvae. Other atmospheric conditions, in addition to temperature, influence larval life, thus the drying out of the larval habitat destroys the larvae since they can only feed on liquid food, but the nidus in which the larva lives must not be too moist since the maggots are easily drowned.

The time required, when nutritional conditions are good, for development throughout the three larval stages varies according to the season of the year. During hot weather larval development may be completed in three days, in cooler weather in a week, but if the prevailing temperatures drop still further this period may be prolonged to several weeks. The mature larva, which is white in colour, usually measures about 10-14 mm. in length, its size depending on the nature and availability, of the food supply and on the degree of crowding at the breeding site. The body, which is conical in shape and which

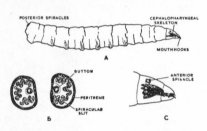

Fig. 116. *A.* larva of *Musca domestica*; *B.* enlarged view of posterior spiracles and *C.* enlarged view of anterior segments.

tapers gradually from the broad posterior end to the much attenuated head, is composed of twelve smooth segments which appear spineless when examined with a hand lens. The first (the smallest) segment, which may be regarded as the head, bears a pair of mouth-hooks which are unequal in size and appearance, a characteristic feature of the genus *Musca*. The mouth-hooks are supported on the cephalopharyngeal skeleton which is visible through the thin integument of the first few segments. The posterior surface of the last body segment bears a pair of spiracles, the posterior spiracles which, in all species of house flies, are D-shaped, with the straight side of each D facing the other. In *Musca domestica, M. vicina* and *M. nebulo* the peritreme, which forms the boundaries of the spiracular plate, is thin but in *M. sorbens* it is very thick. The spiracular openings, which number three on each plate, are sinuous and partly encircle a medianly placed button.

When full grown, the third stage larva, prior to pupation, ceases to feed and migrates, usually at night, away from the breeding material to a distance which may be anything from a foot or so to several yards, according to the hardness of the ground. Having found a suitable site the maggot burrows into the soil, down to a foot or more in loose dry soil, but only to a few inches in firmer soil. The larvae always migrate from the breeding site if the material remains moist, but if it has begun to dry out in the superficial layers, a small number of the larvae may remain in this portion of the material. Knowledge of this migratory habit of mature larvae prior to pupation is of great importance since it has been used as the basis for several methods of control, all of which involve trapping the larvae as they crawl away from the breeding material.

The actual process of pupation consists of a general contraction of the larva within its own integument which darkens and hardens within a period of 6 hours to form a barrel-shaped object, measuring about 6 mm. in length, known as the puparium. The hard puparial case, which affords excellent protection to the pupa lying within, bears traces of the segmentation of the larval skin and the form of the spiracles. Normally the pupal stage lasts 4-5 days during warm weather, but may be prolonged for a week or two in cooler weather; in addition a small proportion of the fly population survives the winter in the pupal stages.

Emergence of the adult fly from the puparium is effected by the separation of a cap which is forced up by the ptilinum, a sac-like structure which the fly protrudes from the frontal region of the head. Having emerged from the puparium the insect pushes its way up through the soil to the surface by the alternate inflation and deflation of the ptilinum, the emptying and filling of which is brought about by the action of certain body muscles causing changes in the blood volume of the sac. On reaching the surface the fly crawls about until the wings unfold and the body

Fig. 117. House fly emerging from the puparium (which usually lies below the surface), with the ptilinum extended.

wall hardens. Having emerged from the puparium the fly takes to the wing in search of food, mating being delayed for a few days.

The house fly is omnivorous, feeding on a vast variety of substances. Since its mouthparts only allow it to take up fluids, it generally feeds on liquid or semi-liquid substances; it does, however, frequently take nourishment from solid material, the surface of which it has previously softened with saliva and vomit. When the house fly is feeding on these different food supplies, the four main types of position taken up by the labella may be described as "the filtering position", "the cupping position", "the scraping position" and "the direct feeding position". On thin or moderately thin layers of such fluid substances as syrup, milk, serum or pus, only the pseudotracheal surfaces of the labella (and not the prestomal teeth) are brought into contact with the substrate (Fig. 118 A-B). In the "filtering position" (Fig. 118 A), used for sucking

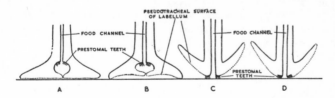

Fig. 118. Diagrammatic representation of the proboscis of the house fly showing the positions assumed when feeding on different types of food. *A.* filtering position (thin films, e.g. milk); *B.* cupping position (moderately thin films, e.g. syrup, serum, pus); *C.* scraping position; *D.* direct feeding position.

fluid from liquid films, the pseudotracheae are pressed against the substrate, whereas in the "cupping position" (Fig. 118 B), used for moderately thin layers (such as drops of syrup or serum), the pseudotracheal surface is cupped; in both these positions liquid, and minute particles, are sucked up through the very small pseudotracheal openings. If the fly feeds on hard and moderately dry substances such as cheese, blood clots or recent healing wound surfaces, the labella are everted, so that the prestomal teeth are exposed and scrape the surface of the substrate; following the act of scraping, the surface is moistened with saliva and the regurgitated contents of the crop (known as the "vomit"). The labella then assume "the filtering position" and the moistened food is taken up by the fly (Fig. 118 C). In the "direct feeding position", as when the fly is feeding on semi-solid or glutinous substances such as human or animal excrement or sputum, the labella are completely everted, so that the prestomal teeth do not function; in this position food substances are sucked up directly into the food channel without the intervention of the filtering action of the pseudotracheae (Fig. 118 D).

House flies are for ever in search of food and because of their high intake of nourishment they defaecate very often, so that a well fed insect may deposit faeces constantly, with as little as 5 minutes interval between each drop of faeces. This constant discharge of excreta is one of the many factors which make the house fly a very dangerous carrier of disease.

Whilst *Musca domestica* and other species of *Musca* are essentially domestic flies and usually confine their search for food to human dwellings or their neighbourhood, nevertheless, this is not always the case, for they are vigorous fliers, and, particularly in less dense suburban communities, they will range over several square miles from their breeding places, such factors as odours and prevailing metereological conditions (temperature, light and wind) playing an important part in their dispersal. In addition, their flight range is influenced by the density of the human population and the general state of hygiene of the community. House flies are active only in the daytime and at night rest in corners of rooms and on such places as the ceiling and on lamp frames.

Whilst house flies are prevalent all the year round in the tropics, in the temperate zones their numbers fall off sharply with the approach of winter, so that they virtually disappear in cold weather. It seems almost certain that a proportion of the flies normally winter as puparia and with the onset of the warm, weather the population may increase very rapidly, particularly in insanitary conditions, unless control measures directed at the breeding sites are undertaken.

House flies and disease

The outstanding importance of house flies as mechanical vectors of disease, particularly of diseases caused by bacteria, is in the main due to two factors. In the first place the house fly sucks up its nourishment from a wide variety of substances, which include such contaminated material from human sources as excreta, sputum, nasal secretions, and the excretions from sores and wounds, and at the same time it shows an equal fondness for food stuffs partaken of by man. Secondly, the fly possesses an external and internal structure particularly well adapted for the taking up and carrying of living organisms from the contaminated material to prepared food stuffs. The various modes of feeding adopted by the fly have a very definite bearing on the size of the particles which it takes up when feeding. During feeding involving the "filtering position" and the "cupping position" all large particles are strained off, so that only bacteria or viruses can pass into the alimentary tract, but the "scraping position", which produces sufficient rasping effect to cut through the proglottid of a tapeworm, and the "direct feeding position" allow various cestode and nematode eggs as well as protozoan·cysts to enter the gut.

In this way the causative organisms of typhoid and paratyphoid, dysentery (both bacillary and amoebic), conjunctivitis, cholera and several other bacterial and virus diseases, and probably various helminth infections, may be transmitted to man by the house fly. This transference may be accomplished in one of three ways. In the first place the fly may carry organisms on any part of the body and particularly on the proboscis or on the glandular hairs of the pulvilli. Secondly, organisms may be ingested with the food of the fly, and, passing through the alimentary canal, may be deposited on food stuffs during the act of defaecation, which usually takes place whilst the fly is feeding. Thirdly, organisms may be conveyed on to food through the agency of the vomit (the "vomit drop") which is so often used by the fly when feeding on solid or semi-solid food that it is of particular significance in disease transmission. Not only may large numbers of bacteria and virus particles be regurgitated from the crop but a limited number of larger organisms such as protozoal cysts may also be deposited on to food in this way.

In addition to its role as an indirect cause of disease, the house fly sometimes affects man directly, since its larva is occasionally found in recently passed stools and, more commonly, in suppurating wounds.

CHAPTER XXVIII

THE FAMILY MUSCIDAE (cont.)

NON-BITING MUSCIDS, OTHER THAN THE HOUSE FLY,
WHICH FREQUENT HUMAN HABITATIONS.

BESIDES *Musca domestica* and other domestic species of *Musca* the only muscid flies commonly frequenting human habitations belong to the genera *Fannia* and *Muscina*, the members of which have an almost worldwide distribution.

The genus *Fannia*

Flies belonging to the genus *Fannia* resemble *Musca domestica* very closely in their general appearance, but since they are somewhat smaller than the

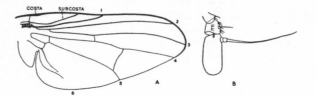

Fig. 119. *A.* wing and *B.* antenna of *Fannia* sp.

house fly (they measure 6-7 mm.) they are commonly designated as "lesser house flies". In addition to their smaller size, they may be distinguished from other domestic muscids, including members of the genus *Muscina*, by their wing venation and by the arista which is bare. The genus *Fannia* contains two species which are commonly met with in dwelling places, *F. canicularis* ("the lesser house fly") which has 3 longitudinal brown stripes on the thorax, and *F. scalaris* ("the latrine fly") which has two such stripes.

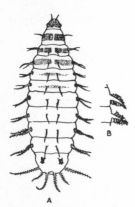

Fig. 120. *A.* full grown larva of *Fannia canicularis* *B.* lateral processes of *F. scalaris* shown for comparison.

F. canicularis lays 50 to 100 eggs in such food materials as decomposing cheese, bacon and dried fish, and in the urine soaked bedding of animals. *Fannia scalaris* lays its eggs in similar substances but shows a predilection for the faeces of man and animals, especially when these are in a liquid state. The eggs of both species hatch in one to two days.

The larvae, when full grown, measure 5-6 mm. and have a characteristic appearance. The body, which is oval in shape and flattened dorso-ventrally, is adorned with a number of conspicuous fleshy processes each of which bears smaller secondary projections. Whereas in *F. canicularis* the main processes are slender and the secondary processes are small and spiniferous, in *F. scalaris* the main processes are large and fleshy and the secondary processes are stout, giving this species a feathered appearance.

Larval life, which is passed in the material in which the eggs were laid, is completed in one to two weeks, but this period may be prolonged if the nidus dries out, as it is apt to do in the case of *F. canicularis* which breeds in a drier medium than *F. scalaris*. At the completion of their development the larvae migrate to drier conditions in order to pupate, the puparium, which is brown in colour, maintaining the form of the larva very closely. The imago emerges in one to two weeks, the whole life-cycle lasting about one month.

The adults of both species often enter houses in large numbers, particularly where insanitary conditions prevail. The feeding habits and feeding mechanisms of both species of *Fannia* are similar to those of *M. domestica* but since they do not tend to alight on human food supplies to the same extent as the house fly they are not considered to be as serious a menace to public health.

Since the larvae of both species have been found in recently passed stools and urine they have been suspected of causing intestinal and urinary myiasis. The ingestion of the larvae with food, the deposition of eggs in or near the urino-genital orifice, and the introduction of larvae by improperly cleaned instruments have been cited as causes of these forms of myiasis, but it should not be forgotten that in these, as in many other instances, the presence of unnoticed larvae in a utensil before its use may give rise to erroneous conclusions.

The genus *Muscina*

Flies belonging to the genus *Muscina* are usually slightly larger than the house fly. The only species which is common in human habitations is *Muscina stabulans* ("the false stable fly"). This species has four longitudinal black stripes on the thorax, and closely resembles the house fly from which it can be distinguished by the wing venation in which the 4th vein is clearly separated from the 3rd at the wing margin.

Muscina scatters its eggs indiscriminately over the surface of decaying animal and vegetable matter such as

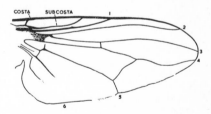

Fig. 121. Wing of *Muscina* sp.

rotting fruit and vegetables, raw and cooked meats and decaying carcases, and on human and animal excrement. About 150 to 200 eggs, which hatch in one to two days, are laid in the course of a single oviposition.

The larva, which resembles that of *Musca domestica*, may be distinguished from the latter by the morphology of its posterior spiracles. Each spiracle is almost round in outline and has a wide, strongly chitinised peritreme, within which lie three crescent-shaped slits. No conspicuous button is present and the

Fig. 122. Posterior spiracles of the full grown larva of *Muscina* sp.

mouthhooks, unlike those of *Musca,* are equal in size. The larvae are omnivorous, and may be predacious feeding on other fly larvae including *Musca domestica.* When full grown they crawl to drier ground to pupate. The pupal stage lasts one to two weeks, the whole life-cycle occupying about one month.

The adults have the same disease-carrying potentialities as *Musca*, but as they are not so closely associated with foodstuffs they are of less significance in this respect. The larvae like those of *Musca* and *Fannia* have been recorded as causing myiasis.

CHAPTER XXIX

THE FAMILY MUSCIDAE (cont.)

The genus *Glossina*

THE genus *Glossina* includes all the so-called "tsetse flies" numbering about 23 species. The word "tsetse" is of long usage and appears to have been derived from an African word meaning "the fly destructive of cattle". Tsetse flies are of great medical significance since they are the vectors, both to man and to his domestic stock, of African trypanosomiasis, which is transmitted by them mechanically (at any rate in the case of cattle), as well as cyclically. The peculiar and commanding place of cattle in African society gives a special importance to a disease which is responsible for large areas of good pastoral country remaining neglected.

The characteristic features of trypanosomiasis in man and in his domestic stock must have long been recognised; indeed as early as the 14th century an Arabian writer described the long illness and subsequent death of a Sultan of the great Malli kingdom in terms which leave no doubt that the disease was sleeping sickness. It was not until 1895, however, that the classical work of Bruce and his associates showed that the cause of the disease in cattle was a trypanosome which was transmitted to these animals by the tsetse. The discovery by Dutton in 1901 of trypanosomes in the blood of a sleeping sickness patient was later followed by the work of Bruce and his collaborators who showed that, as in the case of cattle, these organisms were transmitted by the tsetse.

Both sexes suck blood and are equally capable of transmitting trypanosomiasis. Both "nagana" (an African word signifying trypanosomiasis of cattle) and sleeping sickness (the name given to the disease in man) occur in a well defined area in Tropical Africa which corresponds with the geographical distribution of the genus *Glossina*. This area is almost entirely restricted to a zone lying between, approximately, 15° North and 20° South of the equator, and to a narrow strip of the East African Coast extending to some 30° further South (see Fig. 123). Tsetse flies are not evenly distributed throughout these areas; indeed, there are extensive tracts of country which are unsuitable for their breeding and, therefore, free from their presence.

Fig. 123. Map showing the distribution of the tsetse fly, genus *Glossina*. Some small isolated areas occur outside the distribution shown.

External anatomy of the adult fly

Tsetse flies are elongated, robust, medium sized, yellowish to black-brown flies measuring approximately 6 to 15 mm. in length; whereas in some species

Fig. 124. A tsetse fly in the resting attitude. The species depicted is *Glossina pallidipes*.

the abdominal segments are uniformly coloured, in others they are adorned with light coloured stripes. The tsetse may easily be distinguished from other biting flies by the presence of a very conspicuous forwardly projecting proboscis (which is held parallel to the substrate when the fly is at rest) and by a wing venation which is particularly characteristic. Although tsetse flies possess other anatomical features peculiar to the genus *Glossina*, the medical officer should find this general description quite sufficient for the purpose of recognising the genus.

The head. The head is moderately large and bears a pair of compound eyes, a pair of antennae and a prominent, slender, rigid proboscis, with which is associated a pair of long palps. The eyes in both sexes occupy the sides of the head, and are widely

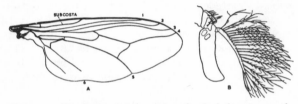

Fig. 125. *A.* wing and *B.* antenna of a fly belonging to the genus *Glossina.*

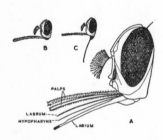

Fig. 126. The heads of tsetse flies seen in profile. *A.* the labrum and the hypopharynx have been separated from the groove of the labium in which they are normally carried; *B.* position of the mouthparts when the fly is at rest; *C.* position of the mouthparts when the fly is feeding.

separated by the frons and vertex. The antennae are highly characteristic, each consisting of three segments, the first two of which are small and not readily visible while the third is large and somewhat banana-shaped in outline. The third antennal segment bears, close to its origin from the second, an arista characterised by the presence of branched hairs on the upper surface.

The proboscis consists of a pair of long, non-segmented palps which enclose and hide from view the fascicle of the insect. The biting fascicle is composed of a labrum, a hypopharynx and a labium all three of which are chitinised. The labium, unlike that of the house fly, is a horny organ which is adapted for piercing the integument of vertebrates and which terminates in two eversible toothed labella. As in all other cyclorrhaphous flies of medical importance there are no mandibles or maxillae. If the units of the fascicle are separated, it will be seen that the largest structure is the labium which consists of a basal bulbous portion extending forwards as a long gutter

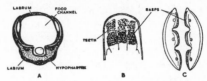

Fig. 127.   A. cross section of the proboscis of the tsetse fly; B. internal aspect of inner wall of labellum; C. section through the closed labella.

and enclosing within its cavity the slender hypopharynx and the relatively broad labrum. The hypopharynx (which is traversed by an extremely fine salivary duct) and the labrum together form the food channel up which the blood-meal travels to the pharynx of the fly.

When the insect is about to feed, it separates its palps and the fascicle is directed vertically downwards (see Fig. 126 C). The labella, each of which is armed with denticles at the tip and with rasps on the inner surface, are pressed against the skin and as the fascicle is driven in, the fly steadies itself by gripping the skin with its claws. Penetration into the subcutaneous tissues is effected by means of the everted labella, the rasps of which enable the fascicle to be drawn into the deeper tissues. The fascicle bends in various directions and when a suitable haemorrhage is formed the fly engorges.

The thorax. The thorax is stout and marked on its dorsal surface with dark brown stripes and spots. The wings which are long have the very characteristic venation shown in Fig. 125 A. The closed cell shown in the diagram as lying between the 4th and 5th veins is sometimes described as the "hatchet" cell, that part of the cell nearer the thorax forming the handle and that nearer the wing margin the blade. When the fly is at rest the long wings which project beyond the posterior extremity of the abdomen are kept folded over the back, like the blades of a closed pair of scissors. The legs are moderately long and are held slightly spread out when the fly is resting (see Plate IX).

The abdomen. Whereas in most muscid flies only four abdominal segments are visible from the dorsal surface, in *Glossina* six segments can be counted. The abdomen may be either uniformly dark brown or black brown in colour, or adorned with transverse light brown or yellow coloured stripes.

The sexes can easily be distinguished from one another; whilst in the female the external genitalia are inconspicuous, in the male they take the form of a circular chitinous plate

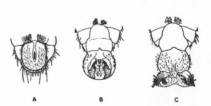

Fig. 128.   Diagrammatic representation of the external genitalia of a male tsetse fly. A. normal resting position; B. appearance when the chitinous plate is turned down with a needle; C. as in B, but with the claspers turned down. The species depicted is G. palpalis.

on the ventral surface of the tip of the abdomen which, if the fly is examined in the lateral view, appears as a knob-like protuberance (Fig. 128 A). If in a freshly killed fly, a needle is inserted between the protuberance and the ventral surface of the abdomen, the plate can be turned back still hinged to the tip of the abdomen (Fig. 128 B) and if the process is continued a second plate hinged to the tip of the first plate can be exposed (Fig. 128 C). This second plate is seen to consist of two lateral chitinised pieces, known as claspers, which in many species of tsetse flies are connected by a median membrane. The morphology of the claspers differs in each particular species of tsetse fly and these differences are made use of by the systematist.

The internal anatomy of the tsetse fly considered in relation to disease transmission

The only internal organs calling for detailed consideration are the alimentary canal and the salivary glands, since an understanding of these structures is essential in following the life-cycle of certain trypanosomes while in the insect host. The food channel, which is formed by the labrum and labium, leads into the short pharynx which is followed by the oesophagus. The oesophagus, which in the fore-part of the thorax terminates in the bulbous proventriculus, gives off a long slender duct which expands in the abdomen to form the large thin-walled crop. From the proventriculus the narrow anterior part of the mid-gut passes through the remainder of the thorax to enter the abdomen in which lies the much convoluted posterior portion, together with the short hind-gut. The four malpighian tubules mark the beginning of the hind-gut which terminates at the anus.

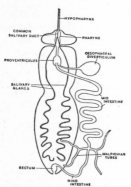

Fig. 129. Diagrammatic representation of the alimentary tract of a tsetse fly.

The peritrophic membrane, which in the tsetse plays an essential role in the life-cycle of the trypanosomes responsible for sleeping sickness, is formed at the junction of the proventriculus and the mid-gut and lines the whole of the mid-gut and part of the hind-gut as an inner sleeve. When first produced in the vicinity of the proventriculus, it is soft and delicate but it becomes tougher as it is passed down the gut.

In proportion to the size of the insect the paired salivary glands, which are slender coiled tubes lying in the abdomen, are enormously long, considerably longer than the insect itself. The salivary ducts lead through the thorax to the head where they become attenuated and unite to form a common duct which leads to the hypopharynx.

When the fly feeds the trypanosomes taken up with the blood-meal pass down the gut until they come to the free edge of the peritrophic membrane in the hind-gut; at this point they "turn the corner" to lie between the peritrophic membrane and the gut wall. Once ensconced between the peritrophic membrane and the gut wall the trypanosomes multiply rapidly. Having completed the first stage of their development the trypanosomes migrate forwards towards the proventriculus in the neighbourhood of which they traverse the peritrophic membrane, re-enter the lumen of the gut in the proventricular region, and pass up the oesophagus to the pharynx.

Most authorities hold the view that from the pharynx the trypanosomes proceed up labrum and, having reached the tip of the hypopharynx, they reverse their journey and proceed down the hypopharynx to the common salivary duct and thence to the glands. In the salivary glands the trypanosomes complete their development to the infective form and are injected with the saliva, when the fly feeds.

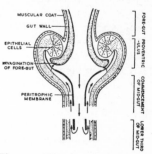

Fig. 130. Diagrammatic representation of longitudinal sections through the fore and midgut of a tsetse fly. The course pursued by the developing trypanosomes after ingestion is indicated by the arrows.

Life-cycle of the tsetse fly

In all the Diptera so far considered it has been shown that reproduction of the species is effected by the laying of large numbers of eggs at varying intervals. In the genus *Glossina*, however, a single egg hatches in as specialised part of the genital canal, known as the uterus, and the resultant larva is full grown before it leaves the parent. It is clear that if this solitary birth is to compete successfully against the mass production of other Diptera, then the single offspring must be very carefully protected. In point of fact, this is the case, and the reproductive system of the female tsetse is specially adapted for looking after the needs of the egg and larva while *in utero*.

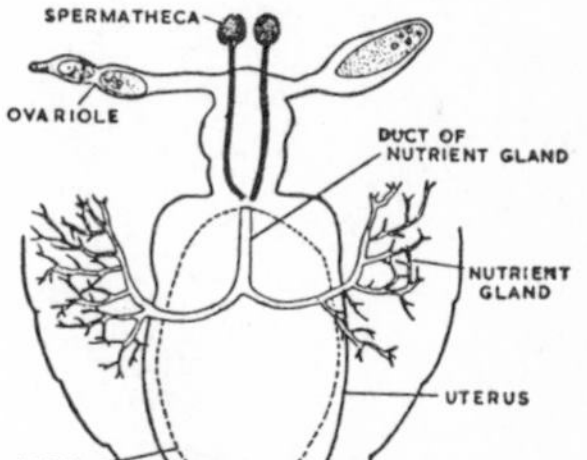

Fertilisation of the female by the male is effected within a few days after emergence, the spermatozoa being stored in the spermatheca in readiness to fertilise the eggs following each ovulation. The egg, which is banana-shaped and white in colour, measures about 1.5 mm. and possesses a distinctly reticulated shell. The larva which emerges from the egg 3 to 4 days later remains in the uterus, the empty egg shell and also the subsequent larval pelts being expelled through the vaginal orifice by means of a special organ known as the choriothete situated in the uterine wall. The uterus which is capable of very great distension is provided with a pair of racemose tubular milk glands (analogous to the accessory glands of certain cyclorraphous flies) the common duct of

Fig. 131. Diagrammatic representation of the internal genitalia of a female tsetse fly, containing a full grown larva.

which enters the uterine cavity at its upper pole. The larva lies in the uterus with its mouth in contact with the opening of the milk gland duct and it feeds by imbibing the white nutrient fluid (the "milk") produced by the glands. Production of adequate secretion from these glands is dependent on good nutrition of the mother and any undue interference with the obtaining of frequent blood-meals, and therefore with the flow of "milk", may result in abortion. It is believed that the oxygen requirements of the larva are supplied through the two additional stigmata, known as the polypneustic lobes. The larva undergoes three instars and becomes full grown in some 8 to 12 days, the period of maximum growth taking place during the third instar and in this, the final stage of pregnancy, the distended uterus occupies most of the abdominal cavity. The cast skins produced at the first two moults are, as previously explained, expelled through the vaginal orifice.

Larviposition lasts only a few minutes, the larva wriggling out of the genital orifice of the female with its posterior end appearing first, so that the birth may be described as a "breech presentation".

The larva, which measures almost a centimetre, is an active, maggot-like creature with some nine, not very marked, abdominal segments. The body, which is of a pale yellow or whitish colour, bears a conspicuous black "collar" at the posterior end terminating in two large, black, shining lobes—the polypneustic lobes (see Plates X and XI).

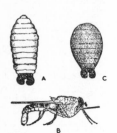

Fig. 132. *A.* the full grown larva of the tsetse fly immediately after deposition; *B.* a tsetse fly in the act of larviposition (after Newstead); *C.* the puparium of the tsetsefly.

The places selected for larviposition are always in the shade, and include such sites as the shelter of trees and bushes, beneath rocks, fallen logs, the mouths of caves, and cavities in trees, and even rot holes in trees above ground level. The ground must be loose enough to allow the larva to burrow and must be reasonably dry, otherwise the nature of the soil selected does not seem to matter very much and varies from humus and rotting leaves, to sand.

As soon as the larva is dropped on to the soil by the female it burrows down one or two inches below the surface and turns into a pupa in about a quarter of an hour. The tsetse fly pupates in the same manner as other cyclorraphous flies, so that pupation takes place within the skin of the 3rd instar larva. The larva contracts considerably to form a barrel-shaped object varying between 5 and 8 mm. in length, with the prominent polypneustic lobes of the larva still clearly visible. The puparium, which retains the form of the larva, is hard and rigid and is dark reddish brown to black in colour. The ease of recognition of the puparium is a point of some practical importance, because it is possible to train even young children to find and recognise the characteristic puparia without difficulty (see Plate XI, Fig. 2).

The adult fly emerges, by pushing off a cap at the end of the puparium, about a month after pupation. When the newly emerged fly has forced its way up to the surface of the soil, it runs about actively on the ground for a quarter of an hour or so, before taking to the wing. It then remains relatively inactive for a day or two, after which it is ready to seek its first blood-meal.

The length of life of the tsetse varies considerably according to the season, hot dry weather shortening the life-span. It is probable that the average length of life is about 2 to 3 months, but that in optimum conditions flies may survive as long as five months. Since the gestation period is usually 8 to 12 days and since repeated coitus is unnecessary, the female tsetse may produce two or three offspring for each month of life.

The only food of the fly is blood. In nature the interval between meals appears to be 4 or 5 days, although this period may be reduced if the saturation deficiency is high, or lengthened (even up to about 10 days) if it is low. Both the male and female flies feed only on the blood of vertebrates and their hosts range from reptiles to large ungulates. Although several species of tsetse feed on reptiles as well as on warm-blooded animals, and although no species of tsetse is known to feed exclusively on one type of host, nevertheless each species shows some degree of host preference. In general, ungulates (including cattle) appear to be favoured as hosts and if these are removed from a district certain species of tsetse, for instance *G. morsitans* and *G. swynnertoni*, will tend to disappear, whilst other species such as *G. palpalis* and *G. tachinoides* show a fall in population numbers.

Shade and a correct degree of humidity are necessary for the adult flies and for their puparia; but whereas the latter have no power of altering their position and must perish unless they remain constantly in a suitable habitat, the former often leave, although only for a short time, such habitats in order to seek their blood-meals. Tsetse flies are associated with woody vegetation of many types and are absent from extensive plains, closely cultivated areas or areas densely inhabitated by human populations. Most species use two types of vegetation, one being used for breeding, whilst the adult flies frequent another.

Ecologically the genus *Glossina* falls into two main groups (1) a group composed of the riverine species such as *G. palpalis* and *G. tachinoides* which inhabit the vegetation along the banks of rivers and lakes, and (2) a group comprising such woodland species as *G. morsitans* and *G. swynnertoni* which live in rather open, lightly wooded parkland away from water.

Tsetse flies breed throughout the year except at the height of the rains, when the excessive humidity and low evaporative power of the air results in a drop in reproduction for about a month. The season of abundance and spread of the flies centripetally is mainly during the period of the early rains, when the temperature, the saturation deficiency and the availability of the food hosts are generally most favourable, and when sites suitable for larviposition are most numerous. In the dry season, the fly population is at a minimum and becomes concentrated in certain limited areas where the vegetation provides a suitable microclimate. Such centres or foci are referred to as "permanent breeding places", "primary foci" or "homes".

Feeding takes place in daylight and, in general, the adults move out into more open spaces and to the edges of breeding grounds in order to hunt for prey. They hunt by sight and, probably to a less extent, by smell; movement rather than form attracts them, and they will follow moving vehicles. The most suitable places for the hunting and feeding activities of the adult tsetse flies are alongside roads, paths, glades and edges of thickets in more open country, on the banks of streams and rivers, animal water holes and ferry jetties.

It should be explained that it is becoming increasingly clear that the distribution and the maintenance of various species of *Glossina* in certain areas are dependent on many factors in addition to those we have mentioned in the foregoing brief account.

A proportion of tsetse succeed in gaining a foothold in previously fly-free country as a result of the wide dispersal which occurs during the rains, for at this season of the year tsetse flies are prepared to fly considerable distances from their homes; others may be conveyed into previously fly-free country by following animals, man, or any moving object. Again, they may enter boats, trains, motor cars or aeroplanes (as in the case of the living tsetse flies which arrived in Brazil in a plane from Africa) and so be mechanically transported into new areas.

Tsetse flies and trypanosomiasis

Any species of tsetse may be a vector of trypanosomiasis to man but the chief vectors are *Glossina palpalis*, *G. tachinoides*, *G. morsitans*, *G. swynnertoni* and *G. pallidipes*.

Glossina palpalis and *G. tachinoides* are riverine species and the main vectors of Gambian sleeping sickness, caused by *Trypanosoma gambiense*. These flies frequent restricted spots at fords and watering places, at lake sides and along banks of rivers where they hunt for a host and they may feed repeatedly on human beings who converge towards the same spot to cross a river or to fetch water, so that a focus of infection may be established in quite a small locality. *G. palpalis* occurs in West Africa and ranges across Central Africa to the region of the Great Lakes—L. Rupert, L. Victoria and L. Tanganyika; it prefers dense humid forest with a woody undergrowth. *G. tachinoides* is limited to West Africa and, although it occurs in riverine forests like *G. palpalis*, it prefers a less dense undergrowth.

The chief vector of Rhodesian sleeping sickness, which is caused by *Trypanosoma rhodesiense*, is *G. morsitans*, and other important species are *G. swynnertoni* and *G. pallidipes*. These flies are found in areas thinly populated by human beings and bite "game animals" and cattle in preference to man; notwithstanding this fact they are responsible for numerous cases of human trypanosomiasis in Central and East Africa. *G. morsitans* has a very wide distribution from West Africa to East Africa and ranges down the eastern side of Africa to Portuguese East Africa. It is found in woodland savannah, where trees and thickets are distributed in close proximity providing a canopy of branches and leaf which is high but not uniformly dense, and here the fly may be found over areas as large as 1000 square miles. G. *swynnertoni* has a restricted distribution in East Africa whilst G. *pallidipes* occurs along a long belt of East Africa. Both these species frequent more open savannah country than does G. *morsitans*.

A pictorial key to some of the more important species of tsetse flies will be found at the end of Chapter LIII.

CHAPTER XXX

THE FAMILY MUSCIDAE (cont.)

The genera *Stomoxys, Haematobia* and *Lyperosia*

IN addition to *Glossina*, at least three other genera of muscids contain species which are blood-suckers and which attack domestic stock and, in the case of one species, man. The three genera concerned are *Stomoxys, Haematobia* and *Lyperosia*; several species of flies in all three genera are important pests of man's domestic stock (particularly cattle, horses and dogs) in various parts of the world but only one species, *Stomoxys calcitrans*, is known also to feed on man.

The stable fly (*Stomoxys calcitrans*)

Stomoxys calcitrans, which has a worldwide distribution is commonly known as the "stable fly" although it is often called the "dog fly" in the United States. It is primarily a pest of domestic animals but it readily bites man if given the opportunity. Although it transmits several diseases of farm animals it is not a proven vector of any parasitic infection to man.

Stomoxys calcitrans, which is about the same size as the house fly, is of a dark grey colour, with four brown-black longitudinal bands on the thorax. The

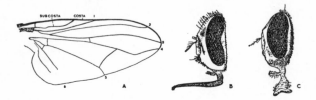

Fig. 133.   *A.* wing of the stable fly (*Stomoxys calcitrans*). *B.* head of the stable fly seen in profile; *C.* head of the house fly for comparison.

wing venation although differing sharply from that of *Musca* and *Fannia* resembles that of *Muscina*. The head of *Stomoxys* is characterised by the presence of a slender, elongate, rigid, non-retractile proboscis, and the antennae bear aristae which show feathering on the upper surface only.

In its general morphology *Stomoxys calcitrans* resembles *Musca, Fannia* and *Muscina* so closely in appearance that it is often mistaken for one of these flies by the layman, who is liable to complain of having been "bitten by a house fly". From members of these three genera it can readily be distinguished by the possession of a rigid projecting proboscis while it differs from blood-sucking flies occurring in the genera *Lyperosia* and *Haemotobia* by the fact that the palps in *Stomoxys* are relatively short as compared with those of flies in the other two genera. In the tropics the only other fly with which *Stomoxys* is likely to be

PLATE IX

A tsetse fly (*Glossina palpalis*) in the resting attitude.
[*Courtesy Mr. W. Petana*]

PLATE X

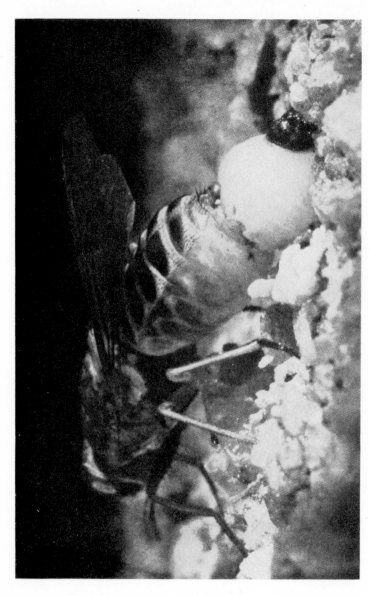

A tsetse fly (*Glossina palpalis*) in the act of depositing its larva.

[*Courtesy Mr. W. Petana*]

PLATE XI

FIG. 1. The larva of a tsetse fly (*Glossina palpalis*).
[*Courtesy Mr. W. Petana*]

FIG. 2. The puparium of a tsetse fly (*Glossina palpalis*).
[*Courtesy Mr. W. Petana*]

PLATE XII

African technicians collecting biting flies by two different methods.
[*Courtesy Mr. W. Petana*]

confused is the tsetse and it can be distinguished from it by its smaller size, by the wing venation, and by the arista. In addition the feeding attitude is often characteristic, for whereas the tsetse keeps its wings folded and buries its fascicle in the tissues, *Stomoxys* feeds with the wings slightly separated and inserts no more than one third of its proboscis.

The life-cycle of *Stomoxys calcitrans*

About 10 days following fertilisation and the taking of a blood-meal the female is ready to lay her eggs. The eggs, which are creamy-white in colour and measure about 1 mm. bear a general resemblance to those of *Musca*. They are usually laid in small groups of 4 to 20, although occasionally they may be deposited in batches as large as 50 to 70. The sites selected for oviposition are horse manure and other animal dung, particularly when mixed with liberal amounts of straw and stable bedding. The eggs are also laid in collections of decaying and fermenting vegetable matter such as grass clippings and farm refuse; in addition *Stomoxys* has been known to breed in grasses and seaweeds thrown up on sea-shores by tidal action.

The eggs hatch in 1 to 4 days; the larva which is an active creature requires, in addition to the food substances already mentioned, darkness and a high degree of moisture. In consequence breeding tends to occur in heaped up decaying vegetable matter, and the spreading of such material (which is a recognised method of control) results in the death of the larvae. The period of time required by the larva to reach maturity is considerably longer than that required by the house fly larva; whilst in warm conditions larval development may take as little as 10 days, in cooler conditions it may take a month or longer.

There are 3 larval stages. The mature larva which measures 11-12 mm. in length is a typical maggot and is creamy-white in colour. The posterior spiracles are rather small, nearly circular in outline and widely separated one from the other. The spiracular plate is dark and no peritreme can be distinguished. The

Fig. 134. Posterior spiracles of the full grown larva of *Stomoxys calcitrans*

spiracular slits are small and S-shaped, and the centrally placed button is poorly defined.

When full grown the larvae, like those of the house fly, migrate some distance away from the breeding site and burrow into the soil prior to pupation. The puparium, which is a dark brown in colour, measures about 5 to 6 mm. in length and may usually be distinguished from that of the house fly by an examination of the spiracles on the pupal case. The pupal stage lasts anything from just under a week to three weeks and the imago on emerging from the puparium works its way up through the soil by aid of the ptilinum, and after drying its wings takes to flight.

Soon after mating the adults fly off in search of food, both the males and females sucking blood. Although they do not habitually bite man, they will readily do so if another host is not available. The stable fly, which requires several blood-meals before each oviposition, gives a painful bite and when attacking in large numbers can prove a serious pest.

Stable flies are diurnal feeders which seek their hosts both in cloudy weather and bright sunshine and bite chiefly out of doors, although they will enter well lit buildings to feed. They are most numerous in the neighbourhood of the breeding sites but may be dispersed by their habit of following cattle and horses.

In the tropics active breeding takes place all the year round, but in the temperate zones the numbers drop abruptly with the onset of the cold weather, the flies passing the winter in the larval and pupal stages. The adults live for about 3 weeks to a month.

Medical importance of Stomoxys calcitrans

Although *S. calcitrans* has long been suspected to be a vector of disease to man, there is no evidence to incriminate it as the transmitter of any infection under natural conditions. It does, however, sometimes constitute itself as a biting pest, particularly in the neighbourhood of farmyards and other areas where it breeds, and at certain times of the year, especially in certain localities in the tropics, it may prove itself to be a scourge. To the veterinarian and the farmer *S. calcitrans* is a dangerous insect, not only because of the irritation caused by its biting activities but because it is a vector of several helminth and protozoal diseases to domestic stock.

CHAPTER XXXI

THE FAMILY CALLIPHORIDAE

IN urban areas and in highly civilised communities as a whole the majority of calliphorid flies, like the majority of parasitic helminths, have ceased to be a medical problem, while in rural areas where people are living in unhygienic conditions only a few species of these flies are of importance. In these circumstances it might be thought reasonable to dismiss the subject with a brief account of the few outstandingly important species. Since, however, calliphorid flies are highly important parasites of domestic stock, and since, as in the case of the blood-sucking muscids, their presence or absence is intimately connected with the well-being and health of primitive people, it is advisable to treat the subject on a wider scale.

The family Calliphoridae is composed of a great number of species (probably more than a thousand) of Diptera, including such well known domestic types as the "blue bottle", "green bottle" and the "flesh flies". Calliphorid flies, although sharing in common certain distinctive morphological features, vary so much in colour that they appear to constitute a somewhat heterogeneous assemblage.

It is difficult to give a simple account of how to recognise members of the family Calliphoridae, while the recognition of the various genera and of the species composing them is a matter for the trained taxonomist. On the other hand it is their association with myiasis* that renders the Calliphoridae of medical importance, and fortunately, it is usually a simple matter to recognise the various genera, and sometimes the species, of calliphorids bred from cases of myiasis, the main difficulty arising when adult flies with no obvious connection with the vertebrate hosts are submitted for examination.

Flies belonging to the family Calliphoridae possess a wing venation of the type shown in Fig. 135. This wing venation, although usual, cannot be relied upon as a character of the family. The arista which is feathered on both sides is similar to that of many other cyclorraphous flies and is of no assistance in classification. As in members of the closely related family Tachinidae, but unlike the family Muscidae, hypopleural

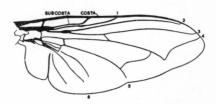

Fig. 135. Type of wing venation commonly seen in flies belonging to the family calliphoridae.

bristles are present, while unlike the tachinids the calliphorids do not possess a well developed mesopostnotum (post scutellum). None of the calliphorid

---

* Myiasis may be defined as the invasion of living tissues or organs by fly larvae.

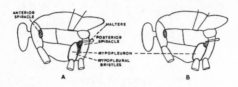

Fig. 136. Diagrammatic representation of the lateral view of the thorax of *A.* a member of the family Calliphoridae, showing the presence of bristles on the hypopleuron, and *B.* a member of the family Muscidae, in which hypopleural bristles are absent.

flies are blood-suckers and all possess retractile mouthparts of the soft suctorial type seen in *Musca.*

Amongst the characters used to define the various genera contained in the family Calliphoridae are the morphology of the squama (particularly as regards the presence or absence of hairs on the upper surface) and the pattern of the stout bristles (dorsocentral and acrostichal bristles) on the dorsum of the thorax.

Larval calliphorids have always been recognised as a common cause of crippling myiasis; this is particularly true of the tropics although the introduction of modern medicine and improved standards of hygiene have resulted in a slow retrogression of its incidence.

Just as it is difficult to define the morphological features characterising the family Calliphoridae and the various species and genera which it contains, so also it is difficult to define what species within the family should be regarded as "true myiasis producing" agents in the human host. Although any attempt to prepare such a list would involve mentioning endless species (see later chapter on myiasis) nevertheless all those calliphorids which are regarded as of practical importance occur in 9 genera divided amongst the two subfamilies, Calliphorinae and Sarcophaginae. The account which follows of the various species concerned can only be regarded as an outline, and those interested in a fuller description of the morphological and biological aspects of the subject should consult the monograph by James (1947)*.

The family Calliphoridae may be regarded as being divided into two subfamilies, the subfamily Calliphorinae and the subfamily Sarcophaginae.

THE SUBFAMILY CALLIPHORINAE

The flies composing the subfamily Calliphorinae may be considered as falling into two groups, the metallic calliphorines comprising flies whose bodies are of a metallic blue, green or purplish colour and a second group, the non-metallic calliphorines, in which the colour of the flies is either black, deep grey or ochreous yellow.

Of the metallic calliphorines the most important genera are *Chrysomyia*** and *Callitroga*, both of which contain many species which normally undergo their larval development in carrion (in which the adult flies have previously deposited their eggs) but which may and often do develop to the mature form in pre-existing wounds and ulcers in the vertebrate host. What renders the two

---

* M. T. James (1947). "The flies that cause myiasis in man". Misc. Publ. U.S. Dept Agric. No. 631.   ** Also written *Chrysomya*.

genera notorious, however, is the fact that they contain two species of myiasis producing flies, *Chrysomyia bezziana* and *Callitroga americana*, which cannot undergo development in carrion and which are obligatory parasites in living mammalian tissues, including those of man. In addition to these two outstandingly important genera other genera of metallic calliphorines, in particular *Lucilia*, *Calliphora* and *Phormia*, although they do not contain species which are obligatory parasites of living tissues, nevertheless often infest wounds and give rise to a secondary type of myiasis.

Of the non-metallic calliphorines, two species, *Cordylobia anthropophaga* and *Stasisia rodhaini*, infest the skin of man and animals whilst a third species, *Auchmeromyia luteola*, although not a cause of myiasis, possesses a larval stage which is blood-sucking.

The full grown or nearly full grown larvae of the two groups can usually be distinguished by their general form, those of the metallic calliphorines being typical cone-shaped maggots, whereas those of the non-metallic calliphorinae are grub-like and more or less oval in form. In the larvae belonging to the subfamily Calliphorinae (in both the metallic and non-metallic species) the posterior spiracles are clearly visible posteriorly and are not

Fig. 137. *A.* the conical form usually assumed by full grown larvae of the metallic calliphorines; *B.* the more oval and more rugose form common to the non-metallic calliphorines.

situated at the bottom of a depression as in the subfamily Sarcophaginae.

In the case of the metallic calliphorine larvae the posterior spiracular plates are pear-shaped with a distinct peritreme and provided with three straight spiracular slits which converge towards the button. Those larvae of the non-metallic calliphorines which parasitise man possess spiracular plates of various shapes; the peritreme is usually indistinct and the spiracular slits which may be either straight or sinuous do not converge towards the button (see Fig. 140).

The metallic calliphorines
The genus *Chrysomyia*

The genus *Chrysomyia*, which occurs only in the Old World where it is limited to certain areas in the tropics and subtropics, includes several species which are the cause of myiasis in both man and animals.

By far the most important species medi-

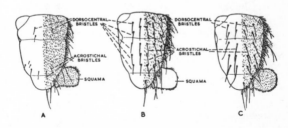

Fig. 138. Diagrammatic representations of dorsal views of the thoraces of flies belonging to the genera A. *Chrysomyia*, B. *Lucilia* and C. *Calliphora*.

cally is *Chrysomyia bezziana*, known as the "Old World screw worm", which is an obligatory parasite of the living tissues of man and animals. It has a wide distribution, being found in the Oriental Region from India to the Phillipines and throughout Tropical Africa. Its importance as a cause of myiasis in man varies according to the locality in which it occurs; whereas in Asia many human cases have been reported, in Africa it appears to favour cattle and does not attack man with such frequency. The adult fly, which measures about 8-12 mm., varies from green to blue-green and even purplish blue, in colour. The dorsal bristles of the thorax (the dorsocentral and acrostichal bristles) are few in number, thus enabling the green varieties of *Chrysomyia* to be distinguished from the various species of *Lucilia* in which the bristles are numerous. The squamae unlike those of *Lucilia* bear hairs on the dorsal surface.

Following fertilisation the female lays several hundred eggs, either on the mucous membranes (particularly when these are soiled by foetid discharges from the natural orifices) or else glues them to the edge of wounds or onto diseased skin. The larvae, which hatch in 8-24 hours, burrow into the tissues where they remain together in groups and reach maturity at the end of 6 to 7 days. The mature larva is a typical maggot, measuring about 1.5 cm., with bands of distinct spines forming rings on the anterior margins of the

body segments. The anterior spiracles consist of five finger-like processes, while the posterior spiracles, which are of the typical calliphorine type, possess a peritreme which is

Fig. 139.   Full grown larva of *Chrysomyia* sp.

incomplete at the button. The larvae of *Chrysomyia* tend to penetrate deeply in the tissues, so that infestations of the head in the neighbourhood of the eyes, ears, mouth and nose may be very serious as the result of the production of foul smelling and extensive ulcers.

Having reached maturity the larvae wriggle out of the wounds and drop to the ground, where they burrow into loose soil to pupate. The duration of the pupal stage is dependent on temperature; in warm parts of the tropics it lasts about a week but in cooler localities it may be prolonged for many weeks, and even months during the winter. The adult flies may be found alighting not only on wounds but also on decaying substances, fresh animal dung and flowers.

The genus *Callitroga* (= *Cochliomyia*)

Flies belonging to the genus *Callitroga* are found widely distributed throughout North and South America, where two species, *Callitroga americana* and *C. macellaria,* have been recorded from cases of myiasis in man. Undoubtedly the most important species is *C. americana,* an obligatory parasite of living tissue which is commonly known as the "New World screw worm" and which occurs in the United States, and as far South as the Argentine as well as in the Caribbean Islands. The adults are blue to blue-green flies and, like *Chrysomyia bezziana,* the dorsal bristles are poorly developed and the squamae bear hairs on their dorsal surface.

Following fertilisation the female lays two to three hundred eggs on the edges of wounds or on diseased mucous membranes. Some 24 to 36 hours later the eggs hatch and the larvae burrow in groups deeply into the tissues, becoming mature after 4 days to just over a week. The third stage larva is very similar to that of *Chrysomyia bezziana,* the anterior border of each segment being encircled by a band of spines. The posterior spiracles closely resemble those of the Old World screw worm but the anterior spiracles bear eight finger-like processes instead of five (see Fig. 140). The larva of *Callitroga americana* is distinguishable (with difficulty) from that of *Callitroga macellaria,* chiefly by the pigmentation of the large tracheal trunks leading to the posterior spiracles, which are darkly chitinised in C. *americana* but lightly chitinised in C. *macellaria.* Many cases of myiasis in man due to the larvae of C. *americana* have been reported. Even the smallest wound or lesion, such as a pimple or a scratch on the skin, may be attacked and infestation of the natural orifices, particularly of the nose but also the mouth, vagina and, in the new born, the navel, may result in serious destruction of tissue and even death. Lesions of the sinuses resulting from the extension of buccal or nasal infestations may give rise to very severe pain.

Following maturity the larvae behave like those of *Chrysomyia,* as also do the adult flies.

The genus *Lucilia*

The genus *Lucilia,* the members of which are known as "green bottles", has a worldwide distribution. The larvae are not obligatory parasites of living tissues and normally breed in carrion, but certain members of the genus readily attack the living tissues of sheep and two species, *Lucilia sericata* and *L. cuprina,* have not infrequently been reported as infesting wounds of human beings in Asia, Africa and America.

The adult flies are green, greenish-blue or copper-green with the dorsal bristles of the thorax well developed; the squamae are bare (see Fig. 138). The eggs are laid on, or close to, foul smelling wounds or ulcers which, if visited by several flies, may contain thousands of eggs. Larval development is rapid and may be completed in 3 or 4 days, although usually occupying over a week. The larvae, which are typical maggots, do not bear conspicuous spines on the segments, as do the larvae of *Callitroga* and *Chrysomyia,* and the spiracular plates possess complete peritremes which surround the button. The larvae of *Lucilia* are very similar to those of *Calliphora* and can only be distinguished from the latter by raising them to the adult form.

On reaching maturity the larvae fall to the ground where pupation takes place in loose soil. The adults, which emerge in one to two weeks, may be seen settling on carcasses, animal excreta and decaying substances.

The genus *Calliphora*

Flies, commonly known as "blue bottles", belonging to the genus *Calliphora* have a worldwide distribution. The larval stages are normally found in carrion and only very occasionally do they cause myiasis in man. Such infestations are usually without serious consequences; indeed, in the past, *Calliphora* and *Lucilia* larvae were used therapeutically to clean up septic wounds. The adults are

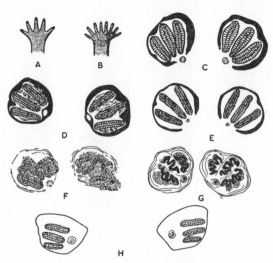

Fig. 140.   Anterior spiracles of full grown larvae of A. *Chrysomyia* sp. and B. *Callitroga* sp. Posterior spiracles of full grown larvae of C. *Chrysomyia* sp.; D. *Lucilia* sp.; E. *Phormia* sp.; F. *Cordylobia anthropophaga*; G. *Stasisia rodhaini*; H. *Auchmeromyia* sp.

large robust flies measuring about 1 cm. in length of a dull blue colour with well developed dorsal bristles; the squamae are hairy. The larvae are typical maggots of about the same size as those of *Callitroga* and *Chrysomyia*, but differing from them in that they have no obvious bands of spines on the body segments.

The genus *Phormia*

Members of the genus *Phormia* resemble small blue bottles from which they may be distinguished by the absence of hairs on the squamae. The larva of one species (*Phormia regina*) has been recorded as infesting suppurating wounds; it resembles those of *Lucilia* and *Calliphora* but may be distinguished from them by the morphology of the posterior spiracles, the peritreme not surrounding the button. This species of fly is not found in the tropics but frequents the temperate and sub-arctic regions of America, Europe and Asia.

The non-metallic calliphorines

Cordylobia anthropophaga, locally known as the "tumbu fly" or "mango fly" is distributed in Africa from Senegal and Ethiopia in the North to Natal in the South. The adult fly is dull yellow in colour with two dark grey, broad, longitudinal stripes on the thorax, and deep brown markings on the abdomen which possesses four visible segments of about equal length.

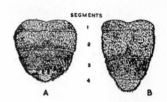

Fig. 141. Dorsal aspect of the abdomen of A. *Cordylobia anthropophaga* and B. *Auchmeromyia luteola.*

The females lay as many as 300 eggs in batches on dry soil or sand which has been contaminated by the urine or excreta of man or animals, particularly rats which are their normal hosts. The eggs, which are banana-shaped and white in colour, are deposited on grains of sand to which they are firmly glued.

The larva hatches from the egg in about two days and perches on a grain of sand. If a host comes into contact with the larva, the latter attaches itself and penetrates the host's skin by means of its mouthhooks. The larva, which always remains with its posterior spiracles in contact with the outside air, produces a furuncular swelling just under the surface of the skin. In the subdermal pocket-like cavity it undergoes two moults, and matures in about 8 days. The mature larva (see Fig. 137) is a grub-like maggot broadly oval in shape with well marked segments covered with spines. It is yellowish-white in colour and measures over a centimetre. The posterior spiracular plates are not provided with a sclerotized peritreme, the slits are moderately sinuous (somewhat in the form of question marks) and the button is indistinct. Another non-metallic calliphorid fly, *Stasisia rodhaini*, occasionally parasitises man in tropical Africa producing furuncular swellings similar to those of *C. anthropophaga*. The spiracular slits of this larva are more sinuous than those of *C. anthropophaga* (see Fig. 140).

When the larvae of the tumbu fly are mature they wriggle out of the host's tissues and fall to the ground, where they bury themselves prior to pupation. The adult flies, which emerge about 10 days later, feed on fruit and animal excreta and readily enter human dwellings.

Any boil-like swelling, occurring in localities where *C. anthropophaga* is common, should be suspected as being due to a tumbu fly larva. The boil is tender to pressure and if the centre is carefully examined a small hole will be seen through which serous fluid—but not usually pus— is exuded, sometimes in considerable quantities. Treatment consists in covering the "boil" with medicinal paraffin so that the larva protrudes its posterior spiracles in an attempt to reach air, and performs wriggling movements, so lubricating the pocket in the skin. After this treatment the larva can usually be gently pressed out; the boil should not be excised and care should be taken not to crush the larva. Human beings often become infested from sand used in latrines, whilst clothing, particularly underclothes and bed linen, when spread out to dry on infected soil, may constitute a source of infection.

Auchmeromyia luteola, which is commonly known as the "Congo floor maggot", is widely distributed throughout tropical and subtropical Africa and is essentially a parasite of man, no other hosts having been demonstrated. The adult fly closely resembles the "tumbu fly", *C. anthrophaga*, in general appearance, but it differs from this species in that the 2nd abdominal segment is twice as long as any of the others (see Fig. 141).

The female lays her eggs in batches of about 50 on soil or sand in the habitations of the indigenous population. The larva, which hatches from the egg 1 to 3 days later, hides in cracks or crevices in the floor of dwelling places or, more typically, under the sleeping mats of the inhabitants. At night the larva, which is an obligatory parasite of man, crawls up to a sleeping individual and drives its mouthhooks into the skin. Having pierced the skin it creates a partial vacuum round the incision by drawing up its prothorax ("shrugging its shoulders") and so forming a cup into which the blood flows and from which it is sucked up into the alimentary tract. Having engorged with blood the larva releases its hold on its victim and creeps away to hide in a crevice or crack where it remains whilst digesting the blood-meal. It is unable to climb, so that persons sleeping on beds or platforms elevated as little as six inches from the level of the ground are safe from attacks by the larvae. The floor maggot never feeds more than once in 24 hours and in nature probably never feeds more than 4 or 5 times in a week; indeed, it is capable of resisting starvation for several weeks should it not be able to find a host. There are three larval instars, a blood-meal being necessary before each moult, larval development in good conditions taking 3-4 weeks although it may be prolonged for several weeks in adverse circumstances. The fully developed larva is a rugose, grub-like maggot devoid of spines and, when engorged with blood, is pink in colour. The spiracular plates, which lack a distinct peritreme, are widely separated (see Fig. 140) and are each provided with three parallel slits.

The mature larva pupates in cracks and crevices or even on the surface of the soil and the adult emerges after about two weeks. The adult flies, which frequent the neighbourhood of human dwellings, readily enter huts or houses where they may be seen resting on the walls. The life-cycle and habits of this fly are closely associated with the mode of life of the African peasant who sleeps on the floor of the huts in which he dwells. The larva of the Congo floor maggot is an annoying pest which, with the progress of civilisation into the remote areas of the African hinterland, is gradually disappearing.

THE SUBFAMILY SARCOPHAGINAE

The subfamily Sarcophaginae is composed of medium to moderately large grey flies (commonly known as "flesh flies") measuring 8 to 15 mm. in length, with longitudinal black markings on the thorax and with a tesselated pattern on the abdomen. In life the eyes are characteristically brick red but the colour fades after death and cannot be made out in dried specimens. The subfamily includes two genera, *Sarcophaga* and *Wohlfahrtia,* the larvae of which are sometimes responsible for causing myiasis in man.

The females of both genera are larviparous, the 1st stage larvae being squirted from the genital orifice of the female on to the chosen site. The larvae of the sarcophagines are typical maggots with pear-shaped posterior spiracles, each of which bears three straight slits converging towards the button. Although sarcophagine larvae generally resemble those of the calliphorines they may

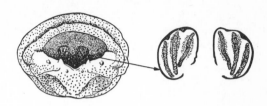

Fig. 142. Diagrammatic representation of the posterior spiracles of a full grown larva belonging to the subfamily Sarcophaginae.

readily be distinguished from the latter in that the spiracles of sarcophagines are situated in a deep pit at the posterior end, so that they can only be seen with difficulty. In our present state of knowledge it is not possible to identify the various genera until after the adults are bred out.

The genus *Wohlfahrtia*

Members of the genus *Wohlfahrtia,* which has a worldwide distribution, comprises flies as big or bigger than a blue bottle. The abdomen is usually light grey with well defined black spots, circular or semi-circular in shape, although in some species the spots may be so large as to be nearly confluent, imparting to the abdomen an almost uniform black appearance. The most important species are *Wohlfahrtia magnifica* of Europe and Asia and *W. vigil* of North America. *W. magnifica* is a serious cause of myiasis in many countries bordering on the Mediterranean and all evidence suggests that this species is a specific myiasis producing fly.

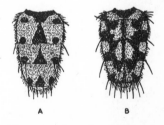

A   B

Fig. 143. Dorsal aspect of the abdomen of A. *Wohlfahrtia* sp. and B. *Sarcophaga* sp..

The females deposit their 1st stage larvae in groups, sometimes numbering five or six dozen, in wounds and sores on animals or man, and in such sites the larvae mature in about ten days. The larvae, as in the case of the other myiasis producing flies, when mature, drop to the ground where they burrow in loose soil, the adults emerging from the pupae in one to two weeks.

The genus *Sarcophaga*

Like members of the genus *Wohlfahrtia,* flies belonging to the genus *Sarcophaga* have a very wide distribution. They are grey flies, varying greatly in size, with longitudinal black markings on the thorax and ill-defined black squares or angulated patches on the abdomen giving the surface a chessboard effect. They only occasionally cause myiasis, and usually breed in carrion or in human and animal excreta.

The gravid female produces 20 to 40 larvae at a time and these complete their development very rapidly, usually in 3 to 4 days. Their subsequent life history is similar to that of *Wohlfahrtia*.

CHAPTER XXXII

THE FAMILY OESTRIDAE

FOR the purpose of this book the family Oestridae is regarded as including all the so-called "warble flies" and "bot flies". Strictly speaking the medical importance of these flies is confined to one species, *Dermatobia hominis*, the larval form of which can complete its development in man as well as in other vertebrate hosts but, in addition, a very limited number of other species, the larvae of which normally infest animals, occasionally parasitise and undergo partial development in man.

Although members of the family Oestridae are only of limited medical importance, many species are of great veterinary importance since they are a common and widespread cause of specific myiasis in domestic stock. The resulting lesions not only affect the health of the animal hosts but also, as a result of the damage done to the meat and hide, cause vast economic losses.

Most, but by no means all, species of oestrids are bee-like in appearance, this similarity being due not only to their general shape but also to the fact that the presence of long hairs on the body gives them a furry appearance. In all species occurring in this group the eyes are set wide apart and the mouth parts, which are covered with a mask-like flap, are non-functional; in consequence the adult flies do not feed, their short existence of probably not more than a week to ten days being devoted to mating and reproduction.

In contrast to the short adult life the larval stage is unusually long, lasting as much as six to eight months.

Although the family Oestridae is here considered as including all warble flies and bot flies, nevertheless it must be noted that most entomologists consider the oestrids to constitute several families, such as the Cuterebridae, the Gasterophilidae, the Oestridae (*sensu stricto*) and the Hypodermatidae. It should be remembered however that the distinctions separating these families are for the most part based on anatomical differences observed in the adults, and that the medical officer is unlikely to encounter any but the larval stages of development.

Oestrid flies have long been known to cause myiasis in animals and as far back as the 19th century the life history of at least one species was known to Linnaeus and other early entomologists. With the arrival of the European in the New World, the serious lesions caused by *Dermatobia hominis* in man and in his domestic stock were soon recognised, but it was not until much later that other species of oestrids were observed to be the occasional cause of aberrant non-specific myiasis in humans.

Since the most important species of oestrid parasitising man is unquestionably *D. hominis* special attention will be devoted to it in this chapter.

Dermatobia hominis (= D. cyaniventris)

Dermatobia hominis, which is known by such local names as "ver macaque" and "berne fly" is confined to the Americas where it has a wide distribution

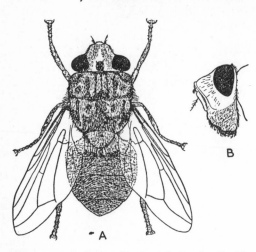

ranging from Mexico to the Argentine but, although it occurs along the shores of the Carribean, it is absent, with the exception of Trinidad, from the islands of the West Indies. The adult fly, which is a little larger than a blue bottle, is a non-hairy oestrid with a purplish blue metallic sheen and, as in all oestrids, the eyes are widely separated and the vestigial mouthparts are covered with a mask-like flap. The larval stages of *D. hominis* are important parasites not only of cattle and other domestic stock (they do not parasitise equines) but also of man. In all these hosts

Fig. 144.   *A. Dermatobia hominis* female; *B.* side view of head showing mask-like flap covering the rudimentary mouthparts.

they produce a very severe, long lasting and painful form of myiasis which may result in permanent deformity or even, in the case of young children, sometimes in death.

D. hominis is essentially a forest inhabiting fly and is found in lowlands or in

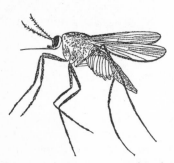

valleys, chiefly in wooded country and along the edges of forests. The females lay their eggs on the underside of various species of arthropods which then act as transport hosts for the eggs. The number of eggs laid on the arthropod carrier vary from five to twenty five according to the size of the host. Whatever species of arthropod may be selected it is always one which tends to alight on animals or on man during its natural activities; mosquitoes, in particular members of the genus *Psorophora*, are important transport hosts, but other arthropods, notably stable flies (*Stomoxys*), house flies

Fig. 145.   The egg mass of D. *hominis* attached to the under surface of a mosquito.

and ticks may also be enforced carriers of the eggs. The larvae within the eggs become fully formed and ready to emerge in about a week: if at the end of this incubation period the transport host alights on a warm-blooded animal the larvae rapidly emerge from the egg mass and fall onto the skin of their new host.

The newly hatched larva, which measures about 1 to 1.5 mm., is cylindrical in shape and markedly spiny on the anterior half of the body. Within a few seconds of having dropped on to the skin it begins to burrow through the epidermis of its vertebrate host and eventually comes to rest in a subdermal pocket, with the anterior end facing inwards and the posterior end (bearing the spiracles) immediately below the aperture in the hosts skin. Larval development, the whole of which takes place in the subdermal pocket, is prolonged, lasting anything from 5 to 10 weeks and even longer. Whereas the second stage larva is pyriform in shape and bears large rose-thorn spines which encircle the anterior segment in bands, the third stage is oval in shape with relatively much smaller spines. The fully developed 3rd stage larva, which measures about one to two and a half centimetres, bears a pair of conspicuous flower-like anterior spiracles while the posterior spiracles, which have three straight slits, are situated at the base of a concavity on the last abdominal segment.

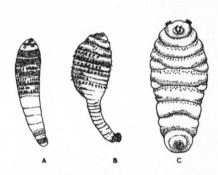

Fig. 146. *D. hominis. A.* 1st stage larva; *B.* 2nd stage larva; *C.* 3rd stage larva. (The 3 instars are not drawn to scale.)

When full grown, the larva wriggles through the skin aperture and falls to the ground, where it pupates very superficially. The adult fly emerges some three weeks to a month later.

A few days after parasitisation has occurred the site occupied in the skin by the larva assumes the appearance of a boil-like swelling which later produces a discharge (sometimes foul smelling) and which usually gives rise to intermittent attacks of excruciating pain. Treatment, which is dependent on the stage of development of the larva, often involves surgical interference. In such instances the aperture in the skin produced by the maggot should be carefully extended, following anaesthetisation of the surrounding skin, and once the incision is large enough the creature should be removed with forceps, care being taken not to crush it, since fluid released from the injured larva may cause a violent reaction in the host.

Oestrus ovis

Oestrus ovis, commonly known as the "sheep nostril fly" is one of the smaller oestrids, being only slightly larger than the house fly. They are inconspicuous, non-hairy flies, which possess the characteristic dichoptic eyes and the masked mouthparts of the family, while both males and females have the dorsum of the thorax covered with small dark-coloured tubercles, so that the flies look as if they had been sprayed with minute drops of tar. Members of the genus *Oestrus* are normally parasitic in sheep and goats, the female flies being larviparous and depositing a number of first instar larvae on the edge of, or just inside, the nostrils of the vertebrate host. The tiny larvae at once migrate to the nasal mucosa and nasal and frontal sinuses; here they undergo further development and after two to twelve months pass out *via* the nostrils to the ground, where they pupate—the imagoes emerging 3 to 4 weeks later.

In the case of man, *O. ovis* has been recorded, particularly from the Mediterranean area, as causing myiasis in the eye, the nose and the mouth; as might be expected, such cases have for the most part occurred in persons concerned with sheep or goat tending. In all cases of human infestation the larvae seldom appear to develop beyond the first instar, at which stage they measure little more than a millimetre, and are provided with spines (confined to the ventral surface) and large mouth hooks.

Hypoderma spp.

The adults are hairy bee-like flies which are very rapid in flight, and which are rarely seen except when ovipositing. Normally the female lays her eggs on the hairs of the legs, and of the belly, of cattle; as soon as the larvae have hatched they penetrate through the skin into the subcutaneous tissues. They then make their way through the tissues to the oesophageal wall from which they migrate until they reach the skin on each side of the spine. A swelling with an aperture (known as a "warble") marks the site of the larva below the skin, and from this site the maggot, on becoming fully mature, emerges, falls to the ground and pupates.

Warble flies, although normally parasites of cattle, occasionally cause myiasis in man, usually in persons tending or milking farm animals. In such instances the larva generally migrates immediately beneath the skin surface leaving a tortuous inflamed line indistinguishable from that caused by certain migrating helminth larvae and known as cutaneous "creeping eruption" or "larva migrans". On rare occasions the larva instead of wandering just below the skin surface penetrates more deeply inwards and undergoes considerable development, even reaching full growth, and thereby causing a warble-like swelling beneath the skin surface.

Gasterophilus spp.

The adults of these flies (which like those of *Hypoderma* spp. are bee-like and not often seen except when ovipositing) lay their eggs on the hair of animals, particularly horses. Having emerged from the eggs the larvae either crawl into the horse's mouth or else are transferred to it by the horse's tongue. Once in the mouth they burrow into the mucous membrane and migrate to the stommach where they re-emerge into the lumen and attach themselves to the gut wall by means of their mouth hooks. When mature they release their hold, are voided in the droppings and pupate on the ground.

Cases of infection of man by *Gasterophilus* are rare and only the first stage larva is concerned. This larva which is a cylindrical creature about 0.5 – 1 mm. long, with most of the segments bearing a single or double row of conspicuous spines, burrows into the skin and migrates immediately beneath the surface where it gives rise to a linear eruption indistinguishable from that caused by *Hypoderma* spp., or by helminth larvae.

CHAPTER XXXIII

A SUMMARY OF OUR KNOWLEDGE OF MYIASIS AS OBSERVED IN MAN

AS already explained, myiasis may be defined as the invasion of living tissue by the larvae of certain species of Diptera; it follows that the invasion of the skin or internal organs by mites or the occurrence of beetles in the intestinal tract does not come into this category.

It is customary and convenient, although lacking in scientific precision, to consider external and internal myiasis as separate entities.

External myiasis

External myiasis or dermal myiasis, the term being used to include invasion of the mucous membranes and conjunctiva, has attracted considerable attention, and the large number of species of fly larvae recorded as causal organisms has led to considerable, and possibly unnecessary, confusion since, just as in the case of the bacteria, any fly larva which is capable of development in dead meat can also develop in dead or moribund tissues, such as occur in septic wounds or malignant growths. Such casual invaders can scarcely be regarded as causal organisms and, if they are omitted from consideration, there remains only a very limited number of species whose larvae can be considered as causing specific external myiasis in man.

These true myiasis producing species, although few in number, are distributed amongst the following eight genera: *Hypoderma, Gasterophilus, Oestrus, Dermatobia, Callitroga, Chrysomyia, Cordylobia* and *Wohlfahrtia*. The first three of these genera (all of which contain species occurring in the temperate zones) are mainly of importance as parasites of domestic stock, and although cases of human infestation are reported from time to time, nevertheless the larvae of these flies must be regarded as rare and accidental parasites of man, in whose tissues they can only survive for a limited period.

Flies belonging to the genera *Dermatobia, Callitroga, Chrysomyia* and *Cordylobia* are essentially inhabitants of the tropics, and each genus contains one or two species the larvae of which, although mainly parasitic in hosts other than man, are of considerable medical importance since they cause severe and widespread myiasis in the human population. The larvae of most species of *Wohlfahrtia* are not obligatory parasites in living tissue, but a limited number of species are obligatory or almost obligatory, and some of the latter are a not uncommon cause of myiasis in the human population, particularly amongst children. Although cases of myiasis due to the larvae of *Wohlfahrtia* spp. have been recorded from both the Old and the New World, cases have not as yet been observed in Europe.

The treatment of the various forms of external myiasis produced by these different species consists essentially in destroying and, in most instances, removing the parasite and then treating the lesions. In the case of open wounds the removal is usually a simple matter, but when the larvae are deeply embedded beneath the skin, as in the case of long lasting *Cordylobia* and *Dermatobia* infections, or when larvae have penetrated into the turbinal mucous membranes, or even into the frontal sinuses, as in certain cases of *Callitroga* and *Chrysomyia* infections, their removal may call for surgical interference. In the case of invasion by parasites of small size, as occurs during the first few days of invasion or where growth of the parasite is stunted—as is usual in cases of infection of the larva migrans type—it is probably quite satisfactory to kill the larva *in situ*, without paying particular heed to its removal. On the other hand, the destruction by means of chloroform or other insecticidal agents, of well developed large parasites, deeply situated in the tissues, without ensuring their subsequent removal, may be fraught with serious consequences. In these conditions an attempt should be made to remove the larvae and, whether or not this proves successful, the wound should be packed with an antibiotic such as a one-to-one mixture of sulphanilamide and sulphathiazole.

The prevention of myiasis is mainly centred on the destruction of the larval and adult stages of the flies responsible, while the particular methods to be employed are largely dependent on whether the larvae of the species to be controlled are obligatory parasites of living tissue or normally breeders in carrion. If they are obligatory parasites, then control should be directed to the destruction of the larvae in the living host and to preventing the further development of any larvae which have escaped and pupated in the soil. If the species in question is not an obligatory parasite additional measures are necessary, in that the flies must be prevented from breeding in carrion by the protection or destruction of carcases. The use of mosquito nets and screening to protect the human population is commonly employed in the tropics but is not usual in temperate climates. The use of repellents is probably of some value, and all lesions of the skin or mucous membrane which are of a type likely to attract flies should be protected by gauze or wool dressings.

Internal myiasis

Cases of internal myiasis are usually classified as being of intestinal or else of genito-urinary origin. There are no specific or obligatory dipterous parasites of man which fall into either of these categories; on the other hand a whole host of different species of larvae (including many of those which cause external myiasis) may, and sometimes do, sojourn for a brief period in the gut or, more rarely, in the genito-urinary tract, but they very rarely undergo full development in these situations and their presence may be looked upon as entirely fortuitous.

In the case of genito-urinary myiasis, infestations are usually traceable to the invading larvae entering a genital or urinary orifice which is either the site of a previous lesion or else an opening from which pus is being discharged. In such instances the larvae may ascend the genital or urinary tract and survive for considerable periods, although it is unusual for such larvae to reach maturity.

In the case of intestinal myiasis, man usually acquires his infection by the accidental ingestion of the eggs or larvae of food-frequenting flies, although cases have been recorded where the route of entry of the larvae has been through the anus. It is probable that almost any species of fly larva may survive in the intestinal tract for periods of time, the length of which is dependent on many factors (including the age of the larvae at the time of ingestion), but certain species appear to be associated with intestinal myiasis more often than others. In this category occur the larvae of a number of species of Diptera whose recognition and life-history have already been described, such as the genera *Musca*, *Muscina*, *Fannia*, *Sarcophaga*, *Stomoxys* and *Lucilia*. In addition, flies occurring in certain other genera, not previously described because they are not otherwise of medical importance, have been reported as causing intestinal myiasis.

Eristalis spp. Flies of this genus bear a general resemblance to hive-bees (although of course the latter possess two pairs of wings) and are often called "drone flies" or "hover flies", the latter name being descriptive of their habit of remaining poised in the air for several seconds. The female flies lay their eggs at the margin of stagnant water while the larvae, which live in the mud and which, when mature, are about an inch in length, take in air from the surface by means of a long tail-like siphon tube, hence the name "rat-tailed larva". When passed in the faeces the larvae are usually dead, but their striking appearance attracts attention and they are often mistaken for helminth parasites.

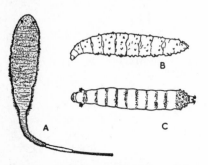

Fig. 147. *A.* the "rat-tailed" larva, *Eristalis* sp., dorsal view, *B. Aphiochaeta* sp. larva, side view; *C. Drosophila* sp. larva, dorsal view.

Aphiochaeta scalaris. This is one of the small lacalypterate, cyclorrhaphous flies, the larva of which only attains a length of less than a quarter of an inch. The larvae and pupae are often found in human stools and statements have been made that the larvae can complete their development in the gut and that the adults can hatch from the pupae and produce a second generation while still in the intestine.

Piophila spp. The larvae or maggots (commonly called "cheese skippers") of this fly normally occur in decaying vegetable and various protein foods, and are particularly common in ripe cheeses. The full grown larvae measure about a quarter of an inch and have a characteristic habit of engaging the mouth-hooks on the hind-end, thus forming a circle; the hooks are then suddenly released from their grip and the larva springs away for a distance of about 2-3 inches. The larvae, which are sometimes passed alive in the faeces, are in these circumstances derived from eating various infested food substances, particularly cheese.

Drosophila spp. These tiny flies, commonly known as "fruit flies", are often seen in dense swarms on, and flying above, over-ripe fruit. The minute larvae sometimes occur in the faeces in vast numbers and may be mistaken by the uninitiated for parasitic helminth larvae.

Varying degrees of intestinal discomfort are reported following the ingestion of these and various other species of fly larvae, but—apart from the use of aperients—specific treatment is rarely necessary. Prophylaxis follows the obvious course of avoiding the ingestion of such contaminated food or water.

CHAPTER XXXIV

THE ORDER SIPHONAPTERA

THE CHARACTERS OF THE ORDER AND THE LIFE-CYCLE OF THE FLEA

THE order Siphonaptera, which contains the fleas, comprises about 1500 species. These insects are small, laterally compressed, wingless creatures, with a holometabolous life-cycle. Whereas the immature stages are all free-living, the adult stages are all parasitic on mammals or birds. While the majority are only temporary parasites, the females of a few species spend their whole life attached to the host. They possess an external morphology adapted to this parasitic mode of life.

Fleas are of great significance in human welfare, not because of the annoyance they cause as a biting nuisance but because of the part they play as vectors of disease. Whilst only a restricted number of species commonly attack human beings, the order Siphonaptera includes many species which although not normally parasites of man, nevertheless occupy a dominant position in the epidemiology of disease, in that they maintain such diseases as bubonic plague and murine typhus in the animal reservoirs, and in certain circumstances leave these hosts to bite man and thus convey the infection to him.

Although fleas are mainly notorious as vectors to man of these forms of plague and typhus, they are also responsible (although only on rare occasions) for transmitting to him certain relatively unimportant cestode infections.

Until the discovery in 1894 of the bacillary nature of plague no progress had been made in understanding the nature of the disease, which in the 6th and 14th centuries had given rise to particularly devastating pandemics, the occurrence of which was everywhere regarded with horror. Simond's epoch-making suggestion in 1898 that fleas were the vectors of bubonic plague led, in the next ten years, to the classical work of the Indian plague commission which proved that fleas are the vectors of the disease, and which for the first time allowed sound measures of control to be introduced. These studies were consolidated by the discovery in 1914 by Bacot and Martin of the mechanism by which these insects transmit the disease.

When studies on the transmission of plague by fleas began, knowledge of the systematics of these insects was in a rudimentary state; it was fortunate, therefore, that as early as 1898 there began an association between two remarkable men, Rothschild and Karl Jordan, who undertook a systematic study of the order Siphonaptera, because they realized that such investigations were an essential preliminary to further biological and medical studies; without the work of these men little would now be known of the epidemiology of plague.

External morphology of the flea

Fleas are small laterally compressed insects, measuring according to the species anything from 1 to 8 mm.. They vary in colour from a light amber to a very dark brown. Although each of the main divisions of the body—head, thorax and abdomen—can easily be recognised, nevertheless there is no sharp demarcation between them, so that the flea has a somewhat compact

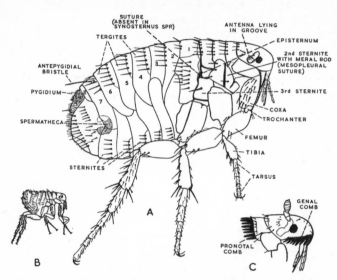

Fig. 148. *A.* the external anatomy of a combless female flea: the species depicted is *Xenopsylla cheopis*. *B.* outline of male to show cocked up appearance of abdomen. *C.* head of a combed flea, *Ctenocephalides* sp. (the antenna is erected).

appearance. Wings or rudiments of wings are never present, whilst the legs which are long and powerful are clearly specialised for the purpose of jumping. The body and the legs are adorned with stiff setae which when the insect is seen under the microscope give it a bristly appearance.

The head. The head, which is usually roughly triangular in outline, and is closely joined to the thorax, bears a pair of antennae, biting mouthparts and, in a large number of species, a row of powerful tooth-like spines, collectively known as the genal comb, or genal ctenidium (pl. ctenidia), arranged on the lower border of the head. The eyes, when present, are simple (not facetted) and are usually obvious, due to the dark pigment which they contain. The antennae, which are situated immediately behind the eyes, lie in distinct depressions (the antennal grooves) which prevent them being injured whilst the flea is wandering about in the fur or feathers of its host. Each antenna is composed of three segments, the first two of which are usually smaller than the third or terminal segment which is commonly club-shaped with a laminated appearance. The antennae, which can be erected out of the antennal grooves, bear structures which are believed to be sensitive to warm air currents thus enabling the flea to locate its host.

The mouthparts, which are prominent and point almost vertically downwards from the forward lower angle of the head, are composed of a labrum, a pair of maxillae, a pair of maxillary palps, a pair of labial palps and a pair of triangular flap-like structures known as the maxillary blades; mandibles are absent. The labrum and the maxillae (which are serrated at their tips) are stylet-like and together form the food canal up which the blood is sucked into the pharynx. The hypopharynx lies concealed in the head and is a small dagger-like structure which discharges the salivary secretions received from the salivary duct into two canals (the salivary canals) formed by the grooved lower extremities of the

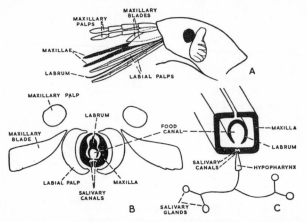

Fig. 149. Diagrammatic representation of the mouthparts of a flea. *A.* seen from the side with the structures separated; *B.* seen in cross section; *C.* schematic representation of the food and salivary canals.

maxillae. Thus, not only do the maxillae assist in the formation of the food canal but they also serve to convey saliva to the tissues of the host. The labium, which is inconspicuous, consists of a small median plate at the root of the mouthparts; it bears a pair of long indistinctly segmented palps, the labial palps, which form a sheath to the labium and maxillae. The maxillary blades, despite their pointed appearance, do not pierce the skin but are said to help in parting the hairs as the flea selects a suitable site on the host's skin in which to drive in its labrum and maxillae; associated with the maxillary flaps are a pair of long, distinctly segmented (maxillary) palps, which are sometimes mistaken for the less conspicuous antennae.

The thorax. The thorax consists of three clearly demarcated laterally compressed segments, each consisting of a dorsal plate, the notum (clearly visible in lateral view) and a ventral plate commonly called the sternum. In some species of fleas the notum of the prothorax bears on its posterior border conspicuous spines which collectively are known as the pronotal comb or pronotal ctenidium.

Only vestiges of most of the pleura can be recognised, but one large pleural plate which covers parts of segments I and II of the abdomen is usually conspicuous (in Fig. 148 A this plate may be recognised lying immediately posterior to the episternum and the 3rd sternite). In a proportion of species a vertical rod-like structure, the "meral rod" or "pleural rod" divides the 2nd sternal plate into an anterior and a posterior region; its presence or absence is of assistance in recognising amongst the combless fleas the vectors of plague. The legs, which are usually covered with bristles, consist of five segments; the coxa and femur are large and laterally compressed, whilst the tarsus, which is divided into five divisions, terminates in a pair of claws.

The abdomen. The abdomen consists of 10 segments, the 9th and 10th being greatly modified for sexual purposes. The 7th tergum in both sexes bears, in addition to a varying number of short hairs, a pair of conspicuous setae known as the antepygidial bristles, so named because behind them, on the 9th tergite of both the male and female flea, there is a small pincushion-like structure (the pygidium or sensillium) which is believed to have a sensory function.

The terminal portion of the abdomen of the male and of the female differ considerably in form and morphology. In the male (Fig. 148B) the abdomen has a rather cocked up appearance due to the presence of copulatory

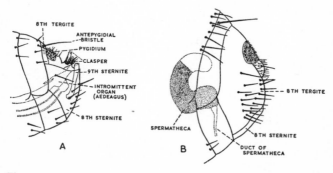

Fig. 150.   Terminal segments of *A.* a male flea and *B.* a female flea.

structures, notably a pair of claspers (which may have several lobes), a pair of rod-like structures, known as the ninth tergites, and the large aedeagus with its chitinous supports. The female lacks external genitalia and her abdomen has a rounded terminal outline; the spermathecae, which are often strongly chitinised, are usually clearly visible in the abdomen of cleared fleas, and in certain species their characteristic morphology is of great assistance in classification.

Aspects of the internal anatomy of fleas which are important in
understanding the role of these insects as vectors of disease.

Since the structure of the alimentary canal of adult fleas is important in understanding the mechanism of plague transmission, a short description of its structure is appropriate at this stage. There is a powerful, spindle-shaped sucking pharynx, which tapers off to become continuous with the oesophagus and leads into a characteristic conical organ, the proventriculus. The proventriculus is lined on its inner surface with a close set series of backwardly directed chitinous rods, converging towards a central point in the lumen of the organ; these rods when pressed together prevent regurgitation of the contents of the stomach into the oesophagus. The stomach is relatively large and is continuous

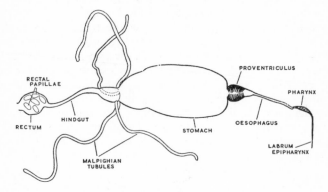

Fig. 151.   Diagrammatic representation of the alimentary canal of a flea.

with a short hind-gut, the most prominent features of which are the four malpighian tubules (these are attached to the hind-gut close to its origin from the stomach) and the expanded rectum with its prominent rectal papillae which extract excess water from the faeces, the latter being passed in an almost dry or semisolid state.

There are two pairs of salivary glands, the common duct of which enters the hypopharynx. The salivary secretion plays no direct part in the transmission of plague or of murine typhus.

The life-cycle of the flea

Both the adult male and female flea are parasitic, the blood of mammals and birds being their sole source of food; whereas in the case of the male, blood is required essentially for the purpose of nutrition, in the case of the female not only is blood necessary as food but it is also essential for the maturation of the eggs.

The female flea, when ready to oviposit, leaves the host in order to lay her eggs in the debris which accumulates in the host's nest, lair or dwelling place. In the case of those species which frequent human dwellings or the living quarters of domestic animals, the eggs are laid in or near to cracks or crevices in the floor. The egg, which is just visible to the naked eye, is a pearly white or yellowish glistening body, oval or round in shape, the chorion showing no obvious sculpturing. The egg possesses a somewhat glutinous covering which sometimes allows it to stick to the hair of animals or to fibres (such as fibres of sacking) and so be transported over considerable distances. During her lifetime, which may be up to six months or even a year, a female flea will lay as many as 300 to 500 eggs, depositing them singly in small batches of up to a dozen at a time. The eggs hatch in anything from two days to about two weeks, both temperature and humidity having a marked effect on hatching time.

The tiny larvae emerge from the eggs, which they split open with the aid of a frontal spine, "the egg breaker". Flea larvae are active creatures which shun light and move freely about their habitat seeking food. They feed on organic debris in the host's nest or domicile, a diet which in the case of many species is supplemented by the partly digested blood evacuated from the alimentary canal of the adult fleas. The length of life spent in the larval stages is very variable and depends not only on the species of flea concerned but also on the availability of food and the climatic conditions. Adult fleas can survive under very arid conditions, due to the efficiency of their rectal glands in abstracting water from the faeces, but the flea larvae are much more susceptible and fail to survive if exposed to a high saturation deficiency; it should be remembered, however, that excessive humidity is also harmful.

In optimum conditions in the tropics the larvae may complete their development in 10 days to 2 weeks, but this period is readily prolonged in adverse conditions. In nearly all species of fleas there are three larval instars, but a few instances are known in which there are only two. The mature larva is less than 1 cm. in length with a distinct pigmented head, bearing a pair of antennae and biting mouthparts; there are thirteen, white to light brown, body segments,

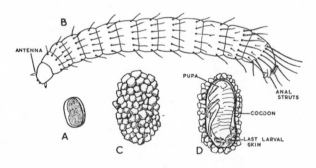

Fig. 152. The immature stages of the life cycle of a flea, *A.* egg; *B.* the full grown larva; *C.* cocoon with adherent particles; *D.* section of cocoon showing pupa and last larval skin.

each of which bears a few slender, simple setae. The last body segment is unlike the others in that it terminates in a pair of fleshy, finger-like processes known as the anal struts, which the larva uses to aid its somewhat clumsy progress.

On completing its development the larva spins an oval-shaped silken cocoon, the outer surface of which it covers with fragments of debris or grains of sand from the host's habitat. The cocoon, due to this camouflage, may be very difficult to distinguish from its surroundings. If the cocoon is dissected open with a pair of fine needles it is seen to enclose the last larval skin and the pupa, the covering of which is so transparent that the adult flea can clearly be seen within. The adult when it emerges is almost colourless but rapidly darkens to the characteristic deep brown colour. The adult usually emerges in a week to a week and a half, but if the cocoon remains undisturbed, emergence may be prolonged for periods of up to a year or more. Whilst all the stimuli which cause the adult to leave the cocoon are incompletely known, it is certain that vibration is an important factor. This probably accounts for the many instances of persons who having entered deserted dwellings, are later attacked by large numbers of fleas seeking their first blood meal.

As previously mentioned the adults of most species of fleas spend only a proportion of their lives on the host animal, the exceptions being the females of such species as *Tunga penetrans* and *Echidnophaga gallinacea* which embed themselves in the integument of their hosts where they remain until, after having discharged all their eggs, they die. Fleas feed frequently, partaking of blood meals from their hosts several times a day; this voracious feeding is necessary since much of the blood taken up is very rapidly passed through the gut and expelled from the anus in a semidigested state. Fleas avoid light and while on their hosts remain hidden in the fur and feathers or, in the case of man, under the clothing, until such time as they leave their hosts and seek out dark recesses in order to hide and oviposit.

Although fleas are not strictly host-specific they tend to limit themselves to hosts belonging to the same generic group. Hungry fleas, however, have more catholic tastes than well-fed fleas and will attack unusual hosts, as is the case with rat fleas of the genus *Xenopsylla* which, although they do not usually feed on man, will do so when deprived of their normal rodent host. Fleas quickly abandon the bodies of dead or dying animals, a fact of great significance in the epidemiology of plague.

Fleas are attracted by the warmth of the body of the host, which they reach by crawling and jumping. When using the latter means of progression they can cover surprising distances, figures of over 6 inches in height, and of one foot in length having been recorded.

Provided that the climatic conditions are suitable, fleas are relatively long lived, and fed insects kept at temperatures below 23°C will live as long as 6 months or more. Plague infection tends to shorten their lives but even heavily infected *X. cheopis* have been shown to survive for well over a month when kept at temperatures below 15°C. Any rise of temperature (particularly sharp increases) causes fleas to seek more frequent blood-meals; this is particularly important in the case of plague-infected fleas which because of their infection either cannot ingest blood or retain the blood which they have ingested, and the consequent dessication to which they are thus subjected causes them to bite much more frequently than is normal. Climatic conditions exert marked influence on the abundance of fleas, the population in the temperate zones being highest in summer, whereas in tropical areas it reaches its maximum during the cooler months.

The classification of fleas and the role of these insects as vectors of disease will be briefly dealt with in the following chapter.

CHAPTER XXXV

THE ORDER SIPHONAPTERA (cont.)

THE CLASSIFICATION OF FLEAS AND THE ASSOCIATION
OF CERTAIN SPECIES WITH DISEASE

THE order Siphonaptera is divided into two superfamilies, the Pulicoidea and the Ceratophylloidea. The characters by which the two super-families may be distinguished from one another would involve a description of morphological details beyond the scope of this book, while the scientific classification of the various species is a matter for the specialist. Since, however, only a fraction (probably no more than a dozen) of the 1500 or so known species are likely to be encountered by the medical officer in the course of his work, the following simplified classification is suggested. Although such a classification cannot be regarded as of any systematic value, it will be found of considerable practical help to the medical officer since it will permit the identification of the genus and sometimes of the species of most fleas collected in or about human dwellings or on animals frequenting such places, and these will be found to include most species of medical importance.

For this simplified classification it is convenient to separate all fleas into two main groups, the first of which comprises all the "combless" fleas, that is, all those species devoid of combs (ctenidia), whilst the second includes all those fleas with either one or two combs—the "combed" fleas.

The combless fleas

The group comprising the combless fleas contains one species, *Pulex irritans,* which is an annoying parasite of man and which occasionally plays a minor role in the transmission of disease, one species, *Tunga penetrans,* the female of

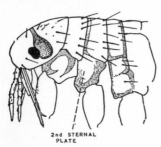

which penetrates into the tissues of the human host and which may cause much suffering and disability and, finally, three species of fleas all occurring in the genus *Xenopsylla* which between them are responsible for the trans-mission to man of the majority of infections with bubonic plague and murine typhus. In the following account only these medically important genera and species are discussed.

Fig. 153. Head and thorax of *Pulex irritans.* Note the absence of a meral rod (mesopleural suture).

1) *Pulex irritans.* This insect, which has a cosmopolitan distribution, is the most common flea parasite of man, having earned for itself the somewhat inapt sobriquet "the human flea". It measures between 2 to 4 mm. in length and possesses a head with a rounded profile. The eyes are

distinct and there is no meral rod dividing the second sternal plate into an anterior and a posterior region.

Not only does *P. irritans* breed in dwellings and visit human beings in order to take a blood-meal, but it also attacks a wide variety of domestic animals. It is often found breeding in the neighbourhood of pig styes where it sometimes proves to be a nuisance to farm workers. Whereas in some localities, such as California, it is an abundant and serious pest, in other areas it is replaced by different species, particularly by the dog flea and by the cat flea.

2) *Tunga penetrans.* Although the genus is composed of several species, only one, *T. penetrans*, commonly known as the "jigger flea" or "chigoe", attacks man. Originally this flea was strictly South American in distribution, but with the inception of the negro slave traffic, it spread to tropical and subtropical Africa and to the island of Madagascar; it has also appeared, but has not established itself, in India. The unfed adults are amongst the smallest of the fleas, being about 1 mm. in size and, when seen under the microscope, they are distinctly less spiny in appearance than most other fleas. The head, which is angulated, bears unusually prominent mouthparts and each of the three strongly compressed thoracic segments bears a pair of relatively long but slender legs.

The life-cycle of members of the genus *Tunga* differs sharply in certain respects from that of other fleas, particularly with regard to the behaviour of the adult female which passes nearly the whole of her existence embedded in the skin of the host. It is this habit of penetrating the skin and its association with severe secondary infection which causes *Tunga penetrans* to be of considerable medical importance.

Fig. 154.   *Tunga penetrans,* female.

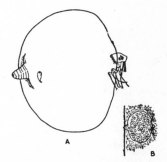

Fig. 155.   Ovigerous *T. penetrans*; *A.* after removal from the host, and *B.* diagrammatic representation of its position in the tissues of the host.

Both the male and the female jigger flea are blood-suckers, but whereas the male leaves its host after obtaining its meal the female, having fed, burrows into the skin where it is soft, commonly between the toes or in the neighbourhood of the nail bed. When the last abdominal segments are almost level with the skin surface the female ceases to burrow and in this situation she matures her ova, the abdomen swelling to a diameter of 6 mm. or more, in about a week. Egg laying then commences and for a period of a week to ten days, 150 to 200 eggs are extruded singly from the vaginal orifice and fall to the ground; once egg laying is completed the female dies in the skin and shrivels up *in situ*.

The egg is similar to that of other fleas and the larvae which emerge after 3 to 4 days incubation are typical siphonapteran larvae, thriving best in sandy soil or in the dust of human habitations. Larval development (which is characterised by two instars) lasts for a period of approximately two weeks and is followed by the spinning of the cocoon in which the pupa transforms into the adult after about a week.

Not only do prophylactic measures include the maintenance of clean conditions in human dwellings, but since the jumping powers of these fleas are limited, and since their attacks are generally confined to the feet, the wearing of proper footwear is the most effective form of protection. Since *T. penetrans* attacks not only man but many species of domestic animals, particularly pigs, it is important to remember these possible animal reservoirs when dealing with local outbreaks of jigger infestations. Human cases are best treated by removing the embedded flea, if possible soon after penetration and before the egg sac is well developed. When the egg sac is fully formed its removal entire and unruptured is a delicate and skilled operation, in the performance of which the local inhabitants are usually highly successful.

Another species of burrowing flea, *Echidnophaga gallinacea*, the so-called "sticktight flea", on rare occasions attacks man. This flea is somewhat similar in general appearance to *Tunga penetrans*, from which it may be distinguished by the outline of the head (truncated in *E. gallinacea* and angulated in *T. penetrans*) and by the presence of stouter setae on the body.

3) *The genus Xenopsylla*. The genus *Xenopsylla*, which comprises about 60 species and subspecies of fleas, includes no more than half a dozen which are of any particular medical significance, chiefly as vectors of plague, and are commonly known as tropical rat fleas. Members of the genus are mainly found distributed in Asia and Africa, although certain species, such as *X. cheopis* and *X. braziliensis*, which are very important vectors of plague, have been carried to other parts of the world by rats which have travelled on ships. Fleas belonging to the genus *Xenopsylla* generally resemble *P. irritans* but may be distinguished by the possession of a meral rod on the 2nd sternal plate (absent in *P. irritans*). Another species of flea, *Synosternus pallidus*, which attacks human beings in Senegambia, closely resembles *Xenopsylla spp.* and like them it possesses a meral rod but, whereas in *Xenopsylla spp.* the episternum of the metathorax is separated by a suture from the 3rd sternite, in *S. pallidus* there is no suture separating the two plates (see Fig. 148).

The combed fleas

The only combed fleas which are likely to be met with by the medical officer are *Ctenocephalides felis* (the cat flea), *C. canis* (the dog flea), *Nosopsyllus fasciatus* (the rat flea of the temperate zones) and *Leptopsylla segnis* (the mouse flea. These fleas are chiefly important as a biting nuisance but in laboratory conditions they have been shown capable of acting as vectors of bubonic plague and endemic typhus and in nature they probably play a minor part in the transmission of these diseases. In addition they act as intermediate hosts of certain cestode parasites which although common in animals are of rare occurrence in man.

1) *Ctenocephalides canis and C. felis.* The genus *Ctenocephalides*, the members of which possess both genal and pronotal combs, includes about a dozen species and subspecies, only two of which, *C. canis* and *C. felis*, are common and widespread. These two species normally feed indiscriminately on dogs or cats in the bedding of which they breed, but they do not confine their attacks to these animals and readily bite man.

2) *Nosopsyllus fasciatus.* This flea possesses a pronotal comb but lacks a genal comb. It is primarily a parasite of rats and although originally confined to

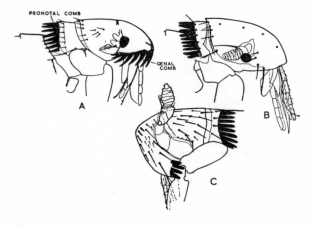

Fig. 156. Heads of *A. Ctenocephalides* sp.; *B. Nosopsyllus fasciatus*; *C. Leptopsylla segnis* (the antenna is shown erect).

Europe has spread to many other parts of the world; in the tropics it is to be found chiefly in sea ports. It does not bite man readily.

3) *Leptopsylla segnis* .This species possesses both pronotal and genal combs but unlike species of the genus *Ctenocephalides* the spines of the genal comb are backwardly directed and there are two spines on the occiput. It is a parasite of mice and, occasionally, rats, and only rarely bites man, whom it shows a distinct reluctance to attack. It is a not uncommon species of flea and may usually be collected from mice in households or other dwelling places.

The medical importance of fleas*

1) *Fleas as a cause of irritation.*

Although fleas are important vectors of disease there is little doubt that in the everyday life of most human communities they would pass almost unnoticed if it was not that the reactions following their bites in sensitised persons are the cause of much irritation and discomfort. Only three species, *Pulex irritans, Ctenocephalides canis* and *C. felis* are of worldwide importance in this respect, but other species may be of local importance, as for example in Senegal where *Synosternus pallidus* is usually the commonest flea frequenting human habitations.

2) *Fleas as transmitters of bubonic plague.*

Bubonic plague, which like pneumonic plague, is caused by *Pasteurella pestis*, is primarily a disease of rodents, man only becoming secondarily infected. Bubonic plague occurs in two epidemiological forms, one of which affects wild field rodents (such as gerbils in South Africa, voles and squirrels in the Western U.S.A. and marmots in Asiatic Russia) and is designated as sylvatic or campestral plague, whilst the second form, which is the extension of sylvatic plague to areas of human aggregations, affects urban rodents (chiefly *Rattus rattus* and *R. norvegicus*) and is known as urban plague.

Sylvatic plague is maintained in field rodents by a number of species of wild rodent fleas from which man occasionally becomes infected with the disease, particularly when handling dead animals. Urban rats acquire plague from infected wild rodents, and the infection is maintained in these urban rodents chiefly through the agency of fleas belonging to the genus *Xenopsylla*. In certain circumstances, particularly during an epizootic of plague amongst urban rats, the fleas leave their normal hosts, attack man and infect him with the disease.

The most important transmitter of *P. pestis* to man is *Xenopsylla cheopis*, but *X. braziliensis* and *X. astia* have been shown to be efficient vectors. As mentioned already, man also acquires plague from wild rodent fleas but the specific identity of the fleas involved in these cases, which are sporadic in occurrence, is not known for certain, and probably a number of species are involved; in the western U.S.A., *Diamanus montanus,* a squirrel flea, and in Russia *Oropsylla silantiewi,* a marmot flea, may have been responsible for some of the cases.

Fleas feeding on plague infected rodents, whose blood contains *P. pestis* in sufficient concentration, take up the bacilli into the stomach, in which site they multiply and extend forwards into the proventriculus. In certain instances, particularly in the case of fleas of the genus *Xenopsylla*, multiplication in the proventriculus interferes with the normal functioning of the valve by forming colonies between the proventricular rods and sometimes causes narrowing ("partial blocking") or complete obliteration ("complete blocking") of the gut lumen. Fleas infected with plague from a rodent host may leave it for a number of reasons, the commonest cause being the death of the animal.

---

* Burrowing fleas of the genera *Tunga* and *Echidnophaga* are omitted as their medical importance has been considered already.

Having done so they seek out a new host, preferably another rodent, but if such a host is not available they will feed on man.

The plague infected flea may transfer its infection to a new host in a variety of ways, as for example through the infected faeces of the flea reaching an

Fig. 157. The development of *Pasteurella pestis* in *Xenopsylla cheopis*. *A*. early stage of development: the proventriculus is still functioning normally. *B*. partial blocking: the proventriculus is no longer forming an efficient valve. *C*. complete blocking: blood is no longer able to pass into or escape from the stomach.

abrasion in the skin, but such methods of transfer are of little or no epidemiological significance and the vast majority of infections occur through the bite of partially or completely blocked fleas. In the case of the partially blocked flea, the insect is capable of taking up blood into the mid-gut but cannot retain it there owing to the non-functioning of the proventriculus and as a result some of the regurgitated blood, mixed with plague bacilli, is delivered back into the puncture wound. In the case of the completely blocked flea no blood can be drawn up into the stomach but the oscillating column of blood in contact with the proventriculus loosens clumps of bacilli and these may similarly gain access to the wound.

In the case of the partially blocked flea the longevity may not be significantly lessened and such fleas may inflict many infective bites during their lifetime. The life of the completely blocked flea is greatly shortened, nevertheless during this shortened life the blocked flea, in its endeavours to satisfy its hunger, bites not once but many times and may attack several hosts in this way.

Fleas as transmitters of endemic typhus

Murine typhus or flea-borne typhus (caused by *Rickettsia mooseri*) following the attacks of infected fleas occurs in many parts of the tropical and subtropical world. The chief species concerned are *Xenopsylla*, particularly *X. cheopis*, *Nosopsyllus fasciatus* and, much less commonly, *C. felis* and *C. canis*. All these species become infected by feeding on the rat reservoir of the disease, man rarely if ever acting as a source of infection to the flea. The ingested rickettsiae multiply in the gut but unlike *P. pestis* do not cause blocking of the proventriculus, and infection results from the faeces or crushed bodies of the fleas coming into contact with abrasions or scratches in the skin.

Fleas as transmitters of cestode infections

Three species of cestodes, *Dipylidium caninum*, *Hymenolepis nana* (the rodent variety) and *H. diminuta*, all of which normally develop in animals, but occasionally parasitise man, have fleas as their intermediate hosts. The eggs of these helminths are taken up by the larval fleas, and the cysticercoids, which are infective to man, are found in the adult insect, so that in normal circumstances infection can only be contracted by swallowing the adult flea. The swallowing of such infected fleas by man is, of course, of rare occurrence, although children and others sometimes acquire the infestation by the too close fondling of domestic pets. As regards the species of fleas most commonly involved, *D. caninum* is usually transmitted by fleas of the genus *Ctenocephalides*, whilst *H. diminuta* and *H. nana* are harboured by *Nosopsyllus fasciatus* and *Xenopsylla* spp.

Fleas are vectors of many protozoal and helminth infections which are not transmissible to man; amongst the former is *Trypanosoma lewisi*, a not uncommon infection amongst laboratory rats.

CHAPTER XXXVI

THE ORDER ANOPLURA

THE order Anoplura (meaning without pleurons, although much reduced pleurons are always present) is made up of dorso-ventrally flattened wingless insects which have a hemimetabolous life-cycle and which are permanent ecto-parasites on mammals, to whose hair (and clothes, in the case of man) they attach their eggs.

Members of the order Anoplura, all of which are known as "sucking lice", possess "sucking" mouthparts borne on an elongated head. These insects must be distinguished from members of the order Mallophaga which are found both on birds and mammals and which are known as "biting lice", possessing mouthparts adapted for chewing and set on a broad head. Although the common biting louse of the dog, *Trichodectes canis,* occasionally acts as an additional intermediate host for *Dipylidium caninum,* nevertheless, biting lice which are common parasites of domestic stock never infest man nor transmit diseases to him and therefore they may be omitted from further consideration.

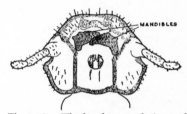

Fig. 158. The head, ventral view, of *Trichodectes canis*, a member of the order Mallophaga, showing "chewing" mouthparts.

The order Anoplura, in contradistinction to the order Mallophaga, includes certain species of great medical importance. If consideration is given to what insects have most affected man and determined his progress in the world, it would probably be agreed that in the tropics he has been more hampered by the mosquito than by any other insect. On the other hand, if man's progress all over the world including the temperate zones is considered, then unquestionably the flea and the louse have been man's worst enemies, and of the two the louse has caused greater and more devastating epidemics than has the flea.

All lice belonging to the order Anoplura, whatever their species, are permanent obligatory ecto-parasites living entirely on mammals (they do not infest birds) and obtaining their nourishment by sucking blood. They are specific in their choice of hosts to a remarkable extent, so that the lice found on man cannot normally survive on any other animal, while similarly the lice from animals cannot live on man. Some species have no eyes and when eyes are present they are rudimentary and appear to be used, as in the case of the flea, to avoid exposure to light. In sucking lice the body is flattened dorso-ventrally to allow the insect to crawl through the hair of the host and is covered with a leathery integument that resists crushing. The legs are stout and thick,

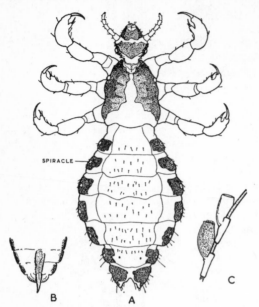

SPIRACLE

C

B   A

Fig. 159. *Pediculus humanus* var. *corporis*. A. female;
B. tip of abdomen of male; C. eggs of *Pediculus* sp.
attached to a hair.

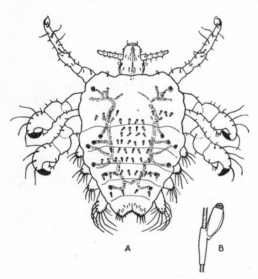

A   B

Fig. 160. *Phthirus pubis*. A. female; B. egg attached
to a hair.

rather lobster-like, and obviously adapted for grasping such objects as the hairs of the host and also, in the case of man, the fibres of his clothing. It will be seen later that many of these biological and anatomical characteristics play a very important part in determining the manner in which lice act as vectors of disease. The order Anoplura is comprised of six families and contains several hundred species, but only two of these species, *Pediculus humanus* and *Phthirus pubis*, occur on the human host.

PHTHIRUS PUBIS

Phthirus pubis, commonly known as the "crab louse" or "pubic louse" has been recognised since the earliest times as a parasite of man, and its form and its distribution on the body have caused it to be distinguished from both the head louse and the body louse. It is a common parasite of man (although not so common as *Pediculus*) and has a worldwide distribution.

In its general anatomy *Phthirus* resembles *Pediculus*, but the two genera can be easily distinguished by the rounded, almost circular, shape of the former and by the fact that whereas in *Pediculus*, all three pairs of legs are about equally developed, in the case of *Phthirus* they are unequal, the front pair being less well developed than the hind. The egg of the crab louse is smaller than that of the body louse and the blob of cement which attaches it to the hair is relatively larger.

The sexes can be distinguished by examining the tip of the abdomen which, in the female, shows the presence of claspers and gonopods, while in the case of the male the aedeagus usually protrudes from the sexual orifice. Both sexes suck blood.

The life-cycle and bionomics of the crab louse resemble those of the body louse but differ from it in that whereas the eggs and active forms of the body louse occur on the host's clothing as well as on the hair of the body, all stages of the crab louse are confined to the body hair. In addition, although the lice of both genera frequently change their position on the surface of the body, crab lice are much more sluggish and more confined in their movements than are body lice.

Crab lice live attached to the hair of the human host, usually in the pubic and peri-anal regions, but they may be found on the eye-lashes, on the hair of the face, in the axilla and elsewhere. They are seldom found on the scalp, probably because of the density of the hair there.

There is no proof that in nature the crab louse transmits any disease to man, although it has been proved to transmit typhus in the laboratory and there is a suggestion that it may do so in China. In some individuals characteristic blue spots (2-20 mm. in diameter) are produced by the bites of the crab louse, a reaction which is caused by the saliva from the reniform salivary glands.

Infection with *Phthirus* is usually acquired through coitus but it is a mistake to consider this as the only channel of infection, for it may be acquired in other ways such as the wearing of discarded clothing, or from infested beds, or from latrine seats. It is probable that in these cases infection is spread by eggs or active forms attached to loose hairs dropped by infected persons.

Modern treatment of crab lice infestations does not involve shaving of the infested areas since DDT and *gamma* BHC are both effective. There is always some risk of dermatitis when treating pediculosis of the ano-genital region, and it is well to remember that this may be caused by the vehicle as well as by the drug.

PEDICULUS HUMANUS

It has long been recognised that infestations with *Pediculus humanus* may be confined either to the head or to the trunk. In the past these two populations were regarded as distinct species and named respectively *Pediculus capitis*, the head louse, and *P. corporis* (syn. *P. vestimenti*) the body louse. These two varieties can be distinguished one from the other by certain small but constant anatomical differences, but the distinction is more of academic than of practical importance and it is now agreed that *P. capitis* and *P. corporis* are varieties of the same species which have adopted different modes of life, due to their anatomical distribution when on the human host, but are able to interbreed freely and produce fertile offsprings.

For reasons which are partially but not fully understood, although both varieties are equally capable of infection in the laboratory with spirochaetal and rickettsial infections, in nature the head louse is a much less important vector of disease than is the body louse.

Pediculus humanus var. *capitis*

Apart from the differences already noted, the life-cycle and habits of *P. capitis* are similar to those of *P. corporis*, and except under the heading of control measures, no further reference will be made to the head louse.

Pediculus humanus var. *corporis*

Still recognizable specimens of lice have been recovered from Peruvian mummies, and their association with man together with the irritation caused by their presence must have been recognised since the earliest times. It was not until 1907 however, that their association with disease was clearly established, at which time Mackie proved that the body louse is a vector of epidemic relapsing fever. Some three years later Nicolle transferred the infection of epidemic typhus from a man to a chimpanzee and demonstrated that the disease could be transmitted by feeding "clean" lice on an infected monkey and, after the necessary incubation period, to a "clean" monkey. During the war of 1914-1918 "trench fever", which in France was responsible for more days off duty than any other single disease, was similarly shown to be louse-borne.

The body louse has a worldwide distribution but in the tropics its occurrence is virtually confined to persons wearing clothing and although the minimal amount of clothing, such as a loin cloth, will support a louse population, the heaviest infestations tend to occur on persons whose whole body is clothed. In consequence, populations of body lice and the diseases associated with their presence tend to reach the maximum in conditions of relative cold.

Members of the genus *Pediculus* have a very characteristic appearance and are not likely to be confused with insects of other genera. The adult female body louse measures 3 to 4 mm. in length, while the males are slightly smaller. Both sexes are flattened dorso-ventrally. Lice have a soft, but nevertheless tough, skin which is of a dirty white to grey colour. The general form of the louse is shown in Fig. 159. This drawing shows that although the body is clearly divided into a head, thorax and abdomen, as is characteristic of all insects, segmentation of the thorax is not noticeable.

The antennae are short and consist of five segments. The eyes are inconspicuous and are placed rather far back on the head. The three pairs of legs end in grasping organs (legs consist of tibia, tarsus and claw) which are obviously adapted for holding on to the hair of the host. There is a single pair of spiracles on the thorax and a pair on each abdominal segment, the latter being very prominent structures. The sexes can be distinguished by the bifurcation of the tip of the abdomen in the female and by the absence of bifurcation and the presence of an aedeagus in the male. Both sexes suck blood and are equally concerned in the transmission of disease.

The mouthparts of the louse are arranged on rather a different plan from those of the other insects so far considered. They consist of a flexible, sucking mouth, the haustellum (*haurire*, to suck), armed on the inner surface with minute teeth with which the louse grips the skin of its host, while the cutting apparatus with which the louse draws blood consists of two stylets, one of which is dorsal to the other, both stylets originating in the ventral diverticulum called the stylet sac. The walls of the stylet sac are continued into the mouth cavity where they form a gutter, within the groove of which the stylets can be alternately extended and retracted. During its meal the louse injects the salivary secretion, derived from the four salivary glands in the thorax, through the hypopharynx which lies in close association with the dorsal stylet. Having cut the skin and injected the salivary secretion, the louse operates its powerful sucking pharynx, so that blood mixed with saliva is drawn from the wound and passes into the buccal cavity. From the buccal cavity the blood is taken up into the oesophagus and gut by means of the pharyngeal tube, which consists of two closely applied half-tubes representing a forward prolongation of the pharynx. The arrangement of these various structures is represented diagrammatically in Fig. 161.

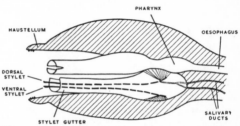

Fig. 161. Diagrammatic representation of the mouthparts and sucking apparatus of a louse as seen in a longitudinal setion cut through the head.

After fertilisation the female body louse lays her eggs either on the hairs of the clothing (almost exclusively on the underclothing, chiefly along the seams of the vests, pants, shirt, etc.) or on the hairs of the body, usually on the more densely hairy regions such as occur in the axillae and on the pubis. In normal circumstances the majority (some 70%) of the eggs are laid on the clothing and the remainder on the body hair.

When the louse is about to lay an egg she grasps one of the hairs of the body or a

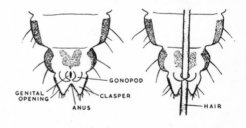

Fig. 162. Tip of abdomen of *Pediculus* sp., female, showing position assumed during oviposition. (Semi–diagrammatic).

strand of the clothing with her legs, in such a way that the stem of the hair or fibre lies along the ventral aspect of her abdomen—after the manner of a

P

man climbing a rope—and is brought into contact with the genital opening by being held between the gonopods. The egg is then passed out of the vagina and during its passage through the oviduct the lower pole is coated with cement from the "cement glands" or "accessory glands". The egg passed through the vulva on to the hair is fixed to it in the characteristic position shown in Fig. 159. The cement attaching the egg to the hair dries extremely hard, and resists any amount of washing or the action of chemicals which are not injurious to the skin; hence the reason why in severe infestations it is only possible to remove the eggs from the body or scalp by cutting or shaving the hair.

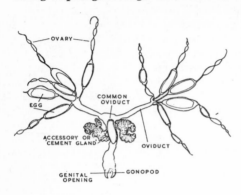

Fig. 163.   Diagrammatic representation of the reproductive system of *Pediculus* sp. female showing an egg, immediately prior to deposition, lying in the oviduct where it receives the products of the "cement gland"'s.

The egg is oval in shape and crowned with a rounded cap or operculum provided with perforations through which the developing louse obtains air; thus the whole egg has the appearance of a pepper pot. These perforations are of importance as they explain why the application of any oily substance which blocks up the air holes, although seldom killing the embryo, prolongs the process of hatching.

Air is required not only for supplying oxygen to the tissues but also to assist the louse in leaving the egg. For this purpose it swallows air which distends the body and thus gives the imprisoned louse a purchase against the side walls of the egg and enables it to press its head against the operculum and burst it open. In normal conditions the developmental period in the egg lasts about a week, but if the eggs are not kept warm, as in the case of discarded clothing in winter, it may be three weeks before the insect emerges from the egg. In no combination of circumstances have eggs hatched after one month's storage, so that previously infested fomites are safe to use after this period.

The female louse lays a steady sequence of eggs at the rate of seven to ten a day throughout her life; as this may last for as much as a month she is capable of producing between two hundred and three hundred eggs in her lifetime. The young larva which emerges closely resembles its parents except that it is smaller and not yet sexually mature.

The nymph undergoes three moults before becoming full grown and sexually mature and, in the case of the female, capable of laying eggs. This growing period usually occupies about eight days; the total cycle therefore from egg to egg under favourable conditions is about sixteen days, made up of eight days in the egg and eight days growing to maturity.

Lice are so essentially parasitic that they perish in about ten days if kept away from the human host, although they may survive longer if they are given a full blood-meal and then kept under favourable conditions. For this reason they do not tend to infest houses, and discarded clothing becomes free from lice in a comparatively short time, dependent upon the temperature and humidity.

Lice are spread by crowding and close contact of humans, especially if facilities for washing and changing the clothes are difficult. It is for this reason that lice and the louse-borne diseases are so often closely associated with such national disasters as wars, earthquakes and famines, although any prolonged crowding together of human beings in insanitary surroundings will produce the same result.

Lice like a warm, moist atmosphere, 30°C being their optimum temperature: at 22°C they cannot lay eggs, and at 40°C lice are unable to feed. These reactions to temperature are of more than academic interest, for when the temperature of a person suffering from a louse-borne disease rises steeply the subsequent migration of his louse population will—if they are successful in finding a new host—cause a spread of the disease. A similar spread of the disease will follow the migration of lice away from the rapidly cooling body of a person who has died while suffering from a louse-borne disease.

The medical importance of lice

It is universally recognised that lice infestation lowers the social status and that the lousy man is looked down upon by his fellows; nor should it be forgotten that the irritation caused by the presence of lice generally results in scratching and may lead to extensive secondary infections.

Body lice and head lice are responsible for the transmission to man of at least three diseases, although, as already noted, the latter play a much less important part.

(1) *Typhus.*

The louse is responsible for the transmission of typhus, of the type known as typhus exanthematicus, epidemic typhus or louse-borne typhus. The causal organism, *Rickettsia prowazeki* (syn. *Rickettsia rickettsia*), after it has been taken up by the feeding louse invades and multiplies in the cells lining the gut. The invaded cells become distended with these organisms and about four days after the infecting meal the cells rupture and release the rickettsiae back into the lumen of the intestinal tract. The rickettsiae do not multiply in the coelom of the louse nor do they invade the salivary glands, hence man acquires his infection with typhus, either by the faeces of the louse gaining entrance through an abrasion of the skin, or, alternatively, by crushing an infected louse and the gut contents coming in contact with an abraded skin area. *R. prowazeki* is one of the few pathogenic organisms transmissible to man which causes the death of the insect host. Hence the louse which transmits the infection to man has a much reduced life span. This may explain why persons suffering from typhus are sometimes found to be free of lice.

(2) *Trench fever.*

The causal organism, *Rickettsia quintana,* when ingested by the feeding louse multiplies in the lumen of the insect's gut, but does not appear to destroy the cells lining the gut, neither does it occur in the haemocoele nor in the salivary glands. *R. quintana,* unlike *R. prowazeki,* does not seem to have any injurious effect on its insect host. Trench fever, like typhus, is conveyed to man by the infected louse faeces coming in contact with a skin abrasion. The organisms persist for long periods in the dried louse faeces and are capable of producing the disease if they enter abrasions in the skin or, possibly, if they are inhaled. People who are themselves free from lice may acquire trench fever as the result of handling fomites contaminated with dried louse faeces.

(3) *Relapsing fever.*

The causal organism, *Treponema recurrentis,* when taken up by the louse with a blood-meal, derived from a person suffering from epidemic (otherwise known as louse-borne) relapsing fever, usually disappears from the lumen of the insect's gut within twenty four hours, only to reappear, some six to eight days later, in enormously increased numbers in the haemocoele. This fresh invasion is almost entirely confined to the blood of the louse and spirochaetes do not occur in the lumen of the gut or in the salivary glands, hence man seldom acquires the infection in other ways than by crushing the louse.

Treatment and control of body lice infestations

It is generally agreed that for the treatment of the individual harbouring body lice the following will suffice. All clothing directly in contact with the skin should be freely dusted with a powder containing 10% DDT. The treated clothing should then be worn for ten days before it is sent to be washed and laundered. If the individual finds it necessary to change the treated clothing before the expiration of ten days, the fresh garments should be similarly treated, and the discarded garments laundered, and dusted with DDT when returned. For treatment of infested communities, blowing DDT in a concentration of 10% in an inert powder under the clothing with a dust-gun is cheap, quick and effective. Shaving of the body hairs is seldom, if ever, necessary.

Control and treatment of head lice infestations

For the treatment of infestation by head lice *gamma* BHC and DDT are both effective, but whereas the former has an ovicidal effect, DDT only kills the active forms of the louse. A single treatment with 2 per cent DDT in aqueous emulsion is stated to secure a cure in nearly every case in which it is properly applied, and to provide protection against reinfestation for at least a fortnight. Cutting of the hair is unnecessary except for the treatment of severe secondary pyogenic infection.

CHAPTER XXXVII

THE ORDER HEMIPTERA

MEMBERS of the order Hemiptera or Rhynchota have a worldwide distribution and although they all possess a hemimetabolous life-cycle they differ greatly in their size, their shape and their habits. Some are very large insects, like certain giant members of the family Belastomidae which exceed 4 inches in length and are capable of killing small fish and frogs, whilst others, such as plant lice, are so small that they pass unseen unless their habitat is examined with a lens. The various species within the order also exhibit great diversity in form. Some species, such as members of the family Hydrometridae which are found on the surface of stagnant ponds, are stick-like in form; others—like certain members of the family Coreidae—closely resemble ants. Whilst many species, which are important because of the damage they do to crops, are scale-like and only recognisable as insects following a careful examination.

In spite of these great variations in size and appearance, members of the order Hemiptera have one easily recognisable character in common; the proboscis, which is always adapted for sucking, is kept bent under the body and the relatively large labium is commonly 3 or 4 segmented.

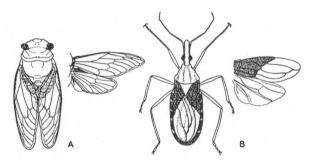

Fig. 164. Semi-diagrammatic representation of *A.* a bug in the suborder Homoptera, showing the membraneous character of the 1st and 2nd wings and *B.* a bug in the suborder Heteroptera showing the thickened and leathery base of the first wing.

Wings are usually present, but in certain species, notably some of the plant feeding bugs and in the medically important species of bugs in the family Cimicidae, they are absent. When wings are present two pairs are always found, and the division of the order Hemiptera into its two suborders (Heteroptera and Homoptera) is largely based on the characters of the first pair. In the suborder Homoptera, in which the wings slope over the sides of the body like the eves of a house, both pairs are similar in texture being uniformly membraneous. In the case of the suborder Heteroptera the two pairs of wings, which fold over each other and cover the abdomen, are dissimilar. Whereas the second pair of wings (as in the case of the Homoptera) are wholly membraneous, the first pair are membraneous only at the extremities, the bases being thickened and leathery. This latter type of wing is known as a hemielytron.

There are no species of medical importance in the suborder Homoptera, all the known species being normally plant feeders. The suborder Heteroptera similarly includes many species which are plant feeders, but it also includes a proportion of species which feed on the body fluids of animals, both vertebrates and invertebrates. Two families of the order Heteroptera—the family Cimicidae and the family Reduviidae—are important to human welfare since they each include several species which habitually feed on man. Those species which are of medical importance are discussed in the following chapters.

CHAPTER XXXVIII

THE FAMILY CIMICIDAE

THE family Cimicidae is composed of wingless bugs which are temporary obligatory parasites of mammals and birds, throughout their life-cycles. They are oval and, when hungry, dorso-ventrally flattened insects which vary from 2 to 6 mm. in length. When unfed they are of a light yellow or brown colour but after a full blood-meal the body darkens to a mahogany

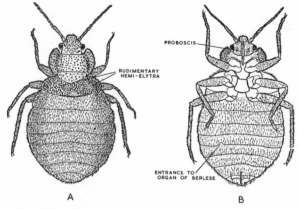

Fig. 165. *Cimex lectularius*, female. *A.* dorsal view, *B.* ventral view.

tint and becomes rounded. The hemielytra are so reduced as to be scale-like in appearance; while the proboscis, which is short and fine, lies in a groove on the ventral surface of the head.

Bugs in the family Cimicidae are chiefly parasites of birds and bats. There are four subfamilies containing over 35 species two of which, *Cimex lectularius* and *Cimex rotundatus* (commonly known as "bed bugs") habitually feed on man, although they will bite a wide variety of other hosts. Other species of cimicid bugs, such as *Leptocimex boueti*, which normally feeds on bats, and *C. columbarius* which is a pigeon parasite, together with bugs of the genus *Oeciacus*, which are parasitic on swallows in the British Isles, will attack man if the occasion arises.

"The bed bugs" : C. lectularius and C. rotundatus (= C. hemipterus)

From early times the bed bug has been known by a wide variety of other names such as "wall louse" and "mahogany flat". References to bed bugs as annoying creatures appear in many early papers, and in 1730 John Southall wrote a treatise on bugs and their control in which he showed a remarkable knowledge of his subject.

Although bed bugs have not been known to transmit disease in nature, nevertheless they have been shown to do so in laboratory conditions, while their presence in dwelling houses is obnoxious and their bites, particularly in sensitised persons, may give rise to considerable discomfort and even chronic ill-health as a result of sleepless nights.

The common bed bug, *Cimex lectularius*, is found chiefly in temperate and subtropical regions but it occurs also in certain parts of the tropics to which it has been carried by man. The most usual form of transport is in ships; indeed, in all parts of the world, bug infested houses are notoriously common in seaports. *Cimex rotundatus* is more restricted in its distribution and is essentially a tropical species; it, like *C. lectularius*, tends to be more common in coastal areas than inland. Since the two species have similar life-cycles and habits and since the methods employed for their control are almost identical, it is seldom necessary for the medical officer to observe the small morphological differences by which they can be distinguished.

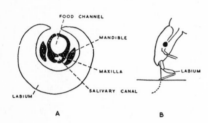

Fig. 166. *A*. Transverse section through the proboscis of a bed bug; *B*. position of the mouth parts when feeding. (Diagrammatic).

In *C. lectularius* and *C. rotundatus* the head is short and broad and bears a pair of small conspicuous compound eyes set on slight lateral prominences; the antennae, which are four segmented, are long and slender. The proboscis is short and lies pressed to the head and prothorax.

The mouthparts of bugs are unlike those of other insects; the labium when straightened out forms a hollow gutter containing the piercing and sucking apparatus, consisting of two mandibles and two maxillae. Their relationship in the labium is depicted in transverse section in Fig. 166; and this shows a different arrangement of the mouthparts from that of the insect groups previously discussed. Whereas in most blood-sucking insects the labrum forms the food channel, in the Hemiptera the labrum is reduced to a little projection, which appears more or less functionless, while the maxillae, when closely applied to each other (which is their normal position), form a two grooved fascicle, one tube acting as the food channel and the other as the salivary canal. The hypopharynx, as in fleas, is reduced to a minute pointed structure projecting into the proximal end of the salivary channel formed by the maxillae. In the Hemiptera the mandibles only act as cutting instruments, for which purpose each mandible is finely serrated and takes no part in the conveyance of food or saliva. There are no maxillary or labial palps.

When feeding, the bed bug places the tip of the labium against the skin which it pierces with its sharp mandibles. Into the cut thus made are inserted the mandibles and the double tube formed by the two maxillae, up one division of which the blood is sucked, while the saliva passes down the other. In order to allow these organs to penetrate deeply, the labium must be shortened, and this is done partly by bending, as in the case of the mosquitoes, and partly by the telescoping of the joints.

The first thoracic segment of the bed bug is distinctly larger than the second and third, and has characteristic wing-like expansions, which give the head the appearance of nestling in the thorax. Although bed bugs lack wings, vestiges may be recognised in the hemielytra which lie over the second and third thoracic segments. The three pairs of legs, the first pair of which is shorter than the second pair, are slender and moderately long.

The abdomen is oval in form with eight visible segments; in the male the tip is more pointed than in the female and from the genital opening may be seen projecting a strong and slightly curved penis. In the female on·the right side of the ventral surface of the apparent fourth segment, there is a nick in the chitin which opens into a saccular organ known as the organ of Berlese (or Ribaga). This organ lies free in the haemocoele and after copulation serves as a temporary reservoir for the sperm.

Life-cycle of the bed bug

Like other members of the order Hemiptera, the bed bug has a hemimetabolous life-cycle. The fertilised female, after a blood-meal, lays pearly white eggs which are about 1 mm. in length and have a characteristic appearance. They are oval in shape and slightly curved at the anterior end which is provided with a distinct cap (or operculum) and are ornamented with a light mosaic pattern. As a consequence of their characteristic form bed bug eggs can easily be distinguished from those of other househaunting insects, a fact which is of value in searching dwellings for evidence of infestation.

Fig. 167. Eggs of *Cimex* sp., hatched and unhatched.

The eggs are laid at the rate of 2 to 3 a day in unexposed sites such as cracks and crevices in the wall or flooring, spaces in the woodwork of furniture and behind pictures and wallpaper. Occasionally as many as 40 or 50 eggs will be found attached close together. During her lifetime (the span of which is very variable and may be anything from a month to a year) the female will lay up to 100 eggs, each egg being laid in an upright position and firmly attached to the substrate by cement. The egg output increases for several weeks and then falls off gradually; since the females have to be fertilised regularly it is not uncommon to find that some of the eggs do not hatch.

The incubation period of the egg is dependent on temperature. Since bugs are house-dwellers, the speed of development of their ova is subject to normal variations in household temperature. The eggs usually take 9 to 10 days to hatch, but at low temperatures this period may be prolonged to several weeks, while at temperatures below 14°C they do not hatch. Temperatures of about 27°C allow hatching to take place in under a week.

Prior to hatching the larva moves up towards the operculum and its red eyes may be seen through the egg shell from which it emerges by pushing off the operculum, leaving behind the characteristic empty egg which may or may not have the cap attached to its rim. The newly hatched larva, which measures about 1.5. mm. and is almost colourless, does not leave the breeding place for some 24 hours, at the end of which time it is ready to seek its first blood-meal.

The bug undergoes five ecdyses before reaching sexual maturity, each instar requiring at least one blood-meal before moulting to the next stage. The cast skins accumulate in the bugs' resting places, and these, together with the eggs, form a valuable means of establishing the presence of bed bug infestations. The time required to reach sexual maturity under optimum conditions is between 6 weeks to 2 months but is often considerably prolonged since it is dependent not only on optimum temperature conditions but also on a constant supply of hosts. All stages and both sexes must feed regularly on warm-blooded animals; they prefer man to other hosts but maintain themselves in or near human habitations by feeding on rodents, poultry and bats. Bed bugs will feed every few days but they can withstand starvation for long periods, sometimes for months. Normally they feed only at night, the height of activity being reached in the early hours of the morning, but in darkened surroundings or if they are particularly avid for blood they feed in the daytime.

Since bed bugs, having no wings are unable to fly, their dissemination is brought about partly by the migration of individual bugs from one building to the other, but more often by the carriage (by land, sea, or air) of infested household goods, chiefly furniture but also drapery and clothing, whether packed or worn on the person.

The bed bug is not known to transmit diseases in nature but its importance as a disturber of the peace and as a degrader of social status is great and its nuisance value should not be underestimated.

As has been stated earlier in this chapter, the presence of bed bugs in an habitation may be established not only by the finding of the living insects but also by the presence of the eggs and cast skins. In addition, it should be mentioned that other useful guides are the presence of the characteristic "bug marks" (due to the insects' excretions) on wall paper and on walls, and the peculiar odour which some persons have the ability to recognise. Once the presence of an infestation has been established it is usually comparatively easy to effect control, for since bed bugs cannot fly and since they must usually cross open spaces to reach their food supply, they readily fall victims to contact insecticides such as DDT and BHC. The thorough spraying of infested rooms has achieved good results in Europe and up to the present resistance has not been reported in Britain. Resistance to DDT and to other chlorinated insecticides has, however, developed in bugs in many parts of the tropics.

CHAPTER XXXIX

THE FAMILY REDUVIIDAE

THE family Reduviidae is one of the largest families in the suborder Heteroptera, being composed of 29 subfamilies. Of these only one, the subfamily Triatominae, comprises species which are blood-suckers, certain of which habitually feed on mammals including man.

Triatomine bugs or rapacious bugs, which are familiarly known as "kissing bugs", "assassin bugs" or "cone nose bugs" are elongated insects generally of a dull colour, although some species have yellow or red markings. The head, which is separated from the thorax by a distinct neck, is long and snout-like and bears on its under surface a fine, straight and relatively short proboscis. The antennae are four segmented and are inserted on the sides of the head in front of the eyes. Triatomines may be distinguished from other reduviid bugs, occurring in sub-families other than the subfamily Triatominae, since in the latter the proboscis is coarse and distinctly curved while the antennae arise from the dorsal surface; these (non-triatomine) bugs are predaceous in habit feeding on other arthropods, and are therefore free from suspicion as disease carriers.

A   B

Fig. 168.   A. Head of a bug belonging to the subfamily Triatominae showing the antennae arising from the sides of the head and the straight proboscis; B. head of a bug belonging to a sub-family other than the Triatominae showing the antennae arising from the dorsal surface of the head and the curved proboscis.

Triatomine bugs are almost entirely American in distribution being found from the United States to the Argentine, but one species *Triatoma rubrofasciata* occurs throughout the tropics, and three species are found in Asia and Africa. Although early voyagers to the New World collected reduviid bugs and observed that certain species sucked blood, and although the morphology of these insects was studied by European entomologists as far back as the 18th century, it was not until 1909, when Chagas in Brazil showed that *Panstrongylus megistus* transmitted *Trypanosoma cruzi* (the causal organism of South American trypanosomiasis), that reduviid bugs attracted the attention of medical scientists. In this connection, Neiva, working in Brazil in 1910, made a detailed taxonomic study of the subfamily Triatominae, such a study being an essential preliminary to further biological and medical investigations.

Today about 100 species of triatomine bugs, occurring in some 11 genera, are recognised, the distinction between the different genera being based on morphological characters outside the scope of this book.

All the species of triatomine bugs so far studied allow the development of *T. cruzi*, and probably a very large number of species are concerned in maintaining the disease in the animal reservoir. On the other hand there are

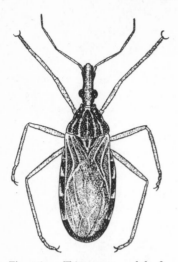

Fig. 169. *Triatoma* sp., adult female, dorsal view.

only a very limited number of species which, by reason of their domestic or semi-domestic habits, transmit the disease to man, and these species are mainly confined to the genera *Triatoma, Rhodnius* and *Panstrongylus*.

Both sexes of triatomine bugs suck blood, and they usually feed at night and in conditions of darkness.

Morphology of the adult bug

Triatomine bugs, which may be recognised and distinguished from other bugs by the characters already given, vary in size from less than one, to over three centimetres in length. Most of the species which attack man are large bugs which are generally of a sombre hue, but in some species the base of the wings and the exposed flanks of the abdomen show patches of red and yellow, giving the insect a banded appearance.

The head. The head is elongated, with prominent dark brown or black eyes, and bears a proboscis which when the insect is not feeding is carried flexed under the head and thorax, with its tip resting in a groove between the first pair of legs. The antennae which are four segmented and, although slender, are very conspicuous, always arise from the sides of the head, either immediately in front of the eyes or some distance anterior to them.

The slender proboscis is composed of a relatively fleshy, three segmented, gutter-like labium, in which lie the long stylet-like mandibles and maxillae. When the insect attacks its host the labium, containing the mandibles and maxillae, is swung forwards and the tip of the labium is applied to the skin of the host. The mandibles and maxillae, which are motivated by powerful protractors within the head, are then driven into the skin, a slight telescoping of the segments of the labium taking place at the same time. The mandibles, which are markedly serrated at their tips, act as anchors of the fascicle, whilst the maxillae probe in various directions until they meet and penetrate a blood-vessel, into the lumen of which they are then thrust. As in the case of the bed bug the maxillae form a double tube (like the barrels of a shot-gun) one tube acting as a food channel up which the blood is sucked, while the other tube acts as a pipe down which the saliva is pumped.

The thorax. The thorax, as viewed from the dorsal surface, shows only the conspicuous pronotum, the mesothorax and metathorax being hidden by the folded wings. The pronotum is somewhat triangular in shape, with projecting postero-lateral angles which give the bug the appearance of having shoulders. Immediately behind the pronotum are two pairs of wings (only the upper pair is normally seen) which are folded scissor-like over the abdomen, covering all except its lateral borders. The first pair of wings are known as hemielytra, since the basal portion is considerably more heavily chitinised than is the distal and more membraneous portion. Below the hemielytra, which arise from the mesothorax, are a second pair of wings; these are membraneous and arise from the metathorax. In addition to the wings, the thorax bears three pairs of long slender legs, ending in paired claws.

The abdomen. The abdomen is broadly oval in shape, the lateral margins, which are up-tilted and which are not covered by the wings, being known as the connexiva. The genitalia are not prominent either in the male or the female and the tip of the abdomen must be closely examined with a hand lens to observe the slight prominence which distinguishes the male.

Life history and habits

Following mating, the females lay their eggs in or near to the resting places of the mammalian—or sometimes avian—hosts from which they obtain their blood-meals. In the case of the domestic and semi-domestic species of these bugs the eggs are found in cracks and crevices in the walls and floors of human habitations and of buildings housing domestic stock, particularly when these are in a dilapidated condition. The eggs of the non-domestic species are laid in the lairs, shelters, and nests of the wild animals or birds on which the active forms normally feed.

Copulation occurs shortly after emergence from the last nymphal instar and the first batch of eggs is laid some 10-14 days after the fertilised female has obtained a blood-meal. Oviposition occupies several days, most triatomine bugs laying their eggs in small batches, and it is unusual for more than 10-20 eggs to be laid in any one day. Once the ovaries are exhausted, the female will not lay again until another blood-meal has been obtained. The total number of eggs laid by one female during her lifetime probably may be anything between 50 and 500, and is dependent not only on the length of the insect's life, but also on the number of blood-meals which have been available.

The eggs, which vary in size and colour according to the species, when viewed with a hand lens are seen to be smooth-shelled oval objects with a well marked operculum at one end. In size they vary from 1.5 to 2.5 mm. in length and whereas many domestic species lay eggs which are pink in colour, certain species produce yellow, and others, white eggs. The eggs are either laid in groups and glued to the substrate, as is the case in *Rhodnius* spp., or they may be laid singly, either free or attached to the substrate, as is the case in most *Triatoma* spp.

After about 10 days, the first nymph (or larva) emerges from the egg by pushing off the operculum. It is a delicate creature, light in colour and generally resembling the adult in form but is without any trace of wings. Although the nymphs are capable of very active movement they usually remain in the hiding places until a few days have passed when they are ready to take a blood-meal. There are five nymphal stages in all, each nymphal stage requiring a full blood-meal before moulting to the next stage. The young nymph will take as much as 12 times its own weight in blood but as it approaches the adult stage the amount of blood taken up becomes relatively smaller, so that by the time the bug has reached the 5th nymphal stage it only takes 3 to 4 times its own weight. Only the adults have fully developed wings, but the wing lobes, which are the rudimentary wings of the future adult, begin to be clearly seen in the 4th and 5th nymphal stages.

Triatomine bugs are for the most part parasites of wild animals in whose shelters and holes they live; they are particularly common in the burrows of armadillos and in the nests of rodents (especially in those of wood rats of the genus *Neotoma*) but many species are not particular and feed on a wide range of wild mammals, domestic mammals and domestic birds. Several species, in particular *Rhodnius prolixus*, *Panstrongylus megistus*, *Triatoma infestans* and *T. phyllosoma* have adapted themselves to domestic conditions and are found especially in wood and mud huts of the poorer class peasant population, where they hide in cracks and holes in the walls in which they find the darkness and microclimatic conditions suitable for their development and breeding. Even if the huts are vacated, this does not necessarily result in the disappearance of the bug population, since the adults, once they have had a full meal, can resist starvation for several months, because of the large quantity of blood they ingest and the unusually slow rate of its digestion. When food supplies are no longer available the winged adults can take to flight to look for new hosts and shelters. The life-cycle of these bugs is an unusually long one and whereas when living in optimum conditions in the laboratory they can complete their development from egg to egg in a few months, it is probably that in nature the life-cycle occupies one to two years.

Medical importance of triatomine bugs

Although *Trypanosoma cruzi* is capable of undergoing development in all triatomine bugs of both sexes, and although the infection is maintained in the animal reservoir by many different species, only three species, due to their habit of living in peasant dwellings in close contact with man and feeding readily on the human host, are important vectors of Chagas' disease to man. *Rhodnius prolixus* is the vector in Central America and in the northern part of South America, *Panstrongylus megistus* in Brazil and *Triatoma infestans* in the Argentine and neighbouring territories. These bugs do not transmit by their bites as the metacyclic forms of *T. cruzi* are passed in the faeces and not in the saliva.

The bugs feed at night and attack any exposed skin areas so that persons sleeping clothed or under bedding tend to be bitten about the hands, neck and face, bites being particularly common around the mouth and eyes. Triatomine bugs usually take 10–20 minutes to obtain a full blood-meal and it is character-istic of many species to pass liquid or semi-liquid faeces during, or immediately after, the meal. If the metacyclic forms of *T. cruzi* are present in the faeces and if these gain access to the tissues through the mucous membranes or abrasions in the skin, infection of the human host is likely to result. In the case of certain species, at any rate, the bite is normally painless and there is no marked subsequent reaction; on the other hand, in the case of sensitised persons there is often a very severe reaction which may be immediate but which is more often delayed for 12-24 hours. The urticaria and scratching of the bitten area, associated with such reactions, probably increases the risk of infection.

In addition to *T. cruzi* another, and apparently benign, species of trypanosome, *T. rangeli*, is transmitted to man by triatomine bugs occurring in the genus *Rhodnius*. In the case of *T. rangeli* development to the metacyclic forms takes place both in the gut and in the salivary glands of the bug; transmission, therefore, is by the bite as well as by the faeces.

Control is largely dependent on housing conditions. Triatomine bugs tend not to frequent well built and well kept houses and any improvement in social conditions which leads to the abandonment of the wood and mud buildings results in the disappearance of the bugs and, consequently, of the disease.

The most effective insecticide appears to be *gamma* BHC, used as a powder (in a concentration of 1.0 gm. of the gamma isomer per square metre) and scattered over the floors and blown into crevices. Some workers claim as good or better results following the use of 3 per cent dieldrin powder at a concentration of 1 gm. per square metre.

CHAPTER XL

THE CLASS ARACHNIDA

THE class Arachnida which is one of the largest of the classes constituting the phylum Arthropoda is usually regarded as being divided into seven orders, three of which contain species of medical importance. Of these three orders, two, the order Araneida (the true spiders) and the order Scorpionida (the scorpions) contain a restricted number of species which are responsible for inflicting poisonous bites and stings; but although these arthropods may sometimes cause serious injuries and although they are often of considerable local importance, they cannot be regarded as of great medical significance. On the other hand the remaining order, the Acarina, in spite of the fact that it is largely composed of free-living species, contains a number of species which are parasitic and which are of very great importance as vectors of certain viral, rickettsial, spirochaetal and bacterial diseases to man.

Arachnids differ greatly from insects, both as regards their morphology and their life-cycles, and a brief account of the characters of the class Arachnida and how these differ from those of the class Insecta is given below.

External morphology of the Arachnida

Unlike the insects, in which the body is divided into three clearly recognisable regions—a head, a thorax and an abdomen—the arachnids possess a body which is either sac-like with no recognisable division between the cephalothorax (evolved from the fusion of the head and thorax) and the abdomen, as is the case in all ticks and most mites, or else it is divided into two recognisable parts (the cephalothorax and the abdomen) as is the case in the remaining arachnids.

The cephalothorax never bears antennae. Eyes may or may not be present and when present they are always simple, and not compound as in many species of insects. The cephalothorax bears six pairs of appendages the first two of which are concerned with feeding and the remaining four with locomotion. The first pair of appendages are known as the chelicerae and the second pair as the palps (pedipalps). The chelicerae are either pincer-like or simple piercing organs, whilst the palps are usually leg-like. In addition to the chelicerae and the palps there is an epistome or "upper lip", usually poorly developed, and a hypostome or "lower lip". The four pairs of legs are chiefly employed in locomotion although occasionally, notably in ticks and mites, the first pair may have in addition a sensory function and serve as feelers. Wings are never present.

The abdomen does not bear appendages. The genital opening, although varying in position, is usually situated ventrally. A terminal anus is always present.

Life history of arachnids

Arachnids are mostly oviparous, but a proportion of species reproduce

PLATE XIII

A triatomine bug (*Rhodnius prolixus*) in the act of feeding.
[*Courtesy Mr. Eric Norman*]

PLATE XIV

The bed bug (*Cimex lectularius*) in a resting attitude.

[*Courtesy Mr. J. P. Brady*]

viviparously. The stage which emerges from the egg, and which is known as a larva, generally resembles the adult in form but it possesses only three pairs of legs. The larva moults to give rise to one or more four-legged nymphal stages, which differ from the adults chiefly in lacking genital organs. There is thus an incomplete metamorphosis in the life-cycle of arachnids and never a complete metamorphosis as in the case of many insects.

CHAPTER XLI

THE ORDER ACARINA

THE Acarina is a large order comprising all the mites and ticks and contains many thousands of species, some of which are free-living forms, found in the soil or on plants, whilst others are parasitic forms which live on vertebrates and on invertebrates. Those species of acarines which are parasitic on vertebrates include many species which are not only troublesome pests to man and to his domestic stock but are also important vectors of disease. Amongst the latter are the "soft ticks", which are the transmitters of tick-borne relapsing fever, and the "hard ticks" which convey tick-borne typhus, tick-borne encephalitis, and possibly tularaemia.

Mites also act as vectors to man of disease, scrub-typhus being conveyed by trombiculid mites and rickettsial pox by laelaptid mites. Two species of mites, *Sarcoptes scabiei* var. *hominis* which gives rise to scabies, and *Demodex folliculorum* var. *hominis,* which is apparently non-pathogenic, occur in the skin of man and are obligatory parasites. In addition, certain other species of mites such as the tyroglyphids, which are non-parasitic and which live in foodstuffs, may, by coming into contact with human skin, cause a troublesome although transient allergic dermatitis.

The worldwide distribution of the acarines and the multiplicity of habitats and modes of life adopted by the various species within the order have resulted in the development of a great diversity of anatomical forms, with the result that it is difficult to define the order within strict systematic limits. All the species of medical importance, however, with the exception of *Demodex,* share certain features in common and the account of the order Acarina, which is given below, is therefore confined to a general consideration of the morphology and habits of these medically important species.

General morphology of the medically important Acarina

Most acarines of medical importance, with the exception of nymphal and adult ticks, are minute creatures which can only be satisfactorily studied by means of a microscope. A hand lens usually suffices for the examination of nymphal and adult ticks, although a microscope is necessary for the detailed study of certain taxonomic features, such as the dentition of the hypostome. All ticks and mites with the exception of *Demodex* possess an unsegmented saccular body and there is usually little or no indication of a division of the body into a cephalothorax and an abdomen; the exception, *Demodex,* is elongated and worm like, and has an annulated abdomen.

Most species have a dorsal plate or scutum which varies considerably in size and form, from the very small cephalothoracic plate which occurs on the scabies mite (*S. Scabiei,*) to the large scutum which, in the case of the male ixodid, covers almost the whole of the dorsal surface. In some acarines distinct ventral plates are also present. The shape and appearance of these plates, or scuta, and the type of setae which occur on these and on other parts of the body surface are of importance in classification.

The mouthparts of both ticks and mites arise from the anterior end of the body and are so disposed as to form a false head, which is known as the gnathosoma (in mites) or the capitulum (in ticks).

The chief structures composing the mouthparts are the palps and the chelicerae. The palps which are essentially sensory organs (in some species they may be modified to assist in capturing prey) are usually distinctly segmented and are often leg-like in appearance. The chelicerae vary greatly in morphology and may be either adapted for tearing, as in *Sarcoptes scabiei*, where they are shaped like pincers, or they may be piercing organs as in the ticks and the mites. In most acarines an upper lip (or epistome) and a lower lip (or hyposto-me) can usually be recog-nised. These structures are not normally conspicuous features of the mouthparts, but in the ticks the hypo-stome is a characteristic and very prominent struc-ture which bears teeth on its ventral surface and which forms an essential part of the creature's feeding apparatus.

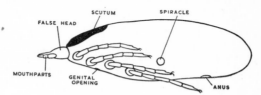

Fig. 170. Diagrammatic representation of a mem-ber of the order Acarina, lateral view.

The legs are six segmented (each consisting of a coxa, a trochanter, a femur, a genu, a tibia and a tarsus) and arise from the anterior half or two thirds of the body; in some species, notably in some species of trombiculid mites, the femur has become subdivided into two segments with the result that the leg appears to be comprised of seven segments. The tarsus may either end in claws as in all the ticks and in the tropical rat mite, *Ornithonyssus bacoti* (=*Liponyssus bacoti*), or it may terminate in suckers or long hairs as in *Sarcoptes scabiei*.

The genital opening is ventrally placed and is variable in location, being situated far forwards in some acarines, such as ticks and laelaptid mites, or it may be relatively posterior as in *Sarcoptes scabiei*. Although sexual dimorphism is well marked in the ixodid or hard ticks and in most species of parasitic mites it is far less evident in the soft ticks.

Internal morphology of the Acarina

The food channel, which is formed by the chelicerae and the hypostome, leads into the fore-gut.

The fore-gut is divided into the buccal cavity, the pharynx and the oesopha-gus, the buccal cavity receiving the ducts of the salivary glands which empty their contents separately into its lumen. The number of glands present and also their morphology varies considerably, and even amongst closely related acari-nes these structures may differ markedly in appearance, as for example in the soft ticks where each gland is unilobular, whilst it is bilobular in the hard ticks.

The secretions of the salivary glands of mites and ticks are considered to be chiefly concerned with the acquirement and digestion of food. In the case of certain species the salivary secretion may act as a vehicle of transmission of various disease-causing organisms from an infected to an uninfected host.

The buccal cavity connects with the pharynx which is provided with powerful muscles, which enable the acarine to suck up liquids into its gut. The pharynx is followed by the oesophagus and leads into the mid-gut which is characterised by the presence of diverticula which are sometimes very numerous. The hind-gut is a straight tube-like structure which may either be uniform in size throughout its entire length or provided with an enlarged distal portion forming a rectum; in many species of ticks the hind-gut often possesses an extremely narrow lumen and, in certain instances, such as in *Ornithodoros moubata*, it may be blind.

The excretory system of the acarines varies considerably from family to family. It may consist either of one or several pairs of coxal glands, or a pair of long, slightly coiled tubes opening into the rectum, known as malpighian tubules, or an assortment of small glands of varying morphological structure (usually associated with some part of the alimentary canal) or a mixture of two and even all three types of excretory organs. In argasid or soft ticks the fluid from the coxal organs may be a vehicle for the transmission of disease from one vertebrate host to another.

Although all ticks possess a respiratory system with well developed spiracles (stigmata), many mites appear to lack a definite system of breathing organs, respiration taking place through the delicate integument.

The order Acarina is usually divided into the following four suborders:

1) *The suborder Ixodides*. This suborder comprises the hard and the soft ticks and these possess a pair of stigmata, surrounded by a rounded chitinised plate (known as the stigmal plate) on each side of the body. The hypostome, which is modified as a piercing organ, is well developed and provided with teeth.

2) *The suborder Mesostigmata*. Members are characterised by the presence of a pair of lateral stigmata, each of which is associated with an elongated chitinised plate (known as a peritreme) on each side of the body. The hypostome is poorly developed, without teeth, and is not adapted for piercing. In this suborder are included the laelaptid mites — *Dermanyssus gallinae*, *Allodermanyssus sanguineus* and *Ornithonyssus bacoti (=Liponyssus bacoti)*.

3) *The suborder Sarcoptiformes*. Mites with no dectable respiratory openings; the palps are reduced, the chelicerae are adapted for tearing and are pincer-like with an apposable and a fixed arm. *Sarcoptes scabiei* is in this suborder.

4) *The suborder Trombidiformes*. These mites appear to be devoid of respiratory organs, but they possess a pair of stigmata near the mouthparts, which are very difficult to see. The hypostome is poorly developed, without teeth and is not adapted for piercing. The palps are often well developed and leg-like, and the chelicerae are modified for piercing and are not pincer-like. The suborder includes the trombiculid mites, such as *Trombicula akamushi*.

Certain medically important members of each of these four suborders will be given detailed consideration in the next five chapters.

CHAPTER XLII

THE FAMILY ARGASIDAE

ARGASID ticks, commonly known as "soft ticks", and in many parts of the world as "tampan ticks", belong to the family Argasidae, members of which lack the shield or scutum characteristic of members of the family Ixodidae, the "hard ticks".

The argasid ticks have a wide distribution in the tropics and sub-tropics whilst a small number of species are sparsely distributed in colder climates including Great Britain. They are found particularly in the drier parts of the tropics, and when they do occur in areas of heavy rainfall they seek out and should be looked for in relatively dry microclimates. Both sexes are entirely dependent on blood-meals for their existence and when seeking their hosts the different species of argasids show marked host preferences. These findings explain why the distribution of a particular species is often patchy and why, when a particular species is present, it is often so in large numbers. Some species prefer avian hosts, others mammals; those species which feed on mammals are found in such places as the burrows of rodents and wart-hogs, in the resting places of bats and in caves visited by various creatures including man. Only a very limited number of species feed regularly on man, and these domestic species will be referred to again when considering their medical importance.

Owing to their coarse mouthparts and their method of feeding many species of argasids inflict a painful bite, but their main medical importance lies in the fact that in the tropics and subtropics they are the only significant vectors of endemic (tick-borne) relapsing fever caused by Treponema duttoni. The scientific demonstration that an argasid tick (Ornithodoros moubata) was a vector of relapsing fever was made by Dutton in 1901, but there is good evidence that at least a century prior to Dutton's important discovery, the indigenous population in Africa associated the bite of this tick with the subsequent onset of a severe and often fatal fever.

The recognition of argasid ticks of medical importance

Three genera of argasid ticks are known to attack man. Of these the larvae and nymphs of Otobius megnini, the spinose ear tick, which are normally parasitic in the ears of domestic animals throughout a wide zone in the tropics, have on several occasions been recorded from a similar site in the human host. Although the removal of the tick from the human ear may prove difficult this species is not known to be a vector of disease to man. The nymph of Otobius megnini is easily recognised by the presence of spiny processes on the body surface.

Ticks belonging to the genus Argas are parasitic on birds and bats and one species Argas persicus which normally feeds on poultry will often attack man and in many parts of the tropics proves to be a domestic pest of some importance. This species is a well known vector of Treponema anserina, the cause of spirochaetosis in poultry, but it is not capable of transmitting spirochaetosis, caused by *Treponema duttoni*, to man, although at one time owing to the finding of spirochaetes in the haemocoele it was suspected of doing so. The genus *Argas* is characterised by the presence of a sutural line, that is, a rim or "edge" which encircles the body and remains present even in gorged ticks.

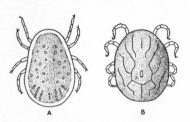

The remaining genus, *Ornithodoros*, includes all known species of argasid ticks which are vectors of relapsing fever to man. These are typical argasid ticks which may be distinguished from those in the genus *Otobius* by the absence of spiny processes on the nymph, and from ticks in the genus *Argas* by the fact that, even when unfed, they show no sutural line, the edge of the body being rounded (see Plate XV, fig. 2).

Fig. 171. *A.* an argasid tick belonging to the genus *Argas*, showing the presence of a sutural line. (Diagrammatic). *B.* an argasid tick belonging to the genus *Ornithodoros*: note the absence of a sutural line. (Diagrammatic).

The accounts which follow are mainly applicable to ticks in the genus *Ornithodoros*.

External anatomy of the adult tick

Argasid ticks are oval or ovate in shape; but the shape varies considerably not only with the species but also with the degree of distension associated with the blood-meals. All species of argasid ticks are possessed of a tough, rugose and leathery cuticle devoid of plates or shields. Eyes may or may not be present; when present they are situated on the lateral margins of the body.

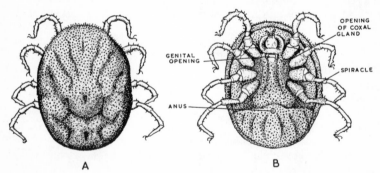

Fig. 172. An argasid tick; the species depicted is *Ornithodoros moubata*. *A.* dorsal view; *B.* ventral view.

In the adult stages of both sexes the capitulum is ventrally situated and is therefore not visible from above, a character which immediately distinguishes adult argasids from adult ixodids, since in the latter the capitulum is more dorsally situated and therefore more easily visible from above. This method of distinction does not hold good for the larvae nor sometimes for the early nymphs, for in these stages of development the mouthparts often extend beyond the body rim, as is always the case in the ixodids.

The mouthparts, which are borne on the capitulum, include a pair of palps, a pair of chelicerae and a toothed hypostome. The palps, which consist of four unequal segments have their apices downwardly directed, and because of their leg-like appearance they are sometimes referred to as "pedipalps". The hypostome and the chelicerae generally resemble those of the ixodid ticks, but the cheliceral sheaths are smooth and not "shagreened" as in the hard ticks.

The genital opening is situated on the ventral surface close to the base of the capitulum, and the anus, which is also ventrally placed, opens at the posterior end of the body. The spiracles are located just above and in front of the 4th pair of coxae, while the openings of the coxal glands lie between the attachments of the first and second pairs of legs.

There are four pairs of legs, the segments of which are somewhat tuberculated whilst the tarsi lack the pads (or pulvilli) which are present in the ixodids.

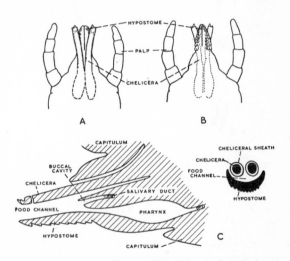

Fig. 173. The mouthparts of a tick. *A.* dorsal view; *B.* ventral view; *C.* diagrammatic representations of the mouthparts as seen in longitudinal and cross sections.

The external anatomy of the two sexes is very similar but they may be distinguished by a careful examination of the genital aperture which in the male is more conspicuous than in the female.

Internal anatomy of the adult tick

Coxal organs (called by the older authors coxal glands) are present in members of the family Argasidae but absent in members of the family Ixodidae; with this exception the internal anatomy of the argasid and ixodid ticks is very similar and the following general description will serve for both.

The alimentary canal is adapted for the accomodation and digestion of the large blood-meals which ticks obtain from a wide variety of hosts. The pharynx is provided with powerful muscles enabling the tick to take up its blood-meal very rapidly, while the stomach, the wall of which is only one cell in thickness, is provided with numerous diverticula so arranged as to accommodate the relatively large quantity of blood representing some 6-7 times the weight of the unfed tick. A hind-gut may or may not be present; when present it appears to be atrophied and cord-like and to serve no useful function. The two malpighian tubules are very long and lie in twisted coils in the haemolymph, which everywhere surrounds them, prior to their entrance into the sacculated, often bean-shaped, rectum. Since it is urine, and not faeces, that enters and is discharged from this organ, the word rectum is really a misnomer and bladder is a more apt term.

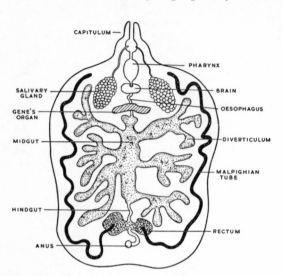

Fig. 174. Diagrammatic representation of the internal anatomy of a tick.

The coxal organs of the argasid ticks often contain a powerful anti-coagulant. These organs are not glands in the true sense, since their function is to filter off unwanted liquids and salts from the blood-meal soon after its ingestion. The spirochaetes which swarm in the haemolymph of infected argasid ticks readily traverse the walls of the coxal organs, to which they seem to be attracted, and may be found in large numbers in the coxal fluid. Certain species of soft ticks produce coxal fluid during or immediately after the act of feeding, other species only after leaving the host. The significance of the coxal organs in relation to the transmission of relapsing fever will be discussed when considering the medical importance of the argasid ticks.

Life-cycle and habits

Argasid and ixodid ticks have a hemimetabolous life-cycle; in certain respects, however, the members of the two families lead very different existences, indeed the habits of the medically important argasids are more akin to those of bed bugs than to those of the hard ticks.

Egg laying occurs following the ripening of the ovaries after an essential blood-meal; it is normally preceded by fertilisation, which certainly increases egg production, although parthenogenesis is not unknown. Unlike the ixodid ticks, which lay all their eggs in a single mass numbering many thousands, and then die, the argasid ticks lay their eggs (following each blood-meal) in some half a dozen batches each of which may contain anything from 10 to 100 eggs, depending on the size of the previous blood-meal. Since the life of the adult female often extends over several years the total number of eggs laid may be a thousand or more.

The eggs are always laid in or near to the resting places of the ticks. In the case of the domestic species they are laid in cracks and crevices in the walls and floors or just beneath the surface of mud or sand floors in human habitations; while in the case of the non-domestic species they are laid in similar situations in the lairs or resting places of wild animals or birds.

The eggs normally hatch in anything from a week to a month; but they are very resistant to adverse conditions because as each egg is passed out from the vulva it receives a coating of waterproof cement applied to it by Gene's organ*. The first active stage in the life-cycle is the hexapod larva; in the case of *Ornithodoros moubata* the larva having broken open the egg remains in the cavity of the shell until it has moulted to the first nymph before seeking a blood-meal; but in the case of most other species the larvae attach and feed prior to moulting. The length of attachment varies with the species and may be anything from a few minutes to several days.

Argasid ticks, unlike ixodid ticks, have several nymphal stages, usually four or five. Each stage requires a blood-meal before moulting to the next and during this stage of the life-cycle feeding is rapid and is completed in 5-30 minutes. The final nymphal stage closely resembles the adult but the genital opening is absent, although a papilla representing the future site is present.

The total length of the life-cycle varies greatly depending not only on the species of tick but also on the number of blood-meals available; in nature it probably averages six months to a year although it can be completed in a much shorter time in laboratory conditions.

The dispersal of ticks is largely effected by the habits of the vertebrate hosts. In the case of ixodid ticks which attach to the hosts for long periods the dispersed ticks may be sparsely distributed over a very wide area; but in the case of the argasid ticks, which in general remain attached only for short periods, the tendency is for the establishment of large isolated colonies, centred in and around the dwelling place of selected hosts. In the case of certain domestic species, such as *O. moubata* and *O. tholozani*, which feed on man, the ticks may travel long distances in the belongings of their human hosts.

Argasid ticks are long lived and can survive prolonged starvation. The longevity in nature is not known but in captivity individual ticks can survive five to seven years after a single blood-meal.

The medical importance of argasid ticks

Although, as previously stated, argasid ticks inflict painful and often

---

* A trunk-like organ which is common to both the ixodid and the argasids and which, during oviposition, is protruded from an aperture above the capitulum.

troublesome bites, nevertheless their real medical importance rests on their ability to transmit "tick-borne" relapsing fever (caused by *Treponema duttoni*) to man. Numerous species are capable of transmitting this spirochaetal infection; some of these maintain the disease in the animal reservoir (which consists not only of rodents but also of wart-hogs and many other animals) and may play a relatively unimportant part by causing infection in persons accidentally coming in contact with such animal reservoirs. A much more limited number of species, all of which are domestic or semi-domestic in their habits, are important transmitters of the disease to man. The most notorious species in the Old World is *O. moubata* which conveys the infection in tropical and subtropical Africa, while in North Africa the outstanding vector is *O. erraticus*. In the Near East and adjoining countries *O. tholozani* is responsible for the majority of the infections. In the United States the disease is somewhat sporadic in its distribution and several species are concerned, amongst which *O. turicata* and *O. hermsi* are the most important.

In the case of *Ornithodoros moubata*, which has been more fully studied than other species, the salivary glands of the adult ticks of both sexes may become lightly infected at an early stage, but this infection tends to diminish and finally die out. On the other hand the salivary glands of the nymphal ticks once infected tend to remain so for long periods. In the case of the adult ticks the greatest concentration of spirochaetes is usually found in the coxal organs, for spirochaetes present in the haemolymph appear to be attracted to these structures and to accumulate in them in vast numbers. In the case of the nymphs the coxal organs, although they are subject to early invasion, tend to lose their infection at a later stage. Similar migrations of spirochaetes occur in the case of other species such as *O. tholozani* and *O. turicata*, but in these instances there is a tendency at all stages of development of the tick for the salivary glands to remain infected, whereas spirochaetes are often absent from the coxal fluid. Finally, in the case of all ticks susceptible to infection with *T. duttoni*, invasion of the ovaries by the spirochaetes is a constant feature and results in hereditary transmission which may persist through at least three generations of ticks. As a result of this transovarian infection it is not uncommon to find that in certain localities a high proportion of ticks of all sizes, and therefore of all ages, are infected with spirochaetes.

The way in which man acquires his infection from an infective tick varies according to the species involved, and the following remarks apply to *O. moubata*. When the infected tick feeds on a vertebrate host it injects saliva at intervals throughout the course of its meal and at this stage infection may result, particularly when the tick is in the nymphal stage. Although infection may reach the human host through the saliva it is also acquired through the coxal fluid for, although certain species of argasid ticks do not excrete coxal fluid until after they have left the host, *O. moubata* almost always does so and it is certain that a proportion, the extent of which is not yet known, of human infections are acquired as the result of the infected coxal fluid reaching abrasions in the skin. Finally, it should be remembered that ticks are often bathed in the coxal fluid which they have excreted so that there is considerable risk in handling such ticks, and this risk is increased if the tick is crushed and the infected haemolymph allowed to reach an abrasion in the skin.

Although infection by the coxal route is probably common in the case of *O. moubata,* in the case of certain other species such as *O. tholozani* and *O. turicata,* which usually produce coxal fluid only when they have left the host, infection is more usually acquired through the bite.

While it is undeniable that man sometimes becomes infected from the coxal fluid and sometimes from the bite, it appears unlikely that he ever acquires infection from the dejecta of the tick, for, although it is not uncommon for the feeding ticks to pass fluid from the rectum during the course of their meal, this fluid seldom or never contains spirochaetes.

It is clear from the foregoing account of the life-cycle and habits of argasid ticks that in order to avoid infection from the non-domestic species personal prophylaxis should always be practised. As regards the domestic species, strikingly successful control, often with complete eradication, has followed the substitution of well built dwellings for the mud and wood houses with cracked floors and walls which are recognised breeding places of *Ornithodoros* spp. Where housing improvement is impossible or uneconomical, a certain degree of control (but not eradication) may be achieved by the use of appropriate contact insecticides.

CHAPTER XLIII

THE FAMILY IXODIDAE

THE family Ixodidae, which numbers many hundreds of species and which has a worldwide distribution, contains all the so-called "hard" ticks. Adult ixodids are large acarines possessing an unsegmented, saccular body which is provided with a distinct dorsal shield (or scutum) smaller in the female than in the male (see Plate XV, fig. 1). The mouthparts, which are clearly visible at all stages of development, when the tick is examined in dorsal view, are composed of a pair of palps, a pair of chelicerae and a well developed hypostome provided with rows of ventrally placed teeth.

Although ixodids, since they are common parasites of domestic stock, had long been familiar creatures to naturalists, it was not until 1893 that Theobald Smith and Kilbourne showed that the cattle tick, *Boophilus annulatus,* was the vector of *Babesia bigemina,* a protozoan causing Texas fever in cattle. This discovery proved for the first time that an arthropod was a vector of disease to domestic animals, and as a result entomologists turned their attention seriously to a study of ticks. The subsequent discovery, made independently by Ricketts and by King in 1906, that the organism responsible for Rocky Mountain spotted fever *(Rickettsia rickettsii)* was transmitted by *Dermacentor andersoni,* gave further impetus to the work of the systematists and resulted in the publication between 1908 and 1911 of the first important monographs on ticks by Nuttall and his collaborators. These monographs have long served as the basis of our knowledge, not only of the morphology of ticks but also of their biology and relationship to disease.

External anatomy of adult ticks

Unfed adult ixodid ticks vary considerably in size, measuring from a little over 1 mm. to over 9 mm., the females usually being larger than the males. When fully fed the females are greatly distended whereas the males, which only take a small blood-meal, show little increase in size. Although many species are of a dull colour, a proportion have coloured ornamentations, bright and often metallic patches of colour being present on the scutum and on the legs.

The scutum is situated anteriorly on the saccular body and is present at all stages of the tick's development. Whereas in the adult female the area of the body covered by the scutum is limited to the anterior part of the dorsal surface, and may be difficult to detect in engorged individuals, it is always readily seen in the adult males in which the scutum covers almost the whole of the dorsal surface, leaving only a small bare area around the edge of the body. In the case of the larvae and nymphs the scutum covers only the anterior end of the body. When eyes are present they will be found laterally on the edge of the scutum. In addition to the scutum the males of many species bear ventral shields or plates; in both sexes the shape, size and colouration of the shields and plates is of importance in classification.

The family Ixodidae

The members of both sexes of certain genera, such as *Dermacentor, Rhipi-cephalus* and *Haemaphysalis,* bear indentations, known as "festoons", on the

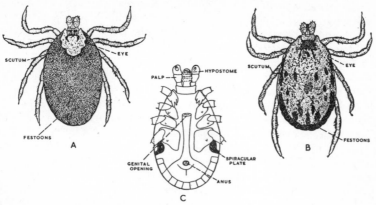

Fig. 175.   An ixodid tick; the species depicted is *Dermacentor andersoni. A.* female, dorsal view; *B.* male, dorsal view; *C.* male, ventral view.

posterior margin of the body. In the fully engorged females of these genera owing to the great distension of the body, festoons are not usually visible, but they are always readily recognisable in the males.

The capitulum (the "false-head") which is always visible from above, and the morphology of which is of considerable generic importance in classi-fication, consists of a basal portion (the "basis capituli") bearing distally a pair of palps, a pair of chelicerae, and a prominent, toothed hypostome. The palps of the adult ixodids, which consist of four segments (each of which is known as an "article"), are quite different to the leg-like palps of the adult argasids, being somewhat club-shaped in appearance. In adult ticks, whereas the first or basal segment is small, segments two and three are greatly enlarged, while the fourth or terminal segment is usually greatly reduced and, since it lies in a pit-like depression on the ventral aspect of the third segment, is difficult to find. In the case of the larvae and the nymphs in which the palps are usually not so highly specialised, all the four segments can be recognised. The chelicerae are powerful cutting organs bearing strong teeth at their tips which are used by the tick in penetrating the skin of the host, each chelicera being closely invested by a sheath bearing small teeth known as denticles. The hypostome, which is situated ventrally, bears a varying number of rows of recurved teeth on its under surface and serves as an anchoring organ. The palps do not enter the skin of the host and are purely sensory organs.

The spiracular plate in the Ixodidae is large and conspicuous and generally rounded or comma-shaped, and lies on the lateral aspect, posterior to the fourth coxa.

The adults and nymphs bear four pairs of legs and the larvae three. The coxae may bear spurs which are of assistance in classification.

Life-cycle and habits

Following engorgement the female ixodid tick drops off her host to the ground, where she either buries herself in the soil or seeks a sheltered spot under stones or amongst roots particularly of shrubs and grasses. Here she remains quiescent whilst she digests her meal and matures her eggs, gestation usually occupying several weeks, although it may be shortened or prolonged, even for several months, according to the conditions of the environment, mainly the temperature.

Once egg-laying has begun it is continued for several weeks during which time all the eggs are extruded, and a few days later the female dies. The number of eggs deposited is usually very large, figures between 3,000 and 8,000 being common. In the case of some species as few as 1000 eggs are deposited, whilst the females of certain other species lay as many as 20,000 or more. The eggs are small spherical objects, which are individually just visible to the naked eye and are laid in a large glutinous mass which is almost as large as the tick itself and which accumulates in front of and on top of the scutum of the ovipositing female. As each individual egg is passed, it is transfered from the vulva to the scutum by means of Gene's organ.

The incubation time of the egg is very variable lasting anything from a few weeks to several months, depending on the prevailing temperature and the species of tick concerned.

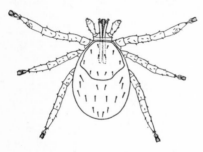

Fig. 176.   The larva of an ixodid tick.

The newly emerged tick, which is known as the larva or "seed tick", measures between 0.5 and 1.5 mm., and is characterised by the presence of three pairs of legs. Small larval ixodids may be mistaken for certain large parasitic mites, but the presence of a toothed hypostome in the tick and its absence in the mite serves as a distinguishing feature.

The larvae do not seek a host immediately after emergence but remain quiescent for a few days. Following this period of quiescence the hungry larvae become intensely active and, moving with surprising speed, swarm over the surface of the soil and up the stems of grasses or other small plants seeking a host. While thus situated they respond to various stimuli produced by passing hosts, such as changes in light intensity, eddies of warm air, vibrations in the soil and various odours. When they first receive such stimuli they raise their forelegs (on which are situated certain sensory organs) and wave them in the air, a behaviour known as "questing". Having contacted a suitable host, the tick attaches itself to certain sites of predilection on its host's body, the exact site varying with the different species of ticks and their hosts.

When feeding the tick presses its mouthparts against the epidermis of the host and lacerates the skin by means of a few rapid movements of the chelicerae. Having penetrated the skin the larval tick remains attached to its host for several days, the hypostome serving as an anchoring organ which is so firmly embedded in the host's skin that any attempt to pull off the tick by force generally causes the mouthparts to be left in the wound and may result in a focus of infection. During the act of feeding blood is slowly sucked into the sacculated stomach, while the tick defaecates rhythmically, the faeces which it produces soiling the wound made in the skin by the mouthparts. The period of attachment of the larva varies a great deal but most species of medical importance usually feed for from three days to about a week. Having completed its blood-meal the larva drops to the ground where it seeks a sheltered spot to digest its meal, digestion usually being accomplished in the course of a few days although it may, in adverse circumstances, be prolonged for many weeks. Having digested its food the larva remains quiescent for a few days after which it moults to become a nymph.

The nymph, like the larva, possesses no genital aperture but it can at once be distinguished from the hexapod larva by the presence of four pairs of legs. In seeking a host the nymph behaves similarly to the larva, but having found a suitable animal on which to feed it remains attached for a longer period than does the larva, taking about a week to ten days to become engorged. Once feeding is completed the nymph detaches itself from the host and drops to the surface of the soil to seek a sheltered spot to digest its meal. When digestion is completed the nymph moults to become an adult male or female for, unlike the argasid ticks which have several nymphal stages, and therefore several moults, there is only one nymphal stage in the ixodid life-cycle. Having become an adult it usually spends a period of about a week in a quiescent state before seeking a fresh host.

The adult female closely resembles the nymph and like the latter has a small scutum but it may be distinguished from the nymph by the possession of a genital opening, and by the presence of a pair of depressions (known as "foveae") which are situated on the dorsal surface of the broad base of the capitulum.

The male differs sharply from both the nymph and the female in possessing a very large scutum which covers nearly the whole of the dorsal surface.

In seeking a host the adult male and female ticks behave similarly to the larvae and nymphs, but whereas all ixodid female ticks require a large blood meal the males of most species engorge only to a moderate extent, whilst in the case of a certain number of species the males do not appear to feed. The females usually remain attached to the host animal for a longer period of time than the nymphs, taking anything from about one to four weeks to become replete. Although the males only take small meals they may remain for long periods on the host, copulating with the females whilst these are engaged in feeding. Engorged females are often difficult to identify and for this reason the finding of pairs of ticks in copula is of assistance, since, as a rule, the identification of the males presents little difficulty.

The female having fully engorged becomes greatly distended, usually several times her original size, and drops to the ground where she finds her way to the shelter of stones or roots of plants, where she digests her meal and lays her eggs. Oviposition may commence as early as 3 to 5 days after the female has left the host, although this preoviposition period is often prolonged for many weeks. The length of time taken by the tick to lay all her eggs is variable, extending from about 10 days to a month or more, the number of ova produced falling off steadily as oviposition progresses. After the female has laid all her eggs she dies without feeding again and usually without moving far from the site of oviposition.

It will be observed that in the above description of the life-cycle of an ixodid tick each stage—the larva, the nymph and the adult—fed on a different animal. Ticks of this type which require three hosts to complete their life-cycle are known as three-host ticks, species with this habit occurring in such medically important genera as *Ixodes, Rhipicephalus, Haemaphysalis* and *Dermacentor.* Whilst most ixodids belong to the group requiring three hosts in the life-cycle, a proportion of species which are of medical or veterinary importance, chiefly members of the genus *Hyalomma*, remain on the same host during the larval and nymphal stages, the engorged nymph dropping to the soil where it moults to the adult form which then seeks a new host; ticks possessing this type of life-cycle, in which only two hosts are required, are known as two-host ticks. A few species, notably members of the genus *Boophilus*, spend the whole of their larval, nymphal and adult life on the same animal, the adult female only leaving its host in order to oviposit; ticks which require only one host to complete their life-cycle are known as one-host ticks. It is obvious that one-host ticks will be less likely to pick up infections of which they are the potential vectors than are two or three-host ticks, and that when such infections are acquired they can only be transferred to a new host by a fresh generation of ticks which have become infected by transovarial passage.

Host specificity is very variable, most species of ticks of medical importance having a wide host range. Generally speaking the larvae choose small animals on which to feed, while the nymphs and adults parasitise larger animals. Man is attacked by all stages—larvae, nymphs and adults—but most of the records indicate that he is more prone to be parasitised by the younger stages—the larvae and nymphs—than by the adult ticks.

Although ticks are able to withstand wide ranges of temperature and humidity and are thus able to parasitise hosts which wander over large tracts of variegated country, the majority of species will not establish themselves in very dry or very wet environments; notable exceptions are members of the genus *Hyalomma* which live in very dry conditions, several species occurring in deserts. A determining factor in maintaining a suitable degree of humidity at the soil surface is the nature of the vegetation covering it and it is not uncommon to find that the occurrence of a particular species of tick is associated with a particular type of vegetation.

Adverse climatic conditions, such as are met with in winter in temperate regions, may greatly prolong the life-cycle of ticks, while failure to find

Fig. 1. A female ixodid tick
(*Ixodes hexagonus*).
[*Courtesy Mr. Eric Norman*]

Fig. 2. An argasid tick (*Orni-thodorus moubata*) in a resting
attitude.
[*Courtesy Mr. J. P. Brady*]

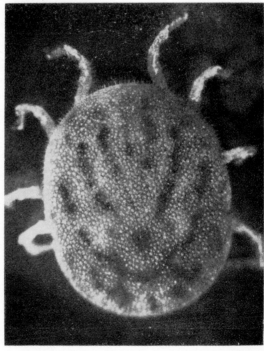

PLATE XVI

FIG. 1. *Porocephalus sp.* lying encrusted in the wall of the colon of an African patient.

[*Courtesy Annals of Tropical Medicine and Parasitology, and Dr. D. A. Cannon*]

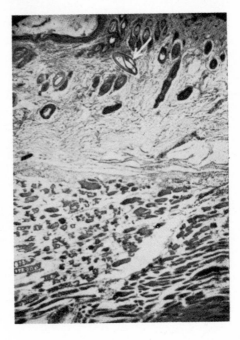

FIG. 2. Section through the skin of a guinea-pig one hour after the infliction of a sting by the hive-bee (*Apis mellifica*) (× 36). The sting, cut in cross section, is indicated by an arrow. Note the oedema and marked muscle necrosis.

[*Courtesy Annals of Tropical Medicine and Parasitology*]

suitable hosts may result in long periods of starvation which may extend the life-cycle by months and even years. Whereas activity of ixodid ticks is usually suspended in temperate zones during cold periods, in the tropics breeding usually continues uninterrupted throughout the year.

Medical importance of ixodid ticks

Although ticks are primarily parasites of animals they frequently attack man, and all over the world their bites are recognised as a common source of irritation and often of secondary infections occurring in man as well as in his domestic stock. It is, however, as vectors of disease that ixodid ticks are medically important, being known as transmitters of certain rickettsial, viral and bacterial diseases, some of which are of great epidemiological importance and have a worldwide distribution.

The persistent presence of the mouthparts of the tick in the human skin, coupled with the injection of salivary secretion, gives rise to much irritation with the result that the victim often tries to pull away the tick from its site of attachment, a procedure which commonly results in the body of the tick being torn away from the imbedded capitulum. Not only may the imbedded capitulum give rise to a septic focus in the skin but, in the case of a tick infected with rickettsiae, the release of the contents of its ruptured gut may produce an infection which might not otherwise have occurred had the tick been removed intact.

In addition to the importance of removing the tick undamaged, it is also necessary to ensure that it is removed with as little delay as possible for it has been demonstrated that rickettsial infections are not usually transmitted to the human host until some hours after the tick has begun to feed, while in the case of "tick paralysis" the amount of toxin injected is directly proportional to the length of time the tick has been attached.

The removal of the offending tick is best effected by dabbing it with chloroform or ether, after which the capitulum should be pressed deeper in the skin (to loosen the teeth of the hypostome) and then gentle traction exerted. If for any reason it is not possible to use a volatile anaesthetic, the tick may be covered with a pledget of cotton wool soaked in medicinal paraffin, but in this case the removal of the tick cannot be accomplished until some hours after the application of the dressing.

Tick-borne typhus, which is caused by *Rickettsia rickettsii*, is found both in the New World and the Old World, in each of which regions it is known by a multiplicity of names. The disease exists chiefly in an animal reservoir and human cases, although not uncommon in endemic areas, are largely sporadic. Tick-borne typhus can be transmitted to man by all stages of hard ticks (the most important species are three-host ticks), the larval ticks having acquired the ricksettsiae by transovarial passage. Under normal conditions, before man can acquire the disease from an infected tick, it must, as previously stated, have been attached for several hours.

In the New World, tick-borne typhus is known mainly as Rocky Mountain

R

spotted fever in North America, and as Sao Paulo typhus in South America. The important vectors of Rocky Mountain spotted fever belong to the genera *Dermacentor* (particularly *Dermacentor andersoni*) and *Amblyomma*, whilst in the case of Sao Paulo typhus another species of *Amblyomma* appears to be the important vector. In the Old World tick-borne typhus is known by a large variety of local names, such as fièvre boutonneuse, Indian tick typhus, South African tick typhus and Queensland typhus. A number of vectors have been incriminated but probably the most widespread and important transmitters of the disease are two species of dog ticks, *Rhipicephalus sanguineus* and *Haemaphysalis leachi*. In certain localised areas, such as in North Queensland where *Ixodes holocyclus* is a transmitter, other species are of importance.

Q fever (a rickettsial disease due to *Rickettsia conori*) is transmitted in the animal reservoir by ticks and, on rare occasions, man also contracts the disease in this way, but the majority of persons acquire the disease through the ingestion of milk or meat from infected cattle.

Tick-borne encephalitis has been reported as occurring widely throughout Europe and Asia where the disease follows the bites of several species of ticks belonging to the genera *Dermacentor*, *Haemaphysalis* and *Ixodes* (*I. persulcatus* and *I. ricinus* being of particular importance). Transovarial transmission rarely occurs. The virus occurs in domestic animals, but is found mainly in rodents and birds which help to disseminate the infection and which act as the reservoir.

Colorado tick fever is a viral infection which is of considerable local importance in the United States, and which has been shown to be transmitted by *Dermacentor andersoni*.

Tularaemia, which is primarily a disease of wild rodents, is caused by a bacillus, *Pasteurella tularensis*, and occurs in North America, Europe and Asia. Man usually acquires the disease by direct contact with infected carcases; in addition, it is said to be transmitted by a number of arthropods, including ticks.

In some parts of the world, notably in Australia, North America, South Africa and South Eastern Europe several species of ticks, particularly members of the genus *Ixodes* and *Dermacentor,* produce a type of ascending motor paralysis known as "tick paralysis" which is sometimes mistaken for poliomyelitis or for acute ascending paralysis (Landry's disease). Tick paralysis is not due to any specific organism but is caused by a toxin present in the saliva of the tick, symptoms beginning to appear several days after the tick has attached. Removal of the offending tick usually brings about a rapid cure.

CHAPTER XLIV

SARCOPTES SCABIEI

Recognition, life-cycle and medical importance

S CABIES, like the louse-borne diseases, has long been associated with war, and with such national calamities as famines and earthquakes, for both scabies and lousiness increase when people are herded together and when facilities for washing the body and clothing are reduced. Scabies, like crab lice infestations, has often been described as a venereal disease, but it would be more apt to describe it as a family disease for it passes between husband and wife, parents and children, and from child to child.

The part played by scabies in war-time and in the aftermath of war has been recorded by numerous writers. Sokoloff described how all ranks suffered from the diseae in Napoleon's Italian campaign (1796-1797) and Erasmus Wilson observed similar widespread infestations amongst the British forces during the Crimean campaign, while in the 1914-1918 war Milian wrote of the French forces "Scabies is a veritable scourge in our armies. Its incidence is extremely high and it incapacitates a goodly number of soldiers".

Figures concerning the incidence of scabies in the 1939-45 war show that it played an important part in curtailing the war effort. Thus it is known that the number of cases in the army in Britain reached as high a figure as 6,000 fresh cases per month. A similar rise occurred in the civilian population, and during 1942, 19,000 people were treated for scabies in the Liverpool area alone. Other countries were much more severely affected, thus, UNRRA, in 1945 reported that in the province of Aquila in Italy 85% of the population in devastated areas had scabies; in Norway there were 9,605 cases notified in 1938 and 68,013 in 1943. It would appear then that Friedman accurately summarized the situation when he wrote "It is, however, no exaggeration to say that there never has been an extended war in which the unwelcomed acarus did not actively, joyously, and in great numbers participate".

Why is scabies important? During the last war the Director of Hygiene made the statement that scabies was the most time-wasting disease of the army in the British Isles. This description of scabies as a time-waster is essentially true, it wastes not only the time of the patient, but the time of the medical staff who have to treat the patient, and the time of the men who have to disinfest the patient's belongings.

Scabies is of worldwide distribution, but the newcomer to the tropics frequently fails to recognise it because it is so often obscured by concomitant skin diseases or secondary infections, which conceal the parasite. Many of these complications have been described as separate entities, thus the "Norwegian crusted scabies" of Europe, "craw-craw" of West Africa and "kas kas" of New Guinea have all been shown to be complications of skin infestations originally caused by *S. scabiei*.

The sarcoptic mites cause skin diseases in almost all species of animals and sarcoptic mange is common in such domestic animals as horses, cattle, dogs and pigs. Formerly it was usual to name the mite according to the host on which it was found. As a result the literature contains descriptions of *Sarcoptes canis* from the dog, *S. ovis* from the sheep, *S. equi* from the horse, together with many other species including *S. leonis* recovered from a mangy lion kept in a zoological garden. Nowadays only one species, *Sarcoptes scabiei,* is recognised and the various mites occurring and causing sarcoptic mange in different species of animals are regarded as varieties. Thus the mite causing scabies in man is known as *Sarcoptes scabiei* var. *hominis* and that in the dog as *Sarcoptes scabiei* var. *canis,* etc. It is important to remember, however, that there are physiological differences between these varieties and that although the transfer of such varieties as *S. scabiei* var. *equi* to man, which results in the infestation commonly known as "cavalryman's itch", is possible, such a transfer never produces typical human scabies but only a temporary invasion which clears up readily, sometimes without treatment.

Sarcoptes scabiei var *hominis* is a small, flattened, disc-shaped creature which is whitish in colour and just visible to the naked eye the female measuring about 350-250 microns, the male about 200-150 microns. In many respects the external and internal anatomy of the mite resembles that of the tick, but there are no obvious spiracles, the hypostome is devoid of teeth and not so well developed, while the chelicerae are of the pincer type.

The adults possess eight short, squat legs, while, as in the tick, the larvae

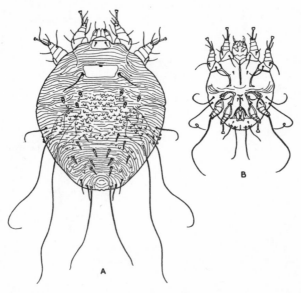

Fig. 177.   *Sarcoptes scabiei. A.* female, dorsal view; *B.* male, ventral view.

have six. In the female the two first pairs of legs have suckers situated at the end of an unjointed pedicel, whereas the last two pairs have no suckers. The male is similar but smaller and the last pair of legs also possess suckers. The individuals of both sexes have the dorsum armed with backwardly directed spines, which facilitate the mite's progress down the burrow.

The female itch mite enters the skin and burrows two or three millimetres during the course of twenty-four hours, working chiefly at night; warmth also increases her activity. The burrows, when visible, appear as raised tortuous lines, a few millimetres to several centimetres in length. The female mite burrows very superficially into the skin, so that the burrow never lies below the stratum corneum. She always selects places where the skin is thin and wrinkled. The areas most commonly infested in order of preference are: the skin between the fingers and on the wrist, on the feet, on the extensor surface of the elbows, in the axillae and, in the male, on the penis and scrotum. In the female, it is not uncommon to find infestations under the breasts. In adults the presence of burrows on the face or neck is unusual, but in children, whose skin is everywhere vulnerable, infection may occur anywhere, including the face and neck.

By placing a mite on the skin it is quite easy to watch how she excavates her tunnel. If this is done it will be seen that she raises the hind part of the body on the stilt-like hairs on the posterior legs, thus bringing her mouthparts into contact with the skin, and in this position by means of the pincer-like chelicerae, she literally eats her way into the stratum corneum, her progress being assisted by the blade-like projections on the

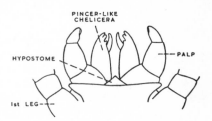

Fig. 178. Diagrammatic representation of the mouthparts of *Sarcoptes scabiei*.

fore-limbs. At first the mite burrows vertically downwards but later she proceeds parallel to the skin surface, the resulting tunnel never extending below the stratum corneum even in very thin skinned individuals.

During her progress down the burrow the female lays some 25–30 eggs, oviposition usually beginning on the 4th or 5th day, and 4–5 eggs being laid each day. In addition to the eggs, the somewhat characteristically shaped faeces also accumulate in the tunnel. Empty egg-shells, since they disintegrate rapidly, are relatively rare. The total length of the tunnel varies from a few millimetres up to several centimetres and is usually tortuous in form. The large eggs (150 x 100 microns) laid in the burrows hatch within 4–5 days and the larvae escape from the parent tunnel and wander on the skin. Many of the larvae perish without further development, but of those which survive, a minute proportion are transferred to new hosts (some authorities believe that the majority of fresh infections are caused by the transfer of pubescent and, sometimes, ovigerous females), whilst the remainder burrow into the intact stratum corneum to construct their almost invisible moulting pockets. Once beneath the skin surface the larva makes no attempt to extend the pocket but feeds and grows until it is ready to moult to an 8-legged nymph. The resultant first nymph either remains in its burrow or leaves it to construct a similar refuge in another area.

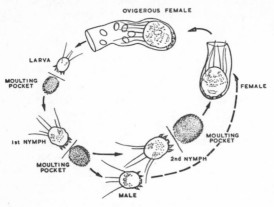

If the nymph is destined to become a female it moults within the pocket to become the second nymph, similar to the first, and either remains in the pocket or leaves it to construct a duplicate refuge. In this last refuge the final moult occurs resulting in the production of the adult female.

Fig. 179.   The life-cycle of a sarcoptid mite.

The adult female remains quiescent in the moulting pocket until she is fertilised by the nomadic male, who usually reaches her by tunnelling through the roof of the pocket. Once fertilised she extends the moulting pocket to a tunnel which gradually takes on the characteristic serpiginous form and in which the eggs are laid. The total life-cycle from egg to egg takes about two to three weeks. The adult female's life-span in the host is about a month, and we know that, under favourable conditions, she can survive for ten days off the host.

The life-cycle of the male differs from that of the female in that the second nymphal stage is omitted.

Theoretically, the only certain method of diagnosing scabies is to demonstrate the presence of mites, larvae or ova in the tunnels, but in practice the presence of typical tortuous tunnels associated with a history of itching is generally regarded as sufficient evidence. In fair skinned people it is often possible to observe a peppered appearance in the tunnel, due to the accumulated faecal pellets of the mites, while at one end there is a little pearl-shaped object with a dark spot on its extremity. This pearl-shaped object is the adult female and the dark spot represents the mouthparts. If the point of a needle is inserted just below the mite it is usually easy to extract the creature and identify it under the microscope. The number of burrows and adult females found on the patient may be as many as 100, but this is very exceptional, the average patient only being infested with some 10-15 adults.

The tunnels made by the ovigerous female must not be confused with the scabies rash. The so-called rash of scabies is a follicular papular eruption which is widely distributed over those skin areas where the burrows of the ovigerous females tend to be absent—the buttocks, the scapular region and the abdomen being the regions most commonly affected. The nature and cause of the rash has long been disputed, but there appears little reason to doubt that it is the result of sensitisation following a previous infection. The rash seldom appears until about a month after a primary infection and until its appearance the patient is often unaware of his infection. The severe pruritus which accompanies the rash gives rise to scratching which often leads to secondary infections which cause much discomfort to the patient and which increase the difficulties of diagnosis.

The control of scabies.

Scabies passes from person to person by any close bodily contact, the closer the contact, the more readily it is passed; this fact, when combined with the previously recorded observation that patients with a primary attack are often unaware of their infection, renders it important that the examination for scabies should be extended to all persons who have been in close contact with the patient. During the war it was shown that the passage of *S. scabiei* by fomites was rare, and consequently the disinfestation of clothing and blankets was generally abandoned. This does not mean that it is unnecessary to disinfest fomites, but only that the time and energy expended on such work is not compatible with the results achieved.

The treatment of scabies.

As regards treatment, the first point to consider is the preparation of the patient. Here again it is a question of time and labour economy. Undoubtedly a hot bath with plenty of soap and the use of a soft nail brush will tend to increase the efficacy of the subsequent treatment, but speaking generally, it only does so to a small extent.

There are two types of drugs at present in use, and both are efficient when properly employed.

Benzyl benzoate: This is the most commonly employed and probably the most efficient drug used for the treatment of scabies, although sometimes it is not well tolerated by young children. When properly used and applied in a dilution of 25% it is reported to cure 90% of cases by a single application. The vehicle employed is usually soap and isopropyl alcohol, or better still, stearic acid and triethanalamine (6 ml. to a litre of water). It is estimated that 2 oz. per person is sufficient for a single treatment.

Organic Sulphur: Two preparations are in use: (a) Mitigal, which is dimethyl thianthrene (dimethyl diphenylene disulphide) which contains 25 per cent organically combined sulphur. This is effective and pleasant to use, but is liable to produce sulphur dermatitis, although to a less extent than inorganic sulphur; it is also expensive. (b) Tetmosol, which is tetraethylthiuram monosulphide, is highly efficient, seldom produces dermatitis and is particularly valuable for the treatment of scabies in children. It has the disadvantage of being slow in action, as compared with benzyl benzoate. When combined with soap it has been shown to act as a prophylactic and slow curative agent.

The number of treatments necessary to produce cure has been the subject of much fruitless discussion. On one point, however, all are agreed; whatever the form of treatment employed, a higher proportion of persons are cured by two treatments than by one—and a still higher proportion are cured by three applications. If more than one treatment is given it is advisable to give the second treatment some 5-6 days after the first, for by that time the eggs, which are the most resistant stage, will have hatched. It has been claimed that one application of "lindane" ointment, which contains benzene hexachloride, destroys the eggs as well as the active stages of the mites, but this claim has not yet been fully substantiated.

CHAPTER XLV

THE FAMILY TROMBICULIDAE

Trombiculid mites, recognition, life-cycle and medical importance

THE family Trombiculidae, which is composed of many hundreds of species of mites has a worldwide distribution. The life-cycle consists essentially of an egg, a larval, a nymphal and an adult stage. The host parasite relationship differs markedly from that of other families of acarines which attack man in that only the larval stage is parasitic, the nymphal and adult stages being free-living. Whereas the nymphs and adults live in the soil near the surface and hence are but rarely seen, the larvae which are known by a wide variety of names, such as chiggers, harvest-mites and scrub-itch mites, move about actively on the ground and on the vegetation and are familiar creatures which may be recognised by their small size (that of a pin's head), yellow to orange colour, saccular body bearing three pairs of legs, and branched hairs on the body and on the legs.

There is little doubt that for centuries past man has recognised the attacks of chiggers as distinct from those of other parasitic arthropods, and indeed there are numerous references to these mites in the early literature of both the East and the West. In Eastern Asia, where they are the vectors of scrub typhus (mite typhus or tsutsugamushi disease) caused by *Rickettsia tsutsugamushi,* they were described by a 16th century Chinese writer as being "so minute as to be hardly visible" and that "when people ... walk amidst growth in the dark, these mites fasten upon them and burrow under the skin, causing a prickly sensation and a red rash".

The association of trombiculid mites with scrub typhus had been suspected well over a century ago by the Japanese physician Ohtomo, but it was not until the epidemiological studies of Tanaka in 1899 that Kitashima and Miyajima demonstrated, in a classical experiment, that "clean monkeys" which had been exposed in field conditions to mites, in an infected district, contracted the disease. Although the organism responsible for scrub typhus, *R. tsutsugamushi,* was not recognised until long after the work of these investigators, it is clear that their studies form the basis of the present understanding of the epidemiology of the disease.

Modern knowledge of the systematics of trombiculid mites dates from the publication by Oudemans in 1912 of an important monograph on the larval stages of these acarines, whilst pioneer studies on the life-cycle of chiggers are those of Kneissl in 1916 on *T. autumnalis* in Europe, and of several Japanese investigators between 1917 and 1921 on the life history of *T. akamushi* and several related forms.

Since the medical officer during the course of his normal activities is unlikely to encounter the nymphal and adult forms, the following account of the morphology of the mite will be restricted to a description of the larval stage, while the nymphal and adult stages will be briefly referred to when the life-cycle is considered.

Description of the larval trombiculid mite

Larval trombiculid mites, which in the unfed condition measure about 0.15 to 0.3 mm. in length are minute, ochre-yellow to orange-red arthropods with a saccular body bearing three pairs of legs. The body and the legs are uniformly covered with fine feathered setae. On the dorsal surface, placed well anteriorly, there is a dorsal plate or scutum (often flanked by two pairs of eyes), which bears 3 to 10, rarely more, feathered setae, similar to those covering the body and legs, and a pair of specialised hairs, known as sensillae, which arise from distinct bases known as sensillary bases. The sensillae may either be flagelliform or expanded distally, and may either be simple or feathered. The

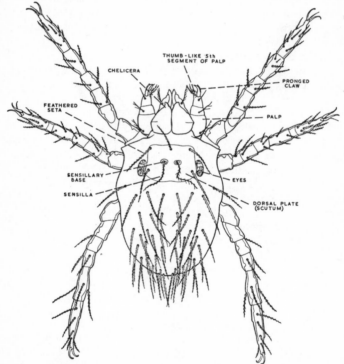

Fig. 180. A larval mite belonging to the genus *Trombicula*, dorsal view.

mouthparts consist of a pair of chelicerae and a pair of palps which, together, give the mite the appearance of having a false head. The chelicerae, which consist of a basal segment and a blade-like distal segment, are modified for piercing, whilst the palp is somewhat leg-like, consisting of five segments, the fourth segment (tibia) bearing a claw (sometimes pronged) which articulates with the fifth segment (tarsus) which is thumb-like. The legs have six or seven segments, a character which is of great importance in classification.

Although chiggers belonging to several genera attack man, only the genus *Trombicula* contains species of medical importance. Members of the genus *Trombicula* may usually be recognised by the possession of a combination of the following characters: all the legs have 7 segments, and the scutum which is roughly rectangular bears five scutal setae, together with the two sensillae which are flagelliform.

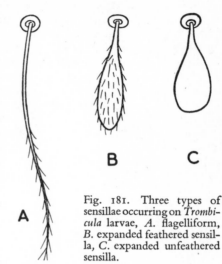

Fig. 181. Three types of sensillae occurring on *Trombicula* larvae, *A*. flagelliform, *B*. expanded feathered sensilla, *C*. expanded unfeathered sensilla.

Life-cycle of the trombiculid mite

Some ten days after having reached adult life and following fertilisation, the female begins to lay her eggs singly at the rate of about 30 to 40 eggs a month. Whereas in tropical areas egg laying goes on uninterrupted for at least a year, in colder areas, as in Japan, there is a suggestion that oviposition ceases during the autumn and the winter. The eggs, which are deposited on the surface of the soil, measure about 150 mm. in diameter and are commonly spherical in shape, usually with rugose markings on the egg-shell.

After seven to ten days the egg-shell splits and the contained larva is exposed but does not emerge, remaining quiescent in the egg-shell for about a week, during which period it is known as the deutovum. Following this period of quiescence the larvae leave the egg-shells and become very active, swarming over the surface of the soil and low lying vegetation.

Since the trombiculid larva is parasitic in habit it seeks a host, which in the case of medically important species may be any warm-blooded vertebrate, on which it must feed in order to develop further and to which it is directed by various stimuli, mainly changes in environmental conditions, such as sudden shadows, abrupt changes in air temperature and so forth. Having found a host the larva seeks a suitable place of attachment choosing a site where the skin is soft and moist, as for example the ears, genitalia, the mammae and around the anus; here the chiggers tend to congregate in closely packed groups. In the case of man the larva usually seeks some constriction between the body and the clothing, where the boot is tight round the ankle or the belt around the abdomen.

The orange-red colour of the larval mites is not due to ingested blood for chiggers do not feed on blood but only on the lymph and the products of digestion of the host's tissues. The mite pierces the skin of the host with its chelicerae and injects saliva into the wound. The semi-digested material is sucked up by the chigger which then injects more saliva, this intermittent injection of saliva resulting in the production of a curious tube-like structure known as a stylostome (histiosiphon). The wall of the stylostome is formed by a sharply defined area of hyaline degeneration extending vertically down-

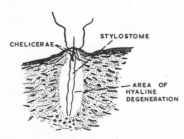

wards to a surprising depth in the skin of the host. The mites remain attached to the vertebrate for anything from a day to a month, the length of time depending on the species of chigger concerned; the trombiculid vectors of scrub typhus remain attached for a period of about three days. At the end of this time the gorged larvae, which are now considerably swollen, release themselves from the host; the detachment of one larva seems to disturb the others which in their turn release their hold and drop to the ground where they conceal themselves in loose soil.

Fig. 182. Diagrammatic representation of the tube-like structure known as the stylostome or histiosiphon produced in the skin of the host by the feeding trombiculid mite.

The larva now once more becomes quiescent (at this stage the creature is known as a nymphochrysalis) and during the next few days a transformation takes place within the larval skin resulting in the formation of the nymph which emerges at the end of a week. The nymph, which measures about 0.5 to

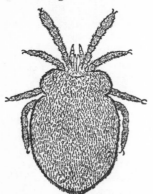

1.0 mm., is usually reddish in colour and the body, which is covered with feathered hairs, is constricted between the 2nd and 3rd pair of legs, giving the mite a figure of 8 appearance. It has four pairs of legs and bears, on the ventral surface, two pairs of genital suckers. Although the mouthparts are generally similar to those of the larva, the nymph is never parasitic and feeds on small arthropods and their eggs. After a period of active life in the soil, the nymph enters a quiescent stage known as the imagochrysalis, from which the adult emerges after about a week.

Fig. 183.   Adult trombiculid mite.

The adult resembles the nymph very closely except that it is larger (measuring 1.0 to 1.5 mm.) and is much more densely covered with hairs. Unlike the nymph which has 2 pairs of genital suckers, the adult has 3 pairs. It has habits similar to those of the nymph and is never parasitic, its food consisting of other small soil-inhabiting arthropods.

The life-cycle of the trombiculid mite is much affected by environmental factors, such as humidity, temperature and the availability of food supplies to the free-living adults and nymphs and to the parasitic larvae.

The survival and persistence of trombiculid populations in nature depends not only on the habits and ecology of the free-living stages (adults and nymphs) but also on the host-parasite relationships of the parasitic stage (the larva), for in order to carry on the life-cycle the larvae must have ready access to hosts which are likely to return them (at intervals corresponding roughly to the attachment period of the larvae) to a nidus suitable for postlarval development, that is to say, one which possesses a high degree of humidity and a plentiful food supply of other soil-inhabiting arthropods. A host which fulfils these requirements is known as a competent maintaining host.

The free-living stages are in delicate ecological balance with their surroundings and even moderate changes in the environment affect markedly such vital functions as feeding and egg laying. The nature of the soil and its water binding capacity, as well as the type of vegetation, are of great importance and may affect the mite population very greatly; for example, low humidity causes the adults to migrate deeper into the soil and egg laying ceases. So delicate is the balance that whereas a patch of ground of no more than a few square yards may prove bo be a good breeding site for the mites, the surrounding soil may be quite unsuitable. These islands, which may vary from a few square yards in extent to areas covering many square miles, are known as "mite islands".

General climatic conditions also affect the trombiculid population, and it is possible to correlate the occurrence of large numbers of mites with seasons of high moisture. In a moist, warm region, such as in southern Asia, there may be five or more generations of mites a year, whereas in colder zones, as in northern Japan, only one or two generations of these acarines occur each year.

Because of the close association of habitat, host and parasite, it has become customary to describe trombiculid mites as "habitat-specific" rather than "host-specific", and it is clear that dispersal by hosts which wander freely over large tracts of variegated territory results in a great loss of larvae.

Medical importance of trombiculid mites

Over a dozen species of chiggers are known to attack man and do so both in the temperate zones and in the tropics. In Africa however, apart from a few instances, human beings appear to be free from their attacks.

Trombiculid larvae affect man in two ways. In the first place they are responsible for a common, widespread and irritating form of dermatitis known as "scrub-itch" or "autumnal itch". In the second place, a very limited number of species act as the vectors of an important rickettsial disease, generally known as scrub typhus, which occurs in South East Asia.

Scrub typhus, which is known also by many other names such as mite typhus and tsutsugamushi disease, is caused by *Rickettsia tsutsugamushi* (=*R.* *orientalis*) and occurs over a wide area of Asia, extending from Japan through South East Asia to India, and also in northern Australia and the neighbouring islands. The disease is acquired by man following the bite of two species* of trombiculid mites belonging to the genus *Trombicula* (sub-genus *Leptotrombidium*), *T. deliensis* and *T. akamushi,* the former species *(T. deliensis)* having much the wider distribution.

Until the outbreak of World War II, scrub typhus was regarded as being a localised disease, but large scale epidemics of the disease followed the military and naval campaigns in the Pacific and South East Asia. These outbreaks are now regarded as being due to an inordinate influx of susceptible human beings into an area with a heavily mite-infested rodent population—the reservoir of the disease.

The infection is maintained amongst rural and forest rodents through the agency of trombiculid mites belonging to several genera, including the genus *Trombicula*. From these wild rodents the infection spreads to other rodents, such as *Rattus*, spp. (south of the tropic of Cancer) and voles of the genus *Microtus* and field mice of the genus *Apodemus* (north of the tropic of Cancer), which live in areas frequented by human beings. Man acquires the disease, from the bite of an infected mite, when he is in a rodent-infested area, and this may be either "bush" country or else cultivated land of a type which provides shelter for the mite-infested rodent population. It appears certain that man very seldom acts as a reservoir of the disease, and that he usually acquires his infection, as in the case of bubonic plague and murine typhus, from the rodent population.

Since the larva only feeds once, the ricksettsiae which it takes up must persist through the nymph and adult stages into the eggs. The larvae which hatch from these eggs are infected with the rickettsiae and are capable of transmitting the disease when they attach themselves to a host to feed; in this way infection may be transferred by transovarial passage for several generations. The proof of the persistence of the ricksettsiae throughout the various stages of the life-cycle of the mite has been demonstrated by the injection, into laboratory rodents, of ground up nymphs, adults and eggs which, although unable to cause infection in nature, nevertheless produce the disease when injected into the test animal.

Control is largely concentrated on separating the infected rodents from the human population by bush clearing of the infested areas, while personal prophylaxis is mainly centred on the use of repellents such as dimethyl phthallate and benzyl benzoate. These give the most prolonged action when smeared over clothing, such as socks, trousers and cuffs, and prevent the mites crawling over these garments on their way to the skin. In addition, where large scale control and protection is necessary, the use of impregnated clothing and the spraying of undergrowth with insecticides such as dieldrin or B H C should be practised.

---

* Some authorities regard these two species as but varieties of one species.

CHAPTER XLVI

MISCELLANEOUS MITES OF MEDICAL IMPORTANCE TOGETHER WITH OBSERVATIONS ON THOSE MEMBERS OF THE CLASS PENTASTOMIDA WHICH SOMETIMES PARASITISE MAN

IN previous chapters two genera of mites containing species of outstanding medical importance have been discussed, *viz* the genus *Sarcoptes* containing the species *S. scabiei* which causes scabies and has a worldwide distribution, and the genus *Trombicula* containing mites which are the vectors of scrub typhus. There remain a large number of species occurring in no less than five families which, although they cannot be regarded as of great medical significance, nevertheless require to have attention drawn to them for various reasons.

The family Laelaptidae

Mites belonging to the family Laelaptidae are chiefly ectoparasites of vertebrates; of these, certain species which are normally parasites of birds and rodents will in certain circumstances attack human beings. Laelaptid mites are mainly important because of the dermatitis which sometimes arises as a result of their bites, but at least one species has been shown to be a vector of rickettsial pox to man.

The following description applies only to laelaptid mites which are of medical importance. They are small oval-shaped creatures, the unfed adults measuring less than a millimetre whilst gorged individuals may be a millimetre or more. Unfed specimens are cream or light ochre, while fed mites (depending on the time when the last meal was taken) vary from red to red black in colour. The body surface is covered with simple hairs. The dorsal surface, in the medically important species, is provided with a single dorsal shield, whilst the ventral surface bears a number of smaller shields. The shape of the shields and the number of setae which they bear is important in classification. The mouthparts are conspicuous and consist of a pair of 5 segmented, leglike, hairy palps and a pair of slender chelicerae which are adapted for piercing the skin of the host. On each side of the body, close to the 4th coxa, is a spiracular opening which is associated with a linear, tube-like structure, known as the peritreme, which extends up to the level of the 1st coxa.

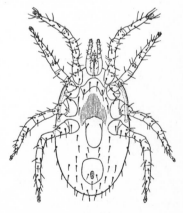

Fig. 184. Adult female *Ornithonyssus bacoti*, the tropical rat mite. (Cleared specimen).

273

The life-cycle of all the laelaptid mites of medical importance is similar, there being an egg, a larval, two nymphal and an adult stage. The eggs, which are minute (just visible to the naked eye), white, oval objects, are laid singly, usually in the resting places of the hosts. The egg hatches to produce a six-legged larva which does not feed but moults in a few days to the first nymphal stage, known as the protonymph, which requires a blood-meal before moulting to the second nymphal stage, known as the deutonymph. The deutonymph (which may or may not feed, depending on the species of mite concerned) moults to the adult male or female, both of which feed on blood. The total life-cycle is completed in a week to three weeks. The adults are long lived, most species being able to survive for several months with only occasional blood-meals.

Over a dozen species have been reported as attacking man, but of these only five are sufficiently common to merit attention. These five species are *Ornithonyssus bacoti* (=*Liponyssus bacoti*) the tropical rat mite, *O. bursa* (=*L. bursa*) the tropical fowl mite, *O. sylviarum* (= *L. sylviarum*) the northern fowl mite, *Dermanyssus gallinae*, the red mite of poultry, and *Allodermanyssus sanguineus*, the house mouse mite.

Whilst all these species, and in particular *O. bacoti* and *D. gallinae*, have been shown to be responsible for outbreaks of dermatitis in man in various parts of the world—both in the tropics and in the temperate zones—the only species which is recognised to be a vector of disease to man is *A. sanguineus*, a parasite of the house mouse in North America, Europe, Asia and Africa, which has been proved to transmit rickettsial pox caused by *Rickettsia akari*. Although *O. bacoti* has not been shown to be a transmitter of disease to man it is known to be a vector, albeit an unimportant one, of murine typhus from rat to rat in the rodent reservoir.

The family Pyemotidae

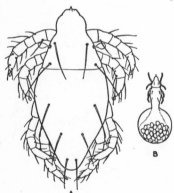

This family of mites includes only one species of medical importance—*Pyemotes ventricosus* (= *Pediculoides ventricosus*).

P. ventricosus is somewhat like a tiny louse in appearance. It is only just visible to the naked eye, measuring less than 0.5 mm., and is elongated, with a segmented body and 4 pairs of legs. A characteristic feature of this mite is a pair of club-shaped seta-like structures lying dorso-laterally between the first and second pairs of legs.

The female is viviparous, the progeny being retained within the abdomen of the parent until they are sexually mature. Since the female may produce as many as 300 mites, her abdomen, posterior to

Fig. 185. *Pyemotes ventricosus*, the grain-itch mite. *A*. adult female; *B*. ovigerous female.

the 4th pair of legs, becomes enormously distended to form a very conspicuous sac. The total life-cycle occupies a week to ten days.

P. ventricosus is not a parasite of vertebrates but feeds on various insects, at times occurring on these arthropods in vast numbers. Human beings handling substances in which the parasitised insects occur such as grain, straw, hay and cotton seed are sometimes affected by the mites which give rise to an allergic dermatitis known as "grain itch". Severe outbreaks have been recorded from many parts of the world, the persons most usually affected being farm labourers or workers unloading cargoes of grain or other foodstuffs.

The families Acaridae (= Tyroglyphidae) and Glycyphagidae

Mites belonging to these two families may be considered together. They are white or yellowish acarines with elongated bodies. Most species of medical importance are sparsely provided with a few long setae, which in some species may be difficult to detect and which are either simple or finely feathered. A transverse suture dividing the body into an anterior and a posterior region may or may not be present. The chelicerae are large, prominent and pincer-like but the palps are small and inconspicuous.

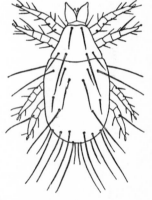

The life-cycle, which is complex, takes about three weeks to complete and includes a curious non-feeding nymphal stage, known as the hypopus which, although not parasitic, attaches itself to other arthropods, thus enabling the mites to be widely dispersed.

These non-parasitic mites live in, and feed on, a great variety of organic substances such Fig. 186. A tyroglyphid mite. as grain of various types, copra and vanilla pods. Persons handling materials in which these acarines occur may complain of a dermatitis, which is regarded as being of an allergic nature and due to previous sensitisation of the individual to some substance present in the secretions or excretions of mites of various genera, the more important of which are *Tyrophagus*, *Acarus* (= *Tyroglyphus*) and *Glycyphagus*. The resultant dermatitis is known by various eponyms, such as "grocer's itch", "copra itch", "miller's itch", "vanilla workers' rash", etc. depending on the occupation of the affected person.

The family Demodicidae

This family contains only one genus, *Demodex*, which is composed of several species, only one of which, *Demodex folliculorum* var. *hominis*, is found inhabiting the hair follicles and sebaceous glands of man.

D. folliculorum var. *hominis* is a minute creature less than 0.5 mm in length which is worm-like in appearance and markedly elongated. The thorax bears

S

eight very short and stumpy legs and the abdomen is annulated. The entire life-cycle is spent in the host's skin.

In man the mites are found in sebaceous glands and hair follicles, particularly in the region of the nose and the eyelids and may be found in the extruded contents of comedones. Although several other species of *Demodex* may be the cause of very severe forms of mange in domestic animals, *D. folliculorum* var.

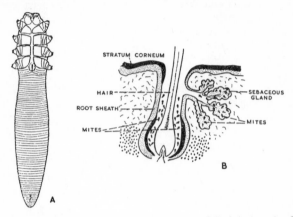

Fig. 187. *Demodex folliculorum* var. *hominis*, the hair follicle mite. *A*. adult; *B*. diagrammatic representation of the sites of development in the hair follicle and sebaceous gland.

hominis does not usually appear to cause any harm to its human host, although there are claims that it may on rare occasions give rise to dermatitis in some subjects. Although these mites appear to be of no medical significance it is important to be aware of their existence, since pathologists are sometimes puzzled by their appearance in skin sections.

MEMBERS OF THE CLASS PENTASTOMIDA WHICH SOMETIMES PARASITISE MAN

Those species which are known to parasitise man occur in the families Linguatulidae and Porocephalidae. These are worm-like arthropods with rudimentary mouthparts which are armed with chitinous hooks; appendages are lacking in the adult stage.

Owing to their elongated appearance and lack of legs or similar appendages linguatulids were for a long time classified as helminths; they are now known to be arthropods, probably related to the arachnids.

Pentastomids have a worldwide distribution, the adults occurring in various species of vertebrates, mainly in snakes and carnivores and also, but only very rarely, in man. The larvae and the nymphs do not normally undergo development in these hosts but do so in many species of herbivorous animals. These immature forms also develop in primates, and man (particularly when living in uncivilised communities in the tropics) is a not uncommon host for at least two species.

In human infestations the cycle normally comes to a blind end at the nymphal stage, but in the case of other animals the body of the infected host may be eaten by the appropriate snake or carnivore host, in which case the immature stages continue their development to the adult sexual forms.

The life-cycle from egg to adult is a long one which, even in optimum conditions, takes from one to two years.

Within the class there are two genera of some medical importance, the genus *Linguatula* and the genus *Porocephalus*.

The genus Linguatula

Members of the genus *Linguatula* which, owing to their shape, are often called "tongue worms", have an almost worldwide distribution. The adult forms occur in the nasal cavities of various carnivores including domestic dogs and cats, while the larvae and nymphs of one species *(L. serrata)* have been recorded on several occasions as parasites of man. It is of interest to note that these human infestations have been observed in Europe as well as in the tropics.

The males are about two, and the females about three centimetres in length, while both sexes are typically tongue-shaped and exhibit the well marked striations shown in the drawing. The fertilised females produce large numbers of eggs which, owing to the irritation caused by the presence of the adults in the nasal cavities, are eventually sneezed out, usually onto low-lying vegetation. If the infected herbage is swallowed by suitable intermediate hosts such as cattle, sheep, goats, rabbits or sometimes man, the eggs hatch and the larvae are liberated in the lumen of the gut. The released larvae in no way resemble the parents but have the appearance of small four-legged mites, about 200 microns in length. These minute creatures burrow into the lymph channels and blood vessels of the gut and become distributed in the mesenteric glands, the lungs and the liver.

In these sites the larvae undergo development to the nymphal forms which closely resemble the adults

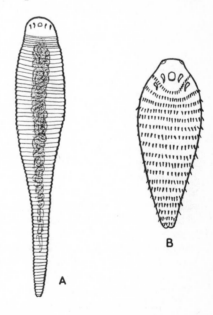

Fig. 188. *Linguatula serrata. A.* adult; *B.* nymph.

but are smaller. Once having reached the nymphal stage the parasites undergo no further development but remain quiescent, and usually encapsulated, awaiting transfer to a carnivorous host.

In man the nymphs are most commonly found in the liver, where their presence, even in large numbers, is not usually associated with any well marked signs or symptoms.

The genus Porocephalus

Members of the genus *Porocephalus* occur mainly in the tropics, particularly in Africa and India. The worm-like segmented adults have an unmistakable appearance, the segmentations of their bodies being separated by a series of

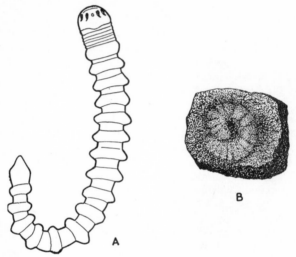

Fig. 189. *Porocephalus* sp. *A.* adult; *B.* nymph as seen in the characteristic coiled position, lying just below the liver capsule.

large chitinous rings. The sexually mature forms, which measure 3 to 12 cm. in length, occur in the lungs of snakes, and the eggs (each of which contains a fully developed four-legged larva) passed by the females are ejected with the snake's bronchial secretions. If the eggs reach herbage or water and are swallowed by a warm-blooded animal some of the contained larvae hatch in the host's intestine, bore their way through the gut wall and become free in the peritoneal cavity. If the host is a suitable one, and may herbivorous animals and primates are included in this category, further development to the nymphal form may take place in almost any organ, but in the case of primates much the most favoured site is the liver. In the liver the nymphs, which already resemble small adults, are usually found encysted and coiled up in a characteristic position just below the liver capsule. In human hosts the life-cycle comes to a blind end at the nymphal stage, while in animals the final development to the adult sexual form can only occur if the cadaver is swallowed by a snake.

In man the invasion of the liver, or more rarely of the gut wall, sometimes produces symptoms and gives rise to a condition referred to as porocephaliasis. More often no symptoms are observed and the condition is only accidentally diagnosed, either as the result of an autopsy or following the taking of an x-ray photograph. (See Plate XVI fig. 1).

Since man only becomes infected by ingestion of the eggs, the control of linguatulid infestations mainly consists in avoiding the consumption of un-cooked vegetables and untreated water, when these are from suspect sources. In uncivilised communities the eating of uncooked or improperly cooked snakes is a common cause of infection.

CHAPTER XLVII

ARTHROPODS DIRECTLY AFFECTING HEALTH, INCLUDING THE SO CALLED "VENOMOUS ARTHROPODS"*

A RTHROPODS may directly affect the health of man either in their role as parasites or as a result of their employing some poison to protect themselves or their territory. It is usual to consider that in both instances the resultant reaction will prove to the disadvantage of the host, but this is not always the case: bee stings, or the injection of the venom obtained from bees, is sometimes prescribed in the treatment of rheumatism, while living blowfly larvae, usually those belonging to the genus *Phormia* or *Lucilia,* have been employed in the treatment of osteomyelitis or for the clearing up of septic wounds. This latter form of treatment has now been largely abandoned, partly because it is repulsive, but chiefly owing to the difficulty of ensuring that the larvae used are free from bacteria and the consequent possibility that tetanus may result. Although the use of live larvae has been largely discontinued, the active substance produced by them, allantoin, is sometimes prescribed. In general, however, the beneficial effects produced by arthropods directly affecting health are negligible, and in the account which follows only their pathogenic effects will be considered.

(1) PARASITIC ARTHROPODS DIRECTLY AFFECTING HEALTH

The following account is intended only as a general survey. The pathogenic effects produced by parasitic arthropods directly injurious to man may be considered under four headings: (a) lesions due to mechanical trauma; (b) lesions due to secondary infections; (c) lesions due to the injection of directly injurious substances; (d) lesions due to previous sensitization of the host. Although these pathogenic effects are considered separately, they may, and often do, occur in conjunction.

(a) *Lesions due to mechanical trauma.* In the case of the puncture or abrasion made by the blood-sucking arthropod, the extent of the lesion produced will depend on the size and nature of the mouthparts and the manner in which they are used. It is, of course, obvious that the large and clumsy skin-piercing organ of some of the Tabanidae (horse flies) and argasid ticks (*Ornithodoros* spp.) will produce more extensive wounds than will the small and delicate mouthparts of the biting midges (*Culicoides* spp.) and the blood-sucking lice, but the difference in the result is not so great as might be expected, since all these arthropods tend to probe the tissues until a pool of blood, sufficient for their purpose, has been produced. In any case, the uncomplicated trauma produced

---

* Based on the original article by one one of us (R.M.G.) appearing in the British Encyclopaedia of British Medical Practice, Volume 2, by permission of the publishers, Butterworth & Company (Publishers) Limited.

by any type of blood-sucking arthropod is seldom sufficiently severe to cause any serious disturbance in the host. When, however, the arthropod extends its activities from sucking blood to tissue invasion, the resultant trauma may be more extensive particularly when it is caused by one of the larger species of myiasis producing fly larvae. On the other hand, however, the invasion of the host tissues by a parasite so minute as *Sarcoptes scabiei*, and one which never penetrates below the stratum corneum cannot be regarded as causing any serious mechanical trauma, and the extensive lesions sometimes associated with its presence must be ascribed to some other cause. Between these extremes there are a host of tissue-invading parasites, mostly larvae of two-winged flies, which cause varying degrees of mechanical trauma in the tissues of their host. As already mentioned, certain forms of myiasis may produce serious lesions, but, with these exceptions and in the absence of complications, the majority of the tissue-invading arthropods seldom produce a degree of mechanical trauma sufficient to interfere with the general health of the host.

(b) *Lesions due to secondary infections.* It has been shown that a few species of fly larvae may produce considerable mechanical trauma. Usually, however, the most serious results of myiasis are those which follow the invasion by bacteria of the wound made by the parasite, and the term "myiasis" generally conjures up a picture of a septic lesion for the cause of which bacteria are more responsible than are the Diptera. In addition to the lesions of myiasis, secondary infection may of course complicate any injury to the host caused by arthropods, the organisms being introduced either directly by the parasite when piercing the skin or subsequently gaining access through the abrasion. It would, naturally, be impossible to consider individually the various species of secondary invaders but attention should be drawn to the risk of tetanus following invasion by the jigger flea, *Tunga penetrans*.

(c) *Lesions due to the injection of directly injurious substances.* The picture of a mechanical injury followed by a secondary infection is often further complicated as a result of the injection by the parasite of a substance inimical to the host. The responsible substance is usually derived from the salivary glands of the parasite, and its employment forms a necessary part of the creature's life-cycle, either as a means of facilitating its penetration into the host, or as a means of aiding it to digest the food obtained from the host. These salivary secretions contain such substances as coagulants, anticoagulants, red-cell agglutinins and haemolysins, together with certain other substances the nature of which has not been determined. In addition, it was thought at one time that the majority of arthropod parasites introduce into the tissues some substance of a toxic nature which causes an immediate or else a delayed reaction in the host which may or may not be severe in character. More recent investigations suggest that only a very limited number of species of parasitic arthropods, including certain ticks and some species of *Simulium*, secrete a substance of a directly toxic nature. Furthermore; although the introduction or anticoagulants and agglutinins may alter the histological picture of the lesions produced, they are not capable of reproducing the marked wheals characteristic of the local reactions so often associated with insect bites and with invasion of the tissues by arthropod parasites.

A form of paralysis which affects man and animals, often with serious and sometimes with fatal results, occasionally follows the bites of ticks. "Tick bite paralysis" is most often associated with species of *Ixodes* in Africa and Australia, and with those of *Dermacentor* and *Amblyomma* in America. There are a few statements that paralysis has been known to follow the bite of an argasid tick.

(d) *Lesions due to previous sensitization of the host.* It has been shown that neither mechanical trauma nor the injection of secretions by blood-sucking and tissue-invading arthropods is necessarily associated with any marked reaction. Nevertheless, it is common knowledge that the bites of certain arthropods, such as fleas, lice, midges, sandflies, mosquitoes, bed bugs and various mites, cause a reaction (which may be severe) amongst a high proportion of persons attacked, while it is commonly believed that invasion of the skin by *S. scabiei* always causes a marked reaction. If, however, the subject is more fully studied it will be found that in persons not previously sensitized the first stage of invasion in scabies is not associated with any marked reaction, and similarly, that individuals bitten for the first time by any of the blood-sucking insects just referred to usually show no immediate obvious reaction. It has further been shown that if the individual continues to be regularly exposed at frequent intervals to the same species of blood-sucking insect, he is unlikely to develop a marked reaction, but that if he is exposed at irregular intervals he is liable, sooner or later, to react violently to the bite in the case of blood-sucking arthropods, or to the invasion of his tissues in the case of *S. scabiei*. It has also been demonstrated that this immediate reaction is capable of passive transfer, that it is highly specific and that persons who react to one species of insect, such as the mosquito or bed bug, will not normally react when bitten by another insect belonging to the same genus but to a different species.

The above observations only refer to a limited number of the common parasitic arthropods, but, in so far as these are concerned, it appears reasonable to consider that any immediate and severe reaction, together with the majority of delayed reactions, associated with their bite or invasion of the tissues is due to previous sensitization and not to the injection of any poisonous or toxic substance. In addition to the localized reaction just described, it is well-known that severe generalized reactions may occur, and it is usually recognized that such reactions are in the nature of anaphylactic phenomena.

Treatment. — The treatment of localized reactions caused by arthropods, in previously sensitized persons, is unsatisfactory. It is known that repeated and regular exposures usually cause the disappearance of the reaction, so that most persons constantly exposed to the bites of arthropods develop what is usually called an immunity but which is better described as desensitization. Unfortunately, however, this desensitization is usually of a transitory nature; while the marked specificity of the reaction suggests that treatment by an antigen prepared from one species is unlikely to make a patient tolerant to insect bites as a whole.

Medicinal treatment, at any rate in so far as local reactions are concerned, seems of little value, and although some writers have claimed that the administration of thiamine chloride reduces the sensitivity to mosquito bites their findings have not been generally confirmed. Reports concerning the value of antihistamine drugs are somewhat contradictory, but it appears that whereas they are of value in controlling general allergic reactions following insect bites, they are seldom effective in reducing the severity of the local reaction. In distinction to the comparative failure of therapeutics, considerable success in protection has been achieved by the employment of certain repellents, particularly dimethyl phthalate.

(2) STINGING, BITING AND VENOMOUS ARTHROPODS

The association between man and arthropods so far considered has been that of host and parasite and, since it is to the disadvantage of the parasite to cause any incapacitating injury to its host, most of the injuries of a serious character arising from this association have been in the nature of accidents caused by the arthropod in its capacity as a vector of disease, or else as a producer of a violent reaction following its injection of a normally harmless substance (usually the saliva) into a previously sensitized person. On the other hand, certain arthropods which are non-parasitic and in no way dependent on man for their existence have developed weapons of defence which they use to protect themselves from interference. These defensive weapons produce harmful effects which vary from the comparatively trivial discomfort caused by a wasp sting to the serious symptoms which may follow the sting of a scorpion or the bite of certain species of spiders. It must not be forgotten, however, that the stings of bites of arthropods regarded as usually only mildly pathogenic, may take on a serious aspect if inflicted on a previously sensitized person.

The use of venom as a means of protection has been developed by arthropods of so widely different character that species of medical importance occur in at least seven different zoological orders.

(a) *Bees, wasps and ants* (order Hymenoptera)

Bees and wasps comprise a large number of species (more than 4,000 species of stinging bees alone have been described), and although the general nature of the poison injected by the different species appear similar, the severity of the reaction varies with the size of the insect and the virulence of its venom. Much research has been conducted on the nature of bee venom, and although its exact composition is still unknown, it has been shown that cobra venom, bee venom and histamine all produce similar pathological lesions when injected intravenously, suggesting that the first-named poisons cause their effect by the liberation of histamine. Although the lesions produced by viper and bee venom are similar, the composition of the venoms responsible must differ, since immunity to snake venom confers no immunity to bee stings. In normal individuals the severity of the reaction following the stings of bees and wasps depends on the site of the sting and on the amount of venom injected and, in such persons, a single sting on the skin is followed by oedema, marked cellular infiltration and some necrosis of the underlying muscle layer. In contrast to the mild effects following stings on the skin, stings inflicted on the tongue and fauces may cause oedema leading to respiratory obstruction and asphyxia. The total number of bee stings inflicted on the skin which is necessary to produce death in a normal healthy adult has been estimated at some 500, if all the stings are administered at about the same time. Death from far fewer numbers has been recorded, but on the whole, severe reactions following a limited number of stings on places other than the mouth and fauces only occur in sensitized persons in whom it is well known that the result of even a single sting may be followed by serious and sometimes fatal results.

Treatment.—The treatment of bee stings in normal persons consists of removing the sting and applying the customary local treatment. The barbed sting of the bee, once inserted, is anchored in the flesh and this results in the tip of the abdomen being torn away when the insect is forcibly removed. Since the poison apparatus remains attached to the sting, any attempt to remove the latter with forceps tends to squeeze more venom into the wound, and in order to avoid this complication the sting should be scraped from the skin with a knife-blade or needle.

In sensitized persons, the sting should be extracted and the usual treatment for allergic reactions, including the giving of adrenaline, should be administered. Successful desensitization has been claimed following the administration of 12-14 intradermal injections commencing with 1:1,000 of a sting, and ending with a dose representing the total venom from the whole sting; it does not appear to be known, however, whether persons desensitized to bee venom are also desensitized to wasp venom.

Ants may injure man by biting, by stinging or by spraying formic acid. In uncomplicated cases, the results of such attacks are seldom serious, but the stings of certain species, such as *Paraponera clavata,* cause agonising pain and may be followed by extensive necrosis of tissue.

(b) *Spiders* (order Araneida)

The original "tarantula" of southern Europe, *Lycosa tarentula,* whose bite was so much dreaded during the Middle Ages, is a harmless creature, while, contrary to popular belief, the large hairy "tarantula spiders" of the tropics seldom cause a serious injury. On the other hand, certain relatively small and insignificant spiders are capable of inflicting highly poisonous bites and are responsible for the majority of authenticated records of severe reactions associated with serious symptoms and even death. The majority of these serious reactions are due to spiders in the genus *Latrodectus,* medically important species of this genus occuring in Australia, New Zealand, South Africa, and in North and South America. These spiders tend to infest such sites around houses as fences, stumps and wood-piles; they also enter buildings, mainly outbuildings, where they hide away from the light and seem to have a particular preference for spinning their webs on the undersides of seats in dry-earth closets. This habit explains the fact that the majority of bites from these creatures are recorded as having occurred on the genitals and buttocks, and that males are more often bitten than are females. The poison, which is injected by the pincer-like fangs of the spider, is a neurotoxin, probably a toxalbumin, which acts on the neuromuscular junction. The local symptoms vary greatly; there may be congestion and oedema or even gangrene, but often the local reaction produced is so slight as to pass unnoticed. Within 15 minutes to several hours after the bite, however, generalized symptoms usually occur. Agonizing muscular pains, increasing in severity and responding poorly to morphine, spread over the chest and abdomen, the latter often assuming a board-like rigidity suggestive of an acute abdominal condition. The patient shows signs of shock; there is profuse perspiration, pallor, and a fall in blood pressure; dyspnoea with respiratory stridor is said to be characteristic. Recovery is recorded in some 95 per cent of cases occurring in adults, but convalescence may be prolonged, and it should be remembered that the prognosis is far less favourable in children.

Treatment.— Specific antivenin is the best treatment, but is difficult to prepare and is not generally available. Local treatment, as for snake bite, should be applied if the bite is on the arm or leg. Most authorities recommend the use of morphine and atropine to relieve the pain, and intramuscular or intravenous injections of calcium gluconate (10 ml. of a 10 per cent solution) to control muscular spasm. Poisonous spiders tend to have a limited distribution and several cases of spider bite may occur within a small area. In such circumstances, recovered cases may be present in the district and it has been suggested that the injection of convalescent serum from such persons is worthy of trial, especially in the case of children. Closets in infested areas should be frequently inspected and sprayed at regular intervals with 10 per cent DDT in kerosene, since it is claimed that DDT in this strength, even when lightly applied to the web, proves rapidly lethal to the spiders using it.

Poisonous spiders occurring in genera other than *Latrodectus*, such as *Atrax* spp. in Australia and *Mastophora gasteracanthoides* (the "pruning spider") in Peru, are of considerable local importance.

(c) *Scorpions* (order Scorpionida)

Members of this order are widely distributed in the tropics and subtropics and probably cause more serious direct injuries than any of the other venomous arthropods. Thus, at one hospital in Trinidad, 689 cases of scorpion bites were admitted during a 5-year period, and during one year the mortality was as high as 4.7 per cent. Whereas the spiders inject venom through the fangs (chelicerae), these appendages are not used as piercing organs by the scorpions, whose entire poison apparatus is carried in the comma-shaped sting at the tip of the tail which, in the act of striking, is swung down over the creature's head and buried in the victim's skin. Some of the larger scorpions, such as *Leiurus quinquestriatus*, inject a large dose of highly toxic venom, and in Egypt, where this species is justly dreaded, the mortality rate amongst children under 5 years of age is above 55 per cent. On the other hand, some of the larger species of scorpions do not possess a particularly poisonous sting and are less dangerous than certain smaller but more venomous species.

The symptoms of scorpion sting are local, severe, burning pain, which usually lessens within 30 minutes, and general manifestations, including profuse sweating, nausea and vomiting. The poison, apart from its local action which may cause inflammation and marked coagulative necrosis of the underlying muscle, appears to act on the nervous system and kills by its effect on the cardiac and respiratory centres. A specific antivenin is much the most satisfactory form of treatment and has greatly reduced the mortality rate especially amongst children in Egypt, the north African coast and Brazil. Local treatment should follow that recommended for spider bite, while the severe pain may be controlled by a local injection of cocaine.

(d) *Centipedes* (order Chilopoda)

Centipedes have a worldwide distribution, but only the large tropical and subtropical species inflict a harmful bite on man. As in the case of spiders and scorpions the venom injected is normally used to kill other smaller arthropods on which these creatures live, but the method of its injection differs in that centipedes possess no fangs or sting and kill their prey by injecting poison through the first pair of leg-like appendages which are modified to form piercing poison claws. The bites of large centipedes are often very painful and may give rise to local necrotic lesions, but they seldom produce marked generalized symptoms, although deaths in children have been recorded. Treatment follows the same general lines as that recommended for scorpion stings.

(e) *Millipedes* (order Diplopoda)

These creatures resemble centipedes in that the body is composed of numerous similar segments each bearing a pair of appendages; zoologically, however, they are widely divergent and may be distinguished by the fact that their segments are rounded, not flattened as in the case of the centipede, and by their tendency to curl up when disturbed. Unlike the other venomous arthropods previously mentioned, millipedes are not predacious and possess no means of injecting poison, their defensive venom either oozing, or else being squirted with considerable force, from special pores arranged along the sides of the body. If this fluid comes in contact with the human skin it may cause considerable irritation or, if it reaches the eyes, severe inflammation. Millipedes rarely enter houses and injuries caused by them are usually acquired out of doors. Nothing is known of the nature of the venom and treatment is palliative.

(f) *Butterflies and moths* (order Lepidoptera)

Apart from cases due to previous sensitization, it is very unusual for adult butterflies or moths to cause irritation of the skin. On the other hand, the caterpillars of many species of Lepidoptera produce a dermatitis of varying degrees of severity. The uticaria which follows direct or indirect contact with the larvae of such species as *Megalopyge opercularia* ("puss caterpillar") *Euproctis chrysorrhoea* ("brown tail moth") and *Lagoa crispata* ("flannel moth") is due to the penetration of the human skin by hairs charged with poison from the subcuticular glands in the larvae. The lesions produced by these and other species of larval lepidoptera are sometimes extensive and, where the insects occur in large numbers, may cause local epidemics of some importance.

(g) *Beetles* (order Coleoptera)

None of the beetles possess a venomous sting or bite, but certain species, particularly those occurring in the families Meloidae and Staphylinidae, secrete a fluid which causes a blister on contact with the skin, or, if it enters the eye, serious inflammation. This vesicant reaction is often delayed, so that the patient is sometimes unable to associate the lesion with its cause.

The local reactions caused by beetles and by the larvae of butterflies and moths are seldom serious, and usually yield to such simple treatment as bathing with warm soapy water and, after drying, a soothing application, such as calamine lotion.

OTHER VENOMOUS INVERTEBRATES

The boundaries of medical zoology are wide and, in addition to certain directly injurious arthropods, there are a host of other invertebrate creatures which wound and poison man by means of stings, bites or the emission of vesicant fluids. Accounts of these creatures will be found in most of the larger works on tropical medicine.

CHAPTER XLVIII

THE COLLECTING OF ARTHROPODS OF MEDICAL IMPORTANCE

THE medical officer is not usually concerned with the collection of arthropods in general, nor yet with the specialised collection of all the available species occurring within a particular group or family. On the other hand, he will often find it necessary to collect a limited number of species of arthropods (at some or all stages of their development) which although occurring in a wide variety of families with very different life-cycles and habits, have one point in common, namely that they are of medical importance.

Before discussing some of the methods commonly employed in the collection of medically important arthropods, it is necessary to consider the particular purpose, or purposes, for which such collections are made, since the ultimate disposal of the material will influence not only the selection of a particular method, but also the subsequent treatment of the arthropods so collected.

Some of the purposes may be summarised as follows:—

(1) Arthropods may be collected for future identification when this cannot be done on the spot, either because there is not sufficient time or because the collector is not sufficiently expert.

(2) Certain arthropod vectors of disease, notably mosquitoes, may be collected with special reference to their numbers, time of biting etc., etc. Such collections are usually undertaken in connection with medical surveys in which it is necessary not only to identify the species concerned, but also to make some estimation of its density and to obtain information concerning its habits.

(3) Arthropods may be collected, in connection with medical surveys, in order that they may be dissected and examined for the presence of parasites. When the information previously obtained concerning the density of a particular arthropod is correlated with its infection rate, the combined result is expressed as the infective density.

(4) Arthropods may be collected in order that a growing stage, which has defied recognition, may be allowed to develop to the imago, which is usually more easily identified. Conversely, fertilised females may be maintained alive in order that the eggs and larvae they produce may be associated with the parent forms.

(5) Arthropods, collected at any stage of their development, may be maintained alive in order to study their life-cycles and biology.

Finally, attention may again be drawn to the great value to teaching institutions of large collections of properly mounted insects for class purposes or for detailed taxonomic studies.

THE COLLECTION OF BITING FLIES AT VARIOUS STAGES
OF THEIR DEVELOPMENT

(a) *Adult stages.*

The collection of biting flies in the adult stage is usually undertaken in order to establish the identity of the species and to study the part it may play in transmitting disease or else directly in causing ill health.

The adults may be captured either when coming to feed on the mammalian host or else in their resting places, the type of resting place often being charac-

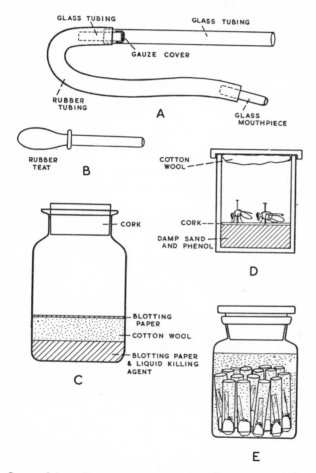

Fig. 190. Some of the collecting and preserving apparatus referred to in the text. *A.* Collecting sucker; *B.* pipette for collecting mosquito larvae etc.; *C.* killing bottle; *D.* relaxing box; *E.* method of storing small tubes containing specimens in a large jar of preservative.

teristic of a particular species of fly. With the exception of the biting cyclorraphous flies, such as the tsetse fly (*Glossina*) and the stable fly (*Stomoxys*), only the females suck blood, so that males are usually absent from collections of flies which have been captured after alighting on the host. Flies settling on the skin may be caught, either by means of a test tube or else by use of a sucker (see fig. 190A). When not feeding the resting males and females generally, although not always, occupy similar sites and should be searched for and collected in their recognised resting places. Some species of biting flies, notably mosquitoes, tend to occupy such man-made habitats as houses and shelters for domestic stock, as well as being found in tunnels and under bridges etc. Other species tend to occupy natural habitats such as caves, burrows in the earth, clefts in rocks and rot holes in trees, while other common resting places are in herbage and on the under surface of leaves. These remarks apply not only to the resting places of most species of mosquitoes but also to those of many important species of sandflies (*Phlebotomus*), the imagos of which are usually looked for either in the dwelling place of the host or else in some sheltered situation in its immediate vicinity. On the other hand, the resting places of the remaining species of biting flies, occurring in the families Simuliidae, Ceratapogonidae, Tabanidae and Muscidae, although sometimes associated with the habitat of the host are more likely to be found in vegetation, often at sites well away from the dwelling place of the host.

Insects found resting in such situations may usually be captured by the use of the suction tube or else in a test tube, but when searching their resting places in vegetation it is often necessary to disturb the foliage and then to capture the insects as they fly out. When capturing small biting flies in flight it is best to use a small (about 6″ diameter) bag made of gauze or muslin, mounted on a light circular wire or cane frame and attached to a short (about 2 ft.) cane handle. The insects should be anaesthetised in the net before transfer to the collecting box or bottle.

(b) *Immature stages.*

The collection of the eggs and larval stages of those biting flies which are of medical importance is usually undertaken in order to establish the relationship between a particular species and its larval habitat. In the case of the mosquitoes and, to some extent, in the case of the black flies (*Simulium* spp.) our knowledge of the morphology of the larva—and sometimes also of the egg—is often sufficiently advanced to render possible the direct identification of the species, but in the case of other types of biting flies it is generally necessary to rear the larvae to the adult stage.

The usual breeding places of the more important species of biting flies have been described in the preceeding chapters, and such likely habitats should be examined by the collector who, in order to carry out an efficient search, must take with him suitable collecting apparatus. It is important to note, however, that the essential equipment is neither elaborate nor costly and that it usually consists of simple materials which are easily obtainable in most villages.

In the case of mosquitoes, the eggs—whether laid singly or in rafts—are best collected either by filtering the water in which they have been laid through fine muslin, or else by skimming the eggs off the surface with a strip of paper. The larvae and pupae may be captured individually with a wide-mouthed pipette fitted with a teat (see fig. 190B) or with a spoon (large enamelled or transparent plastic spoons are particularly suitable), or else they may be obtained, usually in large numbers, by the use of a fine-mesh net or sieve. The most satisfactory techniques for collecting different species in varying conditions can only be learnt by experience, but in general two methods are commonly employed. In the first method, the water to be examined is disturbed as little as possible, the collector concentrating his attention on the eggs, larvae and pupae which can be seen on the surface; this method has the advantage of allowing observations to be made of the natural resting places of the various stages. When using the second method, the collector stirs up the water and mud and pulls out any vegetation which may interfere with his search. Having done this, he can either wait for the water to clear, or else, while it is still muddy, sample it with a net or sieve. This second method generally enables a larger number of larvae and pupae to be collected than does the first method and gives a better idea of the general fauna, but it does not permit observations being made under natural conditions and it is an unsatisfactory method for the collection of eggs. A combination of both methods, in which the undisturbed water is first examined and any floating eggs, larvae and pupae collected, and later disturbed and netted or sieved, generally yields the best result. In the case of mosquito larvae belonging to the genus *Mansonia*, it is necessary to remove likely vegetation from the water and to examine it for the presence of attached larvae and pupae.

In the case of other groups of biting flies the larvae of which lead an aquatic or semi-aquatic existence, a somewhat similar procedure should be followed, but modifications of technique are often required. Thus the eggs, larvae and pupae of *Simulium* spp. are best collected while still attached to easily removable vegetation or stones. The aquatic or semi-aquatic larvae of those species of midges (*Culicoides*) which are of medical importance are best obtained by collecting mud or rotting vegetation from their natural breeding places in pools and tree holes etc. and in rotting stems of cut down vegetation, such as banana plants. In such circumstances the finding of the larvae is made easier if magnesium sulphate is added to the fluid, in a concentration just sufficient to cause the larvae to float to the surface, usually one part of the salt to three parts of water. The egg masses of certain species of horse flies (Tabanidae) which are deposited on vegetation overhanging water or mud are often fairly conspicuous objects and therefore form a guide to the breeding-sites; unfortunately, however, the egg masses of certain medically important species are difficult to detect. The larvae of Tabanid flies come to the surface at such long intervals that direct observation of the undisturbed water is usually profitless, and recourse must be had to searching the superficial layers of mud and rotting vegetation for the presence of the larvae. This search may be expedited and made much less laborious by using a series of metal sieves of ascending fineness of mesh, through which the washings of the mud and rotting vegetation are passed.

In the case of those groups of biting flies the larvae of which lead a terrestial existence, the sites in which the eggs and larvae are found will, as in the case of the aquatic and semi-aquatic types, vary greatly according to the species of fly concerned, the nature of the habitats available and the type of vertebrate on which the adults normally feed. In the case of the sandflies (*Phlebotomus* spp.), although the developing stages are always found in a particular type of microclimate the actual breeding sites of different species must be searched for in widely differing locations. Since sandflies have a very short flight, the larvae are usually found near to the resting places of the adults, and their exact site may be ascertained by trapping the adults as they emerge. Various methods may be employed, thus inverted jam jars may be placed over the mouths of rodent burrows, while pieces of sandfly netting may be pegged out over suspected breeding places in the open. Once the breeding place has been located, the larvae may be collected individually, or, more usually, by removing samples of soil from the habitat and immersing these in fluid of a specific gravity which will cause the larvae to come to the surface.

The larvae of sandflies are usually searched for with a view to establishing the oviposition sites of the adults, such sites being subsequently subjected to insecticidal treatment. Since only a limited number of species of sandflies are likely to be associated with disease transmission, and since the identification of these species is not possible in the larval stage, it is generally essential to retain a proportion of the living larvae in order to breed out the adults.

In the case of the tsetse flies (*Glossina* spp.) the egg is retained in the fly's body and the extra-uterine life of the larva is so brief as to be insignificant; in consequence collections made at the breeding sites are always confined to puparia. The puparia of various species of *Glossina* usually occur in the same type of biotope and should be searched for a few inches below the surface of loose soil or sand occurring in well shaded places, but, although the local conditions surrounding the puparia are thus very similar, nevertheless, as in the case of the sandfly, the exact site of the breeding place will vary according to the species concerned, its association with a particular type of vertebrate host and the nature of the surrounding vegetation.

The finding of the very characteristic puparia is conclusive evidence of the presence of one or more species of *Glossina* in the neighbourhood, but since it is not possible to identify with certainty the species by an examination of the puparia, it is necessary to keep these under observation until the flies have emerged.

The collection of the larval stages of the remaining group of flies—the stable flies (*Stomoxys*) and allied genera—is usually undertaken in order to discover the breeding places (the characteristics of which have been described in a previous chapter) with a view to their subsequent destruction. The larvae of *Stomoxys* and closely allied genera are easily identifiable, and since the identification of a particular species is of little or no medical significance it follows that the collection of the larvae for breeding out purposes is seldom necessary.

THE COLLECTION OF NON-BITING FLIES AT VARIOUS STAGES OF THEIR DEVELOPMENT

This type of collection, so far as the medical officer is concerned, may be divided into two groups: (a) the collection of the adult and larval forms of Diptera likely to be concerned in the mechanical transmission of filth diseases; (b) the collection of the larval, and occasionally of the adult, forms of Diptera causing myiasis in the human host.

(a) *The collection of Diptera likely to be concerned in the transmission of filth diseases.* Adult flies likely to be concerned in the mechanical transmission of disease may be collected at their feeding and resting sites, mainly in buildings, latrines, garbage dumps etc., where they may be captured either with a net or with a test tube in the manner previously described; or else they may be obtained by using various forms of fly traps. Having identified the species likely to be concerned in the transmission of disease, it will then be necessary to search for its breeding places with a view to initiating methods of control. The types of breeding places selected by the various species have been described in the previous chapters, and it is generally possible to identify the genus, and some times the species, without having to resort to breeding out the adults, but, in case of doubt, some of the material from the breeding site, together with the larvae found in it, should be retained and placed in a breeding cage in order to obtain the imagos.

(b) *The collection of Diptera causing myiasis in the human host.* In general this is confined to the collection of the larvae, since the imagos responsible for the larval invasion are either not directly associated with the human host (as in most cases of specific myiasis), or else the adult flies are not available at the time the larvae are first detected (as in most cases of non-specific myiasis). In the case of the non-specific myiasis producing larvae the maggots may be easily picked out of the wound with forceps, and the genus, and sometimes the species, can usually—but by no means always—be identified by such morphological details as are provided by an examination of the posterior spiracles etc. If the larvae cannot be identified, they should be transferred to a breeding cage containing dry earth and a piece of raw meat, such as liver; in these circumstances the larvae will usually continue their development to pupation and may be identified by a study of the emerged adults. In the case of the specific myiasis producing larvae, since it is not possible to rear the growing stages, fully grown larvae, if not directly identifiable, must be collected and placed on dry earth to pupate.

THE COLLECTION OF FLEAS AT VARIOUS STAGES OF THEIR DEVELOPMENT

The collection of the jigger flea (*Tunga penetrans*)—the female of which lives in the skin—from the human host or from the animal reservoir is usually only undertaken to relieve the condition caused by the parasite, or else when specimens are required for class purposes or for special biological studies.

A very different situation exists as regards the collection of the remaining fleas of medical importance, for in this instance the collection of the adult forms may prove an essential part of the work of a medical officer called upon to investigate an outbreak of bubonic plague or, although less commonly, an outbreak of murine typhus. The various species of fleas concerned although responsible for inoculating the causal organisms into man are nevertheless seldom recovered from the human host, but are collected during the course of surveys of the rodent populations which form the animal reservoirs of the human infection. In these circumstances—and for various reasons, including that of personal safety—the fleas are usually collected after they and their rodent host have been killed, preferably with cyanogas, or some other anaesthetic vapour which is lethal to both host and parasite. Dead rodents are usually placed in a cloth or strong paper bag; while, if captured alive in a cage-trap, the cage and the contained occupant may be put directly into the bag. Before tying the mouth of the bag a piece of cotton wool soaked with the anaesthetic is placed inside the bag, the opening of which is then closed and the bag and its contents are placed inside a reasonably air tight receptacle—such as a wooden chest with a close fitting lid. After half an hour, or longer, the bag is opened and all the fleas found free in the bag and cage, together with those obtained by vigorously combing the dead rodent over a sheet of white paper, are collected. When picking up the dead fleas a pair of fine forceps and a camel's hair brush moistened with glycerine will both be found useful.

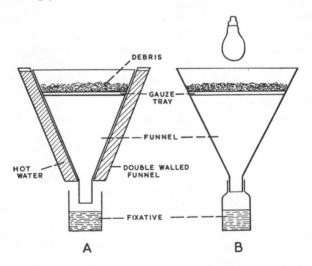

Fig. 191. *A.* Berlese-type funnel in which the heat from a surrounding water jacket tends to drive the insects into a collecting bottle; *B.* another Berlese-type funnel: with this apparatus the light and warmth from an electric light bulb drive the insects into a collecting bottle.

Although the collection of the adult fleas is usually confined to a search of the rodent host, they may also be collected from animal burrows; usually by placing sticky papers ("fly papers" or "tangle foot") at the entrance to the burrow or else by collecting the nesting material and rubbish from the burrow. The material obtained from the burrow may either be placed in a bag and the fleas killed with chloroform, or else the nest and debris may be placed in a Berlese funnel (see Fig. 191) and the migrating fleas killed with chloroform, prior to examination. Finally, fleas and many other parasitic arthropods may be collected from rodent burrows or other likely sites by the introduction of a "test" animal. The test animal is usually a white rat or a guinea pig which has previously been combed clear of any ectoparasites likely to be confused with the fauna which is being searched for in the animal habitat.

As regards the collection of the immature forms, the cocoons containing the pupae are very difficult to detect, but the larvae are more easily found. In the case of those species the adults of which normally feed on rodents this is best done by examining the nests and debris found in the burrow; while the larvae of fleas normally parasitic on man—usually the only species of importance is *Pulex irritans*—may be obtained from the dust and debris found in human habitations.

THE COLLECTION OF BUGS (ORDER HEMIPTERA) AT VARIOUS STAGES
OF THEIR DEVELOPMENT

Medically important bugs occur only in two families (the family Cimicidae and the family Reduviidae) in the Sub-Order Heteroptera.

(a) *The collection of bugs in the family Cimicidae.* Members of the family Cimicidae are not known to transmit, in nature, any disease to man; on the other hand they are unquestionably a source of ill health and the medical officer is often called upon to inquire into the source of the infestations found in dwellings. The methods available for the detection of the presence of the domestic species *Cimex lectularius* and *C. rotundatus* have been described in a previous chapter; the capture of the individual specimens to provide proof of their presence is sometimes necessary and for this purpose pieces of wool damped with chloroform are useful aids when collecting these very active insects. Those species which occasionally attack man—but which are normally parasitic on birds, bats and rodents and in whose shelters and nests they live—should be searched for either by direct examination of the hosts' shelters and nests or else indirectly by placing material likely to contain the active forms into a heated device, such as the Berlese funnel.

(b) *The collection of bugs in the family Reduviidae.* The domestic species, belonging to genera such as *Panstrongylus*, *Rhodnius* and *Triatoma*, which feed on man and which infect him and his domestic stock with *Trypanosoma cruzi*, may be located and collected in native houses by using similar techniques to those employed when searching for the domestic species of *Cimex*. Those species of reduviid bugs which rarely attack man, his domestic stock or the cats and dogs living in his dwellings, but which feed on wild animals and which maintain

T. cruzi in this reservoir, must be searched for in the homes or resting places of the particular animals concerned.

THE COLLECTION OF LICE AT VARIOUS STAGES OF THEIR DEVELOPMENT

Up to the present no species of sucking louse other than the two species (*Pediculus humanus* and *Phthirus pubis*) which parasitise man are known to be vectors, or reservoirs, of any disease transmissible to the human host. In these circumstances, and in view of the fact that both the species mentioned are permanent ectoparasites, the medical officer is concerned only with the collection (either from the body or else from the clothing) of the eggs, nymphs and adults of these two species. The eggs of both species are best obtained by cutting off the hairs on which they were laid. This method is useful also for collecting the nymphal stages of *Pediculus* and for all stages of *Phthirus*. The adult forms of *Pediculus* are best picked up with delicate ("watch-spring") forceps or on the point of a damp camel's hair brush.

THE COLLECTION OF TICKS AT VARIOUS STAGES OF THEIR DEVELOPMENT

Ticks injurious to the health of man occur in the families Ixodidae and Argasidae, and since the habits and habitations of members of the two families differ so markedly, it is best to consider the methods used for their collection separately.

(a) *Collection of ixodid ticks.* Any state of development may be found on the human host, but in practice it is usually only the larval and nymphal stages which are found embedded in the skin. Ticks found attached to the host can usually be removed intact—i.e. without loss of the mouthparts—if the capitulum is grasped with forceps and gentle traction, combined with a slight twisting movement, is exerted. If the mouthparts are very deeply embedded and gentle traction fails to dislodge them, the application of a pledgelet of cotton wool soaked in chloroform, ether or carbon tetrachloride, will usually cause the tick to come away more easily. Various other agents—such as petrol, or the application of heat in the form of a glowing cigarette end—may be used but they are less satisfactory than the anaesthetic fluids just mentioned.

Once a particular species of ixodid tick has been identified as feeding on man in a particular area it may or may not be of importance to inquire into the habits, habitats and hosts of this species at all stages of its development. Such complete investigations are usually beyond the scope of a routine medical survey, but it is often necessary to obtain knowledge regarding a particular aspect, for instance the more important animal reservoir from which man is obtaining his infection, in which case the following methods, amongst many others, may be employed. Suspected host animals other than man—for example dogs—may be examined alive and the ticks picked off with forceps. If the animals have been killed or found dead they may be placed in cloth or paper bags and the techniques previously described for the collection of fleas used to collect all stages of the ticks, some of which will be found loose in the bags or in the fur of the hosts, while others will still be attached to the skin. Again, as in the case of flea collections, the nesting materials and debris from the hosts' burrow may be examined directly for the presence of ticks, or else the ticks may be induced to leave the material by placing it in a Berlese funnel. Finally, ticks at any stage of development may be recovered from herbage, such as grass and low lying bushes, on which they rest while awaiting transfer to a new host. In such sites they may be detected by direct examination (it is not uncommon to find large numbers of larval ticks on a single blade of grass) or by the use of a "drag". A "drag" is a piece of white flannelette about three feet square which it tied—like a flag—to a wooden stick and is then pulled over the grass and other likely habitats, after which it is examined for the presence of any ticks which may have become attached to it.

(b) *Collection of argasid ticks.* Medically important ticks occurring in this family are almost entirely limited to the genus *Ornithodoros.* Certain species in this genus—such as *O. moubata* in Africa and *O. rudis* in the New World—are domestic species which, although prepared to feed on almost any warm-blooded host, normally live in human habitations, and feed on man. Other species within the genus are "non-domestic" or "wild" ticks which feed on various animals, mainly rodents, and which although they do not normally attack man may do so if the latter enters places—such as caves—which are the dwelling places of the ticks' normal hosts. The collection of any or all stages of the domestic species is generally a simple matter, the eggs, larvae, nymphs and adults being found in the cracks and crevices in human habitations. The collection of the non-domestic species of argasid ticks is usually accomplished by using techniques suitable for examining the particular type of refuge occupied by the animal host. In the case of large dwelling places, such as caves and tunnels, a direct examination, similar to that employed when searching human habitations, may be carried out. When the animal's refuge is a small one, as in the case of rodent burrows, recourse must be had to scraping out or digging out the burrow and examining the contained nesting material and other debris.

Ixodid and argasid ticks may be collected from animal habitats by the introduction of clean guinea pigs or white rats, when they are used as test animals in the manner previously described.

THE COLLECTION OF MITES AT VARIOUS STAGES
OF THEIR DEVELOPMENT

In general, the medical officer is interested in the collection of medically important mites occurring in four categories. Firstly in those free-living mites—mainly occurring in the family Tyroglyphidae—which may cause allergic reactions in the human host, and in this category may be included those predacious mites in the genus *Pyemotes* (*Pediculoides*) which cause allergic dermatitis. Secondly, in those skin-burrowing mites which occur in the family Sarcoptidae, thirdly, in those species of mites in the family Trombiculidae which are the vectors of mite-borne typhus, and fourthly in the family Laelaptidae, one species of which has been incriminated as a vector of rickettsial pox.

(a) *The collection of free-living mites suspected of causing allergic symptoms.* The suspected material should be examined under a dissecting microscope and the various stages of the mites found present collected by touching them with the sharp tip of a moistened fine camel's hair brush or else with a fine bristle (a bristle from a clothes brush is usually about the right thickness) fixed by means of melted sealing-wax to a match-stick. Since often more than one species is present it is advisable to secure a representative collection of mites at all stages of development. In the case of the tyroglyphid mites it is unusual to recover the offending mite from the host, but in the case of *Pyemotes* some of the mites are usually found loosely attached to the host and if these are collected they can be compared with the mites found in the suspected material.

(b) *The collection of burrowing mites.* Only one species, *Sarcoptes scabiei*, is commonly parasitic in man. All stages of development, from eggs to adults, may be found in the burrows in the skin; the technique for locating these burrows and for opening them has already been described.

(c) *The collection of trombiculid mites.* The larval forms can be collected from the grass or any low lying vegetation, but their association with man and, or, an animal reservoir is best established by the recovery of the mites from the vertebrate host. In the case of the human host, the site of the mite's attachment generally shows a well marked reaction which surrounds the feeding mite, but as often as not the mite has been scratched out and only the reaction is left; indeed it is surprisingly difficult to recover uninjured trombiculid mite larvae from the human host. When the mite is found *in situ* it should be anaesthetised, by applying a pledgelet of cotton wool soaked in chloroform, and then removed by digging it out of the skin with fine needles. In the case of hosts other than man — most commonly rodents — it is unusual to find any marked reaction at the site of the mite's attachment, but the mites, often in clusters, may be located by examining likely anatomical sites — such as the skin around the ears and nipples — with a dissecting microscope or with a hand lens. It is usually possible to identify the species of the larval stages when these have been recovered from the human host; while a proportion of those found on rodent hosts are similarly identifiable. Once the species of the trombiculid mite larva has been established, it is sometimes possible to find the habitat from which it was derived and hense the breeding places of the adults. This may be done by introducing "bait animals" into suspected areas and comparing the mites subsequently found on them with those previously recovered from human or animal sources.

(d) *The collection of laelaptid mites.* Laelaptid mites which are parastic on rodents may be collected from the hosts or their nests by using a similar technique to that described for the collection of rodent fleas.

THE COLLECTION OF VENOMOUS ARTHROPODS

The term venomous arthropods is generally understood to include not only those arthropods which cause reactions by the injection of venom by means of a bite or of a sting but also those arthropods which cause reactions by ejecting or excreting a vesicant fluid or piercing the skin with vesicant hairs or bristles. The method of capture to be employed will vary according to the species of arthropod concerned and success is largely dependent on patience, common sense and, in the case of the larger and more active venomous creatures such as scorpions and centipedes, a long and strong pair of forceps such as are used for removing specimens from jars in museums.

CHAPTER XLIX

LABELLING AND RECORDING COLLECTIONS OF ARTHROPODS OF MEDICAL IMPORTANCE

INSTITUTES concerned with the teaching of medical entomology often require large numbers of preserved arthropods, in particular common species obtained from the tropics, a plentiful supply being necessary because, when distributed amongst students, it is rapidly lost or damaged. Teaching material of this type generally requires no particular labelling, but apart from this it may be accepted as axiomatic that specimens without a label are valueless, indeed they are often worse than useless for they occupy space that might be better employed.

The purpose of the label, which obviously must remain attached to the specimen, is to carry information. It may bear only a number, referable to a duplicate number in note book (the record book), in which is entered the full information concerning the specimen. Such a system has the obvious advantage in that when a particular specimen is required it may be made immediately available by consulting the record book; but it has the equally obvious disadvantage that if the book is lost or destroyed the specimen can no longer be associated with the information previously collected and it therefore loses its value.

On the whole the ideal system to be aimed at is to record all the essential information on a label, attached to the specimen, to which is added a number identifiable in the record book, which contains the same, or sometimes more extensive information than the label. Notebooks which allow the collector to make three records of the data (the original and two carbon copies) are often useful, particularly when collections are sent to some other locality for identification.

The method of attaching the label to the specimen will vary with the nature of the specimen and the type of mount or the material in which it is preserved. In the case of pinned specimens the information should be written clearly, preferably in printed characters, in indian ink or lead pencil, on good quality hard paper and the pin pushed through the label which, if necessary, has been folded. In the case of specimens preserved in fluid, a similar type of label is usually sufficient although paper specially prepared for the purpose is particularly suitable; if indian ink is used it must be allowed to dry thoroughly before the label is immersed. The label should be inserted, unfolded, in the tube with the specimen and whenever possible a duplicate label should be placed on the outside of the tube since this obviates having to uncork the bottle. A label in the tube with the specimen is necessary because the outer label is often detached or defaced in packing or unpacking, or as a result of exposure to weather. In addition, it is a common experience to find outside labels eaten by cockroaches, particularly if paste is used as an adhesive; to obviate this the outside label may be painted over with melted paraffin wax.

As regards the type and amount of information that should be made available from the label and/or the record book, it is worthwhile remembering that it is unusual for the museum or research institute to which a specimen is sent, to complain that too much information has been given, whereas it is not uncommon for them to complain that the information supplied is not sufficient for their purpose. The nature and amount of information will, of course, vary according to the purpose for which the specimen was collected but in the case of arthropods of medical importance, the following information may be regarded, under ordinary circumstances, as essential.

(1) *The locality where collected.* The sites of collection should be easily identifiable, the name of some small village not usually recorded in gazetteers being of little value. If the site is not indicated on such maps, it is much better to give the general location in regard to an identifiable point, thus—"collected in a small village about 5 miles north-east of Lagos, West Africa."

(2) *The date.* This should include not only the day and the month but also the year and the time of day; it is surprising how often the latter are omitted.

(3) *The name of the collector and his initials.* It is often advisable to add the name of the Service or Institute to which he belongs.

These three items of information must be given in every instance and the following information added if possible and when applicable. (a) If the specimen was bred out this should be recorded and reference made to the previous stage from which the specimen was bred. (b) The nature of the habitat in which the specimen was obtained, for example—"in a fast-running stream"—"inside a native hut"—"on the under-surface of a banana leaf"—"by sweeping long grass" etc., etc. (c) If the specimen was captured when biting, the species of host and the anatomical site on which the arthropod was feeding should be recorded. (d) When parasites have been collected from unidentified small animals, particularly rodents, the name of the host can be subsequently established if the skin and skull are preserved. (e) Meteorological observations are often very helpful, as for example—"caught flying in bright sunlight"—"biting cattle just before dusk". (f) If the specimen is from an aquatic source, it is desirable to mention not only the type of water but also the nature of the vegetation in it. Such information is often of particular value in the case of mosquito larvae; for example—"Anopheline and culicine larvae collected from a small well shaded pool with a rich algal growth; anophelines only at margin in deep shade, culicines more generally distributed, some in patches of sunlight."—"Culicine larvae from small rock pool a few yards above high tide level; the water was distinctly saline to taste; for specimens bred from larvae, see book entry ABC 1234."

CHAPTER L

THE PRESERVATION OF ARTHROPODS OF MEDICAL IMPORTANCE

THE word "preservation" is used here to denote the preservation of dead creatures not intended for further biological studies or for future dissection; the methods to be used for preserving arthropods alive for either of these purposes will be described in later chapters.

The preservation of arthropods with a view to their forming part of an orderly collection in some scientific institute or museum is usually outside the scope of the medical officer. On the other hand, he requires to have knowledge of how to preserve arthropods (often a wide range of different types) which he knows or suspects to be of medical importance, but whose exact identity is unknown to him at the time of their collection. In addition, as already mentioned, he may wish to preserve such insects for the use of teaching centres.

Specimens collected for identification or for teaching purposes need not necessarily be mounted in a uniform manner, for instance, it is not necessary to preserve them with the wings and legs extended; on the other hand, it is essential that the specimens be prepared in such a way as to reduce to a minimum the risks of decay or damage, and that the method of mounting adopted does not mask any morphological details which may be required in a future taxonomic study. The apparatus and reagents required for preserving insects of medical importance in this manner are of the simplest type; indeed it may be said that satisfactory collections of the kind mentioned may be made with the equipment available to most medical officers or which are obtainable from general stores even in small towns. There are, however, certain articles which are not so generally available and the possession of which renders the preservation and mounting of entomological material easier and more satisfactory.

Foremost amongst these requirements are entomological pins. These pins should be of various sizes and should include an adequate supply of the smaller size, commonly known as mosquito pins, and if these are not available fine headless pins generally referred to as stainless steel points. These very fine pins or steel points are almost indispensable for pinning minute blood-sucking insects, such as mosquitoes, simuliid flies and midges (sandflies are best preserved in fluid), and when such pins are not available other methods of mounting—some of which are described later in this chapter—must be employed. The less fine entomological pins can be used for pinning almost any large arthropod which is not to be preserved in a fluid medium; ordinary pins can be used for this purpose but have the disadvantage that their coarseness may damage the insect and sometimes obscures points of morphological importance, while they rust more readily than do entomological pins.

Other forms of very useful—although not essential—specialised equipment are entomological forceps and polyporus strips. Entomological forceps (see fig. 192A) have strong flattened blades which enable the user to handle pinned specimens with a minimum risk of damaging the specimen. When these special forceps are not available, small long-nosed metal pliers or coarse dissecting forceps make a reasonably satisfactory substitute. Strips of polyporus or of pith, or even strips of very soft wood, such as balsa, are used in connection with the mounting of insects, such as mosquitoes and buffalo gnats, which have been transfixed with the fine pins or steel points previously referred to. When polyporus strips or their substitutes are not available cardboard or celluloid strips may be used but these do not give such an efficient grip to the fine pins and should be avoided.

With the exception of pinned specimens the storage of the collected material requires little comment beyond pointing out that unless the specimens have been preserved in fluid, care must be taken to ensure that they are kept free from the attacks of mites and fungi and that, until such time as they are stored in sealed receptacles, they are not destroyed by foraging ants. Freedom from fungi and mites is best insured by painting the inside of the containers, prior to sealing, with a solution such as a creosote and naphtha mixture.* The only safe protection against ants (until the insects are in store boxes) is to place the collections on a table, or other piece of furniture, the legs of which are standing in bowls of water. In general, all pinned specimens must finally be stored in well dried store boxes or cabinets, lined with some material, such as cork sheeting, which will give a secure hold to the pins used to transfix the insects, or used to pass through the polyporus strips into which the fine pins or points supporting small blood-sucking insects have previously been inserted.

Specially made cork-lined boxes which are practically air-tight provide much the most satisfactory store boxes, but good substitutes can be made from well constructed wooden boxes lined with cork sheeting or soft linoleum and provided with well fitting lids.

Before considering the preservation and storage of particular types of arthropods, the medical officer should have knowledge of certain general principles which are applicable to all but a few species.

(1) *The handling of specimens.* Insects should be handled as little as possible (all except stoutly built arthropods are easily damaged) and whatever the method of capture—whether with a net, sucking tube or caught in the fingers — they should be killed as soon as possible. If it is intended to pin the specimen this should be done while the insect is relaxed, at any rate before the internal structures have dried.

(2) *The number of specimens to be collected.* Apart from the fact that museums,

---

* Powdered naphthalene (6 parts), chloroform (1 part), beechwood creosote (1 part), petrol (4 parts).
British Museum (Nat. Hist.) Instructions for collectors. No. 4A. Insects. 3rd Ed., p. 148.

research institutes and teaching centres are always glad of surplus material, it is advisable to obtain a number of specimens of the same species, since points of morphological interest are often more clearly observable in one specimen than in another. In addition, it is often advisable to preserve different specimens of the same species by more than one technique, some being preserved dry and others in fluid.

(3) *Killing agents.* Cyanide of potassium (contained in "killing-bottles") which is commonly used by entomologists, is not well suited for the collection of many insects of medical importance, but chloroform and carbon tetra-chloride are both satisfactory and they are usually available to the medical officer; ether is not often used since it takes longer to kill the insect and in the tropics volatilises with great rapidity. Ethyl acetate (acetic-ether), when available, is on the whole the most generally useful killing agent; it is slower in action than chloroform, but has the great advantage that it does not stiffen specimens and insects may be left in the vapour up to several weeks without hardening or deteriorating. Whatever killing agent is used, care must be taken to insure that the insect does not come into direct contact with the fluid (see fig. 190C).

(4) *Temporary storage.* All insects—including even small nematocerous flies, such as mosquitoes, sandflies and midges—may be temporarily stored between sheets of cellulose "wool" or, if these are not available, crumpled sheets of thin tissue paper; cotton wool is not satisfactory because the appendages of the insects tend to become entangled and are liable to be broken. Such a form of temporary storage is often useful when standard mounting methods are not available or when the collector has not sufficient time to pin all his specimens; it has the disadvantage however, that small insects which have been preserved in this way are difficult to handle and liable to be lost or separated from their labels; while if later it is desired to pin such insects, they must first be placed in a "relaxing box" in order to soften their tissues (see fig. 190D).

(5) *Preserving of arthropods in fluid.* All species of sandflies (*Phlebotomus*), fleas, lice, ticks and mites, at all stages of their development, are best preserved in a fluid medium—advice which applies also to most species of scorpions, centipedes, millipedes and spiders. The eggs and larvae of all species of Diptera and the pupae of orthorrphaphous flies should be preserved in fluid, but the puparia of most cyclorrhaphous flies are best preserved in the dry state. When sufficient numbers of the same species of black-flies or biting midges are available, a proportion of the flies should be mounted dry and the remainder preserved in fluid. When only one or two specimens of such small flies are available they are best preserved in fluid. In addition, the growing refinements in the techniques used by systematists for the separation of closely allied species often involves dissection of a proportion of the arthropods and in such instances specimens preserved in fluid are preferable to dried material.

Many satisfactory preserving fluids have been described, but most of these are intended for specialised studies and only two such media are in common use. The first and most generally used preservative is ethyl alcohol (methyl alcohol may be used) diluted with water so as to give a 75% solution. In order to make a 75% solution of alcohol from commercial ethyl alcohol (which is 95% strength) take 100 ml. of the commercial product and add 27 ml. of water; 3 ml. of glycerine (glycerol) should be added to the final solution in order to prevent specimens from drying out if the alcohol evaporates, but the glycerine should be washed out with alcohol if the specimen subsequently is to be mounted dry. When alcohol is not available a solution of dilute formaldehyde and sodium chloride (known as formol-saline) may be substituted, but it tends to over-harden the specimens. This solution is made up by adding 10 ml. of 40% formaldehyde (commercial formalin) to 90 ml. of water and dissolving in it 1 gram of sodium chloride. Whatever the preserving fluid used, it is wise to transfer the specimens to a fresh solution after a few weeks. The arthropods may be dropped into the fluid while alive—a procedure which causes them to swallow some of the fluid and this aids internal preservation—or they may be dropped first into hot, but not boiling, 40% alcohol and then transferred to 75% alcohol or formol saline. The tubes containing the specimens must be completely filled with fluid to prevent bumping and consequent damage; in the case of delicate insects, pieces of crumpled tissue paper should be added to the tubes. The tubes containing the specimens may be corked and kept separately, but it is often convenient and economical of space to pack the tubes in one or more larger receptacles filled with the same preserving fluid. In such instances, the tubes should not be corked but loosely plugged with cotton wool and stored with the open ends downwards (see fig. 190E), fruit bottling jars with screw-lids being very suitable for this purpose.

In the account which follows the words "in alcohol" signify 75% alcohol to which glycerine has been added; while the words "in formalin" signify immersion in formol saline.

The preservation of Diptera.

All adult Diptera as large or larger than houseflies should be preserved as pinned specimens, the appropriate sized entomological pin being thrust through the insect at a point very slightly to the right of the centre of the thorax (see fig. 192 B & C). When it seems probable that at a later date it may be necessary to examine internal structures or certain external features, such as the genitalia, the flies should be stored in alcohol.

Very small blood-sucking Diptera such as mosquitoes, midges and simuliids may be preserved dry, in which case they should be mounted either on fine pins or else on points (see fig. 192 E & F). When mounting these small insects on steel points, it is best to impale the thorax of the fly on the point to a depth which allows it to reach, but only just reach, the opposite side; in short, the pin should be thrust deeply into—but not through—the thorax. The pin carrying the fly is now turned upside down and the blunt end pushed into a polyporous strip (or pith), which in its turn is transfixed by a large sized pin

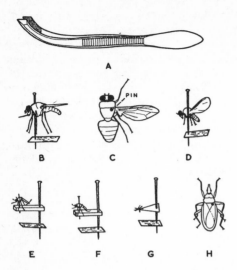

Fig. 192. *A.* a pair of entomological forceps. *B.* and *C.* method of pinning Diptera, as large or larger than a housefly. *D.* one of the small Dipera attached to the side of an entomological pin. *E.* and *F.* method of pinning small Diptera such as the Nematocera. *H.* method pinning one of the larger reduviid bugs through the elytron.

and the mounted specimen placed in the collecting box. Steel points are preferred to mosquito pins since the head of the latter makes it difficult to push it into the polyporus strip. The orthodox pinning position—as shown in fig. 192—is with the dorsum of the thorax uppermost, but if several specimens are available it is well to pin them in different positions; in any case the position is not usually of much importance and is always secondary to the need of avoiding damage to the insect by too much handling. When fine entomological pins or steel points are not available or are not considered satisfactory, pointed pieces of cardboard or celluloid may be substituted; in which case a minute drop of white shellac or shellac gel is applied to the tip of the point and this, in its turn, is pressed against the ventral, or more usually, against the lateral aspect of the thorax (fig. 192G). Another form of dry mounting which is sometimes used for small flies possessing very few scales or bristles—for example the simuliid flies—is to paint a narrow band of shellac about two thirds of the way up a long, but slender, entomological pin, and then to press the band of shellac against the right lateral wall of the insect's thorax (fig. 192D). All mosquitoes, except those intended for dissection, should be mounted dry, preferably on fine pins or steel points, but a proportion of all simuliid flies and midges which have been captured should be preserved in alcohol or formalin.

The preservation of the eggs, larvae and pupae of the Diptera has been dealt with already under the heading, "preserving of arthropods in fluid", and it is only necessary to add that it is advisable to kill the larval stages of nematocerous insects by dropping them into hot dilute alcohol, prior to placing them in the preserving fluid.

The preservation of fleas.

The adults, after they have been killed, preferably with chloroform, should be dropped into alcohol; formalin is not a suitable medium for preserving fleas. The growing stages are best dealt with by dropping them into hot alcohol and then transferring them to either alcohol or formalin. The cocoons and contained pupae are best preserved dry, but when several specimens are available some should be placed in alcohol.

The preservation of lice.

The eggs, nymphs and adult forms of all species of sucking lice should be preserved in alcohol. The nymphs and adults should be killed by dropping them into hot dilute alcohol prior to placing them in the preserving fluid.

The preservation of bugs.

Large adult bugs occurring in the family Reduviidae may be mounted dry as pinned specimens—the pins being passed, not through the thorax, but through the upper quadrant of the right elytron (fig. 192H). Small reduviid bugs—regardless of age or species—and all bugs belonging to the family Cimicidae should be preserved in alcohol. The eggs may be preserved in either alcohol or formalin. Prior to preservation a note should be taken of their colour since this fades rapidly in both media. Chloroform and ethyl acetate are efficient killing agents, but the latter is preferable if the bug is to be pinned, for it leaves the insect relaxed.

The preservation of ticks.

Pinning is a very unsatisfactory way of mounting either argasid or ixodid ticks. Ticks occurring in both these families should be killed with chloroform or ether, or by immersion in hot alcohol, the latter method being the more satisfactory since the tick dies with its legs extended. After death the ticks should be stored in vials containing alcohol, or if this is not available, formalin.

The preservation of mites.

The medical officer is concerned usually only with a limited group commonly referred to as "parastic mites", although on occasions he may wish to preserve certain free-living species, such as the tyroglyphid mites, when these are associated with signs of allergy in the patient. All parasitic and free-living mites are satisfactorily preserved in alcohol and may be kept in this medium until they are required for examination, when they should be cleared in the manner described at the end of this chapter.

The preservation of venomous arthropods of various types.

Bees, wasps and the larger species of ants should be killed with chloroform or ethyl acetate and then pinned in a similar manner to that previously recommended for mounting the larger Diptera. Small, stinging, biting and vesicant arthropods (with representatives amongst the ants, spiders and beetles) are best preserved in alcohol, although some of the larger vesicant beetles may be mounted as pinned specimens. Scorpions, centipedes, millipedes and large spiders should also be stored in alcohol, but formalin, in certain instances, gives as good or better results. Before immersing these large creatures in the preserving fluid it is advisable to inject some of the solution with a hypodermic syringe into their body tissues.

The "clearing" of preserved arthropods preparatory to their identification.

It is sometimes necessary to examine the chitinised structures of an arthropod so that it may be identified. In the case of mites, adult fleas and mosquito larvae it is generally only necessary to remove the specimen from the preservative fluid and to place it in a drop of a clearing agent such as lactochlorophenol,* or if this is not available pure phenol or chloral hydrate. When it is desirable to examine such chitinised structures as the mouthparts or genitalia of larger arthropods, these may be boiled for a short time (usually 5 to 10 minutes) in 5% - 10% potassium or sodium hydroxide, prior to their examination. If permanent specimens are desired the material may be mounted direct in a gum chloral mountant** or else dehydrated and mounted in canada balsam. Specimens which have been cleared in caustic must be washed before mounting.

---

* Lactic acid 20 cc., chloral hydrate 2 grams, phenol crystals (melted) 20 cc.
** Chloral hydrate 160 gm., gum arabic 15 gm., glucose syrup 10 gm., acetic acid 5 gm., distilled water 25 cc.

CHAPTER LI

THE REARING AND MAINTENANCE OF ARTHROPODS
OF MEDICAL IMPORTANCE

WITH the exception of the larvae of some of the "filth flies" and many of the myiasis producing Diptera, medical officers interested in entomological problems are usually only concerned with rearing and maintaining various species of blood-sucking Diptera and then only for short periods. It is true that certain large institutions and research organisations find it necessary constantly to maintain many strains of blood-sucking arthropods of such widely different types as fleas, ticks, bugs, lice and mites, and that some of these are not indigenous in the country in which they are maintained. In general, however, the medical officer is only called upon to deal with the local fauna and although occasionally he may need to breed out a few successive generations of a particular species he is more often concerned either with breeding out immature stages to the adult forms or else with maintaining the adult forms alive for relatively short periods of time. The various types of these short term requirements and the methods best suited for maintaining the insects concerned, may be considered in a number of categories of which the following are some of the more typical.

(1) It is often necessary to keep blood-sucking arthropods alive for short periods, either because they are too numerous for immediate dissection or because it is found necessary to let them digest a previous blood-meal before they are ready for dissection, or in order to ensure that any parasites which may have been present at the time the insects were captured have been allowed to develop sufficiently to render their recognition obvious at the time the insect is dissected.

In circumstances such as these protein meals are seldom necessary; although it is often advantageous to offer "sugar water" (a solution of cane or beet sugar in water) to some insects — particularly mosquitoes — so long as the insects are maintained at the correct temperature and humidity, no further care is necessary. The correct temperature and humidity varies according to the species of arthropod but a temperature of between 24°C. and 26°C. with a relative humidity, at this temperature, of between 70 and 80 per cent, is suitable for most species.

When it is only necessary to keep arthropods alive for such short periods, almost any receptacle—from a jam jar with a piece of muslin tied over the top to a glass fronted box with wire gauze sides—will serve the purpose of a cage. Probably the simplest and most convenient "all purposes" container is an adaptation of the "Barraud Box". This consists of five wire frames, a convenient size being 8" x 8", which can be tied together to form a six sided metal frame, which is then inserted through the wide mouth of a specially shaped net made of "sandfly netting" and carrying a small sleeve at the centre of one of its sides. It is convenient to use coloured gauze which does not reflect light since this increases visibility inside the cage: it is important also to see that the wire frames have no rough edges which might tear the netting. The materials necessary for rapidly assembling 50 to 100 of these breeding cages can be

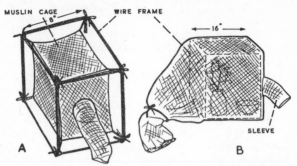

MUSLIN CAGE WIRE FRAME

SLEEVE

A   B

Fig. 193. *A.* a Barraud cage: this type of cage is particularly useful for transporting delicate living insects, such as mosquitoes, over long distances; *B.* an adaptation of the Barraud cage: this type of cage may be used for maintaining and rearing most types of insects even for long periods.

packed in a small suit case, and when put together (and this can be done very rapidly) they will accommodate many separate collections of living insects. When using these types of cages the required humidity may be maintained by laying strips of wet cloth over the tops and sides of the cages or by boiling a kettle of water in the room in which they are kept.

(2) It is sometimes essential to maintain insects alive while investigating their potentialities as vectors of disease. In such instances the insects, which if possible should be laboratory bred specimens, are fed on a person or animal whose peripheral blood contains the parasites responsible for the disease, and which are at a stage of development infective to the insect vector. The insects are then maintained alive until such time as it is considered likely that the ingested organisms will have reached the stage of development infective to the vertebrate host. After this the insects are dissected and examined for visible evidence of their infectivity, or else they are fed on a susceptible laboratory animal which is then kept under observation to see if it will develop the disease*.

In these circumstances it is advisable to carry out the experimental feedings and the subsequent maintenance and re-feeding of the arthropods with a minimum change of habitat. It is the practice of the present writers when working with most species of infected arthropods to place them in glass or perspex cylinders, both ends of which are sealed with gauze and secured with an adhesive tape which has a distinctive colouration, thereby preventing confusion with similar cylinders containing uninfected arthropods. The arthropods remain in these cylinders throughout the feeding processes, and when

* All animals used as hosts in such feeding experiments must be regarded as potentially infected, and either destroyed at the end of the experiment or kept under observation to see if they develop the disease.

it is necessary to transfer them or to remove them for any other purpose, only authorized members of the staff are permitted to open the marked cylinders. Even when these precautions are observed it is advisable to issue stringent warnings regarding the danger of handling such cylinders, a necessary precaution in view of the rapidity with which the contained insects may stab with their probosces through the gauze. Blood-sucking arthropods of the kind usually used in such experiments require little attention beyond regular feeding, the blood-meal being obtained from infected or uninfected animals according to circumstances. The fed insects must of course be maintained at a temperature suitable for the development of the ingested parasites; this is usually a fairly simple matter since the requirements, while in the invertebrate host, of most insect-borne helminths and protozoa are already known.

The foregoing remarks apply to most species of blood-sucking Diptera and also to all species of haematophagous bugs and, with some modifications, to lice; but fleas, mites, ticks and most species of midges and sandflies can only be fed with difficulty, or else not at all, through fine mesh gauze. The various highly specialised techniques employed in attempts to infect these and other blood-sucking arthropods with the diseases which they are known, or suspected, to transmit and the methods to be employed for their subsequent maintenance are beyond the scope of the present volume. Medical officers interested in such transmission experiments should, in the first instance, seek advice from medical or veterinary laboratories whose staffs are investigating the diseases it is proposed to transmit.

(3) When investigating outbreaks of insect-borne diseases it may often be necessary to breed out the immature stages of arthropods in order to identify the species. If the species bred out proves to be a known vector of disease the information acquired regarding the breeding place may be used for control purposes.

If the immature arthropod is in the pupal stage or is in a very late larval stage it is often possible to obtain the imago without making provision for any further food supplies. Even when the larva is at any early stage of development it is frequently practicable to breed it to the adult form without special provision being necessary with regard to its food supply, beyond imitating and maintaining the natural conditions in which the immature stage was found. In practice this is usually quite a simple matter, merely involving the transporting of a generous sample of the local habitat. For instance, when "breeding out" most immature aquatic species such as mosquito larvae it is only necessary to keep them in a sample of the water, weed and mud etc. in which they were found, and to renew this at intervals from the same source, care being taken to ensure that other species of arthropods are not being introduced and that the temperature and light conditions are kept similar to those in nature. The same technique may be used with terrestial species such as sandfly larvae, although in the latter instance the food supply should be augmented with minute quantities of dried rodent faeces. The "breeding out" of the larvae of the Muscidae and of some of the myiasis producing flies has already been referred to in a previous chapter.

The receptacles used to contain the immature aquatic and terrestial forms may be placed inside one of the Barraud cages. The emerging adults will be confined to the gauze cage from which they should be removed with a sucker (see fig. 193B).

The three methods so far described for the housing, feeding and breeding out of the blood-sucking arthropods are mainly concerned with the maintenance of such arthropods for short periods of time, for—as was pointed out at the beginning of the chapter—the rearing of many successive generations of a particular species for observation or for experimental work is for the most part the concern of large institutions and research establishments. On the other hand since so many species of arthropods are now recognised as invertebrate laboratory animals — just as white mice, guinea pigs etc. have long been recognised as vertebrate laboratory animals, — and since these various "strains" of arthropods are now maintained in laboratories all over the world, it is of more than academic interest to know something of these strains and the methods used for their maintenance. Amongst the best known of such strains may be mentioned *Aedes aegypti, Anopheles maculipennis, Culex pipiens, Musca domestica, Ornithodoros moubata* and *Rhodnius prolixus*, all of which, together with many other species, are regularly maintained in Britain. The total number of strains maintained in this way in laboratories all over the world probably exceeds 200, and interested persons can usually obtain particulars by writing to the various Directors of Medical Research in the countries concerned.

These various strains of arthropods are housed in rooms commonly called "insectaria" (insectaries) equipped with thermostats and humidistats which control the heating and humidifying apparatus maintaining the atmosphere at a pre-selected temperature and humidity. In addition the insectaria are usually provided with ultra-violet lamps connected with time clocks which regulate the amount of artificial sunlight to which the arthropods are to be exposed. The various units housed in these insectaria constitute a miniature zoo and, as in the case of a zoo, the inhabitants have to be fed, tended, and have their cages cleaned at regular intervals.

The needs of each species kept in captivity must be studied carefully and since these needs often differ very greatly it is by no means easy for one person to become acquainted with all the requirements of the numerous species now being maintained. Some species, including most of those previously referred to in this chapter, can be reared in great numbers without a large staff or undue expenditure of time, but many others—including tsetse flies and mites of the genus *Trombicula*—can only be maintained with an expenditure of labour which often demands, for these species alone, the whole time services of at least one skilled technician. That these difficulties exist is undeniable, on the other hand it should not be forgotten that when reasonably intelligent and not too expensive labour is available—as is often the case in the tropics— there is no species of arthropod which is maintainable in a modern and well equipped insectarium which cannot also be maintained with simple home made apparatus, although probably with a greater expenditure of labour.

CHAPTER LII

THE DISSECTION OF ARTHROPODS OF MEDICAL IMPORTANCE

THE dissection of arthropods of medical importance is usually undertaken for one of three reasons:—firstly, to study one or more points in their internal anatomy as a means of assisting in the separation of closely allied species with a very similar external anatomy; secondly, as a means of identifying the source of previous blood-meals; and, thirdly, and more commonly, to ascertain whether a particular species of arthropod is acting as a vector of disease and, if so, to what extent it is responsible for the propagation of the infection.

In the accounts which follow certain techniques are described for dissecting various species of arthropods in order to detect in them parasites which are infective to the human host. It is important to remember that these descriptions are strictly limited and that in most medical surveys of insect-borne diseases—particularly in malaria surveys—it is often desirable and sometimes imperative to record other data, such as the age of the vector (as judged by the ovarian development etc.) and the presence of parasites other than those infective to the human host. Descriptions of the techniques necessary to record iuch observations are beyond the scope of the present volume and those snterested should consult one or more of the standard text-books referred to in the foot-note to Chapter LV. No attempt is made to describe the parasites likely to be encountered in these dissections and here again standard text books must be consulted.

Arthropods collected with a view to ascertaining the source of the blood-meal should be dissected as soon as possible after capture; arthropods collected for anatomical examination and those obtained in order that they may be dissected and examined for the presence of parasites should be preserved alive until the previous blood-meal appears to have been digested.

The essential apparatus required for the dissection of arthropods is very simple. It is true that compound dissecting microscopes with built in lighting, together with sets of delicate dissecting instruments (such as those used by eye surgeons) are very convenient and helpful, and if they are available they should be employed, but the fact remains that equally good results have followed the use of much less elaborate equipment. A simple dissecting microscope provided with lenses magnifying 10-15 diameters is essential. The dissecting microscope can either be bought from an optical firm or it can be a home made affair, but in either case it must be provided with some means of focussing the lenses and with a mirror which reflects the light up through the specimen placed on the dissection stage. The necessary dissecting instruments consist of a pair of scissors with fine points; manicure or embroidery scissors are quite suitable, while the spring scissors used by eye surgeons are ideal. The worker should also provide himself with two pairs of forceps with very fine points, such as can be purchased from watchmakers; while dissecting needles of various thicknesses (from gramophone needles to the finest needles used in needlework) make useful tools when mounted in wooden handles. The remaining equipment is of a type found in most medical laboratories. The usual 3″ x 1″ slides and the appropriate coverslips are, of course, essential and it is often helpful to have a stock of ″3 x 2″ slides and a number of very small coverslips which can either be bought, or else made on the spot by dividing large coverslips with a diamond marker. The dissection of arthropods is best carried out in normal saline but, when stained preparations of protozoa are required, it is advisable to replace the normal saline with serum before making the smears. Other essential requirements are Pasteur pipettes with well fitting teats, Leishman or Giemsa stain and such fixing agents as absolute alcohol and formol saline.

DISSECTIONS MADE IN CONNECTION WITH THE IDENTIFICATION OF A PARTICULAR SPECIES OF ARTHROPOD

A limited amount of dissection is sometimes required to aid in identifying certain species of insects, particularly the adult forms of certain species of tsetse flies, mosquitoes and sandflies. Dissections made for this purpose are generally of a simple character and are limited to such operations as the cutting off and mounting of the genitalia—usually the male genitalia—in lacto-chlorophenol or a similar clearing agent (see footnote, Chapter LI). In addition, the identification of most species of sandflies entails an examination, under the microscope, of the buccal and pharyngeal armatures; sometimes this can be done by clearing the whole fly in a suitable medium, but more satisfactory results are obtained if the pharynx and its attachments are dissected out, cleared and mounted. Finally, the identification of ixodid ticks of different genera and species is often assisted if the capitulum is dissected out of the sac-like body and examined separately.

DISSECTIONS MADE IN CONNECTION WITH THE IDENTIFICATION OF PREVIOUS BLOOD-MEALS

The identification of the blood-meals found in arthropods is often of value in determining the part played by them in the transmission of disease. When dissecting arthropods in order to obtain a sample of the previous blood-meal the procedure to be adopted is to place the gorged insect, as soon after capture as possible, on a piece of filter paper of good quality and then to dissect it in the way recommended for the exposure of the gut of arthropods when these are being examined for the presence of parasites. When the gut has been exposed the portion containing the blood-meal is cut off with dissecting needles and smeared out on the filter paper, which is then dried, preferably in a dessicator. The blood stained filter paper is then sent to a laboratory which is competent to carry out precipitin reactions with anti-sera capable of distinguishing blood remnants derived from a wide variety of vertebrate hosts. In order to avoid contamination it is important to clean the needles between each dissection, and to interleaf the filter papers with non-absorbent papers before posting them.

DISSECTIONS MADE IN CONNECTION WITH THE RECOGNITION OF PARASITES LIKELY TO BE TRANSMITTED TO MAN

One of the most important and certainly one of the most interesting aspects of medical entomology is the examination of arthropods for the presence of parasites capable of further development in the human host, after their escape from the insect vector. The methods employed to recognise the presence of such parasites in the vector differ somewhat according to whether the parasites suspected to be present occurs in a group comprised of viruses, rickettsiae, bacteria and spirochaetes or in a group comprising the protozoa and helminths.

For descriptions which are likely to be helpful in the recognition of the various parasites of medical importance which may be encountered in the course of such dissections the reader is referred to standard text-books on parasitology, some of which are mentioned in Chapter LV.

The recognition, in the vector, of viruses, rickettsiae, bacteria and spirochaetes capable of infecting man.

Direct examination of the arthropod is, of course, useless for the detection of virus infections; nor can reliance be placed on the recognition of *Pasteurella pestis* or *P. tularensis* by a similar direct examination of the appropriate vector. On the other hand, the dissection of lice and ticks is sometimes undertaken in order to observe the presence of spirochaetes or rickettsiae, but since the infective stages of such parasites are only occasionally characteristic it is usually necessary to confirm the results of the direct examination of fresh and stained preparations by more reliable methods.

In all instances where the infecting organism is likely to be a virus, a rickettsia, a bacterium or a spirochaete, it is usually only necessary to grind up the whole insect in normal saline and inject the resultant emulsion into susceptible laboratory animals, one or more species of which are capable of being infected with any one of the organisms occurring in this group.* A refinement of this technique, which is often employed, is to dissect out the particular organ likely to be infected—such as the salivary glands or the gut—and similarly inject this into a laboratory animal. Positive results obtained from such experiments allow the observer to state that the arthropod in question is capable of maintaining the parasite or of allowing its development to the infective stage, whilst it is often accepted that such a result proves the arthropod to be a true vector capable of transferring the parasite to its new host, it should be remembered that this is not necessarily the case and that to supply the final proof it is necessary to feed the suspected arthropod on a susceptible host and show that the infection has been transmitted.

---

* In the case of viruses occurring in the sandfly fever and dengue groups, the inoculation of monkeys with ground up vectors known to be infective to man is sometimes, but by no means always, successful.

315

The recognition, in the vector, of protozoa and helminths capable of infecting man.

The methods used to demonstrate the presence of protozoa or helminths infective to man are, in many instances, very different from those used to demonstrate the presence of spirochaetes, bacteria, rickettsiae and viruses, methods which were described in the previous section.

In the first place certain of such protozoal and helminth infections— for example most species of malaria parasites capable of developing in man and the infective forms of *Wuchereria bancrofti*—are not known to develop in any host but man, and, in consequence, the injection into laboratory animals of tissues or tissue fluids derived from arthropods suspected to harbour such parasites is of no diagnostic value. In the second place, whereas it is not possible to state by direct examination of fresh and stained preparations made from a suspected vector, whether or not a particular viral, rickettsial, bacterial or spirochaetal infection has reached its infective stage in the vector, such an estimate is usually possible in the case of protozoal and helminth infections.

This difference is due to the fact that in protozoal and helminth infections an examination of the morphology of the parasite will indicate whether or not it has reached the infective stage, and, in addition, the anatomical site of the parasite in the vector will indicate whether it is or is not ready to pass from its invertebrate to its vertebrate host. In short, if it is found that a protozoal or helminth parasite (known to be able to develop in man) has reached the infective stage in a particular arthropod and that its anatomical site indicates its ability to reach the vertebrate host, then the arthropod in question may be regarded as a true vector of an infection which it is potentially capable of transmitting to man. In consequence of the practical value of such observations, medical officers concerned with insect-borne diseases are often required to undertake the dissection of mosquitoes for malaria, tsetse flies for trypanosomiasis, sandflies for leishmaniasis and a wide range of biting flies for filarial parasites.

(a) *The dissection of mosquitoes for the presence of malaria parasites.* During the course of a malaria survey it is sometimes necessary to record the number of male as well as of female mosquitoes, but only the females are dissected. Having killed the insect with chloroform or other anaesthetic (if none is available the mosquito may be stunned by giving the tube containing it a smart rap on the palm of the hand) examine the insect with a hand lens to identify the species. The wings and legs are then pulled off with the aid of fine forceps, and the fly placed on a slide with its head and thorax resting in a very small drop of normal saline, or of serum, after which the slide carrying the mosquito is placed on the stage of the dissecting microscope. It is only the presence of sporozoites in the salivary glands that warrants the statement that the malaria parasite has reached the infective stage and that it has reached an anatomical site which will ensure that the next time the mosquito bites the bite will be potentially infective. In order to establish whether or not the insect is infective, it is necessary to extract the salivary glands from the thorax; this can be accomplished by various techniques, amongst which the following two are the most commonly employed.

(1) Place one dissecting needle cross the thorax of the insect and the other at the base of the head; the needle across the thorax is used to anchor the mosquito's body while the other needle is pushed slowly and steadily forward thereby dragging the head off the thorax and bringing with it—when the operation is successful—the two salivary glands which, when examined under

a low power lens, appear as minute refractile bodies attached to the base of the head. Both dissecting needles are now used to separate the salivary glands from the base of the head and to transfer them to a fresh drop of fluid, over which a small coverslip (preferably one measuring approximately 0.5 x 0.5 cm.) is placed.

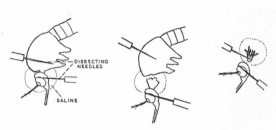

Fig. 194. Most commonly used method for the dissection of the salivary glands of a mosquito.

(2) When using the second method, instead of the head being dragged off the thorax it is cut off cleanly by slicing through the neck with a fine knife (an "eye-knife" or a mounted fragment of a safety-razor blade is suitable); the head is discarded and a small cover slip, similar to that used in the previous method is rested on the decapitated thorax in a sloping position so that its upper edge is above the thorax and its lower edge rests on the slide. The shaft of one dissecting needle is now laid across the thorax and the other needle applied

Fig. 195. Alternative method for the dissection of the salivary glands of a mosquito.

to the upper surface of the coverslip, which is then pressed down with the needle until the thoracic contents begin to exude, and the salivary glands, together with tissue fluids, are squeezed out through the neck opening. At this point the body of the mosquito is pulled away from the cover-slip by a quick, but gentle, movement of the needle placed across the thorax, with the result that the extruded glands are nipped off and retained beneath the cover-slip.

Regardless of which method of extraction was used, the glands are now crushed by pressure on the coverslip, and the preparation examined under the high power of a compound microscope. Sporozoites, if present, usually occur in large numbers and, with very rare exceptions, are present in both sets of glands.

Although it is true that proof that the mosquito is infective rests on the finding of sporozoites in the salivary glands, nevertheless it is of value to determine whether earlier (and non-infective) stages such as oocysts are present. The removal of the gut for this purpose is accomplished by transferring the now headless insect to a fresh drop of saline, after which two small nicks are made, with a dissecting needle, in the chitin on the lateral edges of the penultimate abdominal segment. One needle is now laid across the thorax, after which the tip of the abdomen is grasped with a pair of fine forceps and pulled away from the rest of the abdomen; if fine forceps are not available the tip of the abdomen may be dragged off with a blunt dissecting needle. When the tip of the abdomen is torn off at the level of the nicked segments it drags with it the hind and mid-gut and, sometimes, the

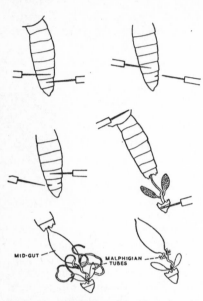

MID-GUT
MALPHIGIAN
TUBES

Fig. 196. Method used for dissecting the gut of a mosquito.

fore-gut and the oesophageal diverticula. At this stage it is convenient, but not essential, to sever the hind-gut at its junction with the tip of the abdomen and to discard the latter with the contained rectum. In addition it is helpful to cut away the malphigian tubules, or else arrange them with a fine needle so that they do not obscure the mid-gut, for any oocysts present will be found in the wall of the mid-gut, usually close to the insertion of the malphigian tubules at the junction of the mid-gut and hind-gut. A coverslip is now placed over the preparation and the slide is transferred to the stage of a compound microscope and examined with a 2/3rd objective for the presence of oocysts. If any suspicious object is detected it must be examined under a higher magnification—the 1/6th or 1/12th—in order to confirm or refute the diagnosis made with the low power objective.

(b) *The dissection of tsetse flies for the presence of trypanosomes.* Kill the insect with chloroform or ethyl acetate and then confirm the sex and species. There is no need to use a compound dissecting microscope and in most instances the extraction of the glands and of the gut can be done by using a low power simple lens or even without any magnification. Pull off the wings and legs and, holding the fly dorsum upwards between the finger and thumb of the left hand, make a median longitudinal incision from the neck to the abdomen. The incision, the object of which is to allow expansion of the thoracic space and so render easier the extraction of the salivary glands, should be a mere scratch, less than a millimetre in depth, and can be made with the point of a small scalpel or with a dissecting needle on which a cutting edge has been ground.

Place the prepared fly on its side in a large drop of dissecting fluid (normal saline or serum) on a glass slide; place one dissecting needle across the thorax and the other in the groove separating the head and the thorax and, using a very slow steady forward movement, drag the head away from the thorax until the membranes and structures which join the head to the thorax rupture. Once these structures have broken, a continuance of the steady pull on the head will partially drag the salivary ducts and the oesophagus out of the thorax. The oesophagus is to some extent anchored in the tissues of the oesophageal diverticulum and as the tension increases it will break off leaving the salivary glands still attached by the salivary ducts to the head. If the steady pull is continued the salivary glands can now usually be withdrawn undamaged. Sometimes one or both salivary ducts break off from the head before the glands have been withdrawn; when this happens it may be possible to grasp their free ends with a pair of finely pointed forceps and, by a series of gentle tugs, to complete the extraction. If the free end of a gland duct contracts back into the thorax, the gland must be recovered from the abdomen, either through a nick made in the side wall of the abdomen, or else, by looking for it during the course of the abdominal dissection.

Once extracted, the salivary glands should be separated from the head — if still attached to it — transferred to a fresh, very small, drop of fluid and covered with a coverslip preferably of small size. The preparation should then be examined under the 1/6th objective for the presence of trypanosomes; if trypanosomes are present, they can usually be seen escaping with the saliva from the torn ducts, but if they are not seen escaping from the ducts the glands should be crushed and the preparation again examined. On very rare occasions only one gland is involved in an infection, so that it is inadvisable to record a negative finding until both glands have been crushed and examined.

The presence of trypanosomes in the salivary glands is evidence of infection with *Trypanosoma brucei*, *T. gambiense* or *T. rhodesiense*. The absence of trypanosomes from the salivary glands is evidence that the fly is not infective to man at the time of its examination, but further examination of the mouthparts may reveal the presence of metacyclic trypanosomes which, although not infective to man, are infective to domestic stock. To carry out the further examination necessary to confirm or disprove the presence of the latter trypanosomes, the labrum and hypopharynx must be dissected out and the whole of, or part of, the alimentary tract removed from the abdomen. In order to do this, place the point of one needle on the bulb at the base of the labium and with the other needle separate the labrum from the labium and drag the former out of its groove. Usually, the hypopharynx springs out from the groove in the labium as the labrum is being separated, but it may remain in its groove; if this happens the hypopharynx must be separated by the use of fine dissecting needles.

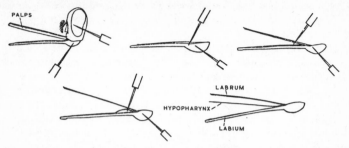

Fig. 197.   Technique used for the separation of the labrum and hypopharynx from the labium of the tsetse.

To dissect the gut it is necessary to place the decapitated body of the fly in a fresh drop of fluid and make two small nicks in the chitin at each side of the penultimate abdominal segment. After this has been done, place one dissecting needle across the thorax and the other across the partially separated abdominal segment, which is then dragged away from the rest of the abdomen bringing with it all or most of the gut. The removed intestinal tract should be transferred to a fresh drop of fluid, cut across at several places with the dissecting needles and, after the application of a coverslip, examined under the high power of the microscope for the presence of trypanosomes. Sometimes it is necessary to examine the proventriculus, an organ which usually comes away with the rest of the gut, but occasionally breaks off and remains in the thorax, when this happens the thorax must be broken up with dissecting needles, the proventriculus separated from the other structures and transferred to a fresh drop of fluid after which it is examined with the 1/6th objective for the presence of trypanosomes. The presence of trypanosomes in the labrum and hypopharynx without the presence of trypanosomes in the gut is suggestive of a *T. vivax* or a *T. uniforme* infection; while involvement of both gut and mouthparts is suggestive of infection with *T. congolense* or *T. simiae*.

(c) *The dissection of sandflies for the presence of leishmania.* The captured females should be killed with chloroform or ethyl acetate and the species identified. If possible the identification should be made before the fly is dissected, but if identification is not possible prior to dissection, the identity of the species can usually still be established after the dissection and examination of the fly for the presence of *Leishmania* spp., provided that the buccal and pharyngeal armatures are preserved.

In order to carry out the dissection the anaesthetised insect is placed on a slide in a drop of normal saline; or if it is intended to stain any protozoa found present, serum or glucose should be substituted for the saline. If the insect contains no blood, or if much of the blood has been digested, the last abdominal segment should be cut off with a sharp instrument—an eye knife or piece of razor blade is suitable—and the upper surface of the abdomen stroked downwards with a needle, in order to expel any contained ova. When the eggs have been got rid of, the head of the sandfly should be steadily pulled off the thorax, using the dissection needles in the manner described for the extraction of the salivary glands from other blood-sucking insects. In the case of the sandfly, a gentle pull will usually result in the oesophagus, salivary glands, oesophageal diverticulum and mid-gut being extracted still attached to the head. If the mid-gut contains much blood, the alimentary tract must be removed in two parts. First the head is gently pulled from the thorax bringing with it the salivary glands, oesophagus and oesophageal diverticulum and, occasionally, the upper part of the mid-gut. After this the rest of the mid-gut can be pulled out of the abdomen with the aid of a needle placed on the terminal abdominal segment.

The presence of leptomonads in the fresh preparation should be confirmed by making smears of the infected organs and staining them with Leishman or Giemsa stain.

(d) *The dissection of mosquitoes for the presence of filarial parasites.* The anaesthetised insect should be identified as regards its genus and species and, the wings and legs having been removed, laid in a drop of saline on a slide, which is then placed on the stage of the dissecting microscope. The head, thorax and abdomen should now be separated with the dissecting needles and transferred to separate drops of saline. The severed head is steadied with one needle, while with the aid of another very fine needle, the labium is split from the base to the tip. If the technique is carried out as described, any larvae in the proboscis will invariably be detected and will almost invariably emerge intact. The thorax, abdomen and the remainder of the head are then teased up and examined as individual fresh preparations under the high power of a dissecting microscope or else under the low power of a compound microscope. If it is desired to preserve any of the worms found, this can be done either by transferring, on the point of a needle, individual worms to alcohol, or else by sucking up the worms with a Pasteur pipette and similarly transferring them to alcohol. If the latter procedure is adopted care must be taken not to over-dilute the preservative fluid.

The presence of infective forms of filariae in the proboscis and, or, head of a mosquito is usually accepted as evidence that the insect—when next it bites—is capable of causing infection in man. It should be remembered, however, that whereas in the case of malaria the presence of sporozoites in the salivary glands of an anopheline is almost certain evidence that the insect is capable of causing infection in the human host, in the case of filariasis, the infective forms found in the head or proboscis, may belong to a species incapable of complete development in man.

(e) *The dissection of simuliid flies (Simulium), tabanid flies (Chrysops) and midges (Culicoides) for the presence of filarial parasites.* The dissections should be made along similar lines to those described for the dissection of mosquitoes, but it should be remembered that, as in the case of mosquitoes, the infective forms found present may not necessarily belong to a species capable of causing infection in man. A proportion of the "ripe" infective forms of *Wuchereria bancrofti* and of *Brugia malayi*, if present, are almost certain to be found in the labium of the mosquito, but the infective forms of *Dipetalonema perstans* and those of *D. streptocerca* occurring in midges (*Culicoides*) may be confined to the head; while a similar localisation may be encountered in simuliid (*Simulium*) flies parasitised by *Onchocerca volvulus*. In the case of flies in the genus *Chrysops* the infective forms of *Loa loa* are seldom encountered in the proboscis, and, although a proportion of the infective forms are almost always present in the head, large numbers are encountered in the thorax and abdomen, the greatest numbers usually occurring in the abdomen.

CHAPTER LIII

THE IDENTIFICATION OF ARTHROPODS OF MEDICAL IMPORTANCE AND THE USE OF KEYS

The identification of arthropods of medical importance

THE accurate recognition of an arthropod, whether it is directly injurious or a vector of disease, and the information this provides as regards its life-cycle, breeding places and habits is an essential preliminary to the planning of practical measures directed to its control and to the elimination or reduction of the lesions it causes or the disease it transmits. Faulty identification of such injurious arthropods has, in the past, led to great wastage in effort and money, and to considerable unnecessary suffering, as is instanced in the following three examples.

Some time after it was shown that *Xenopsylla cheopis* was the vector of plague in South India and Ceylon, it was noted that although the disease occurred in hilly country it was virtually absent from the plains where, what was then regarded as the same species of flea, also occurred. This finding led to a re-examination of the fleas previously collected from parasitised rodents in the two areas. As a result it was discovered that the collections previously labelled as "*Xenopsylla cheopis*" consisted in reality of two very closely related species, *Xenopsylla cheopis*, a very efficient vector of plague which occurred on the hill rats, and *Xenopsylla astia*, a relatively inefficient vector which occured on rats from the plains. Control in the hill districts of *Xenopsylla cheopis* and of its rodent host resulted in an elimination of plague, without any measures having to be taken in the lowlands—a change in tactics which resulted not only in more effective control but also in a marked saving in expenditure.

The second example is that of a taxonomic discovery which finally led to the successful control of a myiasis producing fly, *Callitroga americana*. Until 1933 *Callitroga macellaria* was regarded as responsible for a very large number of cases of dermal and mucosal myiasis in both man and animals in America, and the larval form of this fly was believed to breed in carrion as well as being parasitic and capable of penetrating intact mucous membrane. In 1933 however Cushing and Patton demonstrated that two species, now known as *C. macellaria* and *C. americana,* were being confused together and that whereas the former was essentially a carrion breeder and incapable of penetrating mucous membrane, the latter was strictly parasitic. As a result of this the whole policy of control was altered and funds and labour were directed to the control of, from the Public Health standpoint, the outstandingly important fly, *C. americana.*

The third example is the often quoted story of *Anopheles maculipennis* and its relation to malaria in Europe, following the first World War. After the close of hostilities it was noticed that although this anopheline occurred over a wide area in Europe, malaria which was then rampant in certain districts, showed a distinctly patchy distribution, and it became evident that *A. maculi-*

pennis although present throughout the area was acting as a vector only in certain parts of it. Efforts to recognise differences in the adults and the larvae of *A. maculipennis*, occurring in the malarious and non-malarious localities, failed until it was observed that the malaria and non-malaria carrying forms could be distinguished by morphological differences in the eggs produced by the females collected from the two sorts of locality. In addition it was noted that these differences were reflected in the food preferences of the two types, the type concerned in transmitting being anthropophilic while the type not associated with transmission was zoophilic. This discovery led to the recognition of several subspecies (some authors regard them as species, albeit sibling species) of *A. maculipennis,* which differ from each other more in ecological than in morphological characters. Not only were these discoveries on the "*A. maculipennis* complex" important in limiting control measures to the vector members of the complex, thus saving large sums of money to Public Health authorities in Europe, but they also led to the awakening of an awareness in medical entomologists, and others concerned with arthropod-borne diseases, that fundamental differences may exist in vector potential between two subspecies (or even between two or more morphologically indistinguishable strains) of an arthropod transmitter of disease. As a result of these and other studies it is now clearly recognised that genetic and other factors may greatly modify the behaviour of a particular species of blood-sucking arthropod as a transmitter of disease, a discovery dramatically emphasised within recent years by the appearance, within the species, of strains resistant and non-resistant to particular insecticides.

Nothwithstanding the advent of the "new systematics" which is concerned chiefly with variation in the species and infra-specific categories (such as subspecies, forms, etc.) and the influence of genetic, geographical and other factors, the concept of the "species" in the long accepted sense of the term is still of the greatest significance. In other words, the species still occupies a unique place in systematics and it is with the species, as a basic unit, that we must continue to work.

The first description of a species is known as the "original description".

An adequate account of a species of arthropod is one which includes a reasonably complete and illustrated description of the creature and its immature forms (if these are available), together with an acount, if the material is sufficient, of variability within the species. The characters of the species are usually described in order of importance and the style may be telegraphic. Short remarks on the breeding sites, habits and geographical distribution are helpful and are often appended but it is more common to find such notes accompanying the descriptions of species in synopses (or revisions) of genera, or of larger groups. If the arthropod is a parasite, the name of the host is given and, occasionally, some ecological notes are added.

Although in modern usage it is usual to describe a species from as wide a range of specimens as possible, nevertheless a single specimen of either sex is taken from the series and is designated as the "holotype" or "type" and serves henceforth as a reference specimen. Specimens other than the holotype which the author used when describing the species are known as the "paratypes" and sometimes one of these "paratypes" (always of the opposite sex to the holo-type) is singled out and designated as the "allotype". The locality from which the holotype was collected is known as the "type locality" and if the specimen is a parasite, the species of animal from which it was collected is hereafter designated as the "type host".

Although the descriptions of species and supra-specific groups, such as genera, are to be found widely scattered throughout many types of journals, it is the practice of systematists to collect together all available descriptions and to publish them from time to time in the form of compendia. These compendia, which are variously known as "synopses", "revisions", "monographs" and so forth, are of great value to the non-specialist for not only do they save him an immense amount of time in collating information but they also present him with a comprehensive picture of the classification of the particular group in which he is interested.

The most usual type of compendium is one which deals with a single family

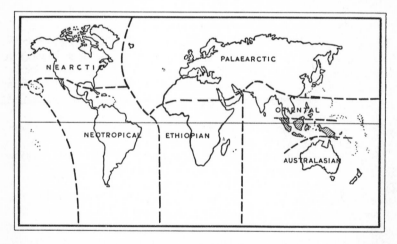

Fig. 198. "The six Zoogeographical Regions, the main divisions of the world so far as animals and plants are concerned. The islands of the South Pacific are linked mianly with the Australasian Region, and to some extent with the Oriental. The volcanic islands of the Hawaiian group belong to none of the Regions, but present an interesting problem in insect migration and colonisation. As stated in the text, there is much overlapping on the borders of the Regions, especially in the Austro-Oriental Region, shown shaded."
(Redrawn from Oldroyd, *Collecting Preserving and Studying Insects*, 1958. By cour-tesy of Hutchinson, London.)

and includes descriptions of all the genera and species but often those devoted to a single genus, such as *Anopheles*, are of great value to the medical officer.

Whilst some of these works are highly technical and only suitable for the use of trained systematists, others have a wider appeal and may be used by workers with only a very limited knowledge of taxonomy. Such compendia of medically important arthropods may have a worldwide range but are usually restricted to one of the six great zoogeographical regions (see Fig 198). Nowadays it is usual to restrict such surveys to still more limited regions, such as those defined by political frontiers or even very restricted tracts of territories such as a county or a magisterial district.

This grouping together of medically important arthropods in zoogeographical regions is not only scientifically convenient but it restricts the number of species to be considered. For instance, whereas the shortest guide to the anophelines of the world occupies some 200 pages, the discussion of the species occurring in the Ethiopian region is limited to 27 pages, while the number of species occurring in a particular magisterial district may often be limited to a brief discussion of only a few of these. It should not be forgotten, however, that as a result of modern travel conditions the range of a species may be rapidly extended over wide areas, as has already occurred in the case of such insects as *Aedes aegypti*, *Xenopsylla cheopis* and *Tunga penetrans*.

The use of keys

In the preceding chapters an account has been given of how to recognise classes, orders and families and, in certain cases, genera of arthropods of medical importance, but only in a very few instances has the recognition of species been dealt with. It is impracticable and very time consuming for the medical officer, and even for the experienced worker, to wade through a compendium of species without some "short cut"; consequently it is the usual practice in systematic works to include a type of scientific shorthand, aptly described as a "key", so as to speed identification.

In order to explain what is meant by a key, perhaps the best method is to use an analytical process, somewhat analogous to that used by the chemist who splits up a compound in order to identify its components.

Let us assume that we are dealing with a region in which only seven species of anopheline mosquitoes occur and that we have in front of us one specimen of each of the following seven species—*A. sacharovi*, *A. algeriensis*, *A. claviger*, *A. coustani* var. *tenebrosus*, *A. multicolor*, *A. pharoensis* and *A. superpictus*.

On examination, these seven mosquitoes prove to consist of one group of species (3 species) with no pale scales on the wings and a second group (4 species) with pale scales on the wings.

We can therefore group the seven species as follows:—

Wings without pale scales . . . . *sacharovi**
                                                    algeriensis
                                                    claviger

---

* It will be observed that in constructing a key to the species the generic name (*Anopheles* in this example) may be omitted.

Wings with pale scales . . . . *coustani* var. *tenebrosus*
multicolor
pharoensis
superpictus

    Each group is now considered separately and it is observed that whereas *sacharovi* has some dark spots on the wing, *algeriensis* and *claviger* have none and, proceeding further, whereas the mesonotum is almost uniformly reddish brown in *algeriensis*, it is greyish brown in the middle with contrasting reddish brown or dark brown sides in *claviger*.

    The key is therefore enlarged as follows:—

1. Wings without pale scales 2
    Wings with pale scales . . . . *coustani* var. *tenebrosus*
                                                     multicolor
                                                   pharoensis
                                                   superpictus

2. Wings with 4 or 5 spots slightly darker than the rest
    of field . . . . *sacharovi*
    Wings without dark spots . . . . 3 .
3. Mesonotum almost uniformly reddish brown . . *algeriensis*
    Mesonotum greyish brown in the middle with con-
      trasting reddish brown or dark brown sides . . *claviger*

    There still remains the group constituted of *coustani* var. *tenebrosus*, *multicolor*, *pharoensis* and *superpictus*. It is found on examination that *coustani* var. *tenebrosus* has the last two segments of the hind tarsus entirely white, whereas the remaining three species have no segments entirely white. Of the three remaining species, *multicolor* has the tips of the palpi dark, while the remaining two species, *pharoensis* and *superpictus,* have the tips of the palpi pale; the latter two can be separated by the presence in one (*pharoensis*) of lateral tufts of scales on the abdomen and their absence in the other (*superpictus*).

    It is now possible to complete the key as follows:—

1. Wings without any pale scales 2
    Wings with some pale scales 4
2. Wings with 4 or 5 spots slightly darker than the
    rest of field . . . . *sacharovi*
    Wings without dark spots 3
3. Mesonotum almost uniformly reddish brown . . *algeriensis*
    Mesonotum greyish brown in the middle with
      contrasting reddish brown or dark brown sides *claviger*
4. Hind tarsi with last two segments entirely white . *coustani* var. *tenebrosus*
    Hind tarsi with no segment entirely white . . . 5
5. Tips of palpi dark . . . . *multicolor*.
    Tips of palpi pale (sometimes narrowly so) . . . 6
6. Abdomen with laterally projecting tufts of scales . *pharoensis*
    Abdomen without laterally projecting tufts of scales *superpictus*

    By using such a key it is possible to arrive rapidly at a tentative identification

of a specimen of *Anopheles* belonging to the particular locality being considered, thus avoiding the laborious and lengthy process of having to read through

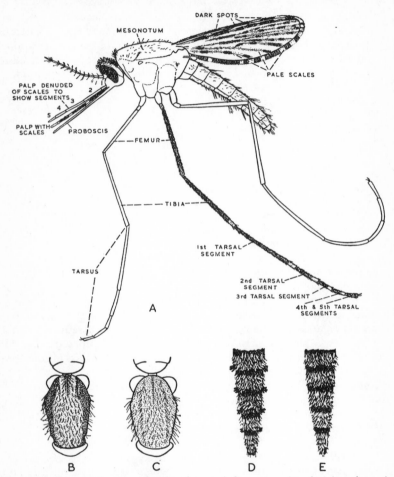

Fig. 199. A. Lateral view of a female anopheline mosquito showing the points
mentioned in the key; B. dorsal view of thorax of *A. claviger*; C. dorsal view of
thorax of *A. algeriensis*; D. dorsal view of abdomen of an anopheline with lateral
tufts of scales; E. lacking lateral tufts of scales.

detailed descriptions of all the seven species before coming to a decision as
regards its identity. Whilst an identification obtained as a result of consulting
a key can never be regarded as final, since the specimen being studied must be
checked against a full description of the species to which it has been "keyed
out", nevertheless it is evident that the key system is a remarkable time-saver.

Not only should the medical officer learn to use keys but he should be prepared, if necessary, to construct them for the species of medically important arthropods occurring in the area in which he is working.

The key given above is an example of one kind of the so-called dichotomous key and is the one in most common use at the present time. Other kinds of dichotomous keys which have been devised may be illustrated as follows:—

The indented key

A. Wings without pale scales.
  a. Wings without dark spots.
    b. Mesonotum almost uniformly reddish brown . . . . *algeriensis*
    bb. Mesonotum not uniformly reddish brown *claviger*
  aa. Wings with dark spots . . . . *sacharovi*
B. Wings with pale scales.
  a. No segment of hind tarsi entirely white.
    b. Tips of palpi pale.
      c. Abdomen with lateral scale tufts . . *pharoensis*
      cc. Abdomen without lateral scale tufts *superpictus*
    bb. Tips of palpi dark . . . . *multicolor*
  aa. Last two segments of hind tarsi entirely white *coustani*
                    var. *tenebrosus*

The serial key

1 (6) Wings without pale scales
2 (3) Wings with 4-5 dark spots . . . . *sacharovi*
3 (2) Wings without dark spots
4 (5) Mesonotum almost uniformly reddish brown *algeriensis*
5 (4) Mesonotum not uniformly reddish brown . *claviger*
6 (1) Wings with some pale scales
7 (8) Last two segments hind tarsi white . . . . *coustani* var. *tenebrosus*
8 (7) Last two segments hind tarsi not entirely white
9 (10) Tips of palpi dark . . . . *multicolor*
10 (9) Tips of palpi pale
11 (12) Abdomen with lateral tufts of scales . . . . . *pharoensis*
12 (11) Abdomen without lateral tufts of scales . . . *superpictus*

In addition to the dichotomous keys given above several other types of keys have been devised including the pictorial key, examples of which are shown in Figs. 200 & 201. This type of key is particularly useful to medical men and non-systematists who wish tentatively to identify certain arthropods, such as tsetse flies and fleas.

Finally, it is pertinent to draw the reader's attention once more to the contents of Chapter L in which the preservation of arthropods of medical importance is discussed. Most of the larger arthropods such as bugs and tsetse flies, and many of the smaller species such as mosquitoes, can usually be identified satisfactorily with the aid of a good hand lens but other creatures such as sandflies, fleas, mites and mosquito larvae can best be identified with a compound microscope following their treatment with clearing agents. If more than one specimen of the species of arthropod to be identified is available, these

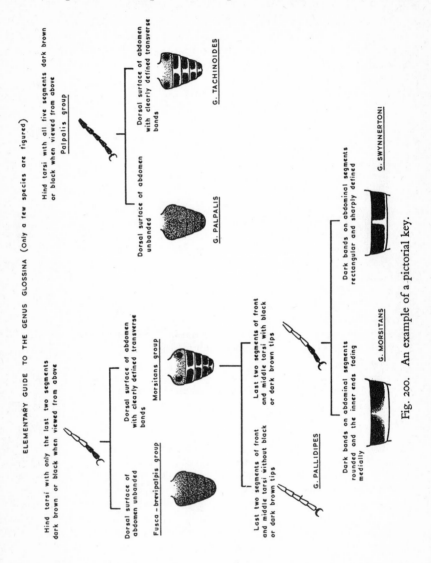

Fig. 200. An example of a pictorial key.

should all be examined since it is not an uncommon experience to find that some delicate structure of taxonomic importance is damaged in a proportion of the material.

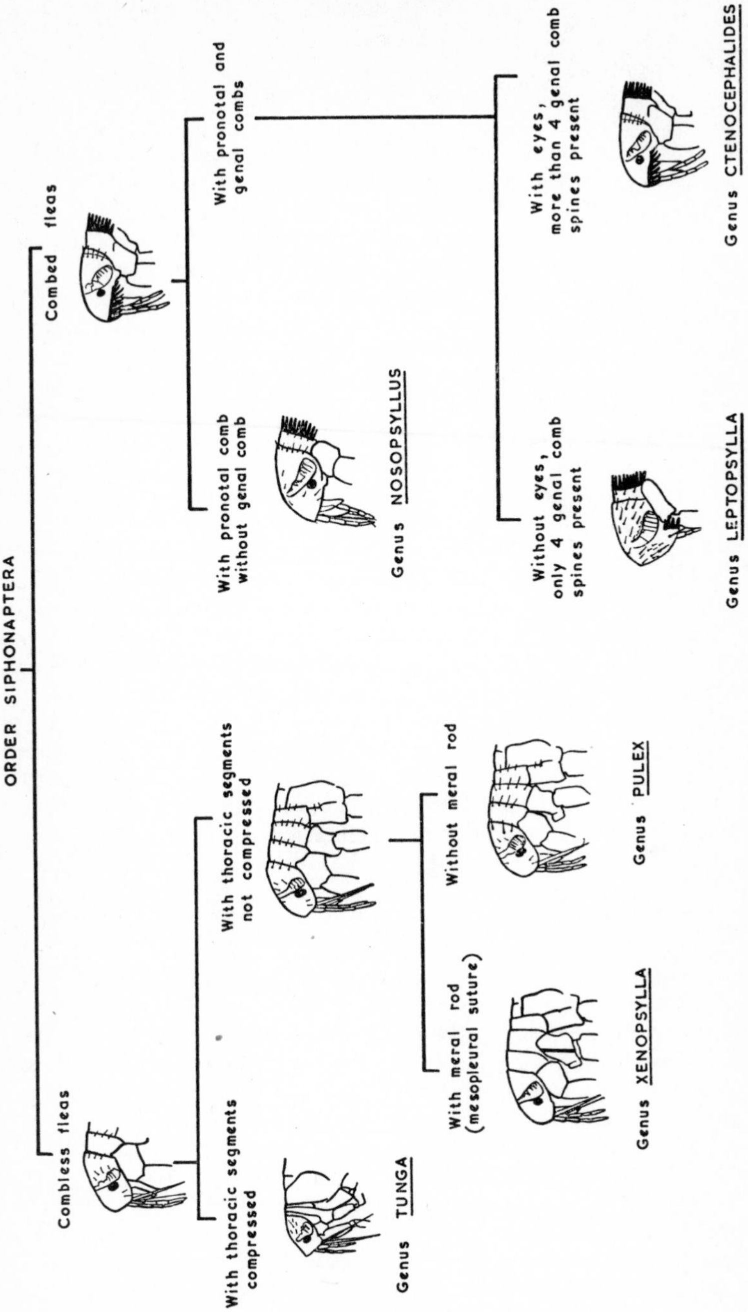

Fig. 201. An example of a pictorial key.

CHAPTER LIV

ZOOLOGICAL NOMENCLATURE

MORE than half a million different kinds of arthropods have been described, and in order to study such a vast assemblage of creatures it is necessary to arrange them into groups. That branch of biology which deals with their arrangement (or classification) is known as systematics, while the principles governing classification are referred to as taxonomy, the terminology employed in the classification being known as nomenclature. It follows that the giving of a name to an animal (as distinct from the naming of a plant) is what constitutes "zoological nomenclature".

In most civilised countries children, at the time of their birth, are given a surname and a first name (christian name). The first name, although it helps to identify an individual, conveys no information regarding his or her relationship to other persons, but the surname links the individual to a particular family and is therefore a guide to lineage. A moment's consideration will show that a knowledge of the generic name of an arthropod is a similar, but much more informative guide, not only to the creature's lineage but also to its morphology, and often to various biological episodes in its life-cycle, provided always that the enquirer has access to the necessary literature. To give an example, the common European vector of malaria is named *Anopheles maculipennis*. Since it is in the genus *Anopheles* we know that it must have the characteristics of the tribe Anophelini, the subfamily Culicinae, the family Culicidae, the suborder Nematocera and the order Diptera. By looking up these various categories in a text book it is possible to build up a detailed picture of the anatomy of this insect. Similarly, we can form a representative picture of many of its biological characteristics. Thus, knowing that it is a member of the order Diptera, it follows that it has a hemimetabolous life-cycle, and since it belongs to the suborder Nematocera and the family Culicidae it is known that the larvae are aquatic and have a characteristic morphology. While, since it belongs to the tribe Anophelini, we know that it lays its eggs singly on the surface of the water, that the eggs are furnished with floats, and that the larvae which emerge are surface feeders and have a morphology characteristic of the tribe Anophelini, as distinct from the tribe Culicini. Finally, since the insect belongs to the genus *Anopheles*, we know that it is a potential transmitter of malaria to man. In short by being given the name of the genus as *Anopheles* we have been furnished with a very helpful guide to many of the characteristic morphological and biological features of this particular insect.

So much for the value of zoological nomenclature; there remain for consideration the methods to be used in its application. In taxonomy the species forms the primary unit (taxon) the usually accepted definition of the term "species" being that all individuals within this primary unit are capable of interbreeding and producing fertile offsprings.

The groups within the species may of course develop characteristics of their

332

own, and we call such groups "subspecies" so long as they are capable of inter-breeding, not only with other members of that particular subspecies but also with members of all other groups within the species. In practice, the application of this fertility test is often impracticable, in consequence it is usual to consider members of different groups as belonging to the same species so long as they do not show any *constant* morphological differences. Obviously this rule needs to be interpreted with caution and common sense, thus males and females of the same species often differ (sometimes very markedly), not only with regard to their genitalia but also with regard to their size, colouration etc. Again, creatures of the same species, but belonging to different castes, often exhibit constant morphological differences which do not warrant the giving of specific rank. Thus, amongst bees, the "workers", the "queens" and the "drones" differ morphologically, nevertheless they clearly belong to the same species.

It is obvious from what has been said that all subspecies fall into "the infraspecific" category and that even further down the scale are the various "forms", "varieties" and "aberrations" which defy accurate classification, beyond saying that they are members of the same species which exhibit differences so small or so inconstant as not to warrant giving them the rank of subspecies.

Amongst the medically important protozoa (and, of course, amongst the medically important bacteria) there are many examples of specific rank being accorded to creatures which, although morphologically indistinguishable at all stages of their development, exhibit certain constant biological differences. In a similar manner certain strains of arthropods which exhibit no constant morphological differences may, at some or at all stages of their development, show constant biological differences, but up to date these differences have not been considered to warrant the giving to them of specific names, although they may be given the rank of varieties or of subspecies.

The various species are in their turn classified into genera, the genera into families, the families into orders, the orders into classes, and the classes into phyla.

The rules or laws governing zoological nomenclature are periodically reviewed by an international body known as the International Committee of Zoological Nomenclature, the object of this body being to name creatures according to an orderly system. These rules have been very admirably summarised by Dr. Hoare in his book entitled "Handbook of Medical Protozoology". In his comments Dr. Hoare has used the names of protozoa and, more rarely, of arthropods to illustrate the application of the rules. With his permission we have substituted the names of arthropods where he has used the names of protozoa and have slightly altered the text accordingly.

Article 1. "Zoological nomenclature is independent of botanical nomenclature in the sense that the name of an animal is not rejected simply because it is identical with the name of a plant."
COMMENT. Though the generic name of an animal may be the same as that of a plant, it is advisable to avoid such duplication.

Article 2. "The scientific designation of animals is uninominal for subgenera and all higher groups, binominal for species, and trinominal for subspecies." COMMENT. Each species is named by a combination of two names, the generic and specific, written in *italics*. This designation is known as binominal, e.g. the housefly, belonging to the genus *Musca* and to the species *domestica*, is designated *Musca domestica*. Subspecies bear three names (trinominal), e.g. human lice belong to two subspecies of the species *Pediculus humanus*, which are designated *Pediculus humanus capitis* (head louse) and *Pediculus humanus corporis* (body louse). If a species is recognised as being constituted of two or more subspecies, one of these subspecies (the original part) is designated by the repetition of the specific name, e.g. *Aedes aegypti* has recently been recognised as consisting of three subspecies, the type form being known as *Aedes aegypti aegypti*, whilst the remaining forms are known as *Aedes aegypti formosus* and *Aedes aegypti queenslandensis*. Units above the species (subgenera, genera, families, etc.) bear one name with a capital initial letter, e.g. genus *Cimex*. When a specific name is repeatedly mentioned in the same publication it is customary to write only the initial letter of the genus, e.g. *C. lectularius*.

Article 3. "The scientific names of animals must be words which are either Latin or Latinized."

Article 4. "The name of a family is formed by adding the ending *idae*, the name of a subfamily by adding *inae*, to the stem of the name of its type genus." COMMENT. Example: the family name Muscidae is derived from the genus *Musca*.

Article 8. "A generic name must consist of a single word . . . written with a capital initial letter, and employed as a substantive in the nominative singgular."

COMMENT. Examples: genera *Anopheles, Phlebotomus, Dermanyssus*.

Article 10. "When it is desired to cite the name of a subgenus, this name is to be placed in parenthesis between the generic and the specific names." COMMENT. Example: the mosquito-vector of yellow fever belongs to the subgenus *Stegomyia* of genus *Aedes* and is designated *Aedes (Stegomyia) aegypti*. The subgeneric name *alone* should never be used in combination with the specific name, otherwise it will be mistaken for a generic name.

When a generic name has been changed the old name may likewise be placed in brackets, provided it is preceded by an equal mark, e.g. *Ornithonyssus* (= *Liponyssus*) *bacoti*, otherwise the name in parenthesis will be mistaken for a subgenus.

Article 13. "While specific substantive names derived from names of persons may be written with a capital letter, all other specific names are to be written with a small initial letter." COMMENT. However, it is customary in entomological practice to write *all* specific names with a small initial letter, e.g. *Anopheles stephensi*.

Article 21. "The author of a scientific name is that person who first publishes the name in connection with an indication, a definition, or a description."

Article 22. "If it is desired to cite the author's name, this should follow the scientific name without interposition of any mark of punctuation; if other citations are desirable (date, *sp.n.*, *emend.*, *sensu stricto*, etc.) these follow the author's name, but are separated from it by a comma or by parenthesis."

COMMENT. Example: *Anopheles marteri* Senevet & Prunelle, 1927, indicates that the species in question was created by the said authors in 1927. When a new species (or other systematic unit) is first proposed, it is designated as such in the original publication, e.g. *Glossina morsitans* sp.n. (or sp. nov.).

Article 23. "When a species is transferred to another than the original genus or the specific name is combined with any other generic name than that with which it was originally published, the name of the author of the specific name is retained in the notation but placed in parenthesis. . . . If it is desired to cite the author of the new combination, his name follows the parenthesis."

COMMENT. Example: *Argas savignyi* Audouin, 1827 was transferred to the genus *Ornithodoros* by Koch in 1844; this change is indicated in the notation *Ornithodoros savignyi* (Audouin 1827) Koch, 1844, or more simply as *Ornithodoros savignyi* (Audouin).

Article 25. "The valid name of a genus or species can only be that name under which it was first designated."

COMMENT. This is the so-called "Law of Priority" and is subject to certain conditions: (a) that the name was published and accompanied by an indication, definition, or description; (b) that the author has applied binominal nomenclature.

Article 32. "A generic or a specific name, once published, cannot be rejected, even by its author, because of inappropriateness."

COMMENT. *Xenopsylla brasiliensis* was first described from specimens collected in Brazil to which it had been carried by ships. It is, however, essentially an Old World species of flea and is much commoner in Africa and Asia than in South America.

Article 34. "A generic name is to be rejected as a homonym when it has previously been used for some other genus of animals."

Article 35. "A specific name is to be rejected as a homonym when it has previously been used for some other species or subspecies of the same genus."

Article 36. "Rejected homonyms can never be used again. Rejected synonyms can be used again in case of restoration of erroneously suppressed groups."

COMMENT. (Articles 34-36). A homonym is one and the same name for two or more different things. Synonyms are different names for one and the same thing.

CHAPTER LV

ON CONSULTING THE LITERATURE

T HE research worker in any branch of medicine can no more carry out his work without the use of a library than he can without the use of a laboratory. But unfortunately, although during his undergraduate days he is taught how to make use of the laboratories that specialize in the needs of the medical practitioner, at no time in his career does he receive instruction on how to make full use of all the resources of a medical or scientific library.

The following notes are written for the guidance of medical officers who wish to "consult the literature" on some specific aspect of medical entomology. They are intended to be a mere introduction to the use of a medical library, and should be understood to indicate only the more obvious paths of approach. To those who wish to know more of the subject, Mr. L. T. Morton's excellent short work on "How to use a Medical Library" (Heinemann, 7s.6d) is strongly recommended.

For the worker who is seeking information on problems of medical entomology, the first two points to be considered are the literature that should be consulted and the places where it is most likely to be available. The literature will be found in text-books, journals and reports, with the appropriate abstracting journals acting as an indispensable guide to all three sources. The location of the libraries housing such works should present few difficulties, for any public library, university library or commercial library (such as that of Messrs. H. K. Lewis and Company Limited, 136, Gower Street, London, W.C.1) will always gladly assist the inquirer. In the larger towns most of the journals that he is likely to need will probably be available in one or other of the local libraries, and those that are not available can easily be traced by means of the "World List of Scientific Periodicals" (which lists all scientific periodicals current since 1900) or the "Union Catalogue of the Periodical Publications in the University Libraries of the British Isles" (which lists periodicals, published both before and after 1900, which are not included in the "World List"), both of which record the libraries in the United Kingdom where they can be found. "Periodicals of Medicine and the Allied Sciences in British Libraries" (British Medical Association) is also useful, though it is a much smaller and less complete work than the "World List" or the "Union Catalogue".

All these resources are available to the medical officer living within reach of a town library. The medical officer who is living in "bush" conditions must either wait until he can visit a centre where a library is available or write for assistance to one of the libraries known to him. Before doing so, however, he would be well advised to ascertain what local information is available upon his particular problem, especially if he is working in the tropics, where almost invariably considerable information can be derived from the back numbers of the local medical journals and from the annual reports of his Medical Department. In previous chapters attention has been drawn to the use of "keys" in the identification of arthropods of medical importance, and to the difficulty of devising keys with worldwide application. The identification of a local species of mosquito, tsetse fly, flea, etc., however, does not necessarily involve a study of all the potential species, for in practice the number of species likely to be encountered are usually quite small, and they can generally be rapidly and accurately separated by the use of a local key dealing only with the species known to occur within a given area. These local keys are quite invaluable and are usually available in most British colonies and protectorates.

Having defined the type of information required and having located a suitable library for his needs, the worker will then proceed to examine the relevant literature, medical, entomological, parasitological and so on. Medical works, though primarily concerned with the patient and his diseases, often give much information on the arthropods which cause or transmit the disease, and parasitological works similarly provide information not only on the creatures which cause parasitic diseases, but also on their vertebrate hosts and (when they exist) on their invertebrate hosts. It would, of course, be quite impossible for the medical officer to search all the relevant literature both past and present that deals with his particular problem, and some method of limiting the search must therefore be used.

The most generally adopted system is to begin by consulting some of the standard text-books on the subject, and from them to compile a list of references or, better still, a card index*. Since text-books, however, no matter how excellent they are, seldom supply all the information required, a wider search of the literature is generally necessary. The most complete index to medical literature is to be found in the "Index-Catalogue of the Library of the Surgeon General's Office, United States Army", a massive work of 58 volumes which lists almost all the printed matter of medical interest from the earliest times up to 1950. It is now unfortunately no longer issued, and for works published after 1950 the worker must consult such other sources as the "Quarterly Cumulative Index Medicus" which lists all works dealing with medicine, surgery and the collateral sciences published since 1870, and the "Index Medicus" (formerly the "Current List of Medical Literature") which is issued monthly. For work dealing with the zoological side of his research, the worker is referred to the *Zoological Record* and to the incomparable "Index-Catalogue of Medical and Veterinary Zoology". Intermediate between periodically issued catalogues containing references to medical entomology and the abstracting journals concerned with this subject, is the *Bulletin Signalétique d'Entomologie Médicale et Vétérinaire* which is issued monthly

---

* Among the wealth of excellent standard text-books the following may be mentioned as of particular value in supplying references: "Stitt's diagnosis, prevention and treatment of tropical diseases" by R. P. Strong; "Textbook of clinical parasitology" by D. L. Belding; "Protozoology" by C. M. Wenyon; "Medical entomology" by R. Matheson; and, for useful references to important papers dealing with general entomology, "A general textbook of entomology" by A. D. Imms.

and which contains lists of published papers classified under various subject headings.

Finally there are the abstracting journals, which list all the work recently published on a given subject and provide abstracts of their contents. For the entomological and parasitological worker the most important of these will probably be the *Review of Applied Entomology, Series B (Medical and Veterinary). Helminthological Abstracts* and the *Veterinary Bulletin.* As a connecting link between them is the *Tropical Diseases Bulletin*, probably the most essential of all the abstracting journals for the worker in the tropics. The value of these abstracting journals lies in the fact that they put the reader in touch with the original articles and enable him to select those that he wishes to study. They must, however, never be allowed to take the place of the original paper, which may throw a light on his subject entirely different from that indicated in the abstract, and furthermore may lead to the discovery of references previously missed by the reader. In cases where the original paper proves to be unobtainable, any published reference to it should clearly indicate that it has been consulted in abstract only.

INDEX

Numerals in bold face indicate main entries

Abrasives, 53
Abstracting journals, 338
Acalypterate fly, 50
Acaridae, 275
Acarina,
 and disease, 244
 classification, 246
 general morphology, 244
 internal anatomy, 245
Accessory glands, 64
Acetic-ether, 304
Adler, 132
Aedeagus, 63, 64
Aedes, **117**
 adult, general morphology, 117
 and disease, 117, 128-130
 and *Eretmapodites*, 121
 and *Psorophora*, 122
 feeding habits, 91, 119
 larval habitat, 118
 larval morphology, 118
 species identification, 119
Aedes,
 aegypti, 117, 118, **119**, 128, 129, 326, 334
 africanus, 119, 128
 albopictus, 129
 caballus, 130
 leucocelaenus, 129
 pembaensis, 127
 polynesiensis, 127, 129
 scutellaris, 129
 simpsoni, 119, 128
 sollicitans, 130
 vittatus, 119, 128
Aedes group, 117
Agglutinins, 58, 88, 281
Alimentary canal,
 acarine, 245
 flea, 212
 general description, 57
 housefly, 168
 louse, 227
 mosquito, 58, 88
 tick, 249
 tsetse-fly, 180
Allantoin, 17, 280
Allodermanyssus sanguineus, 246, 274
Allotype, 325
Amblyomma, 260, 282
Anal struts, 213

Anaplasmosis, 155
Anatomy, internal, and disease,
 flea, 211, 220
 housefly, 168
 tsetse-fly, 180
Anopheles, **99**
 control, 102
 egg, 100
 feeding habits, 106, 107, 110-114
 host-specificity, 107
 larva, 101, 102
 life-cycle, 100
 mating, 106
 medical importance, 99, **108**
 oviposition, 100
 pupa, 104
 resting places, 107
Anopheles,
 abimanus, 110
 algeriensis, 107, 326-329
 aquasalis, 110
 bellator, 106, 110
 claviger, 110, 326-329
 coustani, 326-329
 coustani tenebrosus, 326-329
 culicifacies, 111
 darlingi, 107, 111
 elutus, 113
 farauti, 111
 freeborni, 111
 funestus, 111
 gambiae, 107, 112
 gambiae melas, 112
 hyrcanus sinensis, 113
 labranchiae atroparvus, 112
 labranchiae labranchiae, 112
 leucosphyrus, 106
 maculatus, 113
 maculipennis, 323, 333
 maculipennis atroparvus, 112
 maculipennis freeborni, 111
 maculipennis labranchiae, 112
 marteri, 335
 minimus, 113
 multicolor, 326-329
 pharoensis, 326-329
 pseudopunctipennis, 113
 punctulatus, 113
 punctulatus moluccensis, 111
 quadrimaculatus, 113

Anopheles,
  saccharovi, 113, 326-329
  sinensis, 113
  stephensi, 107, 114, 334
  sundaicus, 114
  superpictus, 114
  umbrosus, 114
Anophelini, 95
Anoplura, 76, **223**
Antenna, 78, 79
Antepygidial bristles, 211
Anthrax, 155
Anthropophilic, 324
Anticoagulins, 58, 88, 250, 281
Antihistamines, 283
Ants, 283
Aorta of insect, 61
Aphiochaeta scalaris, 206
Apodemus, 272
Arista, 78, 162
Arachnida, 41, **242**
  general morphology, 242
  life-history, 242
Araneida, 19, 242, **284**
Argas, 247
Argasid ticks, **247**
  and disease, 247, 251
  bite, 247, 251
  collection, 297
  control, 35, 253
  coxal organs, 250
  ecology, 247, 251
  general life-cycle, 250
  general morphology, 248
  internal anatomy, 249
  longevity, 251
  oviposition, 250
  preservation, 304, 307
  recognition, 247
Arthropoda, 37
  classification, 40
  evolution, 38
Article, tick palp, 255
Asilidae, 153
Assassin bugs, 76, 237
Atrax, 285
Auchmeromyia luteola, 191, **196**
Auditory traps, 55
Autumnal itch, 271
Austen, 12

Babesia bigemina, 12, 254
Bacot, 208
Bait animals, 298
Balsa wood, 303
Barraud cage, 309, 310

Bartonella bacilliformis, 132, 139
Basis capituli, 255
Bats and mosquitoes, 33
Beauperthuy, 11
Bed-bugs, **233**
  and disease, 236
  collection, 295
  control, 236
  distribution, 234
  feeding behaviour, 234
  feeding habits, 236
  general life-cycle, 65, **235**
  general morphology, 234
  oviposition, 235
  recognition of, in buildings, 236
  preservation, 307
Bees, 19, **283**, 333
Bee,
  stings (see stings)
  venom, 283
Beetles, 19, 287
Beneficial arthropods, 14
Benzyl benzoate, 265, 272
Berlese funnel, 294
  and flea collection, 295
  and tick collection, 297
Berne fly, 200
B.H.C., 31, 55, 137, 225, 230, 236, 241,
    266, 272
Bironella, 99, 100
Bites,
  centipede, 286
  insect, 15, 280
  spider, 284
  tick, 247, 251, 259
Biting lice, 223
Biting midge, 148
Black-fly, 140
Blacklock, 140
Blocking of fleas, 220
Blood meals, identification of, 314
Blood, of insects, 61
Blood-sucking muscids, 164
Blue bottle, 189, 194
Body louse (see *Pediculus humanus*)
Boophilus, 258
  annulatus, 254
Boyd-Orr, Sir John, 15
Brachycera, 80, **153**
Breeding out, of insects, 311
Bruce, 12, 177
Bristle, 53
Brown tail moth, 286
Brugia malayi
  animal reservoir, 26
  recognition of, in vector, 321, 322

Brugia malayi,
  vectors, 108, 110-113, 124, 127
Buckley, 108
Buffalo-fly, definition, 140
Bulletin Signalétique, 337
Butterflies, 286
Button, 170

Caddis fly, 77
Calcium gluconate and spider bites, 285
Calliphora, 17, 78, 191, **194**
Calliphoridae,
  distinction from Muscidae, 189
Calliphorinae, 190
Callitroga, 16, 68, **192-194**, 204, 205
Callitroga americana, **192**, 323
  macellaria, **192**, 323
Calypter, 50
Calypterate fly, 50
Canada balsam, 308
Capitulum, 245, 255
Carbon tetrachloride, 304
Carrion's disease, 139
Caudal bristles, 135, 136
Cavalryman's itch, 262
Cell, of wing, 50
Cellulose wool, 304
Cement glands, 64
Centipedes, 286
Cephalopharyngeal skeleton, 163, 173
Cephalothorax, 242
Cestodes and fleas, 221
Cerci, 51
Chagas, 237
Chagas' disease, vectors, 240
Chagasia, 99, 100
Chaoborinae, 83
Cheese-skipper, 206
Chelicera, 242, 245
  argasid, 249
  ixodid, 255
  Sarcoptes, 263
  trombiculid, 268
Chiggers, 267
Chigoe, 217
Chilopoda, 19, 41, **286**
Chitin, 52
Chloral hydrate, 308
Chloroform, 307
Cholera, 173
Chorion, 66
Chrysomyia, 16, 68, 190, **191-194**, 204, 205
Chrysomyia bezziana, **191**, 193
Chrysopinae, 155
Chrysops, 155-161
  dimidiata, 161

Chrysops,
  discalis, 161
  distinctipennis, 161
  silacea, 158, 160, 161
Cimex, (see bed-bugs)
  columbarius, 233
  hemipterus, 233
  lectularius, 233, 234
  rotundatus, 233, 234
Citronella oil, 55
Claspers, 63
Clearing fluids, 308
Clearing of arthropods, 308
Clearing of vegetation, 34
Cleg, 155
Cleland, 12
Climatic pockets, 71
Clubbing, of palp, 97
Coagulants, 281
Cobra venom, 283
Cochliomya, 192
Cockroach mouthparts, 43
Coelomyces, 34
Coleoptera, 19, 287
Collection of,
  argasid ticks, 297
  bed-bugs, 295
  biting flies (adult), 289
  biting flies (immature), 290
  filth flies, 293
  fleas, 293
  ixodid ticks, 296
  lice, 296
  maggots, 293
  reduviids, 295
Collecting net, 290
Collecting sucker, 289, 290
Colorado tick fever, 260
Colours and control, 55
Comb,
  of culicine larva, 116
  genal, of flea, 209
  pronotal, of flea, 210
Combed fleas, 218
Combless fleas, 216
Comstock-Needham method, 49
Competent maintaining host, 271
Cone nose bugs, 237
Congo floor maggot, 196
Conjunctivitis, 162, 173
Connexiva, 237
Control, of parasites,
  chemotherapeutic, 22
  chemoprophylactic, 23
  vaccination, 23

341

Control, of vector,
and type of life cycle, 70
biological, 27, 31
chemical, 28
destruction of hosts, 33
engineering, 35
food supply, 32
hygiene, 36
insecticides, 29
mechanical, 27
new housing, 35
oils, 56, 57
parasites, 33
predators, 33
repellents, 28
seasons, 35
vegetation, 34
Copper aceto-arsenite, 31, 102
Copulation, 63
Copra itch, 18, 275
Cordylobia, 204, 205
Cordylobia anthropophaga, 68, 191, **195**
Coreidae, 231
Costa, of wing, 49
Coxal organs, 246
and disease, 250, **252**
Crabs,
and *Aedes pembaensis*, 127
and simuliids, 144
Crab louse, 224
Craw-craw, 261
Creeping eruption, 202
Creosote and naphtha mixture, 303
Crop, 57
Cross veins, 50
Crustacea, 41
Ctenidium, 209, 216
Ctenocephalides, **219**, 331
and *Dipylidium caninum*, 222
Ctenocephalides
canis, 219-221
felis, 219-221
Culex, **122**
adult, general morphology, 122
and disease, 122, 127, 130
and *Theobaldia*, 125
feeding habits, 123
larval habitat, 123
larval morphology, 116, 123
Culex
annulirostris, 130
pipiens, 122, 123, 127
pipiens fatigans, 123, 127
pipiens molestus, 123
pipiens pipiens, 123
tarsalis, 130

Culex
tritaeniorhynchus, 130
univittatus, 130
Culex group, 122
Culicidae,
classification, 83
recognition, 83
Culicinae,
classification, 95
recognition, 83
Culicini,
distinction from Anophelini, 95
classification, 117
Culicines,
and disease, 115, 127
control, 102
egg, 116
larva, 116
pupa, 116
Culicoides, **148**
and disease, 148, **152**
collection, 290, 291
dissection, 321
feeding habits, 152
flight range, 146, 152
general life-cycle, 150
general morphology, 149
larval habitat, 150
longevity, 152
oviposition, 150
preservation, 304, 305
pupation, 151
resting places, 152, 290
Culicoides
austeni, 148, 150, 152
furens, 152
grahami, 148, 150, 152
Culiseta (= *Theobaldia*), 124, 125
Cushing, 323
Cuterebridae, 199
Cuticle, 52
Cyclical transmission of disease, 20
Cyclops, 12
Cyclorrapha, 80, **162**

Dance of the gnats, 106
Dapple-winged mosquito, 97
Day biters, 92
D.D.T., 31, 55, 137, 225, 230, 236, 285
Deer flies, 155
Deinocerites, 122
Demodex, 244
folliculorum var. *hominis*, 275
Demodicidae, 275
Dengue,
animal reservoir, 26

342

Dengue,
  and monkeys, 315
  vectors, 129
Dermacentor, 258, 260, 282
  andersoni, 254, 260
Dermanyssus, 334
  gallinae, 246, 274
Dermatobia, **200**, 204
Dermatobia hominis, 16, 68, 127, 199, **200**
Dermatitis and,
  Lepidoptera, 286
  beetles, 287
  mites, 264, 271, 274, 275
  organic sulphur, 265
Desensitisation, 282
Dessication, 72
Destruction of vectors,
  chemical, 29
  biological, 31
Deutovum, 269
Diapause, 60
Diamanus montanus, 220
Dieldrin, 241, 272
Diethyl toluamide, 28
Dimethyl,
  diphenylene disulphide, 265
  pthalate, 28, 272, 283
  thianthrene, 265
Dipylidum caninum,
  and dog lice, 223
  and fleas, 221
Dipetalonema perstans,
  animal reservoir, 26
  recognition of, in vector, 322
  vector, 148, 152
Dipetalonema streptocerca,
  recognition of, in vector, 322
  vector, 152
Diplopoda, 19, 41, 286
Diptera, 76, **77**
  classification, 80
  collection, 289
  dissection, 316–322
  general life-cycle, 80
  general morphology, 78
  medical importance, 77
  preservation, 304, 305
  pupation, 80
  rearing, 311
Dissection of arthropods for,
  identification, 314
  identification, blood meal, 314
  recognition of parasites, 315
Dissections of,
  midges for filariae, 321
  mosquitoes for filariae, 321

Dissections, of
  mosquitoes for *Plasmodia*, 316
  simuliids for filariae, 321
  tabanids for filariae, 321
  tsetse flies for trypanosomes, 318
Dixinae, 83
Dog,
  and leishmaniasis, 137, 138
  and biting lice, 223
Dog fly, 186
Dorsal brushes, 104
Dragonfly, 33, 77
Drainage, 35
Drone fly, 206
Drosophila, 206
Drug resistance, 23
Duncan, C.D., 14
Dusts and control, 53, 57
Dutton, 12, 177, 247
Dysentery, 165, 173

Eastern equine encephalomyelitis, 130
Ecdysis, **53**, 61
Echidnophaga gallinacea, 218
Egg, insect, 65
Egg breaker,
  flea, 213
  mosquito, 93
Ejaculatory duct, 64
Empodium, 79
Encephalitis,
  mosquito vectors, 129
  tick vectors, 260
Endochorion, 100
Entomology, definition, 37
Epicuticle, 52
Epidermis, 52, 54
Epidemiology, and climate, 71
Epimeron, 47
Episternum, 47
Epistome, 242
Eretmapodites, 117, **121**
  chrysogaster, 121, 130
Eristalis, 206
Ethyl,
  acetate, 304, 307
  alcohol, 305
Eyes,
  holoptic, 42
  dichoptic, 42
Excretion, 59
Exochorion, 100
Exoskeleton, 38

Faeces of insect, and disease, 60, 240
Fannia, **174**, 206

Fannia
  canicularis, 174
  scalaris, 175
Fan-shaped plate, 103, 104
Fat body, 60
  of mosquito, 60, 89
False-head, 255
False stable fly, 175
Fedschenko, 12
Feeding methods, 15, 280
Fertilisation, 63, 66
Fièvre boutonneuse, 260
Filariasis and,
  ceratopogonids, 148, 152
  mosquitoes, 127
  simuliids, 140, 147
  tabanids, 161
Finlaya, 129
Flannel moth, 286
Fleas,
  and disease, 208, 216, **220**
  and microclimate, 73
  and plague, 220
  and rodents, 33, 218-222
  classification, 216
  collection, 293
  general life-cycle, 212
  general morphology, 208
  habits, 214
  internal anatomy, 211
  larval habitat, 213
  longevity, 214
  oviposition, 212
  preservation, 304, 306
  pupation, 213, 214
Flesh flies, 189, 196
Flora and control, 34
Fly,
  definition, 77
  larvae and wound treatment, 17, 280
  papers, 295
  traps, 28
Food, of insects, 57
Forceps, entomological, 303, 306
Forest mosquitoes, 92
Formaldehyde, 305
Formol saline, 305
Foveae, 257
Francis, 155
Friedman, 261
Fruit-flies, 206
Fungi and mosquitoes, 34

Gad flies, 155
Gambusia, 33
Game and tsetse flies, 33, 183, 184

Gasterophilidae, 199
Gasterophilus, 16, **202**
Genal comb, 209
Gene's organ, 251, 256
Genitalia, 51
Gerbils,
  and plague, 220
  and leishmaniasis, 138
Gills, 38, 39
Gleicher, 165
Glossina,
  and disease, 177, 184, 320
  collection, 290, 292
  control, 33, 34
  dissection, 318
  ecology, 74, **183**
  feeding habits, 183, 184
  feeding mechanism, 15, 179
  general life-cycle, 181
  general morphology, 177
  identification, 75, 330
  internal morphology, 180
  longevity, 183
  mouthparts, 178
  preservation, 305
  pupal habitat, 182
  reproduction, 65, 181
  salivary glands, 180, 319
Glossina,
  brevipalpis, 330
  fusca, 330
  morsitans, 33, 183-185, 330, 335
  tachinoides, 34, 183, 184, 330
  pallidipes, 178, 184, 185, 330
  palpalis, 179, 183-185, 330
  swynnertoni, 183-185, 330
Glycerine, 305
Glycerol (see glycerine)
Glycyphagidae, 275
Gnathosoma, 245
Graber's organ, 159
Grain itch, 18, 275
Green-bottle, 189, 193
Grocer's itch, 275
Growth, 54, 68
Gum chloral mountant, 308

Habitat specificity, 271
Haemaphysalis, 258, 260
  leachi, 260
Haematobia, 186
Haematopota, 156, 160, 161
Haemocoele, 37
Haemocytes, 61
Haemolymph, 37, **61**
  and parasites, 62, 230, 252

Haemolysins, 281
Haemogogus, 117, **120**
  capricornis, 129
  mesodentatus, 120, 129
  spegazzini, 129
  spegazzini falco, 129
Hair, 53
Haltere, 50
Harara, 132, 137
Hard tick, 247, 254
Harvest mites, 267
Haustellum,
  of housefly, 167
  of louse, 227
Heart of insect, 61
Helminthological Abstracts, 338
Helminths, recognition in vector, 316
Hemielytron, 232
Hemiptera and disease, 232
Heteroptera, 231
Hertigia, 131
Hewitt, 165
Hibernation, 60, 89
Hippelates, 162
Histamine, 283
Histiosiphon, 270
Hoare, 333
Holotype, 324
Homoptera, 231
Horseflies, 78, 155 (see also tabanids)
House-fly, **165**
  and disease, 20, 165, **172**
  and microclimate, 74
  control, 170
  feeding habits, 171, 173
  flight range, 171
  general life-cycle, 69, **168**
  general morphology, 168
  internal anatomy, 168
  larval habitat, 169
  mouthparts, 166
  oviposition, 169
  pupation, 171
Hover flies, 206
Hovering dance, 92
Howard, 165
Hydrometridae, 231
Hypopharynx, 44
Humidity receptors, 55
Hyalomma, 258
Hymenolepis
  diminuta, 221, 222
  nana, 221, 222
Hymenoptera, 19, 283
Hypoderma, 16, **202,** 204
Hypodermatidae, 199

Hypodermis, 52
Hypopharynx, 44
Hypopleural bristles, 164, 189, 190
Hypostome, 242, 245, 249, 255, 257

Identification of arthropods, 75, 323
Indoor biters, 92, 107
Index catalogues, 337
Indian tick typhus, 260
Injurious arthropods, 14
Immunity to stings, 283
Impermeability of cuticle, 52
Integument of insects, 52
  and growth, 53
Insecta, 40
  classification, 75
Insecticides, **29–31,** 55–57, 66
Insecticides, resistance to, 31
Insect,
  abdomen, 51
  eyes, 42
  general structure, 42
  genitalia, 51
  head, 42
  leg, 51
  mouthparts, 43
  pleuron, 46
  tergum, 48
  thorax, 45
  wing, 49
Insect-eating birds, 33
Ixodes, 258, 260
  holocyclus, 260
  persulcatus, 260
  ricinus, 260
Ixodid ticks, **254**
  and disease, 254, 259
  collection, 296
  ecology, 258
  general life-cycle, 256
  general morphology, 254
  host-seeking, 256
  host specificity, 258
  one-two-three host, 258
  oviposition, 256, 258
  preservation, 304, 306
  removal of, 296
Ixodides, 246

James, M.T., 190
Japanese B encephalitis, 130
Jigger flea, 217
Jordan, K., 208

Kala-azar, 138
Kas kas, 261

345

Keel, 104
Keys for identification, 326, 336
Kilbourne, 12, 234
Killing agents, 304, 306, 307
Killing bottle, 289
King, 254
Kissing bugs, 237
Kitashima, 267
Kneissl, 267

Labella, 84, 86
Labelling, 300
Labium, 43
Labrum, 43
Lactochlorophenol, 308, 314
Laelaptidae, 273
  life-cycle, 273
  morphology, 273
  medical importance, 274
Lagoa crispata, 286
Landry's disease, 260
Larva migrans, 16, 202
Lasiohelea, 148
Lateral flaps, 103, 104
Latrine fly, 174
Latrodectus, 284
Leg,
  arachnid, 245
  insect, 51
Leishmania
  recognition of, in vector, 320
  vectors, 138
Leishmaniasis, 138
Leiurus quinquestriatus, 285
Lepidoptera, 19, 286
Leptidae, 153
Leptocimex boueti, 233
Leptoconops, 148
Leptopsylla segnis, 219, 331
Leptotrombidium, 272
Lesions due to,
  injurious substances, 19, 281
  mechanical trauma, 15, 280
  secondary infection, 16, 281
  sensitisation, 17, 282, 283
Lesser house fly, 174
Life-cycle,
  hemimetabolous, 68
  holometabolous, 68, 69
Lindane, 266
Linguatula, 277
  serrata, 277
Liponyssus (see Ornithonyssus)
Livingstone, David, 12
Loa loa,
  recognition of, in vector, 322

Loa loa,
  vectors, 161
  animal reservoir, 26
Longevity,
  argasid ticks, 251
  Culicoides, 152
  fleas, 214
  Glossina, 183
  housefly, 172
  mosquitoes, 94, 107
  oestrids, 199
  Phlebotomus, 137
  simuliids, 147
  Stomoxys, 188
  tabanids, 160
Louse (see Pediculus and Phthirus)
Lucilia, 17, 78, 191-193, 280
  sericata, 193
  cuprina, 193
Lung books, 38, 39
Lycolopex vetulus, 138
Lycosa tarantula, 284
Lyperosia, 186
  irritans, 140

Mackie, 12, 226
Magnesiun sulfate, 291
Malaria,
  and animal reservoir, 26, 108
  and drug therapy, 23
  and hibernating mosquitoes, 60
  and mosquitoes, 95, 108
  mode of transmission, 20
  vectors, 106-108, 110-114
Mal-de-caderas, 155
Mallophaga, 223
Malpighian tubules,
  insects, 59
  ticks, 246, 250
Mandibles, 43
Mango fly, 195
Manson, 12
Mansonia, 124
  and disease, 124, 127
  and Theobaldia, 125, 126
  collection, 291
  control, 34
  feeding habits, 125
  general morphology, 124
  larval habitat, 34, 124
  larval morphology, 124, 125
Mansonia
  annulifera, 127
  annulata, 127
  dives, 127
  indiana, 127

346

Mansonia
  longipalpis (= dives), 127
  uniformis, 127
Mansonia group, 123
Mansonella ozzardi, vector, 152
Mahogany flat, 233
Marmots and plague, 220
Martin, 208
Mastophora gasteracanthoides, 285
Match stick hairs, 136
Mating, 63
Mayne, 155
May-fly, 77
Maxilla, 43
Mechanical transmission of disease, 19
Mechanical trauma, 15, 280
Medical Entomology, 5, 37
Megalopyge opercularia, 286
Megharinini, 95
Meloidae, 287
Meral rod, 211
Mesopostnotum, 48
Mesostigmata, 246
Metamorphosis, types of, 68
Methyl alcohol, 305
Microclimate, 71, 73
Micropyle, 66
Microtus, 272
Midge, 140, 148
Milian, 261
Miller's itch, 18, 275
Millipedes, 41, 286
Mite islands, 271
Mite typhus, 267, 271
Mitigal, 265
Miyajima, 267
Monkeys and,
  epidemic typhus, 226
  dengue, 315
  lice, 226
  sandfly fever, 315
  scrub typhus, 267
Monographs, 325
Morton, L.T., 336
Mosquito,
  abdomen, 87
  anatomy, internal, 88, 97
  anatomy, external, 84
  and disease, 84, 95, 108, 127
  antennae, 85, 96, 97
  collection, 290, 291
  colouration, 83, 87, 97
  control, 35, 102
  dissection, 316, 321
  fat body, 60, 89
  feeding habits, 86, 91

Mosquito,
  genitalia, external, 88
  larva, 102, 116
  larval habitat, **93**, 101, 118-126
  life-cycle, general, 69, **91**
  longevity, 94, 107
  mouthparts, 85
  oviposition, 92
  preservation, 304, 305
  reproductive system, 89
  resting places, 92, 290
  salivary glands, 58
Moth flies, 131
Moths, 286
Mounting, of insects, 302
Mouthparts (adult)
  acarine, 245
  bed-bug, 234
  calliphorid, 190
  Culicoides, 149
  cockroach, 43
  Dermatobia, 200
  flea, 210
  Glossina, 44, **178**
  housefly, **166,** 171
  laelaptid mite, 273
  louse *(Pediculus)*, 227
  Mallophaga, 223
  mosquito, 44, **85**
  Phlebotomus, 133
  Sarcoptes scabiei, 263
  Simulium, 141
  Stomoxys, 186
  tabanid, 44, **157**
  tick, argasid, 249
  tick, ixodid, 255
  triatomine, 238
Mouthparts (immature),
  Culicoides, 151
  flea, 213
  housefly, 170
  mosquito, 102
  Phlebotomus, 135, 136
  Simulium, 144
  trombiculid larva, **268,** 270
Mummies and lice, 226
Murray River virus, 130
Musca domestica, (see housefly)
  nebulo, 165, 170
  sorbens, 165, 170
  vicina, 165, 170
Muscidae,
  and Calliphoridae, 189
Muscina, 175
  stabulans, 175

Myiasis, 16, 173, 175, 176, 189-203, **204,**
281
definition of, 189
collection of, flies, 293

Nagana, 177
Nabarro, 12
Neiva, 237
Nematocera, 81
classification, 81, 82
larvae, 82
medical importance, 81
mouthparts, 81
Neotoma, 240
Nervous system, 54
New housing and control, 35
New systematics, 324
Newstead, 12, 131
Niche, 71
Nicoll, 12, 226
Night-biters, 92
Norwegian crusted scabies, 261
No-see-ums, 148
Nosopsyllus fasciatus, **219,** 221, 222
Notum, 48
Nuttall, 254
Nymphochrysalis, 270

Ocelli, 78
Odours and control, 55
Oeciacus, 233
Oestridae, 199, 204
Oestrus ovis, 65, **201**
Ohtomo, 267
Oils and control, 56, 57, 66, 103, 104
Onchocerca volvulus,
recognition of, in vector, 322
vectors, 140, 147
animal reservoir, 26
Onchocerciasis, 140, 147
Oocysts, 318
Operculum, 66
Organic sulphur and scabies, 265
Ornithodoros, 248, 280 (see also argasid
ticks)
erraticus, 252
hermsi, 252
moubata, 247, 251-253, 297
rudis, 297
savignyi, 335
tholozani, 251-253
turicata, 252
Ornithonyssus,
bacoti, 245, 246, 274
bursa, 274
sylviarum, 274

Oropsylla silantiewi, 220
Oroya fever, vector, 132, 139
Ostia, 61
Otobius, 248
megnini, 247
Oudemans, 267
Outdoor-biters, 92, 107
Ovary, 64
Oviduct, 64
Ovipositor, 168
Oviposition, 65
Owl midges, 131
Oxygen requirements, 56

Palmate hair, 103
Pangoninae, 155, 156
Panstrongylus, 238
megistus, 237, 240
Papataci fever, 132, 138
Paralysis, tick, 259, **260,** 282
Parasites and reservoirs, 25
Paraponera clavata, 284
Paratype, 325
Paratyphoid, 173
Paris green, 31, 102
Pasteurella pestis,
recognition of, in vector, 315
vectors, 161, 260
Patton, 323
Pecten, 103, 116
Pediculoides ventricosus, 274
Pediculus humanus, 225
Pediculus humanus var. *capitis*, 225, 226
and disease, 229
collection, 296
control, 230
Pediculus humanus var. *corporis*, **226**
and disease, 229
collection, 296
control, 230
distribution, 226
life-cycle, 227
mouthparts and feeding, 227
morphology, 226
oviposition, 67, 227
preservation, 304
propagation, 229
Pediculus vestimenti, 225
Pedipalp, 242, 249
Pentastomida, 41, 276
Peritreme, 170
Peritrophic membrane,
general description, 59
tsetse, and trypanosomiasis, 59, 180
Phenol, 308

Phlebotomus, **131**
and disease, 132, 134, **137**
collection, 290, 292
control, 136,
feeding habits, 137
flight, 136, 146
general anatomy, 132
general life-cycle, 134
larva, 135
longevity, 137
oviposition, 134
preservation, 304
pupa, 136
resting places, 137, 290
Phlebotomus,
argentipes, 138
chinensis, 138
longipalpis, 138
major, 138
mongolensis, 138
papatasii, 137, 138
perniciosus, 137, 138
sergenti, 138
verrucarum, 139
Physiology and adaptation, 71
Phormia, 191, **194**, 280
Pins, entomological, 302
Piophila, 206
Pistia, 34
Plague,
and fleas, 220
and vaccines, 23
mode of transmission, 20, 221
Plasmodia,
recognition of, in vector, 316–318
Plasmodium,
falciparum, 108
knowlesi, 108
malariae, 108
ovale, 108
vivax, 108
Pleural rod, 211
Pleurite, 47
Pleuron, 46
Polyporos, 303, 305
Porocephaliasis, 279
Porocephalus, 278
Potamon niloticum, 144
Potassium,
cyanide, 304
hydroxide, 308
Predators, effect on vectors, 33
Preserving fluids, 304
Preservation of,
fleas, 306
flies, 304, 305

Preservation of,
lice, 307
bugs, 307
ticks, 307
mites, 307
venomous arthropods, 307
Prescutum, 49
Prestomal teeth, 167, 171
Prevention of contact between vector and
host,
biological barriers, 27
mechanical barriers, 27
chemical barriers, 28
Procuticle, 52
Pronotal comb, 210
Protozoa, recognition of, in vector, 316
Proventriculus,
general description, 57
of flea, 57, 212
of flea and plague, 220
of tsetse and trypanosomes, 181
Pruning spider, 285
Pseudopod, 80, 136, 144, 159
Pseudotracheae, 157, 167, 171
Psorophora,
and *Dermatobia*, 121, 200
medical importance, 117, 121
morphology, 122
Ptilinum, 171
Pubic louse, 224
Pulex irritans, 18, **216**, 220
distinction from *Xenopsylla*, 218
Pulvillus, 79, 249
Punkies, 148
Pupa, "naked", 80
Puparium, 80, 163
Pupipara, 80
Puss caterpillar, 286
Pyemotes ventricosus, 274
Pyemotidae, 274
collection, 298
Pygidium, 211
Pyrethum, 56

Q fever, 260
Queensland typhus, 260
Questing, 256

Rattus, and plague, 220
and scrub typhus, 272
Rectal papillae
and water resorption, 59, 73
of fleas, 212
Redwater fever and ticks, 12, 254
Reduviids, 237
Reed, Walter, 12

Reference journals, 337
Relapsing fever,
    and lice, 230
    and ticks, 252
Relaxing box, 289, 304
Repellents, 28, 55, 272
Reproduction, 63
Reproductive organs,
    female, 64
    male, 63
Reservoirs, animal, and parasite, 26
Resistance to insecticides, 31
Review of Applied Entomology, 338
Revisions, 325
Rhagionidae, 153
Rhodnius, 238, 239, 241
    prolixus, 240
Rhipicephalus, 258
    sanguineus, 260
Rhynchota, 231
Ricketts, 254
Rickettsia
    akari, 274
    conori, 260
    mooseri, 221
    orientalis, 272
    prowazekii, 26, 229
    quintana, 230
    rickettsii, 254, 259
    tsutsugamushi, 267, 272
Rickettsiae
    recognition of, in vector, 315
    and animal reservoir, 26, 272
Rickettsial pox, 274
Rift valley-fever, 130
Robber flies, 153
Rocky Mountain spotted fever, 254, 259
Rodents and,
    leishmaniasis, 137, 138
    endemic (murine typhus), 221, 274
    plague, 25, 33, 214, 220
    rickettsial pox, 274
    scrub typhus, 25, 272
Ross, 12
Rotenone, 57
Rothschild, 12, 208

Sabethines, 120, 126
Sabethes choropterus, 129
Saddle, 104
Saddle hair, 104
Saliva,
    producing sensitisation, 17, 18
    nature of, 58
    of tick, 246
Salivary glands,

general description, 58
    tsetse fly, 58, 180
    louse, 227
    mosquito, 58, 88
    flea, 210, 212
    tick, 245, 250
Sandflies, 131, 140, 148, (see also Phlebotomus)
Sandfly netting, 309
Sandfly fever, 132
    animal reservoir, 26
    vector, 138
Sao Paulo typhus, 260
Sarcophaga, 197, 206
Sarcophaginae, 196
Sarcoptes scabiei, 261
    and disease, 16, 263, 264, 281, 282
    control, 265
    diagnosis, 264
    life-cycle, 263
    morphology, 245, 246, 262
Sarcoptes,
    canis, 262
    equi, 262
    leonis, 262
    ovis, 262
Scabies, 261
    diagnosis, 264
    treatment, 265
Scabies rash, 264
Scale, 53
Scepsidinae, 155
Scoop, 103, 104
Scorpionida, 19, 242, 285
Scorpions, 285
Screw worm, 16, 68
    New World, 192
    Old World, 192
Scrub itch, 271
Scrub itch mites, 267
Scrub typhus, 267, 271
Scutal setae, 269
Scutellum, 48, 49
    of mosquitoes, 97-99
Scutum,
    acarine, 244
    insect, 48, 49
    ixodid, 254
    trombiculid, 268
Season, effect on vectors, 35
Seed tick, 256
Seminal vesicle, 64
Sense organs, 55
Sensilla, 53
    of trombiculids, 268
Sensillium, 211

Sensitisation, **17,** 108, 147, 220, 241, **281-** 286
Sheep nostril fly, 201
Shellac, 306
Shield (see scutum)
Simond, 208
Simulium, **140**
  and disease, 140, 147
  collection, 290, 291
  control, 30
  dissection, 321
  feeding behaviour, 142, 146
  flight, 146
  general life-cycle, 142
  general morphology, 140
  larval behaviour, 143
  longevity, 147
  oviposition, 142
  pupation, 145
  preservation, 305
  resting places, 146, 290
  saliva, 281
Simulium
  callidum, 147
  columbaschensis, 147
  damnosum, 142, 144, 146, 147
  metallicum, 143, 147
  neavei, 144, 147
  ochraceum, 143, 146, 147
Siphon, 116, 159, 206
Siphunculina, 162
Slavery and Tunga, 217
Sleeping sickness, 177
Smith, Theobald, 12, 254
Snake venom, 283
Snakes and *Porocephalus,* 278
Snipe flies, 153
Sodium hydroxide, 308
Soft ticks, 247
Sokoloff, 261
South African tick typhus, 260
Southall, J., 233
Spaniopsis, 153
Species, 324, 332
Spermatheca, 63, 64
  of fleas, 211
  of mosquitoes, 98
  of *Phlebotomus,* 132
Spermatozoa and egg production, 63
Spiders, 33, 284
Spider bites, treatment, 285
Spine, 53
Spiracles, 56
Spirochaetes, (see *Treponema*)
Sporozoites, 317
Squama, 50

Squirrels
  and plague, 220
  and leishmaniasis, 138
St Louis encephalitis, 130
Stable-fly, 186
Staphylinidae, 287
Stasisia rodhaini, 191, 195
Steel points, 302
Stegomyia, 119, 128, 129, 331
Sternum, 38, 45
Sticktight flea, 218
Stigmata, 56
Stigmal plate, 27, 103, 104
Stings,
  bee, 283
  scorpion, 285
  wasp, 283
Stings, treatment,
  bee, 284
  scorpion, 286
Stomoxys, 186, 200, 206, 290
Stomoxys calcitrans,
  collection, 290, 292
  life-cycle, 187
  medical importance, 188
  morphology, 186
Stone fly, 77
Storage,
  cabinets, 303
  jars, 289
  temporary, 304
Strains of insects, 312
Stylet (of louse), 227
Stylostome, 270
Subcosta, 50
Subspecies, 333
Sucking lice, 223
Suction tube, 289, 290
Sugar water, 309
Summer diarrhea, 165
Surra, 155
Synopses, 325
Synosternus pallidus, 218, 220
Systematics and medical entomology, 12
Swarming,
  general description, 63
  Culicoides, 152
  mosquitoes, 63, 106
  tabanids, 63, 160
Symphoromyia, 153

Tabanids, **155**
  and disease, 155, 161
  collection, 290, 291
  dissection, 321
  feeding behaviour, 15, 160, 280

Tabanids,
   flight, 160
   general life-cycle, 157
   general morphology, 156
   larval habits, 158
   oviposition, 157
   preservation, 304, 305
   pupation, 159
   resting attitude, 156
Tabanus, 156, 160
Tabaninae, 155
Tachinidae, 189
Taeniorhynchus, 124
Tampan tick, 247
Tanaka, 267
Tangle foot, 295
Tanytarsus and allergy, 81
Tarantula, 284
Tarsus,
   of insect, 51
   of acarine, 245
Temperature receptors, 55
Tergum, 48
Testes, 64
Test animal, 295, 297
Tetanus and Tunga, 281
Tetmosol, 265
Tetraethylthiuram monosulphide, 265
Texas cattle fever, 12, 254
Theobald, 12, 115
Theobaldia, 124, **125**
   distinction from Culex, 126
Theodor, 132
Thorax, 45
Thiamine chloride, 283
Tick,
   paralysis, 259, 260, 282
   bites, 247, 251, 259, 280
   removal, 259
Tick bird, 33
Tick-borne encephalitis, 260
Todd, 12
Toxins and saliva, 281
Trachea, 56
Tracheole, 56
Transmission of disease,
   cyclical, 20
   mechanical, 19
   transovarial, 272
Trench fever, 226, 230
Treponema,
   and animal reservoir, 26
   behaviour in louse, 230
   behaviour in tick, 250, 252
   recognition of, in vector, 315

Treponema,
   anserina, 247
   duttoni, 26, 247, 248, 252
   recurrentis, 26, 230
Triatoma, 237, 239
   infestans, 240
   phyllosoma, 240
   rubrofasciata, 237
Triatomines, **237**
   and disease, 237, 240
   collection, 295
   feeding behaviour, 240
   general life-cycle, 239
   general morphology, 238
   preservation, 307
Trichodectes canis, 223
Trombicula, 269, 272
   akamushi, 267, 272
   autumnalis, 267
   deliensis, 272
Trombiculids, **267**
   adult, morphology, 270
   and disease, 267, 271
   and rodents, 272
   and rickettsiae, 272
   collection, 298
   control, 272
   ecology, 271, 272
   larva, morphology, 268
   larva, feeding method, 270
   life-cycle, 267, **269**
   nymph, morphology, 270
Trypanosoma,
   brucei, 319
   cruzi, 60, 237, 240, 241
   evansi, 155
   equiperdum, 155
   gambiense, 184, 319
   lewisi, 222
   rangeli, 241
   rhodesiense, 26, 184, 319
   simiae, 320
   uniforme, 320
   vivax, 320
Trypanosomes,
   recognition of, in vector, 318
Trypanosomiasis, African, 177
   and drugs, 23
   and tabanids, 155
   and tsetse flies, 184
Trypanosomiasis, South American, 237
Tsetse flies, (see Glossina)
Tsutsugamushi disease, 267, 272
Tularaemia, 20, 161, 260
Tumbu fly, 195

Tunga penetrans,
and tetanus, 281
collection, 293
control, 218
life-cycle, 217
morphology, 217
Type, 324
host, 325
locality, 325
Typhoid, 165, 173
Typhus,
mode of transmission, 20
endemic (murine), 221, 274
epidemic, 229
Indian tick, 260
Sao Paulo, 260
Scrub, 267, 271
South African tick, 260
tick-borne, 259
Queensland, 260
Tyroglyphidae, 275
Tyroglyphus, 275

Union Catalogue, 336
Utricularia exoleta, 34
Uric acid, 60
Urotaenia group, 127

Vagina, 64
Vanilla worker's rash, 275
Vas deferens, 64
Venomous arthropods, collection, 298
Ventral brushes, 104, 116
Ventral fins, 104
Veins,
cross, 50
wing, 49, 50
Ventral hair tuft, 116
Ver macaque, 200
Veterinary Bulletin, 338
Viper venom, 283
Voles, 220
Vomit drop, 173

Wall louse, 233

War,
and scabies, 261
and scrub typhus, 272
Warble flies, 202
Warileya, 131
Wasps, 283
Water conservation by insect, 59, 60, 72
Water plants and mosquitoes, 34, 124
Western equine encephalomyelitis, 130
West Nile virus, 130
Wild,
mosquitoes, 107
ticks, 297
Wilson, E, 261
Wing venation,
terminology, 49, 50
variation of, 79
Winter malaria, 60
Wohlfartia, 197, 204
magnifica, 197
vigil, 197
Wood rats, 240
World List, 336
Wuchereria bancrofti,
recognition of, in vector, 316, **321,** 322
vectors, 108, **110-114,** 117, 121-124, **127**
and animal reservoir, 26

Xenopsylla, distinction form
Pulex, 218
Synosternus, 218
Xenopsylla, 214, **218,** 221, 222, 331
braziliensis, 218, 220, 335
cheopis, 218, 220, 221, 323, 326
astia, 220, 323

Yellow fever,
animal reservoir, 25, 128
history, 12
mode of transmission, 20
vectors, 127, 128
vaccination against, 23, 25

Zoological nomenclature, rules, 333
Zoological Record, 337
Zoogeographical regions, 325